IMPLICIT AND EXPLICIT KNOWLEDGE: AN EDUCATIONAL APPROACH

edited by

DINA TIROSH

Tel Aviv University, Israel

Human Development, Volume **6**

The Tel Aviv Workshop in Human Development

Sidney Strauss, Series Editor

ABLEX PUBLISHING CORPORATION
NORWOOD, NEW JERSEY

Library of Congress Cataloging-in-Publication Data

Implicit and explicit knowledge : an educational approach / edited by
  Dina Tirosh.
    p.   cm. — (Human development ; v. 6)
  Includes bibliographical references and indexes.
  ISBN 0-89391-743-5
  1. Implicit learning.   2. Cognition in children.   3. Knowledge,
Theory of.   I. Tirosh, Dina.   II. Title: Explicit knowledge.
III. Series: Human development (Norwood, N.J.) ; v. 6.
BF319.5.I45I45   1994
153.4—dc20   94-4458
                                             CIP

Ablex Publishing Corporation
355 Chestnut Street
Norwood, New Jersey 07648

This book is dedicated to the memory of
Tamar Globerson,
a sorely missed member of the Unit
of Human Development and Education.

Contents

Human Development: Preface to the Series

Sidney Strauss

Series Editor

This book series is the product of annual workshops held by the Unit of Human Development and Education in the School of Education at Tel Aviv University. Whenever a new publication comes out, the person responsible for it feels compelled to answer the question: Why a new X (journal, book, book series)? I do not feel exonerated from asking and answering that question. The purpose of the series is to address topics of theory, as well as conceptual and methodological issues that reflect the diversity and complexity of human development. It aims to address four needs in our field, as they relate to edited books.

There are few attempts to deal with important developmental phenomena in a concentrated manner in most of the book series in our field. They generally contain a collection of chapters on unrelated topics. There is a need to have leading experts present their views about relatively circumscribed issues. Our books will be organized around a topic where contributors write chapters that fit into a larger picture the editor will be illuminating.

A second need in our field is to have more interdisciplinary work. We generally read books written by developmental psychologists for developmental psychologists. Restricting inquiry to the psychological realm promotes a rather narrow view of human development. The view of man as a biological entity and cultural producer and consumer as well as a psychological being has been deeply neglected, and an element that will characterize our books is the inclusion of representatives of intellectual disciplines to discuss topics we believe to be of importance for our field.

Most work in developmental psychology is published in English and written by Americans. Much of the Western and Eastern European work is unknown to the vast majority of developmental psychologists, and the same can be said with more emphasis for work being done in Latin America, Asia, and Africa. Whenever possible, we will bring leading intellectual figures from these continents to contribute to our deliberations.

The fourth need is to attend to the applied parts of developmental psychology. Some of the later books will revolve around issues relating developmental psychology and education. We chose this out of the conviction that educational issues force one to face the depth of human complexity and its development in ways that traditional academic developmental psychology often turns away from.

The topics for the books are chosen with an eye towards directions our field is taking or we think should be taking. In some instances we will have a book about a topic that has been discussed in the literature and is ripe for a summary or stocktaking. In other instances the book will be around a topic that has not been discussed at all or has only begun to be written about. In still other cases the book will be about a topic that was once a subject of inquiry and then dropped. We will publish a book around that topic if we believe it should be resurrected because of developments in the field.

It is the hope of the members of the Unit of Human Development and Education that this series will reflect the lively and stimulating workshops that have been held at Tel Aviv University, and that the community of developmental psychologists will find interest in the issues discussed in these pages.

Sidney Strauss
Ramat Hasharon
August 1985

Introduction

Dina Tirosh

Tel-Aviv University

Many researchers find it both necessary and useful to discriminate between different types of knowledge when attempting to answer fundamental questions related to the evolution of knowledge, such as "How is knowledge organized?" and "How does novel knowledge come into existence?" Within the cognitive psychology literature, a distinction is often made between explicit and implicit knowledge. This distinction concerns the awareness dimension of knowledge: While explicit knowledge is generally interpreted as consciously accessible knowledge, implicit knowledge usually means knowledge that is represented in the mind of the individual but of which he is unaware.

These two types of knowledge are largely accepted as playing an important and distinct role in inventing, understanding, thinking, speaking, and learning. Yet leading researchers in cognitive psychology have argued for many years that, until recently, their domain has not devoted enough attention to central issues related to the structural and functional distinctions between actions governed by explicit knowledge and those governed by implicit knowledge. Topics that are repeatedly mentioned in this context as not having been thoroughly investigated include the contribution to thinking and learning processes of a change in the state of the knowledge from implicit to explicit, the sources of these two types of knowledge, and the types of intervention strategies that can help learners become aware of their implicit knowledge and its role in their ways of thinking. It is noticeable that researchers in cognitive psychology as well as in other domains such as language acquisition, mathematics and science education, have recently been showing a growing interest in these issues.

This volume provides an interdisciplinary perspective of the recent, yet on-going discussion on implicit and explicit knowledge. Its chapters reflect the work and thoughts of a group of cognitive psychologists, philosophers, science and mathematics educators, and language acquisition researchers whose contributions in issues pertaining to implicit and explicit knowledge are widely acknowledged. Many of the issues presented in this volume were illuminated and sharpened by the fruitful discussions that were held at Tel-Aviv University during the Sixth Annual International Workshop of the Unit of Human Development and Education.

In this introduction, the major theme of each chapter is briefly summarized. Then, some central themes in the chapters are discussed.

Chapter Summaries

Chapters 1–4 deal with issues related to implicit and explicit aspects in the development of knowledge and its representations, and with the selection of relevant inputs for learning. In the first chapter, diSessa presents a generic/causal program of the development of knowledge and intelligence. He suggests that cognition consists of a bundle of resources, each of which is determined, to a substantial degree, by the history of its development. Four factors are involved in the genesis of each resource: a problem, prior resources, the mechanisms of feedback on positive solutions, and the principles of invention.

diSessa organized the consideration of resources and their genesis under three levels. The alpha level concerns the basic capabilities that a general information-processing system must have (e.g., abstracting, representing knowledge, and conditional control). The beta level specifically involves generic resources for representing and processing knowledge. The gamma level is the level of specific knowledge. With reference to this level, diSessa gives a detailed description from his own work on how general resources might evolve from intuitive knowledge in physics. On the basis of the framework suggested in this chapter, diSessa points to possible extensions and reinterpretations of Piaget's perspective on the development of ideas.

In an attempt to articulate the theme of implicit and explicit knowledge within his chapter, diSessa argues that very little, if any, of the prior resources are evident or reflectively accessible and that none of the beta level resources is open to reflective consideration. For the gamma level, he argues that algebraic and propositional forms of knowledge are generally considered explicit, as it is possible to display them and to reason about them. Yet, he comments that even these forms of knowledge cannot operate without inarticulate, implicit processes that interpret the symbols, find referents, coordinate accesses to get information about referents, and so on. diSessa argues that both our implicit and explicit knowledge remain active throughout the successive stages of intelligence and continue to influence our thinking processes. Throughout the chapter he emphasizes that implicit ideas play a large part in learning specific subject matter.

In line with diSessa, Gelman (Chapter 2) views the learner's implicit knowledge as an extremely important factor that influences the learning of specific subject matter. Her chapter deals with the issue of characterizing the nature of relevant inputs for learning within a constructivist theory. She argues that young children share a universal set of innate, implicit, content-dependent skeletal principles that determine how they interpret situations in their environments. These initial principles serve to define the class of stimuli that are potentially relevant to further learning in a specific domain. Thus, inputs are relevant if they are structured in a way that is consistent with the organization of the innate, domain-specific principles that assimilate them.

Gelman supports her conjecture by evidence from studies in various content domains (i.e., blind children's acquisition of the meaning of nonagentive verbs, sign language acquisition, and infants' learning about objects). The data she presents challenge deeply entrenched assumptions about learning (e.g., learning in the young proceeds necessarily from the sensory through the perceptual to the abstract). Furthermore, the data show that learners sometimes consider as relevant some input that we either treat as irrelevant or are even unaware of.

Gelman notes that the task of selecting relevant inputs needed to promote learning is not easy because (a) we need to know a great deal about the nature of the implicit principles that the learner brings along to the learning setting, and (b) pupils interpret presented materials in ways that do not match our expectations. Her own study on how kindergarten, first-, and second-grade children interpret commonly used instructional materials for learning that fractions are numbers illustrates that in the absence of implicit principles for recognizing an input for what it is, learners might overgeneralize their existing principles and produce a distorted assimilation of the input. Mastery of the idea that fractions are indeed numbers requires the learning of principles that go beyond the implicit fundamental idea that numbers are what you get when you count things.

The inquiry into what counts as relevant input should examine how students interpret instructional materials. In the case of fractions, young children are exposed to the number line as well as parts and wholes of shapes more often than to symbolic forms of fractions. The former are frequently described as concrete, the latter as abstract, and the tendency is to start with the concrete. Gelman argues that the physical objects that are often considered as concrete representations of numbers are not mathematical objects and have to be interpreted by the mind if they are to stand for mathematical terms.

Her findings confirm her hypothesis that young children assimilate data commonly used to represent fractions (i.e., the number line) to a conceptual scheme appropriate only for positive integers. Moreover, children's ability to correctly interpret "concrete" representations of fractions goes hand in hand with their ability to work correctly with the symbolic representations of fractions. Based on these findings, Gelman suggests that more attention should be paid to the role of symbolization in acquiring the concept of fraction. She notes that withholding information about mathematical symbols might amount to withholding the data needed to transcend the principles that guided early learning of mathematics. Gelman emphasizes that children must always remain the final source of validation and input as to how to tinker with, alter, or even change their curriculum.

The role of symbolization in making implicit knowledge explicit is extensively discussed in the third chapter of the book that deals with the acquisition of symbolic competence in children. In accordance with Piaget, Olson and Campbell argue that the beginning of symbolization is to be found at about the age of two in pretend play where one object or event can stand for another. Olson and Campbell suggest that children's first symbols do not represent particular objects but generalized meaning (for instance, dogs in general and not a particular dog). At this stage symbols are relations between signs and meanings and not between signs and referents.

A second stage in using symbols, at about the age of three, is reached when a child comes to see that a symbol may be used to represent a particular thing or situation (i.e., the child may see a dollhouse not only as representing a house but as a representation of a particular house). The authors suggest that at this stage the child is acquiring the first truly metarepresentational predicate for relating a symbol to a state of affairs. For the first time, the child distinguishes the meaning of the symbol from its reference and is able to refer to the object that symbolizes a house as if it were a particular house.

The third stage occurs when the child comes to understand that a representation may misrepresent a real situation. At this stage, when children are about four years old, they acquire a concept or predicate for ascribing properties to their symbols, the critical ones being truth and falsity. Olson and Campbell argue that children's understanding of false belief is a major achievement because it involves perceiving a representation as false, which requires the concepts of truth and falsity. Thus, it is only at this stage that children can be said to have a concept of belief and can apply the concepts of truth and falsity both to themselves and to others.

The authors' perception of the role of symbolization in the development of thought is in accordance with those of Pierce, Bruner, and Goodman, who view the development of thought as a matter of acquiring symbolic means for representing oneself and the world. Olson and Campbell argue that since symbolism is essential to any form of thought, it is crucial to teach children how formal symbol systems can serve as representations of their own implicit knowledge. However, it should be remembered that if the implicit knowledge is not in place and accessible in the form of intuition, the formal symbolization is impossible to learn.

While Chapter 3 deals with one central type of representation, namely symboliz- ation, Fischbein's chapter (Chapter 4) is devoted to a different type of representa- tion: mental models. Fischbein argues that although symbols and models are both related to certain objects that they may replace in our cognitive activities, there is a basic difference between them. A model has an inner structure, and due to this structure it may correspond to a certain original, replacing it in certain conditions. A pure symbol is not structured and thus cannot carry any information by itself.

Fischbein defines the term "model" in the following manner: Given two sys- tems, A and B, B may be considered a model of A if, on the basis of a certain isomorphism between A and B, a description or a solution produced in terms of A may be reflected, consistently, in terms of B and vice versa. He then suggests three dichotomies of models: intuitive versus abstract, analogical versus paradigmatic, and implicit (or tacit) versus explicit. The main part of the chapter is devoted to implicit models.

Fischbein argues that implicit models influence the reasoning strategies and decisions of an individual from behind the scenes, that is, without the individual's being aware of this influence or at least of the extent of it. These models share several properties: spatiality, substantiality, manipulativeness, familiarity, and ro- bustness. Fischbein distinguishes three typical situations related to tacit models: (a) intuitive, spontaneous models of which the individual is completely unaware; (b) learned models that become tacit and continue to influence the individual's way of reasoning even after the model has become obsolete; and (c) conscious models, tacitly influencing the solution decisions.

Fischbein points at a central, didactical problem related to implicit models. He states that in the teaching of science and mathematics the student often needs intuitive support for the abstract concepts that are taught, and thus the teacher introduces the concepts through a model. However, there is almost never an absolute correspondence between the concept controlled by the formal definitions and the concept controlled by the model. The model imposes its own constraints on the concept. After formal learning, the student has to give up her primitive model and rely only on formal definitions, but it seems that the initial model has become so deeply rooted in the learner's mind that it continues to exert unconscious control over mental behavior. Furthermore, a complete detachment from the initial, usually concrete model would risk the inhibition of the productivity of the reasoning processes since the concrete model inspires and stimulates these processes. Fischbein argues that the only solution to this problem is to resort to metacognitive procedures, namely, to help learners develop abilities that will enable them to become aware of the influences of the tacit models and control their impact on their thinking. In his opinion, the success of an instructional process depends to a great extent on our knowledge about the tacit models and on the degree to which we meet the target of developing instructional devices for helping students become aware of the impact of the implicit models on their thinking, and also helping them build efficient conceptual systems that could control the impact of these models.

Chapters 5–9 deal with issues related to the role that implicit and explicit knowledge play in specific content-domains. In Chapter 5, Tirosh and Graeber discuss preservice teachers' implicit and explicit knowledge of multiplication and division. They describe three studies aimed at (a) examining the extent to which preservice teachers' conceptions of multiplication and division are influenced by two models that are used in school to represent these operations: the repeated addition model of multiplication and the partitive model of division; and (b) determining the effects of two interventions, both aimed at raising preservice teachers' awareness of the impact of their explicitly and implicitly held beliefs about division on their performance in solving word problems.

Tirosh and Graeber's findings reveal that only one of five constraints imposed by the learned models was explicitly held by a substantial number of preservice teachers. Yet, preservice teachers' performance in solving multiplication and division word problems was heavily influenced by the other, apparently implicitly held constraints imposed by these models. Two other results were found. First, it was found that the conflict teaching method was very effective in releasing preservice teachers from their explicitly held belief that the quotient must always be greater than the dividend. And second, it was found that preservice teachers' performance in solving division word problems significantly improved after working with a tutorial computer program that provided counterexamples to the implicitly held belief that the divisor must be smaller than the dividend. Yet, the fact that 40% of the preservice teachers were ready to adjust the result of their correct computational example to their explicitly held misbelief suggests that when using the cognitive conflict approach, care should be taken to assure that students are highly confident in the task used to trigger the misbelief. Furthermore, the apparent success of a drill and practice program that did not include specific references to the implicitly held misbelief raises concerns about the importance of explicitly describing "appropriate propositions" in instructional devices.

Chapter 6 and 7 are both embedded in a Piagetian constructivistic framework. In Chapter 6, Steffe offers a detailed model of children's construction of meaning for arithmetical words. In contrast to Gelman, Steffe believes that the acquisition of initial mathematical concepts is not governed by an innate set of counting principles, but rather that human beings actively construct numbers, and that the development of meaning for initial mathematical concepts (e.g., unit) follows a sequence of stages starting with the ability to count perceptual items via counting figural unit items, then motor unit items, verbal unit items, and finally abstract unit items. Steffe analyzes why children in each stage solve problems the way they do, describes qualitative changes within each stage and between stages, and emphasizes that explicitation plays a vital role in the shifts between stages. In each stage, the outcomes of operating in a preceding stage are made explicit in the sense that they can be used as materials for reprocessing, which, in turn, leads to a stage shift.

Steffe's model is largely based on observations made while actually teaching six-year-old children over a period of two years. The teaching experiments are aimed at understanding the ways and means of influencing children's knowledge and the progress they make over extended periods of time when there is no intention of teaching a predetermined way of operating. Each teaching experiment consists of a sequence of teaching episodes and thus allows for observing modifications children make in their schemes. The conceptual analysis of the children's cognitive constructions attempts to develop an understanding of children's mathematics so that their actions can be seen as rational and sensible. The methodology derives from Piaget's clinical interview. Steffe's main aim is to specify numerical concepts and operations in children and make those the conceptual foundations of number in school mathematics.

Steffe argues that the mathematics of children is a legitimate mathematics. In his opinion, the mathematical concepts and operations that one hypothesizes the child might learn should be based on experiential abstractions from interactive communications with children. Educational programs in mathematics should not be based on how adults understand mathematics nor on a view of mathematics education as a process of transferring information printed in textbooks. Rather, they should strive to build programs that are harmonious with children's ways and means of operating. Steffe's current chapter suggests that children's numerical knowledge is strikingly different from what appears in school mathematics textbooks. There is often a large gap between the operations available to the children and what is demanded of them in the school program.

Ferreiro's chapter (Chapter 7) relates to literacy development from a constructivistic outlook. Ferreiro argues that young children approach written language as a conceptual task. An alphabetical writing system, she claims, is a representational system that retains some of the properties and relations of the real object but leaves aside others of its recognized properties and relations. When children construct a writing system, they look for an answer to a very general question: the nature of the link between the real object and its representation.

Ferreiro mentions that some of the ideas children construct about writing systems are in accordance with socially established writing systems, and some are not. She emphasizes that from a constructivist point of view, those former ideas could not be dismissed simply as being wrong. There is a need to distinguish between ''wrong ideas'' that are shared by many children and those that are shared by some children but do not express a kind of consensus among children at a given point in their development. It is of crucial importance to identify wrong ideas that fulfill the function of allowing the next development and to understand their roles in literacy development. One example of such an apparently wrong idea is the minimum quantity principle, namely, the idea that a given minimum number of letters (usually three) is needed to have a written string capable of receiving a meaningful interpretation. This hypothesis, which is pervasively kept by children in various countries where many common written words are actually composed of only one or two letters, fulfills the function of maintaining a distinction between the elements of writing (the letters) and a meaningful piece of writing.

With respect to the usefulness of making children aware of their inadequate ideas about the alphabetical writing system, Ferreiro argues that since some of these have an intrinsic rationality and a positive role to play in literacy development, they should not be treated as being simply wrong. Instead, she suggests contriving situations that encourage children to pass themselves through the steps necessary to become convinced of the appropriateness of a certain idea. Ferreiro concluded that pedagogical research needs to devote a much greater effort to the relation between knowledge constructed outside school settings, which could be viewed as implicit knowledge, and knowledge explicitly taught in school.

In line with Ferreiro, Levin and Gardosh (Chapter 8) propose that children's prior knowledge in a domain should be carefully taken into consideration when designing a curriculum. Their study on interactions between the broad, everyday concept of speed as a relation between time and any change and the confined, linear concept of speed typically introduced in school was aimed at examining whether children distinguish between linear and rotational meanings of speed.

Subjects at different grade levels (third, fifth, seventh, and ninth and university students), who had either not received any formal instruction related to speed or had received formal instruction related only to linear speed were asked (a) to determine the speed of two different kinds of objects: those proceeding on a linear track (an ant and a car), and those moving rotationally (a drill, a mixer, and a record); (b) to compare the speed of linearly moving objects with that of rotating ones; and (c) to formulate the speed of a linear object and of a rotational object. It was found that the majority of subjects in each of the five grade levels differentiated between the two types of speed and described each object by the speed relevant to its motion. These data indicate that prior to instruction children construe rotational speed when dealing with rotational motions and are able to differentiate between linear and angular speed. Moreover, students' ability to make this differentiation is not impaired by the fact that speed in the curriculum is identified with linear speed.

These results challenge the assumption that linear speed is easier to grasp than angular speed, an assumption that dictates the current, mainly linear interpretation of speed presented in school. Levin and Gardosh argue that the confined, linear interpretation of speed presented in school creates a gap between the everyday and the school-based meanings of speed, which may be detrimental to learning. They suggest two ways by which this discrepancy could be bridged: (a) introducing real motions into the classroom and dealing with them in terms of numbers and (b) introducing nonlinear motions earlier in school and leading students to distinguish between their everyday concept of speed, which is not necessarily spatial, and the school concept, which is confined to spatial progression. The authors conclude that dealing with nonspatial and with rotational speeds in classrooms could help make school more relevant to children's everyday life and ideas of motion.

While Levin and Gardosh's chapter refers to novices' intuitive conceptions of a notion used in daily life as well as in physics, Clement's chapter (Chapter 9) discusses experts' use of physical intuitions. Clement provides evidence from thinking-aloud data that indicates that concrete physical intuition schemas play an important role in expert thinking. These intuitions are knowledge structures that reside in long-term memory and are concrete, elemental, and self-evaluated. They have modest generality and stand without further explanation or justification. Reported uses of intuitions, which are often accompanied by hand motions, or acknowledgments of using dynamic, visual, and kinesthetic imagery in an imagistic simulation suggest that these intuitions often involve a perceptual motor schema accompanied by kinesthetic imagery. Such intuitions presumably develop from prior experiences with physical objects and can serve as basic assumptions that form the foundations for later inferences related to the system.

Clement argues that certain intuitions are implicit while others are explicit. He proposes three levels on a dimension running from more implicit to more explicit knowledge: tacit knowledge, conscious but nonverbal knowledge, and conscious and verbally descriptive knowledge. Clement clarifies that the term "tacit" does not necessarily mean forever inaccessible but indicates the object in question is not yet accessible to conscious attention. He hypothesizes that imagistic simulation is a mechanism by which some of the implicit knowledge in physical intuition schemas can be made more explicit.

Clement discusses the limitations of the problem-solving power of physical intuitions (vulnerable to error, some simulations are difficult to carry out, often ineffective in determining exact quantitive relationships) as well as their advantages (a primary source of knowledge in the solution, increase in the understanding of a physical system, increase in confidence in predictions). His data clearly indicate that expert knowledge is not always formal and abstract and that experts find it desirable to retain concrete cases as anchoring assumptions in their thinking. He remarks that focusing only on experts' use of abstract verbal principles is inappropriate. More efforts should be directed toward investigating how subjects select and refine useful physical intuitions and how they coordinate them with other types of knowledge.

In the concluding chapter (Chapter 10), Berg presents a philosophical view of the implicit/explicit distinction. Berg argues that any kind of knowledge, be it implicit or explicit, is necessarily true. What is not true can not be knowledge. At most, it is a false belief. Since several chapters discuss misconceptions (false beliefs), he suggests referring to implicit and explicit beliefs and not to implicit and explicit knowledge.

Berg notes that the implicit/explicit distinction is generally applied in linguistics. In that context, any part of a message or an utterance that lies beyond its literal meaning is viewed as implicit. In his view, the attempt to extend this distinction beyond the realm of linguistic content and to define implicit belief as a belief the individual is unaware of holding is problematic. For instance, within the Freudian framework an implicit belief is interpreted as one that a person would deny having yet without which some of his actions would be unexplainable. Berg argues that it is strange, if not absurd, to ascribe to people beliefs that they deny having. Defining implicit beliefs in terms of the logical consequences of one's beliefs is also problematic as there are many statements that could be viewed as logical consequences of one's beliefs that the subject actually does not hold, and, therefore, there is no reason to assume that those implications of his beliefs of which he is unaware are, nevertheless, his beliefs.

Berg mentions that another notion of tacit knowledge, suggested by Polanyi (1969), involves a triad that consists of subsidiary items bearing on a focus by virtue of an integration performed by a person. The subsidiary element of knowledge is dynamic and may function as subsidiary in one instance and as focal in another. Berg argues that in Polanyi's view there is no strictly explicit knowledge and consequently the implicit/explicit opposition does not hold in this paradigm.

Berg states that implicit knowledge is sometimes described as the knowledge a person uses but cannot express (e.g., we know how to speak grammatically, but explicitly stating that knowledge is notoriously beyond us). He argues that on this view implicit knowledge amounts to implicit method, where implicitly having a method means having a way of doing something without being sufficiently aware of it to be able to spell it out.

Berg suggests that in educational theories the concept of implicit knowledge could be supplanted by two pedagogically more significant concepts: implicit method, in the particular sense previously described; and misconceptions, namely beliefs of whose falseness one is unaware. He explains that without being aware of it, a student may acquire a way of doing something that either does not work so well or works well only in a restricted domain of application. The teacher must become aware of this method in order to help the student become aware of its inadequacy.

Similarly, he explains that false beliefs can lead students to wrong conclusions. Since one of the teacher's aims is to correct misconceptions, the teacher must be aware of them. Berg concludes that, in his opinion, theories formulated in terms of implicit methods and misconceptions are preferable to those working with notions of implicit and explicit knowledge as they are more easily accommodated by the conceptual apparatus we already have.

Chapter Themes

A fundamental issue discussed in the chapters concerns the definitions of implicit and explicit knowledge and their interrelations. In this section of the introduction, I attempt to describe various perspectives of this issue.

Implicit and Explicit Knowledge: Definitions and Relationships

As stated in the opening of this introduction, implicit knowledge is often defined as knowledge the individual is unaware of, while explicit knowledge is interpreted as knowledge accessible to one's consciousness. In most of this book's chapters, these notions are understood more or less in that way (see, for instance, diSessa, page 50; Olson and Campbell, page 92; Fischbein, page 98). Yet, several concerns were raised in respect to the use of these notions and to their relationships.

1. Implicit/explicit knowledge—a legitimate distinction? The terms "implicit knowledge" and "explicit knowledge" are constantly used in the psychological, educational, and language acquisition research literature. While some researchers view this distinction as imperative for the study of human cognition (Chomsky, 1980; Polanyi, 1969), others have questioned its usefulness and even its legitimacy (Campbell, 1986).

The various chapters of the present volume describe different approaches to this issue. While diSessa, Gelman, Olson and Campbell, Fischbein, Tirosh and Graeber, Steffe, and Clement use these terms constantly, Ferreiro argues that she is not convinced of the usefulness of the dichotomy implicit/explicit knowledge in psychological research. She bases her concern on two arguments. First, the dichotomy implicit/explicit conveys the meaning of an heterogeneous amount of other dichotomies, and it is possible that some of the other dichotomies are more applicable to psychological research. Second, it seems that the dichotomy is not versatile enough to allow explanations for the complex cognitive processes involved in the movement from implicit to explicit knowledge. However, Ferreiro argues that this dichotomy could be useful within pedagogical research. She notes that the relation between knowledge constructed outside school versus knowledge explicitly taught in school settings could be expressed through this dichotomy.

A more radical stand against the distinction is taken by Berg, who argues that it is irrelevant to theories of education since any kind of knowledge, including implicit and explicit knowledge, is always true. Beliefs, on the other hand, could be either true or false, and since one of the main aims of teachers is to become aware of the implicit, false beliefs that their students hold, a distinction should be made between implicit and explicit beliefs and not between implicit and explicit knowledge.

These different positions call for a more thorough examination of the relations between the implicit/explicit distinction and other, related terms in an attempt to define the uniqueness of each distinction. The following section deals with this issue.

2. Implicit and explicit knowledge: A dichotomy or a continuum?
Traditionally, these two notions have been discussed as dichotomous. In the last several years, some researchers have questioned the usefulness of such a dichotomy. Karmiloff-Smith stated that "It is my general argument that two level dichtomies used up to now, such as implicit/explicit, procedural/declarative, . . . are insufficient to capture the complex nature of the processes leading to conscious access" (1986, p. 104). She noted that all authors agree that computational processes are never open to introspection and that only the results of computations, or the elements on which they operate, are potentially accessible. Yet, it is difficult to avoid circularity here, because everything that can be consciously accessed is considered a product, and everything that cannot be accessed in that way is considered a process, and vice versa. Karmiloff-Smith suggested four levels of explicitation: implicit, primary, secondary, and tertiary. This distinction between implicit representations and different levels of progressive representational explicitation is conceptualized within a developmental perspective.

In the present book, two chapters discuss the dichotomy/continuum issue. Fischbein, who assumes a dichotomy between implicit and explicit models, comments that this dichotomy does not represent a clear-cut distinction and that absolute classifications are impossible. He argues that there is no intrinsic difference between the two categories of models, and that there is a continuum from unconscious to conscious models through semiconscious ones. Similarly, Clément claims that a strict dichotomy between implicit and explicit knowledge is not useful. In contrast to Fischbein, though, he does not suggest a continuum but proposes three distinct levels on a dimension running from more implicit to less explicit knowledge: tacit knowledge, conscious but nonverbal knowledge, and conscious and verbally descriptive knowledge. This scale takes into account the extent to which the knowledge element is conscious, differentiated from its context, and verbally or mathematically labeled or described in discrete symbols.

It is hoped that the various approaches to the dichotomy/continuum distinction and the attempt to describe different, distinct levels of explicitation would lead to a more thorough examination of the characteristics of each of these two types of knowledge and to a further examination of the relation between differentiation, verbalization, and consciousness.

3. Implicit knowledge, explicit knowledge and their relations with related terms.
The need to clarify the relations between various different but related terms is recurrently discussed. Both in everyday life and in the research literature, different connotations are given to the same terms, or, quite contrarily, different terms convey similar connotations.

In our book, terms such as implicit, tacit, intuitive, inarticulate, inaccessible, nonformal, and unconscious are often used interchangeably. The term explicit, on the other hand, is often replaced by articulate, accessible, formally studied, conscious, reflective, and symbolic (symbolized). Relations between the terms implicit and explicit knowledge and other terms are directly addressed in two chapters.

In Chapter 7, Ferreiro lists several dichotomies (i.e., unconscious versus conscious, intuitive versus organized, common sensical versus scientific) and argues that it is hard to find a common denominator throughout these varieties of meanings. In Chapter 9, Clement discusses the relations between the terms implicit knowledge, explicit knowledge, and intuition. He argues that while some theorists have used the term implicit to mean intuitive knowledge, he takes the position that certain intuitions can be implicit and others explicit. Explicit intuition is defined as an intuitive expectation that is conscious during a real or imagined event and is described verbally or mathematically. Intuition is described as implicit in the sense that the subject is unaware that she possesses a certain knowledge or as implicit in the somewhat weaker sense of being conscious but nonverbal and difficult to describe. Clement provides examples of implicit intuitions as well as explicit ones and explains how implicit knowledge can become explicit. It is worth mentioning that diSessa, in Chapter 1, argues that intuitive ideas are necessarily tacit.

A discussion of the relations between the terms implicit/explicit and other, related terms can also be found in Campbell (1986). We agree with Dennett (1985), who argues that it is essential to understand and differentiate between related terms, such as awareness and consciousness, and to better conceptualize the relations between them. There is work to be done here.

4. From implicit to explicit—a one-way road only? In the present book, most chapters deal mainly with explicitation, that is, the route traveled from implicit to explicit knowledge. Gelman describes children's implicit knowledge as innate, skeletal, domain-specific principles that serve to direct children's attention to inputs, which, in turn, lead to explicit, culturally shared knowledge in that domain. Olson and Campbell propose that what is involved in making habitual, implicit knowledge explicit is representing that knowledge in a symbolic code such as language or diagrams. Tirosh and Graeber describe two means by which students can be helped to explicitate their implicit, inadequate beliefs: the conflict teaching method and the counter examples method. Steffe describes various actions and goals that were previously implicit and were made explicit by counting. He argues that in each of the five stages of the counting schemes he describes, the products of a preceding stage are made explicit in the sense that they can be operated on.

Two chapters refer to both explicitation and implicitation. Fischbein describes several examples of mental models that were originally explicit and became implicit. He argues that explicit models may become implicit as an effect of routine or if their explicit use contradicts newly learned principles. Fischbein further argues that an individual may become aware of his implicit model by an analytical effort made in response to a question. Clement suggests that imagistic simulation is one means of making implicit knowledge more explicit. He mentions that this is the opposite direction from automatization, where a procedure learned explicitly becomes routinized and, hence, implicit.

In the research literature there are many descriptions of knowledge that initially was explicit and then became implicit (see, for instance, Freudenthal's [1983] description of knowledge clogged by automatism). Similarly, there are many discussions on the importance of explicitating knowledge of which the learner is unaware (see, for instance, Bialystok [1983] on inferencing; Forrest-Pressely, MacKinnon, & Waller [1985] on metacognition; and Schonfeld [1985] on problem solving). Yet, these discussions leave many questions open for further consideration. I now mention only two central ones: Are the mechanisms that can account for explicitation of knowledge similar to those involved in the implicitation of knowledge? And, What factors influence one's access to knowledge? These questions have been addressed by Karmiloff-Smith (1987) and by Prawat (1989). Both these researchers state that these issues have become particularly important for developmental psychologists and that more work should be devoted their to exploration. We hope this book provides some stimulation for the debate about these issues.

An Epilogue

This introduction attempted to provide the reader with a preliminary flavor of the book. It presents a brief synopsis of each chapter and of the various perspectives related to the definitions of implicit and explicit knowledge and their relationships, their importance for developmental psychology, and their usefulness for education. Other issues and themes are embedded in each chapter. At this point we will let the authors of the chapters tell their own story, so that the reader may explore the explicit as well as implicit ideas that interweave to form the fabric of this volume.

References

Bialystok, F. (1983). Inferencing: Testing the "hypothesis-testing" hypothesis. In H. W. Seliger & M. H. Long (Eds.), *Classroom oriented research in second language acquisition* (pp. 104–123). London: Newbury House Pub.

Campbell, R. N. (1986). Language acquisition and cognition. In P. Fletcher & M. Garman (Eds.), *Language acquisition* (2nd ed., pp. 30–48). Cambridge: Cambridge University Press.

Chomsky, N. (1980). *Rules and representations.* New York: Columbia University Press.

Dennett, D. C. (1985). *Content and consciousness* (2nd ed.). London: Routledge & Kegan Paul.

Forrest-Pressely, D. L., MacKinnon, G. E., & Waller, T. (Eds.). (1985). *Metacognition, cognition and human performance.* New York: Academic Press.

Freudenthal, H. (1983). *Didactical phenomenology of mathematical structures.* Dordrecht: Reidel.

Karmiloff-Smith, A. (1986). From meta-processes to conscious access: Evidence from children's metalinguistic and repair data. *Cognition, 23,* 95–147.

Karmiloff-Smith, A. (1987, April). *Beyond modularity: A developmental perspective on human consciousness.* Paper presented at the annual meeting of the British Psychological Society, Sussex.

Polanyi, M. (1969). *Knowing and being.* London: Routledge & Kegan Paul.

Prawat, P. S. (1989). Promoting access to knowledge, strategy, and disposition in students: A research synthesis. *Review of Educational Research, 59,* 1–41.

Schonfeld, A. (1985). *Mathematical problem solving.* New York: Academic Press.

1

Speculations on the Foundations of Knowledge and Intelligence

Andrea A. diSessa
University of California, Berkeley

Motivation: How Complex Are Minds?

This chapter asks, from a particular genetic epistemological stance, the simple question: "What are the fundamental problems of knowledge and intelligence, and how have humans solved these, to the extent that they are solved?"

The approach taken here is motivated by two quite opposite thrusts. The first is ancient, but certainly became prominent in eighteenth- and nineteenth-century European philosophy of mind. It presumes a basic *simplicity* to the mechanisms of mind; indeed, it may seek to enumerate them.

> Though it be too obvious to escape observation that different ideas are connected together, I do not find that any philosopher has attempted to enumerate or class all the principles of association—a subject, however that seems worthy of curiosity. To me there appear to be only three principles of connection among ideas, namely, *Resemblance, Continuity* in time or place, and *Cause and Effect*. . . . A picture naturally leads our thoughts to the original [Resemblance]. The mention of one apartment in a building naturally introduces an inquiry or discourse concerning the others [Contiguity]; and if we think of a wound, we can scarcely forbear reflecting on the pain which follows it [Cause and Effect]. (Hume, 1962)

Following the information-processing revolution, distinctly new approaches in this direction have emerged. One of the more pure, and one to which I shall refer in some detail, is the Physical Symbol System Hypothesis, formulated by Alan Newell and others, which claims to lay out in a small set of axioms the definition of a physical symbol system. The axioms are formulated so as to make clear that symbolic processing on a digital computer is an archetypical physical symbol system. Newell puts forward the hypothesis that having a physical symbol system is more or less a necessary and sufficient condition for intelligence. Thus, human beings are intelligent pretty much because they are, like computers, physical symbol processors, and any system can be (more or less) intelligent that is such a

This work has benefited immensely from the conceptual and editorial criticism of Steve Adams, Melinda diSessa, Susan Newman, and Jack Smith. Special thanks for careful criticism and encouragement go to Sid Strauss and Dina Tirosh. Others who made contributions were Efraim Fischbein and Don Ploger. I apologize to those whose contributions over this year I have neglected to acknowledge.

symbol system. More recently, Newell himself, along with John Anderson and others, has developed more elaborate theoretical systems that are claimed to constitute the basic architecture of cognition.

Opposed to this thrust toward simplicity are perspectives that see a hugely rich and diverse phenomenology of cognition and hold little hope for a simple central core. In fact, a great deal of the psychological literature has played out unintentionally in this direction, having announced candidate after candidate of fundamental mechanism or phenomenon at various levels of cognition, from associative bonds to cognitive dissonance. Unfortunately, after some consideration, these seem not up to the job of really implementing, in any general terms, what we might call a cognitive system. They leave us with the impression that minds might indeed be enormously complex, to be understood cumulatively through the discovery of one after another interesting little corner of cognitive mechanism.

I see Piaget's work as having, equally unintentionally, played itself out in the direction of complexity. Though Piaget aimed at finding the basic structures of intelligence through genetic studies, in the end one is most impressed by the richness and diversity of phenomena—on the large scale, things like conservation, object permanence, and so on, and on the small scale hundreds of interesting little filigrees of development in his beautiful examples of children's reasoning. On the grand scale of universals of development, too many questions remain: Exactly where and, indeed, what are structures? Are stages real, substantial chunks of cognitive development or artifacts of children having finally put together only some little subview of the world the way adults do? What are the very general developmental mechanisms like equilibration, and can they really account for the emergence of intelligence?

My own position on this spectrum is that of a slightly disappointed physicist, knowing that the power of science is in simplicity and perspicuity, yet chastened by a careful look at one interesting domain of cognitive phenomena. This domain is what I call intuitive physics—how people reason spontaneously about the physical world and how that knowledge evolves, particularly toward "school" physics. Part of my investigation into intuitive physics (diSessa, 1993)[1] was to take a careful look at some of the initially plausible candidates for a simple, systematic view of this development. Do children start with strong beliefs in misguided alternatives to Newtonian physics, "misconceptions" that must be undermined by explicit articulation and argumentation? Can we respectably view the relevant changes as theory change (say, from an "impetus theory" to a Newtonian one)? Or, perhaps more modestly, can we view them as an ontological shift (from motion as a *process* that needs a cause, to motion as a *natural state* that needs no explanation except when the motion changes)? The disappointment is that the data seem quite clearly to undermine these views, leading me to consider them simplistic rather than sim-

---

[1] Much of this chapter is motivated and empirically grounded in diSessa (1993). That paper will be a constant reference for both details and general perspective.

plifications. Conceptual development seems to proceed on a subconceptual or at least subtheoretical scale, and there are many details at this level to attend to.

This is not to say that there are not some generalities, some candidates for new simplicities that emerge from this work. For example, although intuitive knowledge is hardly systematic enough to be called theorylike, it is not at all without character, with more and less central elements and some fairly coherent subsystems. A second simplification that seems not to be simplistic is that the basic structural character of intuitive knowledge must change in fairly dramatic ways, from a rather fragmented, diverse system, to one that is still somewhat fragmented and diverse but can with some reliability manage to think about a very broad range of phenomena on the basis of a very small number of general constructs.

Still, these results are unsettling. These new systematicities are strongly data dependent; one cannot make predictions without knowing a great deal about the system at early stages. Even then, predictions are limited to announcing more or less plausible developmental routes rather than required ones. With respect to basic structural change, we may see a fundamental epistemological problem that needs to be solved (such as the emergence of a much stronger systematicity), but we do not know how it is solved—or rather, we expect that a great diversity of mechanisms are involved in solving it.

This chapter, then, represents a renewed attack on the diversity and complexity of cognition. The hypothesis is that having learned some important lessons about what kinds of simplicity we cannot expect, we can come back to the search for universal mechanisms of cognition and take some steps toward making such presumptions pay. In contrast to Hume, Newell, and Anderson, my approach is fundamentally developmental. Following Piaget, I think we can unlock many of the secrets of intelligence by considering its genesis. Developmental studies are important in that they show us what kinds of simplicity we cannot expect and sometimes hint at what kinds of simplicity can remain. On the other hand, the sense of underlying mechanisms displayed here is more like that of contemporary cognitive science than Piaget's.

This chapter tries to lay out the beginnings of a program rather than its conclusions. In this way, it is clearly speculative. The program is presented as a set of questions and a frame for thinking about answers. Answers offered here are intended to clarify what the questions mean, to consider what might constitute an answer, and to suggest how one can argue about these issues.

Framework for Analysis: A Causal Scheme

John Searle (1984) asks the provocative question, "What causes minds?" Similarly, this is precisely the central question I try to answer here, at least schematically. Searle's reply is equally provocative. He says, "Brains cause minds." In contrast, I say, with an equivalently elliptical phrasing, that *developmental history causes minds*. The central focus is the effective structure and operation of minds, and the project is (a) to enumerate the factors involved in genesis of that structure and (b) to say what parts of structure are determined by which factors, and how the "determining" gets done.

Causality is a notoriously difficult notion to pin down, though it seems a pervasive mode of analysis in humans. I take this absence of accepted definitions as an opportunity to create a meaning for cause that helps us think about the structure of minds, rather than to appropriate models from other contexts like billiard balls propelling each other in regular ways.

As with billiard ball causality, events are central constructs here. I take events in mind construction to be defined by *problems* not satisfactorily solved by previous events of construction. The causal event itself is the construction of a new structure that, at least to some degree, solves the described problem. In a very crude way, we may say that some organisms have solved the problem of remotely sensing objects by developing eyes. I am after the cognitive equivalent of this.

What is the microstructure of events? Is it some continuous evolution or can we unfold any event into a sequence of microevents? I needn't take a position on this. Instead, I wish to pursue a deliberately synoptic view of causality as a series of events to see how insightful that can be.

To make sense, problems must be such that the system can know that an advance has been made—there must be appropriate *feedback*. From a phylogenetic standpoint, this feedback might well take the form of evolutionary success; solving certain problems—like being able to see prey or predators—confers on organisms a survival advantage. From an ontogenetic perspective I presume as well that changes in the system are driven by success in terms that can be "perceived" by the system.[2]

Identifying feedback presents complications that will need sorting out. Phylogenetic advantages may play themselves out ontogenetically in ways that are not perceptible as local, individual improvements, nor even in ways that appear locally responsive to "perceptible" problems. For example, the "development" (triggering) of instincts may be at present a maladapted expression of what was once a great advantage to the species. Nonetheless, in some way changes in processing should be sustainable only if some appropriate level of system (e.g., phylo- or ontogenetic levels) receives feedback in some version of success and failure. In the case of instincts, we can be fairly sure that at some stage they had quite direct survival value.

In some cases, apparently unguided development may be explained by principles that may themselves have come to exist as structural features of the system. Aspects of biological maturation may not be directly attributable to feedback. Cognitively, one might claim "humans seek coherent views." Principles that do not involve immediate feedback may be needed, but we need to cash them out in specific terms and to describe how those terms emerged from a situation of effective feedback.

---

[2] Of course, I should remove all the anthropomorphic tone from these descriptions. But I take this not to be too difficult a task, so I won't complicate the reader's task by using arcane descriptions that avoid the appearance of anthropomorphism.

How were those principles perceptible as effective to some level of living, changing system?

In addition to *problems* and *feedback*, there are other slots in this causal scheme that must be filled in. First, what are the *prior resources* out of which the problems are solved? Much of the time, prior resources will undoubtedly have been created in some previous causal event. Some prior resources may be provided by entirely other levels of development. For example, resources provided to the species may be used by the individual to solve problems, out of which further developments become possible. Similarly, social theorists may hope to show that solutions to essentially social problems by essentially social means provide basic resources to individual cognition. This is a central claim of Vygotskian analysis.

Finally, we need *principles of invention* by which the appropriate level of system (individual, species, social group) changes itself. These principles may be very simple. For example, chance provides, to first approximation, the origin of new species in Darwin's theory. Or, principles of invention may reside in resources specifically provided by earlier developmental episodes. For example, a human designer creates innovative resources for himself by realizing that, in a particular act of design, he has produced a schema for solution of a general class of problems. A computer program may be abstracted as a general algorithm, and presumably the designer at some point learned how to abstract algorithms.

So, in a nutshell, the program is to look at cognition as constituting a bundle of resources for successfully negotiating circumstances. Each resource must have been provided in some past causal event for which we want to be able to announce (a) the *problem*, (b) the mechanisms of *feedback* on positive solution, (c) the *principles of invention*, and (d) the *prior resources* on which the invention is based. In general we would apply the program recursively on the resources involved in any causal event. At the risk of appearing to engage in anthropomorphism, I will mnemonically call these causal events *design episodes*. Typically, a designer engages the same aspects: a problem, some creative or inventive resources, structural materials out of which to fashion a solution, and some principles of judgment on which he may be satisfied by his invention.

Unlike other causal schemata that might directly supply the structure of the outcome simply and directly from the articulation of the context of the causal event, this one only provides a ground for further argumentation. Thus, the really important discussion begins upon determining what fills in these four slots. On the basis of the detailed characteristics of each of these contributing factors, we argue that features of the solution are due to particular features of the contributing factors, or to specific relational features of their combination. I refer to this line of argumentation as determining the *propagation (or morphosis) of structure*. The need for situation-specific argument concerning the propagation of structure reflects the assumption that we are dealing with complex systems and complex evolutionary processes. No simple universal analysis is likely to suffice for tracing the emergence of new structures out of old ones. I only maintain (hypothetically) that all such analyses will follow this fourfold scheme and postpone particulars. Contrast a collision causal schema wherein every aspect of all possible collisions can be specified in advance, by conservation of momentum and energy.

The basis for this work, then, is that this fourfold analysis of causal events constitutes a minimal and natural schematization in terms of which to determine the propagation of structure and thus to understand the genesis of knowledge and intelligence. Each of the four aspects can be motivated independently. For example, it makes little sense to think that some new state of an evolving complex system can be understood without reference to the structure of prior states out of which it evolved (prior resources). More and more, this constructivist principle seems central to the analysis of learning, to take one case. As well, we must generally suspect that features of cognition are responsive to describable needs (problems) and that unless there is some mechanism by which the meeting of those needs can be fed back into the system, we might just as well believe in the spontaneous development of intelligence in the total absence of need. Finally, unless there are principles by which new structure is generated (invention), feedback will have nothing new to "approve."

Collectively, once we have identified a niche for change, a principle that can enact such a change, the prior structures out of which the change may be fashioned, and processes that validate the need for change operationally, nothing much remains except to argue the details of propagation of structure.

This genetic/causal program for studying complex systems has had enlightening successes outside of cognition. I've already referred to Darwinian evolution. Biology provides several other examples. An organism clearly needs some way informationally to propagate its evolutionary successes from one generation to the next. In principle, some kind of reproducible linear coding sequence would be an ideal solution, provided subsidiary problems can be solved, such as mechanisms by which that code can be transformed into working structure. We have come to understand that essentially one solution to this problem, along these specific lines of an easily reproducible linear code, is characteristic of all life on this planet. Similarly, all organisms need to utilize energy. We have come to understand that all living organisms use and recover energy largely in the form of one specific molecule—adenosine tri-phosphate (ATP). And although organisms can extract energy from a wide range of fuels, all the major fuel molecules ultimately converge into one final common pathway (the Krebs tricarboxylic acid cycle). This pathway is central to energy production in all plants and animals. In the context of the genetic/causal program, we can interpret ATP and the TCA cycle simply as (a central piece of) the solution to a universal biological problem.

I seek simplicity by focusing on *fundamental* problems that determine resources, major structural features of cognition. Although we may hope to find a simple mapping from need to structure, a priori I suspect that such universality is rare. Thus, important and general problems for cognition may be solved in multiple ways, in multiple contexts of invention. In such cases, we preserve simplicity by indexing cognitive structures by problems rather than by solutions.

Aims and Limitations

On a grand scale, I imagine unfolding the development of knowledge and intelligence backward, through resources and episodes that created those resources to hopefully unproblematically physical resources, problems, and principles of invention. At best, this unfolding will proceed seamlessly back into biology and chemistry. Needless to say, I will not press the program that far here. On the other hand, I do need to present some sense of what are more primitive resources. I will generally assume connectionist resources as very low-level capabilities, which here will need no genetic analysis. In other cases, what resources are prior will need specific argument.

In addition to not pressing the program too far back in genetic history, I will not be able to carry it out at any stage in great detail. I will apologize only this once for gaps in the presentation and hope that the insights afforded while suppressing obvious details are good enough to encourage future work.

While the genetic/causal program aims at simplicity, it also seeks to ensure that each described design episode is grounded in particulars of prior resources, characteristics of feedback, and available principles of invention. So a productive tension between simplicity and complexity seems deeply embedded in the approach.

Indeed, because of this tension the whole program may fail in an interesting way. It may well be that cognitive infrastructure develops by an intricate complex of idiosyncratic solutions to idiosyncratic problems at very small scales of design. What emerges may be a physical symbol system, but with a great number of mostly independent resources, in varying degrees of approximation to Newell's (or any) ideal model. That would make it impossible to draw illuminating mappings between simple functional models and the realized system. But the thrust of this chapter is to consider that there may be important modules of cognition (or at least central characteristic problems that are to be solved in idiosyncratic ways, perhaps repeatedly) and to look for them.

It may be that details in the propagation of structure clinch the case for any proposed design episode. We may know that some subsystem developed from some other subsystem in a certain way because characteristic features of prior resources, or of mechanisms of feedback, propagate into the offspring resource. Indeed, this is the way I expect some of the story to work out. Thus, we may be able to deconstruct rationality—to find its purpose and heritage from its characteristically human form. Limitations may serve as artifacts that are as informative about design episodes as knowing the fundamental problems.

Levels

I will organize consideration of resources and their genesis into three rough levels. The first, which I call *alpha*, has to do with information-processing infrastructure— basic and generic capabilities that a general information-processing system must have. The second, *beta*, has to do specifically with knowledge representational capabilities. Though the alpha level may be capable of supporting these beta resources, the presumption in looking at the beta level is that knowledge representation problems may more fundamentally drive development according to our causal scheme. Representation may, in some respects, precede general information-processing capabilities, or the two may be simultaneously realized, with alpha capabilities "incidental" to beta. Another way this may work out is that the alpha level may constitute such primitive resources that too little structure is implied by them to be insightful in the functional/causal way we wish.

The *gamma* level is the level of specific knowledge. Of course I wish to know how specific knowledge evolves, but the primary reason this level is interesting here is that general resources might evolve out of quite particular knowledge, a hypothesis to which I will repeatedly turn.

Deconstruction at the Alpha Level

What capabilities might constitute the minimal "machine" capabilities necessary to build an intelligent system? Apparently people have these in their brains by virtue of whatever neural processes exist there. However, how do we characterize these in ways more illuminating than "brains have them"?

The theory of computation provides a suggestion. In studying the intrinsic capabilities of various classes of computing systems, it has been discovered that essentially all known computational machines are absolutely equivalent in the set of algorithms they can implement. This includes every common digital computer, from the largest mainframe to the smallest micro—and even considerably more modest systems that, on the face of it, seem simply not of the same league as typical computers. These are called *Turing equivalent machines.*[3]

Artificial intelligence and cognitive science have proceeded largely on the basis of cognitive modeling systems defined in terms compatible enough with the theory of computation that their status as Turing equivalent machines is entirely evident. Spurred especially by researchers such as Newell and Simon, it became a tacit and sometimes explicit assumption that intelligence requires a Turing equivalent machine, and nothing much more.

Newell in particular championed this idea and provided a characterization of Turing equivalent machines in terms that highlight the role of symbols in them. He called these systems *physical symbol systems* and framed, with Simon, the hypothesis that intelligence is, more or less, the same as being a physical symbol system. For our purposes, I take the axioms of physical symbol systems as an archetypical alpha level specification.[4,5]

---

[3] For these purposes, the speed with which a computation can be made is ignored. Consult any good text on the theory of computation for details.

[4] Newell in his SOAR system, Anderson in ACT*, and others have provided extensions of the idea of physical symbol systems that might serve as alpha level specifications. However, these are too complex to be discussed here.

[5] Recently, advocates of connectionist architectures have claimed that physical symbol systems are too rigid to model human cognition. For two reasons, they are less interesting to discuss here. First, the

Table 1.1. Functions That Define a Symbol System

Function	Subfunction	Explanation
Abstraction	*Assign*	Naming
	Quote	Controlling reference; variable/literal distinction
	Copy	Supporting isomorphism as well as identity
Representation	*Read* symbol at position *R* from an expression	Fetch
	Write to position *R* in an expression	Mutate
Control	*Do*	Sequence
	Exit if . . .	Conditional
	Continue if . . .	
I.O.	*Input*	Input
	Behave	Output

Let us look at the component capabilities of physical symbol systems, according to Newell (1980), and slightly recharacterized by diSessa (1986) as shown in Table 1.1, to see if we can understand these as reasonable human resources, generated from preexisting resources to solve perceptible problems on the basis of plausible inventive capabilities. In short, our inquiry is to try to understand the cognitive/developmental niches that may correspond to the resources that define Turing equivalence. These resources fall into four general classes: capabilities related to abstracting; capabilities related to representing knowledge; capabilities to compute based on knowledge (internal state); and the ability to read in information as symbols and to produce output actions on the basis of internal states.

Abstraction

Naming. It is difficult to avoid discussing the linguistic capabilities of humans, since these are so powerful that many resources we might mention simply "come along for free" for processors that have linguistic capabilities. Naming is one of these. Yet, I will avoid discussing language for three reasons. First, I cannot pretend to have carried out a genetic/causal analysis for language. It seems immodest even to start. Second, I do not wish to beg the question of stating what problems naming solves in general terms independent of language. Third, it should be illuminating to understand some nonlinguistic versions of the resources that may stem from the same problem, in part to keep in mind that many apparently linguistic resources may also be nonlinguistic resources, and in part to understand what

computation theoretical status of connectionist systems is murky. And second, their basic mechanisms are so weak that connectionist capabilities are unlikely to support any of the kind of argumentation of the sort envisaged here. Instead, the more interesting question is how could connectionist resources be crafted to provide a basis for solving higher level problems?

resources might be available in prelinguistic cognition that might serve in the construction of language.

I take naming in a linguistic sense to be one version of the more general problem of reinstatiating a mind state (knowledge relating to the thing named) on the basis of a much more compact representation, a name. So, for example, one can retrieve all sorts of information about Joe by keeping his name in mind. Note, however, I am not necessarily dealing with naming a physical object nor with getting worldly access to it, such as finding it. That would fall more properly into the category of representation (see later discussion). Instead, naming can be an internal feature for the cognitive processor's private needs. In this form, there seems no doubt that this is a fundamental needed capability. It is a version of "chunking" (Newell, 1990; Simon, 1974).

If one asks why a processor would need to chunk rather than reinstantiate the full state, two answers come to mind. The first has specifically to do with limitations of the processor. Perhaps it cannot reinstantiate and keep active very complex knowledge states. Indeed, this is undoubtedly the case. Research on short-term memory indicates that one cannot keep arbitrarily large amounts of mind state ready for direct access. So computation may need to be "spread out" in space and time by using symbols as abbreviations for more complex mind states. In this form, the need to chunk makes sense as a general problem for which general resources might be useful.

However, framed as a problem in this way, I see no immediate way of identifying the other needed components of the genetic/causal program. It seems too big a jump to see a general chunking capability arising out of an unstructured connectionist system. Perhaps we need intermediate states of development, more local and manageable problems to solve on the way to solving this one. On the other hand, it may be profitable to assume chunking as a primitive resource for the purpose of investigating other resources built upon it.

The other need for chunking comes again more properly at the representational (beta) or even knowledge (gamma) level. That is, one may need to build packages of knowledge that can be known to be needed on the basis of some partial mind state, but of which only an appropriate subpart may be relevant to the current problem for the processor. Thus, Joe's name may occur to you when you need the telephone number of your brother-in-law at work, but it serves its role in this case only as an efficient index that allows you to recall his number (perhaps in an intermediate form as a physical index involving the partially extramental process of looking him up in the phone directory). The name Joe might have served all sorts of other purposes. But in this case, other parts of your mind state cause lookup of his phone number rather than, say, mental inspection of an image of him to determine if he has a beard. In general, appropriate resources for unpacking a chunk are necessary for this kind of chunking to make sense as a resource.

This kind of chunking is simply a manifestation of the power of developing efficient common resources. It is probably the same reason specialization take place in cultural roles, and why freeways are built instead of a greater number of smaller roads. If, in fact, any kind of resource is difficult to generate or maintain, one expects that certain of these resources will become central and "overused" because they exist and can do work in multiple ways. In the cognitive domain, a "Joe" package might exist simply because it can do so much work that other perhaps better tuned resources might be able to do, but at the cost of developing and maintaining them. I expect this to be a common and important macromechanism in cognitive development, the crystallization of modular common (meaning "joint") resources for multiple functions.

Such resources must satisfy an important set of constraints. First, they must be capable of a broad range of cognitive work. This probably means they sit at the nexus of more particular resources that can tune them to particular needs—the "unpacking" capabilities previously mentioned. Undoubtedly, the general resource must develop so as to be responsive to some needs of these ancillary resources (thus, a modest compatibility structuring—resources structured not only by their abstract function, but by the resources that use them). So freeways have exits to join preexisting local roads. Second, the central resource must either develop prior (so as to obviate the need for more special resources) or it must be more efficient in some ways to "crowd out" more special resources. It seems almost any form of difficulty in generating or maintaining new resources will be sufficient to crowd out noncentral ones in favor of central, frequently used ones. Forgetting and evolving connectionist weights on the basis of frequency of use seem plausible place holders for this needed "crowding out" mechanism.

Chunking for the purpose of crystallization of common resources would also seem necessarily to operate in many diverse circumstances—wherever multiple needs can be served by centralized chunks. As such, the development of meta resources to solve at once *every* instance of building common resource chunks seems unlikely.[6] Instead, chunking to create common resources is a mechanism that will work in many circumstances to produce solutions that are particular to the confluence of resources that the crystallization absorbs.

The variable/literal distinction. Even within language, the distinction between a token and that to which it refers is a problematic accomplishment that humans cannot regularly enact.[7] Further, it is difficult to see any general problem to which this supplies an answer, and what feedback is provided by solving it, let alone to know the resources with which to implement the solution. For example, symbols meet their primary needs as previously discussed, in chunking or referring. The need for a metalanguage to consider and describe tokens, while evidently important for linguists and for the capability of a programming language to describe itself, seems beyond basic cognitive needs.

Certainly there are much more specific problems where resources similar to the token/referent distinction need to be enacted. For example, in case of a problem in

---

6 However, this seems precisely the intention of SOAR.
7 This is an impression about which I am, of course, open to experimental data.

interpretation, you may need to distinguish between what you inferred and the literal words somebody said to you. A much weaker version, "knowing" the distinction between a memory and current experience (which is constructed in part with schemata that are themselves "memories" of prior experiences) would seem to have a very different genetic route and to require very different resources to solve. It seems safest here to presume the variable/literal distinction exists in multiple formats that are solved at least partially in each, rather than to assume that a general resource exists.

Copying. The capability to copy data, say, into a new problem-solving context seems a useful resource. However, I do not discuss it here for several reasons. First, this resource is quite particular to a class of cognitive architectures. With appropriate modularity constructions, we could well assume that essentially no copying needs to be done, but that common resources are used in multiple contexts.[8] Second, the more serious problem would seem to be learning, deciding which substructure to copy, rather than the copying itself. Literally copying data structures, at least on first blush, would appear to be too low level a system capability to have a well-defined cognitive/developmental niche.

Representation
Newell characterizes representational capabilities by example as being able to read a symbol from some position in a compound structure, and to write a new symbol into such a position. Certainly representation is an important resource for cognition, but one I will treat mostly at higher levels. We have the same difficulties with this level and version of representational resources as with copying. First, it is a quite particular version of representational resources. Second, the other slots in our causal scheme seem very difficult to fill in if the problem is sketched at this level. For example, it is hard to know how prior resources could set up for the invention of this symbol reading and writing capability, while not already substantially possessing it. And once again, learning "when" seems the much harder and at least as important question as learning "how." The problems of knowing when to save data in an appropriate structure and when to access it may be the central-most problems of knowledge. But stated in this way, these problems are at much too high a level to support genetic/causal analysis. It seems also too difficult to approach those problems without presuming other aspects of representation (which I treat later) in order to escape dramatic underspecification of the design context.

There is one aspect of the representation component of the Physical Symbol System Hypothesis that I find intriguing with respect to the present program. Let me focus, for the moment, on the physical instantiation of symbols per se. This is an easy concern to miss, for assumptions about it are distributed among the axioms. In particular, I ask how the individual identity of symbols is established. We all can

---

[8] Say, an uncopied structure is used in each instance that a copy might be needed, but in a larger data structure that contains an instance index.

recognize symbols like "Joe" when we see them, even when written somewhat irregularly. Computers can internally do the equivalent or else we would say they were having memory errors. But how is the equivalence class of states that count as "Joe" established genetically? I am asking for the propagation of structure from prior resources, problem contexts, inventive processes, and feedback structures to establishing the equivalence classes of physical states that count as the same symbol.

The fact of symbol identity mechanisms is, by itself, not problematic. In digital computers registers and memory locations contain binary codes that establish symbol identity. Starting from a connectionist architecture, some versions of symbol identity are also unproblematic. Say, for example, in the midst of processing a conditional, the connectionist processor needs to check the memory contents of a data structure. This is implementable, in its essence, in the network in Figure 1.1. Node 1 represents querying the particular condition in question. Node 2 is connected to a distinct part of the network that provides the answer to the conditional with the activation, or not, of that particular node. Node 3 reads node 1 and node 2 (only) and provides a "yes" (active state) only if both are active. We presume the rest of the computation depends on node 3 in such a way as to have the desired control effect.

Node 2 symbolizes the truth value of a predicate using tokens equivalent to 0 and 1. The rest of this small network provides the interface so as to be able to use that symbolization effectively. But note how restrictive the notion of symbol identity is here. Without considerably more structure, it is only this node that can count as having this particular symbol 1. There is no possibility of general fetching, moving around, and comparing of symbols.

Contrast digital computers where one certainly has a dramatically broader and more complex notion of symbol identity. This is provided in the various fundamental data types that may be transferred to and occupy essentially any slot in memory. Numbers and characters each have a finite set of generators of their particular symbol subset. This is in contrast, for example, to symbol sets arbitrarily filling the

Figure 1.1. A connectionist conditional.

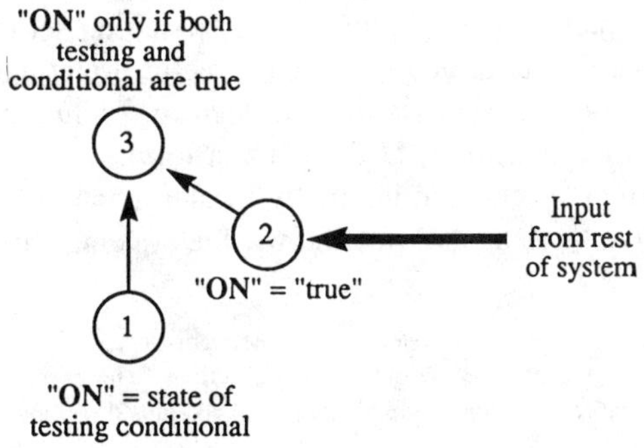

"ON" only if both
testing and
conditional are true

Input
from rest
of system

"ON" = "true"

"ON" = state of
testing conditional

state space of the computer, as, for example, programming with data composed only of binary words.

Such diversity in solutions to the symbol identity problem poses again in sharp terms the starting question. Genetically, what determines the general character of symbol identity and the particular ranges of symbol sets?

Surprisingly, one can take some hints from the answers to this question for digital computers. First, the symbol identity set might be contributed by the supplied architecture, as exemplified in the extreme by binary words in a digital computer. Even more extreme, consider nodes in a connectionist architecture. But this still begs the developmental question of how the architecture came to exist or, in the connectionist case, how a net might decide to use some nodes in its state as symbols.[9] More enlightening, note that common symbol sets in computers are defined by particular use. For example, the representation of numbers is determined by the specific subarchitecture tuned to processing them (e.g., IEEE standards, which exist, in part, so that arithmetic coprocessors can do their job efficiently). Consider also that character strings are present basically to provide efficient I.O. to the external world, namely, to humans who like to see at least approximately familiar linguistic representations of code.

It seems reasonable to conjecture that some versions of these reasons exist in the genesis of any physical symbol system. Thus, some symbol sets may exist for efficiency or compatibility with particular subsystems. A version of this is that symbol equivalence sets exist solely for their role in prior versions of the processing system. Thus learning and change may provide substantial problems to consider along the lines of transforming symbol sets into new symbol sets appropriate to more advanced systems. My expectation here, again, is that the mind has not solved problems computer scientists would believe dubious, to produce some universally appropriate symbol set (Fodor's speculations notwithstanding). Instead, the transition from one symbol set to another, or the development of new symbol sets, constitutes a constant, central problem of cognitive evolution and learning. In the case of intuitive physics, I believe this problem translates almost directly into important and necessary continuities from intuitive to formal physics. That is, in serving the role of an explanatory system concerning the workings of the physical world, school physics is constrained to begin with the same vocabulary (symbols) as intuitive physics. This is true because intuitive physics contains (with some qualifications I shall suppress here) the only workable starting set of symbols that can interface appropriately to prior and to some degree invariant mental apparati, such as the perception of objects, motion, and mechanism. I return specifically to these issues, in slightly modified form, at the gamma level.

Note that this latter speculation implicitly locates symbols, at least sometimes, close to the primitive "meanings" of a knowledge system. This is a version of the

---

[9] If we were to implement a symbol system in a connectionist net, undoubtedly many nodes would serve support roles to implement the various symbolic actions. Those supporting nodes that, say, implement a fetch or a store of symbols would not, in all likelihood, be interpretable as symbols.

conjecture that symbol sets are always strongly tuned to some context, that data representation and the specific processing that runs over it are not independently determined. I certainly do not mean, however, to preclude symbols that are *not* directly representational in the sense of being related to external circumstances, like symbols for world objects. Indeed, later I argue that some of the essential infrastructure of representation cannot be assigned representational meaning. If symbol systems implement this infrastructure, the symbols involved will not be representational in any direct sense. In the gamma level section, I discuss how notions of agency evolve from attributions to the physical world to a part of the infrastructure of reasoning with Newtonian mechanics. As part of Newtonian thinking, however, agency is no longer attributed as an objective feature of the world. If we believe symbols implement the concept of agency, this is an example of representational symbols evolving into nonrepresentational ones.

To close this subsection, note that a strong independence of data symbols from processing system characteristics, such as apparently presumed in Newell's characterization of a universal capability to inspect and mutate data symbols, may lead to very fragile processing systems. If an arbitrary symbol can be inserted, in principle, in arbitrary locations, then small errors in processing could result in dramatic performance errors. If a visual memory symbol is inserted in an aural memory location, or worse, in a motor processing location, spectacular performance errors would no doubt result. Thus, we expect subsystems to keep track of their own symbol sets. As a result, except for the needs of intermodule communication, these sets need not be at all universal.

I treat the last two classes of symbol system capabilities briefly.

Control

Sequential and conditional control do not seem to be a serious problem. Even connectionist systems should not have a difficult time implementing local versions of them. Consider the connectionist conditional mentioned previously. However, strong and broadly applicable methods require a degree of structure that may be very unusual, including hypotheticals and substantially more control over which knowledge applies to a situation. (I return to this problem at the beta and gamma levels. At the gamma level, one problem with developing a Newtonian physics is that intuitions need to be distinguished from more principled means of reasoning about a situation.) I presume as a default, however, that the major parts of this structuring are built anew in each knowledge domain. That is, the general capabilities are very little, if any, more than automatically emergent properties of richly developed knowledge systems. In a related case, the architecture to implement goals and plans may emerge automatically in the course of developing knowledge in a domain. Thus it would not make sense to consider goal and planning structure as a general resource, but one built incidentally in each domain (with undoubted resemblance of common structure, but without any common resources).

As is generally the case here, I cannot argue these presumptions in detail. However, consider: If plans are built out of gradually abstracted descriptions of personal performance and expectations about particular world states that will emerge from some chosen action, there seems little need for general planning structure. Equivalently, interfacing general planning knowledge to the particular knowledge in some domain might be so intricate as to effectively demand that planning emerge anew in each substantial domain. The current psychological literature on physics problem solving does not point to any central role for general planning knowledge. Most of the work seems to be done by physics-specific schemata. On the other hand, some related AI work on qualitative physics implies very systematic and elaborated planning-like structures to consider and evaluate possibilities (see de Kleer, 1982; Forbus, 1984).

Input and Output

Input and output seem relatively uninteresting for our present enterprise in that lower forms of life seem to have mastered these capabilities at least as well as humans have. That is, if we are interested in intelligence in forms that are rather distinctly human—problem solving, learning physics, and so on—we can assume input and output are solved phylogenetically. What should be extraordinarily interesting, however, is to investigate how particular I.O. capabilities, as prior resources, might influence the development of "higher level" cognition. Newell's formulation of basic cognitive resources does not give us any hints for this. For example, we might want to trace (and I will) how spatial perceptual capabilities might get embodied in more general thinking resources. More dramatically, one of my favorite conjectures is that the problem of invariant recognition (the ability to recognize an entity through a very broad range of presentations) is solved phylogenetically initially in the sensory apparatus, and those capabilities propagate into general intelligent processing. If we take a "nearly hardwired" view of perception on the sensory input side, then perhaps the central-most problem to be solved in liberating invariant recognition capability as a general resource is to get the process to operate on arbitrary new tokens that are part of newly developed capabilities, rather than being tied to more directly perceptual processing. That is, what is needed is to invariantly recognize diverse patterns of arbitrary brain state, rather than patterns only in specifically sensory brain state, such as what is connected to the optic nerve.[10] Generalizing invariant recognizing capability to operate on arbitrary internal state (as opposed to only more directly external sensory state), through arbitrarily parameterized variations (rather than, say, just variation due to perspective), may constitute one of the earliest, most general, and most important phylogenetic resource advances. A possible genetic mechanism for reusing specific brain resources in this way and, indeed, the plausibility and potential importance of such a mechanism are discussed in Rozin (1976).

---

[10] Generating new tokens representing a nonsensory recognition seems somewhat less problematic, as, presumably, new tokens need to be generated as the result of learning to invariantly recognize novel objects in purely sensory systems.

A second example of propagation of structure out of sensory apparatus is similar to the compatibility of symbols between two communicating subsystems previously described. It seems unlikely that a powerful sensory system like vision would not induce compatible but more general capabilities in neighboring resources, with compatible data representation for interresource communication. Thus, given how much input comes in a visual form, it seems unlikely that some general capability would not develop to operate on data in nearly visual form more flexibly than sensory processing allows. Humans should be able to imagine a scene with eyes closed and reason about changes in it, with conclusions drawn also in nearly visual form so as to link directly to standard motor routines. I certainly could not presume to describe how veridical these nonsensory resources would be. But later I discuss some surprising possible uses for such imagistic capabilities.

Alpha Retrospective

I can summarize how the Physical Symbol System Hypothesis fares as a candidate problem-generated resources for the genetic/causal view of cognition. First, it seems much too broad an accomplishment to have been achieved in a single stroke of design. Even the pieces of the hypothesis suffer the same problems: Specific feedback is hard to imagine on most, if not all pieces; how does the evolving system get feedback on being able to read and write symbols? Many of the capabilities seem so high level (variable/literal distinction), or so low level (copying), that it is hard to imagine the resources out of which they might have been built—as opposed to being "built in" for all practical purposes. We seem to need many intermediate levels of development to support any plausible design episodes. As well, the Symbol System Hypothesis is stated in terms of unlikely modularities: The hypothesis does not help us to understand how phylogenetically primitive capabilities, such as sensory recognition, might have provided structural help for later problems (general invariant recognition). Instead, these capabilities are described only as "input." Other implied modularities, such as that between representation and control seem much too strong. Starting with a primitive processing model like connectionism that has the data/control distinction all but invisible, how and why do representational tokens (symbols) split off from other processing infrastructure? I have argued, however briefly, that if the connection between data and process is not intimate, there would be no apparent design criteria for symbol sets, and processing might be delicate and prone to dramatic errors.

All this, of course, does not directly undermine the Physical Symbol System Hypothesis. I have sought to keep away from such an argument, either remaining agnostic or actually assuming the hypothesis in order to ask questions of development. Its advocates did not put forward the hypothesis as a genetic analysis of intelligence, so we should not demand it do that work.

The discussion here does suggest, however, that we may find no clean position on the continuum from a responsive but unintelligent system to an intelligent being that has cleanly achieved physical symbol system status. Instead, it seems likely that such a status is achieved in fits and starts, and in degrees of approximation that may be revealing of the situations out of which development arose, including of the characteristics of prior resources from which symbol system capabilities were built. Human beings might be "exotic" symbol processors with a broad range of implementations of each of the basic symbol system capabilities, each implementation specific to particular mental contexts. These implementations might be different only for genetic/historical reasons, or there might be more profound reasons the implementations are not mixed, such as robust performances in the face of errors. Be this as it may, from a psychological point of view the nature of humans' exoticism as symbol systems may be the most important thing we need to learn about them as information processors.

On the positive side, this brief exploration has uncovered at least one meta-developmental principle of invention, the crystallization of common resources, which would seem to work to refine systems in a wide range of circumstances. As well, I have repeatedly remarked that problems are not necessarily in the least isomorphic to their solution (as in the discussion of planning). So we may expect that, indeed, central problems may define the development of cognitive resources, but that they may be solved multiply in different contexts and with different resources. Finally, I have remarked that learning and change may be potent constraints that pose difficult problems for a processor—that, even if intelligence is adequately described as a physical symbol system, the capability to evolve that intelligence, as exemplified by the evolution of symbol sets, may provide as challenging and characteristic a problem as becoming a symbol system in the first place.

The Beta Level: Representational and Reasoning Infrastructure

No one can doubt that it is useful, in some sense, for a processor to be Turing equivalent. However, after the considerations of the last section, it seems that the capabilities of such machines do not match particularly well with the genetic/causal program I am pursuing. Being Turing equivalent does not seem directly to solve any practical and sensible problems. Hence, it seems, the developmental path to physical symbol systemhood is too complex for us to imagine in any detail at this point.

So, it is time to raise our sights above processing resources and attend to requirements for effectiveness in dealing with situations in the world. On the face of it we should at least have an easier time describing plausible problems and feedback. I address these issues in stages, first attending to generic resources in representing and processing environmental information (beta level). Then, in the next major section I address knowledge per se (gamma level), specific rather than generic capabilities.

Motivating the Beta Level

Perhaps the first person historically to consider basic representational resources as characteristic of intelligence was Immanuel Kant. Kant was concerned with what he called the form of knowledge, as opposed to its content. He posited a system of categories including basic notions of space, time, matter, and causality as absolutely and even a priori necessary for cognition. In some ways his program was a spectacular failure in that things he announced as indubitable and belonging to the very forms in which the cognized world must appear proved not only eminently doubtable, but simply false. We have come to understand that space is not necessarily conceived of as Euclidean and three dimensional (Einstein says it is, in fact, curved and four dimensional), matter is not conserved, nor is a proper subpart necessarily "smaller" than the whole (infinite subsets are not necessarily smaller than their supersets). Even more telling, we have come to understand that the cultivated adult common sense that Kant proclaimed as necessary is only gradually constructed. Children, who seem like reasonably cognitive beings in many respects, come to possess these categories only gradually and in various degrees of approximation. (I announced a similar possibility with respect to the issue of being a symbol system in the last section.) In fact, one can view Piaget as having pursued a strongly empirical version of the deconstruction problem that is characteristic of my efforts here—given evidently useful adult capabilities, how did they develop?

Despite their shortcomings, Kant's ideas are an important legacy in several respects. First, of course, I am pursuing in this section a version of his program, and I maintain the coherence of the concept of a generic representational level, at least hypothetically. Second, Kant's categories remain influential. Space, time, and causality, at least, will play important roles in the rest of my story, though not necessarily viewed as the same kind of general cognitive infrastructure that Kant imagined. Instead, I scan more broadly for generic representational problems and try to see how resources developed for other purposes may provide, through recrafting, resources at the beta level. For example, we shall come to see important, general, and very abstract resources like logic built at least in part on spatial or imagistic capabilities.

We clearly come to the idea of representation with substantial differences in assumptions from Kant's day. First, we have a quite different, post–information-processing common sense about cognition to guide us. This will lead to considering different sorts of beta-level programs and resources such as "appropriate persistence of mental states." Second, I will not assume beta resources are established once and for all. Generic problems may have to be solved multiple times in multiple contexts. Finally, we expect our arguments to be much more tentative. This follows from our genetic approach where prior resources may strongly determine succeeding problem solutions, and even their plausibility as problems. As with any history, prior history, to which we may have little access, may be important to the way things develop.[11]

In a similar way, the present genetic/causal program differs from Piaget's program and more generally from traditional developmental approaches to structural change. In developmental theory, discussions of "structural change" (as

---

[11] Perhaps, however, one may hope that characterizing the deepest and central-most problems is not historically contingent in this way.

compared to less deep changes, say, changes in "mere" knowledge) frequently beg the central question of defining *central* or *fundamental* structure. The definition is necessary since *any* change when viewed in a sufficiently elaborated theory, especially a computationally elaborated one, will involve changing structure. Thus if we can discover particular beta-level resources, then we can define structural change through new ways to solve these central or universal problems. Again, I hasten to point out that there is no necessity for any unique module that solves any particular problem. Universal problems might still be solved in numerous ways according to circumstances. But if there are unique modules that solve central problems, certainly one may expect them to define broad characteristics of the processor's state of development of intelligence.

I approach the beta level in three, successively more abstract stages. First, I discuss a case study of recrafting resources, the development of logical capabilities primarily out of spatial capabilities. The description of the relation of logic to other capabilities is provided by others, notably Johnson-Laird (1983). What I add to that description is to assimilate it to the genetic/causal frame; then, within that frame, I generalize the phenomenon. As an aside, I take a very brief look at a close partner to logic, propositions.

Second, I discuss the general issue of meaning. Computational theories of mind have been assailed as syntactic, as providing no account of meaning—the relation of mind states to world states. I argue that it is highly implausible that meaning is established as a one-to-one relation of symbols to referents. However, far from a general indictment of the program to provide computational explanations of mind, I take this as an opportunity to inquire what problems must be solved to create something that we might call meaning or representation.[12] Implicitly, I argue that this is a productive avenue to pursue in coming to understand meaning and representation in general terms.

Finally, I consider some other processing problems that seem quite general for real-world cognizing. These problems have to do with coordinating various forms of the same knowledge, with evoking knowledge in appropriate circumstances and maintaining it as long as may be needed. They will turn out also to apply quite well at the knowledge level (gamma).

Logic and Mental Models

Cognitive beings represent the world and reason about it. I do not undertake to defend such a proposition, but only to use it to focus on plausible cognitive resources.

---

[12] Some have claimed that it is absurd to look into the mind for representations. A mechanistic specification of the mind is impossible, they say, because cognition is fundamentally relational: It depends on both mind and the world. My position is that this is like describing the Guernica mural as fundamentally grey and black splotches—correct, but not particularly adequate. We know the relations are maintained on an everyday basis by mechanisms in the mind; it would profit us to have a bit more specification of them. These critics might, however, be pleased to see that I critique simplistic notions like single token reference and operationalize representation as classes of coordinations across the mind/world interface.

In the category of reasoning, logic has frequently been taken as an archetypical resource, if not the central or only resource. Again, I need not take a position on these matters except to note that people do, sometimes and after a fashion, reason logically. And therefore we may wish to deconstruct this capability according to the genetic/causal program.

Johnson-Laird (1983) proposes that logical processing for some classes of reasoning is built on a "mental modeling" basis involving spatial deployment of tokens representing individuals with various abstracted properties.[13] The logical reasoning itself is done by scanning exemplary tableaus of tokens, called models, and inspecting their properties. Sometimes it may be necessary to add, subtract, or move individuals to improve the initial tableau. Sometimes, indeed, additional tableaus must be constructed.

As an example, take the quantified syllogistic problem, "All men are mortal; some philosophers are men; therefore, what can we conclude?" A reasoner can build an exemplary array of tokens that are marked as "men," and a parallel array marked as "mortal beings." These arrays have a special relation from the first premise. That is, each man *is* a mortal being. We might represent this in the tableau in a number of ways. We might lay tokens out in two parallel columns, one-to-one, to show that for each man, we have a mortal being (see Figure 1.2a). Perhaps by syntactic convention, we put the men on the left, as the first mentioned type. As an alternative presentation we might draw arrows from each man to the mortal being that he is also. Or, more dynamically, we might imagine that each man, when focused upon, brings to our attention a mortal being, or even that the man turns into a mortal token.[14]

We probably should make sure to put extra tokens of mortal beings into the tableau that are not aligned with any man token. But, if our rules of tableau construction conform to the implied logic, we must have no men without corresponding mortal beings. We might encode this by reading that the column on the left is "shorter than" the column on the right.

The second premise, another pair of columns, might well be placed to the left of the preceding pair, as its right column belongs to the type "men," and we can then identify the right column of the second premise with the left column of the first (Figure 1.2b). Here, we have some unpaired members of the philosopher column. Now, what do we conclude? We might straightforwardly observed, by following a pair of pairings, that some philosophers are mortal, the judicious "some" following from the existence of extra tokens in the first column. We might also observe from the unpaired philosophers that some philosophers are not mortal. Unfortunately,

---

[13] Johnson-Laird's theory is more detailed and differs slightly from what is presented here. I do not think this does violence to the spirit of his analysis. The changes I have introduced are largely for simplicity's sake.

[14] These processes may be mediated by a number of particular dispositions and capabilities. For example, if you are told that some *x* have some property, you might be inclined to think that some *x* do not have the property, so "look for" some that do not. Then you might put such representatives in your tableau. Or, you might mentally encode "all *x* are *y*" with an "entailed properties" disposition to enter a *y* in your tableau whenever you encounter an *x*.

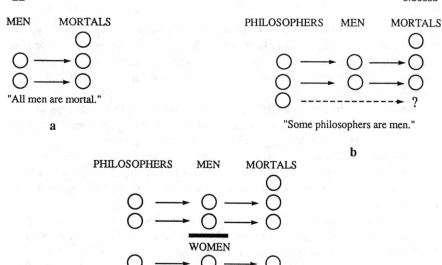

Figure 1.2. a. A tableau representing "All men are mortal." b. Adding "Some philosophers are men." Some philosophers are mortal, but are some philosophers not mortal? c. Patching the tableau to see that it may not be true that some philosophers are not mortal.

this last does not follow as there may be links between philosophers and mortals not mediated by men tokens. The interpreter doing this reasoning and, somehow, noticing that this incorrect conclusion sometimes occurs, might patch the construction of the arrays by always introducing parallel and exemplary companions of established mediators, in this case, men. These might be semantic companions, women, or they might be more logical companions, say, nonmen. Thus, we might easily modify our array by inserting a woman who is paired as a philosopher, and note that this woman might well be mortal, as most real women are (Figure 1.2c). Thus we would defeat the invited but incorrect conclusion that it is necessarily true that some philosophers are not mortal. From another point of view, women philosophers represent counterexamples to the proposed necessity that nonmen philosophers are immortal.

Notice the properties of this hypothetical logic interpreter. First, it operates on a substrate of spatial and imagistic (in a general sense, at least) reasoning.[15] In

---

[15] I am not convinced we should take the integrated spatial array involved here in any literal sense. However, it does not seem difficult to sketch piecemeal replacements for the array of the dispositional form suggested in the last footnote. Any such "improved theory" would describe prior resources differently, but we would reach exactly the same conclusions as far as the intent of the arguments in this chapter are concerned.

addition, some other capabilities are presumed, specifically skill at interpreting tokens as representing individuals *as they belong to characterized classes.* In particular, two tokens under different classes do not represent two individuals if they are "linked." Note also that this interpreter has a class of "invited conclusions" that seem to follow—in a way analogous to the correct conclusion that some philosophers are mortal—directly from producing the two primary array deployments from each of the premises. Further, provided this processor has at least occasional access to careful processing that notes a difficult with uncontrolled reading off arrays, it might generate an appropriate patch, a disposition to place salient and meaningfully paired, but complementary, tokens (in this case representing women) in the array to forestall inappropriate conclusions. "Careful processing" might be reasoning about a particular case—say, discovering a false conclusion violated (by women) in a world situation supposedly analyzed by the unpatched and defective logic interpreter. That case analysis, with a bit of added cleverness in adding the "try a counterexample in the form of unmentioned exemplars of an implied class," would produce the augmented and improved interpreter.

I read this as a genetic story of developing resources. First, I presume that logic of this sort is useful and has appropriate feedback for successful implementation. People do sometimes get information that is useful to them in verbal forms like this, and I believe they can check their own guesses against the possibilities in particular cases. Next, I presume the processor already possesses prior resources that I have framed as strong spatial and individual-as-token-of-class representational skills.[16] Then, by some (unspecified, but, I hope, not implausible) process of invention, the processor creates a first pass spatial method of implementing logic. Characteristics of the implementation, which in this case may be interim mistakes or limitations, are evident in the processing, as well as characteristics of the "ideal solution," logic. Patches such as those that introduce counterexample strategies may develop later to overcome shortcomings. At first these patches might only work reliably in special semantic situations, for example, when "what about women?" comes to mind easily when thinking about men. Later, patches might be more "logical"; the category nonmen is a more general patch mediator.

Even more compactly, we have base resources, need and (plausible) inventive capabilities. We also have substantial propagation of structure revealed in glitches in the processor ("invited" but false) conclusions. Indeed, many such glitches and other characteristics of processing (such as latency or an increased number of errors if multiple models are needed) are actually observed in human behavior.[17]

Work by Falmagne and others (Falmagne, Singer, & Clement, undated; Clement & Falmagne, 1986) tells a story interesting in its similarities to the present interpretation but also enlightening in its differences. Perhaps most important, this work appears to offer some developmental data in support of an ontogenetic status for the previously mentioned "evolving logic interpreter" idea. People actually appear to

---

[16] Or one might need capability with "entailed properties dispositions," and so on.

[17] It would be best to consult Johnson-Laird's more careful version before trying to guess the glitches or other processing implications.

go through a stage in which certain particulars in a situation are necessary in order to complete a bit of logical reasoning. I interpret these as incomplete patches to the interpreter, like using counterexamples generated by semantic rather than logical means in the previous discussion. In fact, the incomplete mechanism in question is precisely counterexample generation. Deprived of situation particulars that allow generation of counterexamples, people cannot reason logically.

At earlier stages the reasoning cannot be done even in the presence of those particulars, analogous to not having formulated the basic token tableau model idea. And at later stages, the particulars are unnecessary, parallel to counterexample generation via "nonman" rather than "woman."

The logical capabilities investigated by Falmagne are even simpler than the ones previously discussed. For example, one might ask, "If John is wearing a red shirt, then he is looking at himself in the mirror; he's not wearing a red shirt; what can you conclude?" Note that this is an indeterminate form: If x then y; not x; nothing can be concluded. (In particular, one cannot conclude not y—a conclusion that is found empirically to be invited.) The particulars necessary for generating counterexamples in this case are the ability to form salient images of the situation in question. For adults, Falmagne finds strong evidence that imagistic reasoning is necessary to conclude that one cannot draw any definite conclusion: John may or may not be looking in the mirror. Subjects apparently generate a counterexample to defeat the potential conclusion that John is not looking in the mirror; they form an image of John looking in the mirror but not wearing a red shirt, and they note this is not inconsistent with the premises. In the absence of a situation that is imageable, subjects have much greater difficulty with these problems.

At earlier stages, children cannot reason about even easily imageable situations; young children generally fail in all circumstances to be able to characterize these indeterminate syllogisms appropriately. The data about later stages is actually about different forms of syllogism. In cases of "If x then y; x; what can be concluded?" (modus ponens) or, "If x then y; not y; what can be concluded?" (modus tollens), imageability is simply not necessary for adults.

There is one important point of difference between the interpretation here compared to Falmagne's. That is, she presumes that some part of the encoding of logical knowledge is always formal and pure in long-term memory, that imagistic or "mental model" reasoning is only necessary to translate linguistic or world information into a form on which pure logical knowledge can work. Thus, the competence to reason on imageable problems is attributed to formal logical competence, which is somehow limited at intermediate developmental stages.

In contrast, I note that asserting the formal nature of reasoning capability begs the question of the form of this "pure" encoding and begs also any of the details of its development. The presumption that whatever exists and controls or uses imaging capability is formal is in danger of asserting that competence is formal simply because we have no analysis whatsoever of it. My program would be most successful if it were true that "pure logical" reasoning is all of the type displayed in this genetic story, built on prior resources in comprehensible steps, except that some of it may be "crystallized." That is, the problems of rapid and reliable, sufficiently broad context application have been solved so that the reasoning appears "pure and formal."[18] In the Johnson-Laird analysis, I have taken some care to suggest some plausible prior resources.

It may certainly be the case that some part or all of the reasoning may become so effective as to appear to be a closed module, pure and formal in the sense that, within its range of application, it effectively pays attention only to logically relevant aspects of world situations and does not need more than them to process effectively. Part of this formality might be achieved by gradually abstracting out unused aspects of imagistic reasoning. One does not any more imagine shapes of individual tokens, say. Or one might generate more abstracted descriptions for the purpose of counter-example generation, descriptions with a broader range of application, for example, nonman (but potentially a philosopher) may serve in place of woman.

Even when the interpreter appears formal in everyday operation, properties of the implementation might become visible in more taxing situations like learning mathematical symbolic logic. New and broader contexts of use might stress a module that is effective according to some standards into betraying internal structure, and one might see propagation of the genetic implementation structure into new learning.

Simple Modeling Relationships

Johnson-Laird refers to the hypothetical internal tableaus as mental models. This term has been used in a variety of other contexts to describe "mental stimulations," perhaps mechanistic ones, or other versions of semantically rich internal representations that may replace supposedly more abstract knowledge (Gentner & Stevens, 1983). Mental models are frequently extolled as either an efficient method of processing or as a characteristically human mode of reasoning, even if they are not efficient. The preceding discussion allows us to generalize the notion of mental model, to see its effectiveness as a natural consequence of its meaning, and, perhaps, to make the concept more precise at the same time.

Abstracting from this scenario of part of the development of logical thinking, we may say that a *simple modeling relationship* exists when a new resource is developed out of some significant prior resource, or small set of prior resources, in such a way that the old resources are not recrystallized. Not recrystallized means that the implementation of the new resource on the basis of the old still shows itself to us either in characteristics of processing (mistakes, limitations, etc.) or in specific further learning that needs to take place. The basic idea is that the older resources provide material out of which new capabilities are "modeled" or "simulated" in some degree, but such that the properties of the modeling materials show through the properties of the new resource. This is clearly a very generic kind of developmental relationship of resources, though one that is certainly not universal. In many

---

[18] I provide more details on "rapid and reliable" processing in the last subsection of the present section. For now, this may be considered a generic form of the problem that at some stages, some situations cannot be effectively engaged in logical reasoning.

situations it might be that many resources are composed in complex combination to create a new one, so little insight can be gained from understanding the prior resources individually. It might also be true that the new resource so thoroughly absorbs and refashions a prior resource that understanding the old resource, again, does not help in understanding the new one.

Naturally occurring simple modeling relationships are necessarily effective to some degree, or competence would have followed other paths of development, or not developed at all. It might well be that many of the cognitive systems that have been called mental models are actually simple modeling relationships, though very little genetic analysis has been performed on these. Mental models of physical devices, for example, might exist primarily in virtue of spatial reasoning capabilities in composition with some basic causal schematizations. In the next section I describe a particularly interesting case of a simple modeling relationship.

Propositions. I conclude this subsection with a note on propositions. From the point of view of producing a logically reasoning being, propositions and syllogistic reasoning capabilities would seem to be corequisites. It does not make sense to have one without the other (though, perhaps propositions are the more likely to be modularly invented, see later discussion). Thus, one may expect propagation of structure in that it is quite likely that deficits in the implementation of syllogisms will be reflected in features in the implementation of propositions, and vice versa.

Let me briefly consider possible independent needs for propositions that might serve to drive development further than needed for logical reasoning. Within the structure of language, of course, propositions seem to have a clear niche as part of a compact, modular infrastructure of meaning. Sentence units might always be interpreted one at a time as propositions with truth value. Indeed, it may be true that the expectation of propositional evaluation of sentences can be important meta-knowledge about language that can help both a listener interpret a speaker consistently and also a speaker know how the listener is interpreting. Yet, that propositions should have developed purely and solely inside language seems unlikely to be a complete solution to our resource development questions. In the first instance, to assert that propositions developed as a subproblem in the context of language resources leaves a great deal of detail unspecified about the problems solved by language. Without some view of that, we have trouble understanding in any detail the context of need in which propositions might have been invented. More directly, while general arguments might suggest that propositions would aid the efficiency of language in any context, it seems quite clear that sentences are not purely propositional. Sentences satisfy too many other communication needs (e.g., expressing emotion, making requests) to be uniformly and exclusively interpreted as propositions. So while propositional interpretation might be appropriate for some sentences, other sentences need nonpropositional interpretation; thus, sentences should also embody structure appropriate for other modes of interpretation and should not be expected to be understandable purely in propositional terms.

So, I argue that the identification of propositions as linguistic structures— sentences—is helpful but a limited insight into the origins and operating context of propositions. If we believe results such as proposed by Johnson-Laird and by Falmagne, that spatial and imagistic reasoning is part of the implementation base of syllogistic reasoning, then it seems even less likely that propositions are exclusively linguistic—this time the argument is on the basis of resources involved in processing them rather than on the basis of need.

Representation

Representational issues have been implicit in what has been said so far. In particular, spatial representation played a central, though not separately analyzed role in the discussion of logical reasoning. Now I take on representation directly with one central question, "Are there objects of mind (symbols) that denote entities in the world?" The question is a representative though somewhat extreme version of an important class of questions about relations between objects of mind and the "real world." Thus, I am addressing, from a genetic/causal point of view, how plausible it is that very simple relations exist.

The argument will be of the following form: While the advantages of common resources might press toward such compact representations as symbols for world objects, relations, and so on, there are limits. In order to solve problems, I argue that the minimum module must be significantly larger than a token. And the optimization to single token reference within such a module appears doubtful.

How can we describe a problem to which (single token) reference might be an appropriate solution? To begin with the archetypical case, what opportunities do physical objects provide? Opportunities, of course, are a kind of problem to the extent that we may "wish to" take advantage of them.

Let us consider an object as a space–time localized nexus of opportunities to coordinate various information accesses and operations. Thus, all attributes intrinsic to the object are findable in proximity to each other—if you want to find the color of the object, you can locate it using any features, then examine its color. "Examining its color" involves a very particular and inarticulable shift of attention. In general, "shifting attention appropriately" may be a good first-pass model of what is involved in some central aspects of coordinating access.

Kant provides a good example of the kind of things that may be involved in appropriate coordination of accesses. Here, generally speaking, the specific problem is to prestore knowledge about something that may be needed in quick access later when the object might even be out of sight. Imagine examining a house a bit at a time, your eyes wandering almost at random across the scene. It is important to interpret what is seen at each point of focus in a particular way. Certainly one does not interpret the door as having caused the window, even if one sees the door immediately before the window and in spatial proximity to it. Instead, one collects bits and pieces of information relevant to interpreting what one sees as rigidly related parts of a single object.

One collects the totality of parts provided the scan is judged as complete. (This is not so simple as it might seem. As Piaget did, ask a child to count the blocks in a multilayer tower.) Local relations gradually get built into an effective model of the object. Two windows are on either side of the door; there is a second story with more windows. Sometimes one can offload observational or encoding chores into reasoning. Hence, if you see the roof is above the second floor, there is no need to observe or separately to remember that the roof is above the first floor. All of this implicates a great deal of knowledge about objects and about our own activities of scanning—how one coordinates scanning and local interpretations (e.g., causal versus geometric) to patch together sensory reports into an appropriate whole.

Viewing people as objects provides examples of an extraordinarily broad range of coordination in multiple sensory channels. We see a person, hence we expect self-motion, and, for example, search for the person appropriately in her absence. That is, we do not necessarily expect to find the person in the same place we last did. Features of personality that might be gleaned in part from interpretation of visual (expression) or auditory patterns affect our stance toward interpreting what is said. Generally, accesses in multiple channels have implications and expected outcomes in other channels—is the individual close enough to hear; does she like to be alone and work late, hence is her office a good place to look after hours?

It might be argued that we could short-circuit the more complex problem—coordinating aspects of access and operations—by asserting that the problem is to provide reference for symbols in the interpreter. In this way, we provide "meaning" in a simple way to the interpreter, a simple relation between the mind and the physical environment. Thus some internal "Joan" that refers to Joan is all that is necessary at the core. All the rest is just knowledge about Joan that may be helpful in solving problems concerning her.

However, I argue that the expanded form, coordinating accesses and operations, is more generic. It seems almost obvious that such coordinating according to regularities afforded by the world should be done. It reduces redundant accesses and encoding effort. It provides for generic means of interpreting accesses. For example, successive observation of features should sometimes be interpreted as "next to" and sometimes as part of "causes." Thus I claim that coordination is, in fact, the general problem to be solved, and we are left to consider why it might be that coordination via a single token reference is particularly effective.[19]

I argue that single-token reference, in some respects, is insufficient to coordinate and in some respects coordinates too tightly. Obviously a single token cannot contain all the information processing necessary to coordinate multiple aspects.

---

[19] If such capability were provided as primitive resources, we might be in a position to argue for it as part of a solution to coordination problems. Indeed, if we have people to interpret computer programs, it might make sense to have some version of single token reference involved in the program. But, in the genetic case, we must have a single processor do all the work, and it is in this context that the emergence of single token reference is implausible. Following this line, *externalized* language may approach the appearance of single token reference, so long as there is a person to interpret it.

There must be significant structure outside the token to do that work. Consider as an illuminating special case what micro coordinations (auditory attention and received information with future attention and expectations) and distinctions must be linked to major coordinations in other modes (recalling emotional stance and relevant facts that might be conveyed in a greeting) when one identifies a friend above the din of a cocktail party conversation and prepares to greet him. Or, what does one do to examine the trumpet line in an orchestral performance?

Thus, a minimal implementation of effective access would involve some lookup of the token to find an appropriate class of access strategies for that token. And these would have to be modified or completely revamped according to knowledge needed in the circumstance, say, according to whether you need to access emotional state or physical state information concerning an individual.

Why should coordination be constrained to operate through the mediary of a single token? Indeed, it seems much more efficient to have multiple interpretations of the individual—sometimes treated as a physical object in order to coordinate, sometimes as a disembodied personality, and so on. Thus, if one has specific structure to coordinate in and across each of these projections of the individual, in most instances, one need not use any individual identification at all in order to coordinate, let alone a unique token.

Perhaps only coordination specific to unique-individuals-in-a-single-interpretation (e.g., Joan as a physical body) can remain as a plausible candidate for single token reference. Indeed, it seems plausible at first blush that such individuals might be identified by unique tokens (names), though this is a different, much more specific function than initially proposed. The actual work of coordination still needs to be done with other processing structure. Yet it does not seem difficult to counter even this restricted proposal. In the first instance, almost all processing can go on without unique individual identification, as I argued previously. Choosing to view Joan as a physical body independent of her other individual features does many coordination tasks. Strong token–individual binding is rarely (if ever) needed.

Second, in the general case identification of individuals is a highly refined and knowledge-intensive activity. One reasons about aspects of the sensory array and about aspects of "the individual" to determine if they are the same. In such a context, it would make much more sense to encode the decision that the sensory array is in fact the individual in question together with memory state reflecting the grounds for the decision, rather than only choosing to use a particular unique token. Throwing away information relevant to identifying an individual in favor of a token representing the conclusion of reasoning is, minimally, a fault intolerant strategy.

The very question of the meaning of individual may become an issue. For example, is the automobile every part of which has been changed still the same automobile? Having to decide once and for all what constitutes an individual or changing one's whole memory data structures if one decides such a question in a new way (so that unique tokens may have to be removed from memories of individuals who no longer satisfy the criteria of individuality) seems a very bad route toward implementing intelligence. Learning quantum mechanics (which has a substantially altered notion of individual) should, implausibly, induce a basic change in the learner's implementation of intelligence. Of course, it is possible to argue that learning quantum mechanics and replacing every part of a car are rare events and need not impact everyday reasoning and hence revamp prior cognitive resources. But I give arguments later that similar events may not be so rare at all and may be central to ordinary learning and development.

There are other arguments against single token reference's playing an important role even in the task of identifying unique individuals. From a learning point of view, one asks when should the learner generate a new token to represent a new individual? Surely it makes more sense to reason *only if need be* about the identity of a perceived individual on the basis of descriptions that one knows are more or less characteristic. So, in this body of "more or less characteristic" descriptions, including generalities about identification, such as that names in this culture are pretty good indices, we are more likely to find the knowledge that solves the problem of identification, to the extent that this problem needs to be solved. We can think of "the lead trumpet in this particular performance" or "a trumpeter with Roger Voisin's tone quality" on the basis of a description without serious commitment as to the general usefulness of integrating a unique token into an already existing knowledge system, and without other commitments, such as which of these two closely related individuals we mean by a particular token. In fact, if the Morning Star and Evening Star are internally encoded as a single token representing Venus, then we stand to lose important differences in access actions that are appropriate to each of these descriptions. Why, at the base of it, is identity more important than access routes?

Instead, I claim that descriptions (e.g., "the guy who was just here," "the readable thing over there on the table"), names among them, and a complex attendant knowledge about more or less characteristic descriptions constitute sufficient solution of the problem of coordination of unique-individuals-in-a-single-interpretation. Unique tokens are neither plausible nor useful.

I have one final argument against simple token/world entity relations. This argument is on the basis of corequisite resources. I have been using examples largely from what is perhaps the strongest body of knowledge humans possess, that having to do with physical objects. If one deals with much weaker knowledge systems, such as intuitions about physical mechanism, people rarely can identify with certainty the existence of particular phenomena in a situation, or its entailments. So it would make little sense to use unique tokens, which presume the possibility of such determination. If there are no relatively certain entities in the world of a certain sort, it makes little sense to develop structure such as reference via unique tokens.

In this argument I have exposed some interesting opportunities for modules of processing much more plausible than any involving single token reference. It seems eminently plausible that certain central classes of coordination should become general resources for an individual. From Piagetian work, we know that establishing appropriate persistence for knowledge related to physical objects (e.g., to keep them in mind when they are out of sight), which is called object permanence, is neither entirely built into primitive capabilities nor easy to learn. Similarly, events have substantially different coordination needs compared to physical objects. Time is centrally implicated—one can never observe an event twice (save through recording technology); actions as well as objects play a role in event identity. (Actions, as well, constitute a plausible class of coordinations.) Indeed, the very distinction between individuals and types may be understood as a basic cut in coordinating knowledge; individuals represent the deepest level of differentiation that still respects basic constitutive, form, space, and time continuities.

So I have cast a particular slice of Kant's program into the form of our present program. We understand a certain kind of basic ontological structure as a series of problems and opportunities to coordinate among and across perceptions and actions. Unlike Kant, however, we cannot see these all as prior to any cognition. Indeed, we expect incomplete construction in the sense that these coordinations need not satisfy any strict rules of classification or simplicity. Unless the intrinsic computational landscape for considering the world is considerably more channeled than it appears, we shall have to accept invention and variation as part of the picture. Types in aboriginal dream time and quantum wave functions both represent kinds of coordinations; neither is particularly obvious nor necessary, though both must serve their respective purposes.

It would be important to know how general or specific these modules of coordination are. Those possibilities previously mentioned seem plausible, but much more specific ones may exist. In fact, it is possible that "deep learning difficulties" may arise, even in school subjects, when a new type of coordination is necessary that is not available in existing beta resources. So, conceptual change may be distinguished from routine learning precisely by implicating new beta resources like new modules of coordination. It is difficult to know whether coming to be able to "see" forces in the world— to be able to identify individuals of that class, to regularly abstract and coordinate central features, and so on—is a sufficiently difficult problem that a simple patching together of prior coordinating resources is inadequate. Personally, I find it plausible that learning the concept of force is this difficult, and in this particular way. In fact, one might conjecture that *every* substantial episode of conceptual change requires new coordinating resources. More generally, given a good map of central problems or necessary beta resources, one could index instances of conceptual change by these.

Processing
At the beta level so far we have examined logic, a particular hypothetical case of a very generic relation between resources and prior resources. Second, we examined the plausibility of very simple relations between world objects and mind objects as the basis for representation. While I rejected the strongest version of this, I maintained that coordinating accesses and actions (especially concerning various different kinds of "objects") is an important problem that might generate specific, modular resources. Now I turn to one final class of problems related to representa-

tion in the broadest sense. This one, it turns out, seems to be a problem as apt to describe gamma development as beta development. The astute reader will notice that I have presaged several aspects of these problems in the immediately preceding subsections.

Consider a particular version of the learning and transfer problem. I view transporting a mind state established in some particular circumstance involving the external world (roughly, that which is learned in an experience) to other circumstances as a generic and problematic situation. An example of this would be noticing a particular configuration of circumstances in which an event regularly occurs. For any version of "noticing regularity" and transporting that noticing to some new circumstance in which the event may be "expected," the following must be established. First, cuing: Some mind state involving the expected event ("represented," in the weakest sense) must be established on the basis of appropriate circumstances. The more general the regularity, the broader the range of superficially distinct circumstances should cue. This poses a version of the invariant recognition problem, though what is recognized is not a thing, but a context. In general, the full range of intelligent processing can be brought to bear on the problem—in finding and incorporating cues to the circumstances in which the expectation is relevant.

Cuing needs to be accompanied by the establishment of appropriate persistence. That is, the cued "expectation" should last as long as necessary to do its work. If the circumstances pass, the expectation should also. Or, if a new view provides strong "evidence" that the initial cuing circumstance is not really characteristic of the expectation, the expectation should pass. In general, I speak of *appropriate persistence* to describe the full class of mechanisms that keep active certain partial mind states for as long as necessary to do their work, and, more specifically, I speak of *reliability processing* to refer to the processing that establishes postrecognition situation appropriateness. Short-term memory might be a generic persistence mechanism to keep around needed results of prior reasoning for involvement in future reasoning.

I note that some degree of complementarity is necessary between cuing and reliability processing. Hence, if very distinctive and easily perceived cues are available to a context, little reliability processing would be necessary. But the reliability that existed would likely complement the particular characteristics of the cuing. Recognizing people may be an easy job in general. But if Joe has a twin brother, you are likely to check the mole on his cheek that distinguishes Joe from his brother before proceeding with the assumption that you have met Joe. "Checking the mole" counts as reliability since, presumably, it happens only after your automatic facial recognition resources cue "Joe" to you.

A much more severe problem of cuing and reliability occurs if we note that the *same* knowledge may be needed under very different conditions. Any processing capability is subject to multiple pressures. In particular, I note two very general ones. First, one may need "run-time" knowledge that is *rapid* but need only be very *specific* both in terms of what is recognized, and also in terms of actions to be taken. On the other hand, there should be great pressure toward ''deep structuring,'' that is, toward single structures of knowledge that handle all relevant occasions. Not only does this follow from the general pressure toward creating common resources, but, more specifically, from the need for localizing knowledge for credit and blame assignment, and for centralized ''improvements.'' Thus, if you have multiple encodings of the same principle, changing it or deleting it if it turns out to be false would be much more difficult than with a single instance of the principle.

Problems of run-time efficiency press toward multiple cuing paths to specialized versions of actions, probably each with limited persistence necessary. In contrast, deep structuring presses toward the localization of cuing to a smaller number of cuing structures, or, more likely, toward a great breath of cuing resources targeted toward a small number of more general knowledge structures. And persistence of the more general structures is a much more substantial problem than in the run-time case, sometimes involving resources as expensive as general problem-solving capabilities to reason out, for example, an appropriate situation-specific action. Therefore, in general, deeply structured systems will be slow to ''compute'' situation-specific responses.

Scientific knowledge provides a good case to exemplify the issues. Physics has basic principles that govern all electromagnetic phenomena. But circuit theory has branched off as its own subject so that the implications of the general laws of physics can be specialized into principles dealing with circuits per se. And indeed, general circuit theory has broken into many subdomains so that humans can, in a reasonable time, deal with the problems specific to the subdomains, say, digital logic, or high-frequency analog circuity. No one has the time to compute the implication of Maxwell's equations anew for each circumstance in which they are needed.

Like the physics case, many cognitive systems will have both run-time and deep structuring needs. So they may develop multiple specific and some more general processing structures. Such multiplicity, however, leads to the problem of coordinating the versions.

In the physics/engineering example previously discussed, discoordination of Maxwell's equations and engineering principles seems not a serious threat. On the other hand, individual cognition may be much more prone to such difficulties. Consider children learning algebra. They are very likely to use specific cues and develop specific rules to govern their manipulations. One thinks of the heuristic of ''moving unknowns to the same side of the equation.'' The spatial description is appropriate to the notational context but generalizes uncertainly to operators other than addition. It certainly does not capture a mathematician's sense of explanation, neither for the appropriateness of the action nor even for its correctness. So a child is not prone to think of squaring both sides of an equation to undo a square root via an inverse operation. And it is easy to forget that one must negate terms when ''moving them to the other side.'' A child may, in some circumstances, understand the generalities that underlie algebra (such as principles that govern inverse operations), but if they are not appropriately coordinated with specific run-time structure, the net knowledge system is weak and error prone. "Run-time versions" versus "compact, deep structural versions," of course, is not only relevant to problem solving, but also to, say, telling oneself or another about what one knows and considering its general validity. Language, more particularly written language, axiomatic deployments, and so on, may be viewed as (very advanced and complex) solutions to the problem of localizing knowledge into deep structural modules such as laws stated as equations. But each system to provide compact representation of core principles requires diverse ancillary knowledge and specializations to actually operate in problem-solving situations.

The developmental literature, Piaget in particular, has highlighted the importance of hypothetical thinking. Hypotheticals are a particularly apt structure to aid in the coordination of run-time and more localized and compact knowledge. Returning to the model situation of developing and transporting expectations, a hypothetical would involve a specially tagged version of an expectation which provides that arbitrary reasoning involving the expectation may be appropriate, while any committed action responses need to be withheld.

I have introduced the problems of (a) establishing appropriate cuing and persistence and (b) coordinating deep structural and run-time processing at the beta level to suggest that there might be generic resources, like hypotheticals, for instance, to deal with such problems. Moweover, it appears (as I describe next) that these problems have a significant presence at the gamma level and frequently show idiosyncratic rather than general solutions.

Intuitive structures of which people have little cognizance or control are involved in their predictions and expectations in physical circumstances. This lack of control may be described as insufficiently organized persistence or reliability. People often simply do not represent aspects of situations that, from a physicist's point of view, are relevant to deciding appropriate use of an expectation. In a well-documented "misconception," people seem to believe that objects go in the direction they are pushed in a much broader range of circumstances than are really governed by such an expectation (diSessa, 1982). Specifically, they apply the expectation regardless of whether the object is in motion or not. In this case, people certainly know the difference between rest and motion but seem not to think this distinction is relevant. Knowing that motion is relevant is tantamount to having the fact of motion be a reliability check on the expectation that a push gives rise directly to motion.

Persistence is more generally a trouble spot. Frequently, people can make appropriate analyses once, but completely lose track of their reasoning so as to be unable to reproduce it. In interviews with children, one finds they can often make surprisingly fine distinctions and analyses, but they do not have sufficient control to make those analyses work consistently.[20] Moreover, integration with other appropri-

---

[20] A striking case of this occurred to me in an interview with a 10-year-old about a pendulum. The child initially distinguished at least three rates: what physicists would call the speed of the bob, the angular speed of the bob, and the rate of decay of the swinging. Yet, in subsequent analyses, he could not maintain these distinctions and lost productive use of them.

ate subsystems, such as the use of linguistically formulated definitions, and so on, may be weak, leading to discoordinations. A child may not be able to describe in words, even approximately, insights that can still lead him to proper predictions. On other occasions, a child can say the right thing but cannot formulate situation-specific actions to carry out. Or strategies may be used that are entirely disconnected from what is said.

Cuing is a serious problem in that intuitive structures may be very appropriate to physical analyses, but they are activated in the naive state only in a restricted (or at least different) set of circumstances. Thus, intuitive feelings for conservation and symmetry may be relevant to respectable physical analyses, but they need to be attached to situations in ways that are "surprising" to the naive knowledge system. Similarly, one can find problems that more expert students can solve if they are told to use conservation of energy, but the idea will not be spontaneously cued.[21]

Consideration of specifics in this way tends to undermine the expectation that there can be structures (beta resources) to solve these very general problems once and for all. Many solutions may be knowledge intensive. That is, solutions may involve integrating quite specific knowledge into quite specific niches in the existing knowledge system. Some "check" should come to mind in reaction to the instinct to predict future motion only from push characteristics. More than that, some knowledge systems (intuitive physics being a major example) seem weakly developed and also only weakly integrated with stronger systems like language. So, the capacity for generic solutions to these difficulties is unlikely until they are at least partially solved in specific terms. A generic hypothetical capability makes no sense without the specific checks and specific subsequent processing that make it useful in the first place. Finally, weak versions of hypothetical processing seem very easy to achieve with rather primitive resources. Basically, some kind of conditional needs to be inserted into the "instinctive" processing. Of course, none of this is to deny, for example, the usefulness of a generic hypothetical processing. Rather, it is to suggest that taking the perspective of problems and resources, hypothetical capability may frequently emerge either bottom up from specific new knowledge being properly coordinated or may emerge as a side effect of substantial other knowledge developments, such as linguistic capability, or the combination of linguistic capability together with specific developments that connect an existing knowledge system to language. Thus, someone may acquire competence at articulating their physical intuitions and, having done so, can question and thus refine them.

Beta Retrospective: Long Loop Causality
I close this section on the beta level by remotivating the concept in the context of our genetic/causal program.

---

[21] For example, conservation of energy solves the problem of finding the speed of water coming out of a hole in the bottom of a can full of water. But even graduate students may not think to try this, though they can easily apply it if it is suggested.

It is perfectly evident that everyday mental events cause everyday physical ones and vice versa. Now this seems very strange to some (e.g., Fodor, 1986) because purely physical causality seems always to be tightly locked to circumstances while mental events are very subtly related to them. The mind seems to be uncoupled in that it can choose what to pay attention to and ignore, and the things it pays attention to are not evidently causal features of the physical world. The way out of the paradox is to realize the mind has had a very long history of coupling with the world to create a wonderfully complex structure that makes the local coupling flexible to the point that it seems nonphysical. But, of course, it is locally physical (photons, neurons, and the rest). The nature of that local coupling seems unusual because it is only the smallest part of the real coupling. The local mechanism has been created by a long evolutionary and developmental history, each part of which was completely compatible with physical causality. History prepares the mind to react to very delicate physical differences, and not to react at all to some other very substantial ones, in ways that reflect its own (invisible) state and apparently nonphysical (conceptual) invariances. Our local reactions loop far back into the past through the infrastructure for coordinating ourselves effectively with the world. Beta resources should capture this infrastructure as resources for further development or learning.

Gamma Level: Knowledge

In this section, I turn to the question of the development of knowledge per se. I make two related analyses. The first is an interpretation in the genetic/causal framework developed here of my own more empirical work on intuitive physics (diSessa, 1993), which motivated the basic scheme and many of the particular analyses that have already been discussed. In large measure, the previous sections of this chapter have aimed at independent motivation, refinement and explication in other contexts of ideas that were generated in this prior work. Thus, returning to the motivating context may well put these ideas in their best light. The cost for this, however, will be the need to rely on complex arguments that cannot be presented in full here. Readers who are unsatisfied with sketches of this other work may need to consult it.

The second analysis is of some paradigmatically Piagetian ideas. The aim is to point to possible extensions and reinterpretations of Piaget based on the framework sketched here.

Prior to making these analyses, it will be to our advantage to summarize and reiterate some of the main ideas developed to this point.

Schematic Review

Consider intelligence to be a collection of resources, each of which has a character that is determined in substantial degree by the history of its development. Model that history, schematically, as a series of events in which prior resources are recrafted by means of certain principles of invention in a context of feedback to solve some identifiable problem (or, equivalently, take advantage of a particular opportunity). My claim is that such a collection of analyses constitutes a minimal and natural cluster of analyses for understanding the genesis of knowledge and intelligent processing. A major principle is that of "propagation (or morphosis) of structure," in which solutions to problems, as neatly defined as the problems and ideal solutions might be in the abstract, are likely to reflect particular characteristics of prior resources, characteristics of channels of feedback, and characteristics of principles of invention. This propagation may be easiest to imagine as limitations in one of these channels that propagate into the following resource (though, from another point of view, a problem is in part defined by the *capability* resources may provide for solving it). Incomplete solutions to a particular problem can give important information about the cognitive ecology in which the solution arose. For example, incompletenesses may indicate particular gaps in available resources or incompletenesses in prior resource constructions. Incompletenesses may also indicate insufficient need, or systematically imperfect feedback. All of these may be telling from a psychogenetic point of view.

In the best of circumstances, some particular causal event might result in the solution of a problem, generating resources which then constitute a module responsible for negotiating a wide range of circumstances in which the problem operates. So, mental tableaus might always be used to reason about syllogisms. In other cases, the generic problem would have to be solved in multiple cases, resulting in multiple versions of resources that may still be effectively described, at one level of abstraction, by the same problem.

Among the subtle complexities in this basic analysis is the fact that multiple simultaneous demands on the same resources, multiple problems, will lead to compromises and trade-offs of design that undoubtedly require much· more fine-structural analysis than I have attempted in any of the cases so far. So, for example, language may gain modularity and reliability through having strict grammatical paths for combining meaning; yet the need for innovation and the possibility of arbitrary word sequences becoming idioms may constantly short-circuit a purely grammatical mapping from words to meanings. At this point, we can scarcely decide such issues. Incomplete solutions such as not-quite-regular grammars may also be evidence for competing problems without independent solutions.

I have proposed the notion of a simple modeling relation as a generic relation among prior resources and newly developed ones. A simple modeling relation exists provided that a major aspect of the implementation of some new resource is given by a single resource or simple combination of resources in such a way that substantial structure is propagated from prior to new resource, perhaps to the detriment of ideal resolution of the problem. If the basic resource were entirely cannibalized and recrafted to new ends so that the characteristics of the modeling material are no longer evident, we would not speak of a modeling relationship. I use the term *modeling* since some new, ideal capability is modeled or simulated with prior resources as raw materials. Like a real model, the properties of the resources show through in the properties of the creation. So a paper airplane flies somewhat like a real one but tears rather more easily, betraying its construction. In the same way, people may reason logically, but fail to do so in ways that show the heritage of their reasoning capabilities. Positive aspects of propagation of structure in the case of logic include realizing a surprising isomorphism between operations on visualizable tableaus (plus appropriate control structure) and syllogistic reasoning. At the same time, this isomorphism is limited; it may require recruiting other resources such as imagistic capabilities associated with the situation in question. Errors and difficulties show up which are characteristic of partial construction.

I have proposed a number of general problems that seem to provide opportunities for interesting inquiry. For example, how do mental constructs, especially general ones, acquire the appropriate breadth of cuing and the appropriate persistence? How can one maintain coordination of real time resources with "deep structural" resources? Or, how does one develop deep structural resources at all, given real time limitations in human processing? With respect to the problem of coordinating within and across aspects of access and action to "real-world" situations, I've discussed the opportunity to build particular modules of coordination. Object permanence appears to be an observed example of such coordination, which happens simultaneously to be an example of a solution to the problem of appropriate persistence of a particular class of ideas, loosely, those we construe as thinking about objects.

At the same time, I have rejected as problems those that are so far from plausible solutions or involve at this point unimaginable principles of invention. For example, it is difficult to imagine the problems and prior resources out of which symbol system capabilities might have developed. In general, it seems easier to specify a bundle of resources, principles of invention, and so on as one moves toward specific knowledge. So I conjecture tentatively that resources, in general, tend to migrate from specific to general. That is the story behind syllogisms where spatial knowledge and example generation in domains gradually becomes syllogistic reasoning. And it is a story that will continue to be played out in the examples to come.

Intuitive Physics

The issue at hand is to understand the evolution of intuitive ideas about the way the physical world works into a part of school physics, mechanics. I claim the relation between these two resources is a simple modeling relation; to wit, intuitive physics provides most of the basic resources out of which experts have built their Newtonian sense of mechanism (which I specify in more detail later). And in this recrafting, much of the character of the intuitive resources is retained. Again, this section is a slightly reinterpreted summary of diSessa (1993).

Prior resources. People's intuitions about how the mechanical world works constitute a broad and only slightly systematic collection of knowledge structures I call p-prims. P-prims themselves have a relatively simple immediate genetic history. They are in general simple abstractions of relatively common phenomena. The terms in which the abstractions are made, of course, are prior resources, prominently spatial terms or time-varying amplitudes and body agency, kinesthetics such as effort, and so on.

P-prims are relatively simple, describable usually as configurations of a few parts. A few examples of p-prims are

- More work or effort begets more results.
- Motion tends to die away.
- An object trapped between two equally pressing other objects is held stably in place (clamping).
- "Squishy" objects compress an amount proportional to the pressing effort.
- Being "in equilibrium" is a natural state for objects, which will return to their equilibrium if perturbed.
- The strongest of a collection of "competing" influences generally gets its way.

Saying that the collection of p-prims is unsystematic means, in part, that there is no simple central core that can derive the whole collection. Instead, p-prims are crafted rather idiosyncratically to the very broad range of experiences people have with the physical world. There are systematicities, owing, for example, to clusters of related p-prims with common "base vocabulary," but these are rather weak, and I will not describe them here.

P-prims are graded in the sense that some are felt to be more deeply explanatory than others in particular situations. For example, people know that things that become unsupported simply fall down. However, a better explanation is that there is a legitimized agency, gravity, that wants things to move downward and causes them to fall. Genetically, this gradient is produced by a gradual sorting of p-prims into those providing more and less generally reliable explanations, based on accumulated evidence in multiple episodes of use.

This ultimate gradient is still quite limited. It tends to be local—depending on particulars of the situation. Thus, there is no strong, general ranking of p-prims. Further, even if a better explanation in certain directions is sought, such a search frequently fails. Even if it succeeds, confidence in the explanation can frequently be shaken if competing explanations and counter arguments are encountered.

Problems. At one level, saying that what is needed is appropriate resources on which to build the conceptual framework of Newtonian mechanics is sufficient statement of the problem. However, one can be more precise. Intuitive physics does not provide the mathematical resources for Newtonian physics, such as algebra, graphing, and so on. Nor does it provide the central "deep structural" conceptual core, per se, or people would have strongly Newtonian common sense, though perhaps without sharp mathematical expression; much data show they do not. Instead, I claim intuitive physics provides knowledge elements out of which much of the core conceptual structure of Newtonian mechanics can be built by relatively simple selection and reorganization. "Relatively simple" does not by any means mean absolutely simple. The complexity of the reorganization is one of the most important parts of the story. However, I claim that such a reorganization is much easier than a competing possibility, that Newtonian physics is built out of much more generic knowledge than naive physical intuition.

So, some of the *deep-structural core* of Newtonian mechanics is provided by intuitive physics. But as well, I claim intuitive physics provides a great repository of pieces out of which to build the attendant *run-time and situation-specific interpretations* in the same manner of gradual selection and integration. I explain in more detail in the following discussion.

Both of these particular problems, seeding core notions and providing appropriate run-time structure, are as much opportunities provided by intuitive ideas as problems in an absolute sense, as I explained may typically be the case in genetic analyses. The first problem is a slightly more specific version of our most general issue, to understand the particular resources that are involved in the construction of a new resource; and the second problem is one of the general problems that I identified as likely to be important in very many particular cases. I claim that the genetic analyses I am sketching for Newtonian mechanics are important in understanding the specific learning difficulties involved. Finally, note that I am, in this section, assuming that the solution to both these problems is at the knowledge level rather than based directly on (or generating) resources at the alpha or even beta level.

A further cut providing more specificity in describing problems involves identifying particular concepts and capabilities needed to do Newtonian mechanics. This might appear to be a standard task analysis. However, citing problems in an a priori fashion is insufficient. What is needed is to specify, to some degree of precision, the full set of genetic/causal components. This I do in some of the following cases.

Consider the centerpiece of Newtonian mechanics, Newton's Second Law, $F = ma$, which prescribes that the force on a body causes an acceleration, modulated by the fact that bigger bodies (with more mass, m) will accelerate less. This schematization meshes with some of the most basic schemata of intuitive physics having to do with interventive causes, agents. It says a bigger, more powerful cause gets a greater effect. And even the effect of mass can be understood as a kind of "resistance," another commonsense category.[22]

Though F and a are algebraically undistinguished—just terms related by direct proportionality—they must be conceptually distinguished in particular ways. At the first level of approximation, these distinctions are quite commonsensical. F is a cause, and a is an archetypical patient response—more motion. The important directed nature of $F = ma$ causality (from F to a) is captured in common sense as agents passing effects to patients, acceleration being an effect passed on by pushing agents. The interpretation of F as a cause is insufficient in many ways (it needs refinement to involve strictly Newtonian causes, and to rule out many nonlocal

---

[22] Jim Minstrell (personal communication, 1989) reports even young elementary school children appear quite competent in describing the effect of increasing mass in contexts of constant effort.

influences and the possibility of nonrelational forces—objects containing their own self-thrusting capabilities), but it *does* rule out the identification of any number of world phenomena as forces. Similarly the intuitive gloss of acceleration as "more motion" is not up to, for example, the quantification needs for full Newtonian comprehension. But it is a good start.

Mass is a highly technical term in Newtonian mechanics. It is not a generalized resistance, and it must even be distinguished from closely related notions as weight, or even gravitational mass (the mass that is the source of gravitational force, as opposed to the mass that resists forces). But, again, mass as a kind of "heft" that is directly felt when pushing objects around is a sufficient first approximation to give intuitive plausibility to $F = ma$. It also provides some effective localization of accesses in problem solving: Not even the most naive student will have difficulties understanding that she should find out something about an object related to the "amount of stuff" there in order to fill in the m term in $F = ma$.

These illustrate one sense in which intuitive physics provides knowledge "of the right kind" to begin the encoding of core ideas in mechanics: compatibility. Of course, the compatibility is not at all accidental in that mechanics and intuitive physics are about the same thing, with important qualifications. However, one should be reminded that, even if they are about the same thing, this compatibility of intuitive and theoretical ideas need not be so strong. Suppose, for example, that the world did not admit a Newtonian approximation to quantum mechanics. Physicists, after all, know that the world does quantum mechanics rather than Newtonian mechanics. Then, learning (quantum) mechanics would be a rather different matter, building on other resources much less directly related to common sense about the physical world. I would likely not be talking about intuitive physics as part of the resource base, and the characteristic problems of learning school physics would be very different. Intuitive physics would not exist in a simple modeling relation with school concepts.

The second contribution to which I claim intuitive physics is apt is toward solving the generic problem of generating run-time structure appropriate to a very broad range of situation specific detail. This problem is exacerbated by two particulars of mechanics. First, it is the general nature of scientific notions to be reductionist in that they succeed by building as compact and highly reliable a core as possible. This is one reason mathematics is so often involved—mathematics provides one of the sharpest and most reliably processed pools of knowledge available to humans. On the other side, the application context of Newtonian theory is one of the richest and most diverse ranges of phenomenology imaginable. Contrast puzzle domains and, perhaps, some subdomains of mathematics per se. The situation is especially difficult since the phenomenological boundaries of mechanics are so indistinct, at least for nonexperts. A very broad range of phenomena are understandable in Newtonian terms: starting from projectiles and tumbling objects; fluid flow, air currents; statics (such as the spread of load in a bridge); and some aspects of material properties (strength, resilience, etc.). But each of these requires a great deal of specific conceptual innovation in order to apply the same general laws.

Check any textbook for some confirmation of this fact in separate chapters and theorems that reuse $F = ma$ in multiple circumstances. Worse, some similar phenomenology is simply not comprehensible in Newtonian terms, such as other aspects of material properties (transparency, causal factors determining strength, etc.). So one absolutely needs a very rich knowledge system to appropriately discriminate problems that may yield to the core and interpolate between the contexts of those problems and core theory.

It is useful to separate out the fact that intuitive physics is content appropriate for doing Newtonian physics, as previously emphasized, from the fact that it is also to some degree form appropriate: It is heuristic (though the directionality of heuristics may need to be somewhat recrafted). It is phenomenologically very broad. More elements are relatively easy to generate, new p-prims that may be needed. And even the mechanisms of development—a gradual sorting, linking, and prioritizing— seem appropriate to developing expertise if expertise consists in large part of a broad and complex heuristic system to categorize and redescribe world situations as Newtonian ones. Again, if my take on the nature of Newtonian expertise is correct, one develops expert intuition in basically the same way one develops common sense.

Let us consider some examples of run-time structure evolved from naive physics. Most of these come from diSessa (1993).

- The intuitive attribute of agency provides not only a genetic ancestor to $F = ma$, but also appropriate run time structure to help focus attention in problem solving (without playing any sanctioned role in the core concepts of Newtonian mechanics). So, for example, the learner can effectively say to himself, "What is the agent causing this thing to move?," rather than being forced to rely entirely on technical definitions of force that are weakly understood, especially in early stages.

- Many of the intuitions experts use in special situations are identical to, or at least structurally similar to, common intuitions. Everyone knows heavy objects are more sluggish and tend to move slower; so experts know that frequency is inversely related to mass in a simple harmonic oscillator. A harmonic oscillator is an abstract system that works like a mass attached to the end of a spring which is fixed at the other end. Among the results one learns about this situation are that the frequency of oscillation is proportional to the square root of the spring constant (stiffness), and inversely proportional to the square root of the mass. The latter is intuitively glossed as heavier things move slower, and the former as stiffer things move or vibrate faster. I claim experts use these intuitive glosses to reason quickly and effectively in particular circumstances.

- In diSessa (1983) I discuss a major development in learning Newtonian mechanics, coming to appreciate the fact that every object in the world is "springy." That is, a table supports a book on it by flexing under the stress of the book until the table resists the book's weight sufficiently to keep it from flexing the table more. Springiness is formally unsanctioned as a central Newtonian concept, but

I claim this intuitively derived idea is required to make a particular class of situations, those involving "rigid" objects, sensible in Newtonian terms.

- Intuitive notions of balance and equilibrium are sometimes quite different from Newtonian ideas. And one frequently sees difficulty in students' appealing primitively to these as explanations (problems in propagation of structure). On the positive side, quite productive use of such ideas seems evident in students' coming to understand, for example, conservation of energy. The plausibility of certain classes of quantities balancing each other supports algebraic representations that also are described as expressing balance.[23]

- Experts develop, I claim, many "approximately naive" intuitions that support quick thinking about specific situations. For example, in the case of two masses connected by a string around a pulley, experts treat the two as a rigid mass that is numerically the sum of the masses of the objects. If one had no intuitions of rigidity and the tendency to synoptically consider complex things as simple ones, this strategy would make much less sense.[24] Roschelle is responsible for a number of related analyses (Roschelle, 1989). For example, he shows an expert solution in a fairly complex situation to be essentially isomorphic at the strategic level to typical novice solutions. Both experts and more naive problem solvers use schemata of balance and overcoming to plan the solution, but experts use the appropriate Newtonian entities to "balance," while novices use inappropriate ones.

Principles of invention. Without going into great detail, I have hypothesized that the mechanisms that recraft intuitive knowledge into the resulting slice of expert physics are not much different from those that made the knowledge system in the first place. The prior knowledge system is weak, diverse, and inarticulate; and there seems no substitute for broad ranges of experience that gradually decrease the use of inappropriate intuitions, increase the use of appropriate ones, and link them in place in the emerging network. Hence, I claim the principles of invention are structurally relatively unproblematic, though expertise is not at all instantly achieved.

There are evidently two levels of detail that need to be added to this sketch. One would like to have a more elaborated model of the general structural properties of "recruiting and refining" knowledge elements, or generating new ones. Some of this is done in diSessa (1993), but much remains unspecified. As well, in each case of conceptual development, one needs to know a great deal about the particular

---

[23] The boundary between run-time structure and encoding core ideas is sometimes unclear if we are talking about the run-time structure that allows a concept to operate in paradigmatic situations. I do not try to sort this out here.

[24] It is possible to characterize this way of thinking as a theorem, as it may, in fact, be proved. But one essentially never finds the theorem proved in textbooks, a tribute to its intuitive obviousness. And, indeed, many novices use the theorem without having been instructed in it and before they are capable of proving it.

knowledge resources available and about how they may be recrafted into expertise. This is largely an empirical task.

At broader levels we do not really know how important an appropriate metaconceptualization of the learning task is, whether students who come to understand some of the features of the evolution of intuitive knowledge into physics have a significant advantage over others. And finally, I have no model to present of the processes that crystallize a complex, evolving, intuitive-Newtonian system into effective expertise, if such a crystallization actually happens. In other words, there is no clear notion of a distinguished end state nor of distinct stages in that development. My story of evolution is fairly local, based on crude (but probably correct) notions like "successful elements are gradually recruited and become applied in more refined ways."

Feedback. In any instructed situation, it is misleadingly easy to see the feedback students get. After all, they are told the correct ideas in lecture and in the text. Their problem solutions are graded and perhaps corrected. More subtly, they have some sense when their ideas are sufficient in problem solving if for no other reason than they may or may not reach a plausible conclusion.

But at the next level of detail, things are not so simple. Instructors and texts are at best subliminally aware of the contributions of intuitive ideas to the development of Newtonian understanding. How can they explain them and their contributions? Nor has instruction concentrated much on providing clean models of core intuitive ideas, and on specific help integrating and refining them. These constitute open avenues for improved development by improving feedback.

Undoubtedly, instructors display their own run-time structures in presentations and problem solving, though these are likely to be highly nonsanctioned. And on the students' side, how are they to get a sense for what is this operative but inexplicit knowledge, even given some opportunity to observe its action in their instructors? Texts are, in all likelihood, much worse in this regard since it is standard practice to omit how one actually thinks about physics problems, producing only the cold logic of what amounts to an after-the-fact proof of what is known true.

Still, many low-level learning mechanisms will work in such a context. Problem situations that are not extremely artificial and abstract will cue intuitions that will be explored unconsciously as productive ideas and presumably linked in for their success. Doing many problems will evolve substantial run-time structure of some sort. But there is effectively no data on the microstructure of this kind of feedback by success. It would be especially interesting to chart how students' general sense for what is an appropriate explanation for physical problems evolves. Students attuned to the virtues of effective reductionist programs should appreciate the growing breadth of the small core of Newtonian ideas and more likely find appropriate places for intuitive precursors without subverting the Newtonian core. I will not pursue the details of internal feedback of this sort here except to say that it should appear as an effective drive toward a coherent, parsimonious view,

Newtonian or otherwise. I believe there is evidence for both productive and unproductive drives of this sort.

Propagation of structure from intuitive resources. I have already described some particulars of the great continuity in specific and structural terms between intuitive physics and the experts' sense of physical mechanism. More can be found in diSessa (1988, 1993). Historically, however, the emphasis has been on the propagation of incorrect intuitive ideas into the process of learning Newtonian mechanics. In the "misconceptions" literature, these are viewed as an annoying accidental importation of prior ideas into the learning process. If the view here is correct, however, these are more like little glitches that we must accept and learn to deal with if we are to pursue the "easy road" of engaging the resource of intuition into learning mechanics. The alternative might be some hypothetical, and I think dubious, abstract route to learning physics. In contrast to the misconceptions formulation, my projection is that future research will result in an equally large and important literature on specific and general commonalities between naive and expert ideas. As the fine structure of feedback and other aspects of this development are uncovered, we should be in a position to greatly facilitate the knowledge evolution.

At larger scales than individual elements, I note probably the central-most difficulty in building Newtonian mechanics on an intuitive base. That is, the expert's sense of mechanisms to dramatically more connected and directed toward a sparse core of theoretical ideas compared to intuitive physics. We can view this as an unfortunate propagation of a systemwide characteristic, fragmentation, from intuitive ideas into learning Newtonian physics. In particular, providing for effective coordination of centralized, core representations and diverse run-time structure is a dramatically difficult and enduring task. I give only a few examples here.

- Much run-time structure can be viewed as intuitive theorems that apply general ideas effectively to specific circumstances. Now, of course, all these ideas must in some sense defer to the core notions. In particular, every expert knows that, when questioned, she has an obligation to justify these theorems. So, there is no question that two masses connected by a string around a pulley are not a rigid body, and an expert will proceed with a proof that, in some circumstances, it is still appropriate to consider it such. But a more novice student may (and does!) simply claim it is obvious that this it is appropriate to treat the pair of masses in this way, mistaking run-time appropriateness for deep justification. Similarly, it is frequently entirely obvious to novices that kinetic energy is the sum of a linear energy and a rotational energy computed by ignoring the motion of the center of mass. After all, energies always add the way masses or numbers of items do. But the additivity of energy in this way is a subtle theorem; it is not at all evident, and, in fact, it is beyond the capabilities of most first- or second-year physics students to prove. We should ask how textbooks can possibly get away with using a hard-to-prove theorem in first-year college problems (rings and disks rolling down ramps) without even mentioning let alone proving the theorem!

- Newton's first two laws, summarized in $F = ma$, describe the effect of a force on its patient. The Third Law, "equal and opposite action and reaction," adds an important feature to the first two laws specifying that the agent is always affected the same as its patient, but in an opposite direction. But, unfortunately, the Third Law typically becomes an isolated and self-justifying explanation for movement in situations where both action and reaction are evident—a rocket moves because the action of the exhaust produces the reaction in movement of the rocket. This is an appropriate run-time gloss of a rocket's propulsion mechanism, but it does not obviate the applicability of $F = ma$. Many students will refuse the suggestion that $F = ma$ should apply to the rocket, instead taking the Third Law as a primitive, self-sufficient explanation.

In summary, novices must come to be able to apply with great reliability and confidence the few central ideas of Newtonian mechanics in a tremendously broad and treacherous range. I describe it as treacherous because Newtonian mechanics will not always apply, and even when it does, it may apply in highly nonobvious ways. There seem to be few resources available or easily crafted to help with this task, so that broad and appropriate application of the few, central Newtonian concepts is likely to remain a characteristic problem rather than one that is solved simply or by generating a general new processing module that solves the problem.[25]

Comments on Piaget

I have always taken Piaget to be an extraordinarily insightful generator of fruitful tasks and to be as insightful as an interpreter, at the first level, of children's behavior in those tasks. In particular, I will use as examples Piaget's contributions to understanding the development of the concept of physical quantity and the development of the concepts of speed, distance, and time.

On the other hand, I do not think Piaget has answered in a respectable manner what we should make of the children's behavior, particularly as to what drives the development that one sees. It seems clear, as Piaget asserts, that direct empiricism is insufficient to convince children to conserve, and that such partial conserving ideas as identity, reversibility, and compensation are somehow involved. But how, exactly, is conservation constituted and incorporated into a very generic mental structure, concrete operations? Indeed, what exactly are concrete operations, what function do they serve, and how can we see them to apply in the broad ranges of circumstances in which they supposedly must work? Similarly, equilibration is a highly unspecified dynamic of the evolution of complex systems. It certainly has

---

[25] I am arguing against the proposal that by making explicit the core notions of Newtonian physics and the processes of applying them, students will be able to "follow the prescriptions and checklists" and avoid the need to recruit intuitive knowledge, along with the difficulties that accrue from doing that. See Reif (1987) for a contrasting view.

not served as the basis for any even plausibly machine-implementable explanation of learning or development. Shouldn't equilibration apply to each of the developments discussed in this chapter? But if so, how, and if not, why not? Piaget just does not provide a convincing account of the causality of development.

In this section I briefly try to expand Piaget's perspective with comments on each of the factors of development we have been considering. I think this is, by itself, useful. However, some detail projected from the lessons learned in the study of intuitive physics will be of additional utility. The point is not so much to criticize Piaget, nor to provide any sort of complete explanation of the kind of intellectual development that he took as central to his mission. Instead, the point is to expand and shift the perspective based on the issues uncovered here in a way that I hope will be productive in future work.

Prior resources. Piaget does not question the origins of the "obvious" initial pronouncements that children make in learning conservation, for example, that a higher level of water means more water. Yet, if there is one thing his work shows, it is that the obvious is not necessarily always perceived as such; consider conservation itself! We would like to have a theory of the obvious, which, in other words, is a description of *prior resources* available to children, which may most ambitiously be given recursively as a genetic description of those prior resources. In particular, one must understand how those resources are in some sense effective—which is seldom done for early intuitive knowledge.

For example, I believe it is helpful to note that (plausibly) the most commonly observed phenomena in dealing with liquids is that the more you pour, the higher the liquid gets in the container. Indeed, in a context of control, say, controlling your own pouring of liquid into a container, the uncompensated correlation that more is higher is sufficient. A second related p-prim may be abstracted in pouring water on a table. A little spreads out a little, and more spreads out more. More implies wider. But this is less often observed and not nearly as important to a youngster who mostly needs to control the milk he pours into his glass. Concomitantly, youngsters sometimes, but less often, use wider implies more compared to higher implies more. What is important to children constitutes a skewing in terms of *restricted feedback.*

A similar restricted feedback seems to explain why some fragments of the concepts of speed and time appear much earlier than others. In the context of on-line controlling of one's own movement, it is always true that more time (in a given motion) means greater distance. So, in this light, consider a situation of two objects, one of which travels a greater distance, but, travelling much faster, traverses it in less time. Children might plausibly insist, given abstractions from the restricted context of on-line self-control, that because one object went farther, it must have traveled longer. Indeed, one does find some children who insist that if an object has gone farther, then it must have traveled for a longer time.

If the small scale of knowledge elements such as p-prims in intuitive physics is typical, then development may involve a much broader and intricate composition of phenomenology than the few, central elements of identity, reversibility, and compensation. So, for example, it would seem that children need to develop rationale to reject "counterexamples," such as the fact that pouring a cup of water into a bathtub does not (perceptibly) raise the level. Thus, they would need to be able to reason about very small increments being invisible before conservation could take its strongest foothold.[26] Or it may be that just preconservation children might insist on the water in the bathtub must go up on adding a cup of water, despite not being to see it happen. This would indicate that a significant strength exists in the fragment "more implies higher," though not in the contexts typically used to test conservation. And indeed, adding water to an existing body seems superficially different from pouring water from one container to another.

Knowing prior resources means not prejudicing the quality of these resources according to the quality of later ones (e.g., by calling them misconceptions). In particular, what attributes constitute the world vocabulary at early stages is extraordinarily difficult to ascertain. For example, while Piaget studied "speed," he insightfully remarked that in his studies it seemed children responded to the word "harder" better than to the word "faster" (Piaget, 1971). Thus children are seeing effort and energy as much as speed in their judgments about speed, time, and distance. As in the case of intuitive physics p-prims, direct abstractions of personal states in the control of the world are prominent. So, for example, Levin (1982) shows that children mistakenly involve attributes like brightness and size in judgments of time. These judgments are much less surprising if we see those attributes as close to the child's version of "speed." Prior resources provide important information especially on beginning stages of building new resources. In this case, brightness and size may be seen as indications of strength and effort. Of course, these correlate with "result" and thus become involved in judgments of speed and time. Brighter objects may be judged to be trying harder, hence going faster independent of distance covered per unit time.

It may be appropriate to interpret Piaget's operations as beta level resources. Certainly they are intended to be very generic and are, in part, Piaget's answers to Kant, whose ideas I have argued deserve consideration as specifying possible beta level resources. In this light, I suggest that in his search for beta level development, Piaget may have underestimated the importance of gamma level particulars, and he may have underestimated the impact of restricted feedback (such as innovation only for the purpose of personal control). If we expect beta resources regularly to emerge from gamma ones, and we take propagation of structure seriously, then we must understand more about the particulars of encoding of prior resources and about the contexts in which children are developing these resources.

With respect to *propagation of structure*, Piaget also gives less attention to the structure of intermediate states in learning than may be appropriate. Though he certainly admits stages where a child gives mixed responses to conservation ques-

---

[26] I do not know of any data on when such reasoning appears, but its correlation with conservation might be interesting.

tions, his descriptions generally leave intermediate stages characterized only as partially constructed later stages. But a lot of information should be available in the particulars of those states about prior resources, principles of innovation, and the form of feedback. We might be able to make a great deal from, for example, which fragments and contexts lead and which lag in development, if we could see and describe the intermediate states well enough. Does the more-implies-higher idea in the context of control overcome (lack of) perceptual reinforcement in the cup of water into the bathtub case? A refined theory of conceptual change should predict characteristic bugs and easy early accomplishments in these intermediate states, such as overgeneralization from a prominent context allowed by impoverished phenomenology (lack of resources) that might have inhibited that overgeneralization.

Within the present framework, we are obligated to consider plausible mechanisms that could drive development, *principles of invention*. Presumably a young child does not spend all of her time doing and thinking about things that contribute to her learning conservation. When exactly is she doing and thinking those things, and what do they contribute? An important question is whether the development is strictly cumulative, or whether there are a few crucial events. Perhaps the critical thing is the gradual development of a problem context; "the solution" comes in one or a few critical episodes; and finally, odds and ends of more extended cuing and more reliable use of the full cluster gradually fall into place. These latter two are specific structural replacements that might pin down what *decalage* means and explain a certain kind of equilibration. Work on intuitive physics suggests looking for accumulated phenomenology, the making of relatively simple observations, which cumulatively contribute crucially to development. For example, the experience of squeezing mud or clay in one's fist and feeling it force its way out the ends is quite a graphic demonstration that thinner carriers with it *necessarily* longer. Some experimenters have reported that in addition to the standard Piagetian explanations for conservation, children sometimes respond to questions about why the amount in the narrow glass is higher by asserting the sides squeezed it up. How do we assess the breadth and importance of the observations that give rise to explanations like this one? Could we simply ask children what they think of such phenomena?

Given the great breadth of common phenomenology, one should expect there is a need to undermine negative or competing p-prims as much as there is need to collect the positive core. Conservation should correlate with the defeat of some key observable "counterexamples" to conservation, either through understanding how it is not a counterexample, or at least through "excuses" entering the knowledge base. Development might turn crucially on the capability to differentiate contexts in which ideas apply from those in which they do not, so counterexamples may be automatically discounted. Perhaps widening experimentation on the intermediate states would be insightful in finding out how counterexamples are defeated—asking about what happens when liquid evaporates, when people drink. Finally, the confidence of recently conserving children could be tested with counterexamples and general arguments and compared with that of later conservers to see if there is a continuing increase in sophistication and confidence, or if there is, instead, a quick transition to fully operating conservation. I believe that thinking of the transition to conservation, in part, as *developing confidence* is a useful experimental heuristic, with the implied gradual accumulation of arguments and a general shift toward believing some phenomena as fundamental and others as less generally important.

I suggest we might be able to make more of larger scaled relationships in development than simply recruitment of individual, p-prim–like elements. Piaget and Inhelder do remark that the rise of atomistic ways of thinking seems to coincide with conservation, but perhaps one can make stronger statements. Atomistic models lend a plausibility to conservation, seeing shape change as mere rearrangement of number-conserved parts. As well, atomism could impart confidence from number conservation's possible involvement in justifying quantity conservation. More speculatively, atomism might exist in a simple modeling relation with quantity conservation, hence provide central resources for recrafting into conservation.

To summarize, I have suggested that it is profitable to consider development of ideas like conservation as gamma level resources that may gradually come to have beta level status, if ever we can see them as such. I have suggested that it might be profitable to characterize the prior resources involved in developing such concepts as p-prims, abstracted in early stages in important contexts like personal on-line control. Indeed, understanding such contexts may shed important light on the meaning of attributes in terms of which children have abstracted their experience. P-prim resources are likely to be fairly dramatically fragmented, so integration of a broad range of them across differing circumstances constitutes a fundamental and probably extended problem. In contrary manner, the natural discriminations of contexts ought also to be correlated with concept development, but they may be independently researched and characterized. In net, propagation of structure as seen in the fine structure of development with many different vectors impinging and coming into a complex coordination seems a relatively untapped resource in understanding general principles of development.

Implicit and Explicit Knowledge

It is important to the mission of this volume that I take a moment to articulate the theme of implicit versus explicit knowledge in relation to this chapter. In some ways this is very easy to do, for the whole enterprise is one of ferreting out the relations of prior systems to present ones. In most of the cases discussed here, very little of prior resources will be so evident or reflectively accessible so as to count as explicit knowledge. Indeed, the whole of intuitive physics seems not to have been noticed possibly until Piaget. In a sense Piaget also missed the importance of the contribution of intuitive (and hence tacit) ideas to learning specific subject matter, as opposed to the somewhat negatively characterized contributions of intuitive ideas to succeeding stages of intelligence.

Beta level resources, if they exist, will all be tacit essentially by definition. It seems hard to imagine that any of the basic infrastructure of intelligence would be open to reflective consideration. Certainly examples like how one does logical reasoning or the existence of modules of coordinating access and action do not encourage us to think beta resources are explicit.

One of our core problems, the coordination of core structural and run-time knowledge seems to split rather cleanly across the explicit/implicit divide. Core Newtonian structure would seem to be explicit. A lot of our confidence in Newtonian mechanics as a highly organized subject comes from our ability to assert and demonstrate in great detail that one formulation, $F = ma$, effectively covers essentially the span of the knowledge system. In general, algebraic and propositional forms of knowledge can lay claim to being explicit in that we can certainly display them and in some ways reason about them. And explicitness goes along with reliability, arbitrary persistence, and interaction with diverse knowledge subsystems such as language. Contrastingly, heuristics and run-time intuitions have only relatively recently had any notice in studies of learning physics, let alone in physics texts.

On the other hand, there are reasons to beware identifying explicit with core knowledge. In my arguments generally I have found important roles for inarticulate and hence inexplicit knowledge, even where there are overt knowledge-like things to point to. Recall, for example, that I argued that symbols, which in external form would seem explicitly to represent their referents, simply cannot do their job without the processes that interpret the symbols, find referents, coordinate accesses so as to get information about referents and so on. Even in the capital of the territory of explicit knowledge, tacit knowledge seems to be the machine under the facade.

Finally, p-prims constitute a rather well-elaborated model of one of the central forms in which tacit knowledge works. I have told a theoretical story about the origins of this kind of knowledge, how it develops, and, in particular, how it contributes to tacit but necessary processes of interpreting symbols like $F = ma$.

Conclusion

Where have we come to in all this? I claimed initially to be searching for simplicity but, in the end, have found substantial complexity.[27] In part, we can say in retrospect that taking a genetic perspective seeded our downfall, for the development even of simple things may be tremendously complex.

There are a few compensating things to be said. First, there are some simplicities in what I have claimed. The basic program is simple, yet it contains very particular claims that are subject to refutation. It might be true that principles of development simply do not all follow the evolutionary scheme I have presented, for example,

---

[27] There is clearly irony in accusing Piaget of overlooking details in a chapter such as this.

involving feedback at every stage. Second, I have delivered at least a few candidates for quite general, perhaps overarching problems for cognition—exploiting opportunities to coordinate among and between accesses and actions or coordinating between deep structural and run-time capabilities. If such problems are characteristic of the problem of developing intelligence, they almost certainly will transcend particular examples like object permanence or difficulties in learning Newtonian physics.

The framework is also one for exploiting details and complexities in the pursuit of evidence for overarching structural patterns. I believe the detailed study of expert and naive behavior shows that intuitive physics is substantially the substrate on which formal physics is learned. Similarly, Johnson-Laird and Falmagne show that spatial and imagistic knowledge is implicated in logical reasoning through little glitches in the implementation.

There are also a few simple but powerful caveats to take away from these analyses. For example, something has been learned about the limits of the meaning and import of the Physical Symbol System Hypothesis by considering it in a genetic light and with respect to substantial problems that sentient beings must solve to be more effective as life forms rather than with respect to the abstract accolades due a mathematical category of uniformly powerful processors. I hope the genetic/causal view can provide more such examples.

Finally, there is some solace in realizing that the world may really be complicated, and the issue is really only to find reasonable simplifications without denying the complexity.

Things should be made as simple as possible . . . but not simpler.

—*Albert Einstein*

References

Clement, C., & Falmagne, R. J. (1986). Logical reasoning, world knowledge, and mental imagery: Interconnections in cognitive processes. *Memory and Cognition, 14*, 299–307.

de Kleer, J. (1982). Qualitative and quantitative knowledge in classical mechanics. Artificial Intelligence Laboratory Technical Report TR-352, Cambridge, MA: MITAI Laboratory.

diSessa, A. A. (1982). Unlearning Aristotelian physics. *Cognitive Science, 6*(1), 37–75.

diSessa, A. A. (1983). Phenomenology and the evolution of intuition. In D. Gentner & A. Stevens (Eds.), *Mental models* (pp. 15–33). Hillsdale, NJ: Lawrence Erlbaum Associates, Inc.

diSessa, A. A. (1986). Notes on the future of programming. In D. A. Norman & S. W. Draper (Eds.), *User centered systems design: New perspectives on human–computer interaction* (pp. 125–152). Hillsdale, NJ: Lawrence Erlbaum Associates, Inc.

diSessa, A. A. (1993). Toward an epistemology of physics. *Cognition and Instruction, 10*, 105–225.

diSessa, A. A. (1988). Knowledge in pieces. In G. Forman & P. Pufall (Eds.), *Constructivism in the computer age* (pp. 49–70). Hillsdale, NJ: Lawrence Erlbaum Associates, Inc.

Falmagne, R. J., Singer, J., & Clement, C. (undated). Imagery and linguistic processes in conditional reasoning. Unpublished manuscript, Clark University Department of Psychology, Worcester, MA.

Fodor, J. A. (1986). Why paramecia don't have mental representations. *Midwest Studies in Philosophy, X*, 3–23.

Forbus, K. (1984). Qualitative process theory. *Artificial Intelligence, 24*, 85–168.

Gentner, D., & Stevens, A. (1983). *Mental models*. Hillsdale, NJ: Lawrence Erlbaum Associates, Inc.

Hume, D. (1962). An inquiry concerning human understanding. In A. Flew, *David Hume: On human nature* (p. 38). New York: Collier Books.

Johnson-Laird, P. N. (1983). *Mental models*. Cambridge, MA: Harvard University Press.

Levin, I. (1982). The nature and development of time concepts in children: The effects of interfering cues. In W. Friedman (Ed.), *The developmental psychology of time* (pp. 47–85). New York: Academic Press.

Newell, A. (1980). Physical symbol systems. *Cognitive Science, 4*, 135–183.

Newell, A. (1990). *Unified theories of cognition*. Cambridge, MA: Harvard University Press.

Piaget, J. (1971). *The child's conception of movement and speed* (G. E. T. Holloway & M. J. Mackenzie, Trans.). New York: Ballatine Books.

Reif, F. (1987). Instructional design, cognition and technology: Applications to the teaching of scientific concepts. *Journal of Research in Science Teaching, 24*, 309–324.

Rozin, P. (1976). The evolution of intelligence and access to the cognitive unconscious. In J. M. Sprague & A. N. Epstein (Eds.), *Progress in psychobiology and physiological psychology* (pp. 245–280). New York: Academic Press.

Searle, J. (1984). *Minds, brains and science*. Cambridge, MA: Harvard University Press.

Simon, H. A. (1974). How big is a chunk? *Science, 183*, 482–488.

Exercises

1.   How secure is my claim that development must be judged by some form of success and failure, and judged ultimately by external feedback? I say "ultimately" since we certainly must allow for developing internalized principles of feedback. But still, these internal resources must have come from somewhere; so I expect all such principles to trace back to some form of external feedback. Perhaps there is a problem in that "feedback" can cover such a broad range of situations that the framework may break down in some way.

2.   Build a computer model that shows a particular instance of crystallization of common resources. You may use any plausible form of "crowding out" of the fragmented resources, such as forgetting or gradual strengthening of associations with the common resource, and weakening of associations with the diverse forms. Perhaps an appropriately simple situation might be the use of a name as an common intermediary to multiple, more specialized versions of reference such as: John-as-personality, John-as-physical-object, John-as-index-to-wife-Mary, etc.

Extra Credit: Mathematize this phenomenon so that it is a theorem for a certain class of cognitive dynamics.

Extra Extra Credit: Extend this mathematization to cover all interesting cases of the "crowding out" phenomenon.

3.   Deconstruct planning knowledge. That is, develop some plausible models that start from a system without any planning capability and describe contexts of need (or opportunity), feedback, principles of invention, and prior resources that can produce a form of planning. Your models may have stages indicating more and

less problematic aspects of producing a general planning scheme, the levels of partial capability. You may use an existing planning model as your goal, or you may invent simplified models to make the task more tractable. If you succeed convincingly without invoking elaborate domain-specific knowledge, you may wish to critique any claim that planning may emerge largely anew in each knowledge domain.

4. Deconstruct goals as cognitive entitics. Some formulations of cognitive infrastructure use goals as low level and given resources, for example, Newell in his unified theories of cognition. But if we take the genetic problem seriously, we might ask what prior conditions and resources might be available in the construction of goals, and what problems goals really satisfy. Do any plausible developmental scenarios result in the generation of goals as defined by the processing structure of which goals are a part in existing theories? How might goals migrate from specific knowledge systems in which they might be generated to a more general processing infrastructure? Is it at all plausible that goals emerged in motor or sensory processing (somewhat as invariant recognition capability may have originated in sensory processing) and then became generic resources?

What corequisite characteristics of content knowledge systems, like physics or mathematics, might be necessary to make goals useful entities. For example, if you have no very general methods that are not bound tightly to contexts, goals are implausibly useful. If goals make strong demands on the corresponding content knowledge system—so strong that true goal-directed behavior requires only a minimal additional structure—then perhaps goals might essentially emerge anew in each system that satisfies the strong prerequisites.

5. Prove that in a connectionist implementation of a physical symbol system there are nodes that are not interpretable as symbols.

2

Constructivism and Supporting Environments

Rochel Gelman

University of California at Los Angeles

Introduction

A major question organizes this volume, "How can educators lead learners from implicit to explicit understanding, especially in the domains of mathematics and science?" This chapter focuses on why it may be difficult to achieve this goal. For one, learners can and do find interpretations that differ from those intended by experts. Our work on fractions will be used to develop some of the implications of this point. In addition, we still do not know how to characterize relevant inputs for learning within a constructivist theory. In order to educate children about explicit theories, we need guidelines for selecting relevant inputs. Constructivist theories have yet to develop these. Our beginning efforts to fill this lacuna are woven throughout the manuscript.

The absence of a constructivist theory of supporting environments is a significant issue in its own right. But even if there were one, we still would be well advised to adopt a wait-and-see stance that is skeptical about new programs and teaching materials, for a foundational assumption of constructivist theories is that learners are actively engaged in selecting and interpreting inputs for and by themselves. Therefore, it is always possible that novices will ignore and/or misinterpret the environments we offer them, forcing us to return to the drawing board—even if we are sure that our new offerings are grand.

Even granting that we now know a great deal about the initial states of a novice's knowledge and that we should build our armament of teaching props to acknowledge these, it is still the case that our pupils could—and probably will—find interpretations that do not match the ones we intended. This follows once we grant that the mind constructs representations on the basis of what it brings to the learning setting as much as what it is offered. We should be prepared for such "failures" of attention and/or interpretation and stand ready to tune or change a program *after* it is put into the arena of learning.

Support for the reported research and preparation of the manuscript came form NSF grants BNS 8916220 and DBS-9209741. Thanks to Iris Levin for working with me on the Inside-Outside data; Betty Meck and Jason Macario for their help with the chapter; and Sid Strauss; Dina Tirosh, Tamar Zelniker, and other members of the Unit in Human Development in the School of Education, Tel Aviv University, for their insightful comments on an earlier draft of this chapter.

On the Need for a Constructivist Theory of Environments

Cognitive developmentalists (especially those influenced by Bartlett and Piaget) have converged on the position that children play an active role in the acquisition of their own knowledge (see Gelman & Brown, 1986, for a review). No longer do we treat young learners as passive recipients of whatever we deem to be good for them. Instead we acknowledge that even young children can find, choose, and sometimes make up inputs that foster development of the representations they are busily constructing. Even when early knowledge is implicit in form, it still influences how settings at home, in school, and the culture at large are interpreted.

Educators too talk of the importance of acknowledging the constructivist tendencies of their students. Especially in the areas of mathematics and science education, much has been written about learners' tendencies to develop systematic and organized knowledge bases about numbers, electricity, substance, the way physical objects move, the animate–inanimate distinction, and so on, often before entering school and often without any obvious guidance from others (see Carey, 1986, for one review). There is a growing realization that instructional efforts have to take into account these active tendencies of learners to make sense of inputs in terms of what novices (as opposed to experts) take for granted (Glaser, 1987). Everywhere there are efforts to characterize the nature of the representations that learners bring to school with them. There is even some work on the mechanisms by which such representations are acquired and could be modified (see other chapters in this volume). Still, surprisingly little attention has been paid to a topic of central importance for educators, namely, how to characterize the nature of supporting environments once it is assumed that learners actively interpret and select inputs on the basis of their knowledge bases. In the absence of such an account we have an incomplete constructivist theory of learning and development.

To say we still need a constructivist theory of the environment and its use is to say we need to characterize its laws of learning. For example, what laws parallel or replace the association laws of frequency and contiguity? What kinds of data are foundational, that is, serve as primitives during early cognitive development? Does the associationist answer that such data are sensory bits hold for a constructivist answer to this question? If not, what alternative does? Are we committed to the notion of a tabula rasa at birth? And so on.

On Relevance

As soon as we give to the mind the ability to define what is relevant, we give over a great deal of our control of selecting inputs to that very same mind. The result is that we no longer can hold the longstanding view that we, be we scientists and/or educators, know what counts as relevant inputs for learning about X, Y, and Z. This consequence is not widely appreciated. For example, wittingly or unwittingly, we continue to act as if we know what the relevant data are—no matter what the child or novice learner of any age thinks. We continue to have the idea that those data that experts take to be relevant will also be viewed as relevant by novices.

Constructivist Theories of Mind: Empiricist Theories of Learning?

If we assume that children construct representations, that they are active participants in the buildup of their own knowledge, we must acknowledge that they also have considerable control over the definition of relevant inputs. The young might even use different data than expected and therefore construct different representations than the experts. If they do, their definition of supporting environments for learning will not converge upon ours. What kinds of assumptions about learning do we need so that novices will build knowledge bases that converge with those of their elders?

Tabula rasae? Can we incorporate the widespread assumption that our young have no representations, that they do not start out sharing knowledge with their elders? If our young have no representations, let alone any in common with us, then they are free to interpret all inputs anyway they want, in any of an infinite number of ways. On straightforward grounds of probability, the odds are that they will generate interpretations of a given input that differ from ours. Similarly, in the absence of any representations to constrain initial interpretations, the odds are high that the young will vary widely amongst themselves in their interpretations of a given input. As a result, members of the next generation should differ from their elders and among themselves in how they interpret seemingly identical inputs.

Since our commonsense observation is that our own young do come to share with us a common core of knowledge, how can we capture this observation within a constructivist account of knowledge acquisition? Feldman and Gelman (1987) offer one solution, in what they call their rational-constructivist account of cognitive development. They assume that young children share some initial knowledge that is common to ours. The knowledge is assumed to be skeletal in form, to be but outlines of some domains of knowledge. These outlines serve to define the class of stimuli that are potentially relevant to further learning about the concepts of the domain. To the extent that they do this, they also serve to direct children's attention to inputs that will nurture the domain's development, that will lead children to seek and respond to those inputs we consider relevant for learning more. Similarly, these structures serve as file drawers of memory about the noted inputs, making it possible for the child to collect relevant data about the body of knowledge.

By limiting the innate knowledge base to *some* skeletal principles, Feldman and Gelman make clear their commitment to the need for learning and development. They also provide an account of how the knowledge that is acquired by the young can converge on the shared knowledge base of the domain. These skeletons do more than focus attention on relevant data. They provide a core around which assimilation and accommodation can take place. Bits and pieces of noticed data are assimilated to an existing structure that serves to keep data in an organized and coherent way. As these skeletal structures are applied they nurture themselves, leading to their own fleshing out.

There Is More to the Nature of Environment Than Meets the Eye (Ear, etc.)

On the nature of foundational inputs. Even if we assume our young share some skeletal cores of knowledge with their elders, they still may treat as relevant some inputs that we take to be irrelevant, or nonexistent. One consequence is that learners sometimes treat as relevant some inputs that we take to be irrelevant or are not aware of! Work on language and concept acquisition in blind and deaf children helps illustrate these points. It leads to the conclusion that those who know the least about a domain are sometimes more ''expert'' on the subject of relevant inputs than are those whose who have mastered that domain. When this does happen, we can look at their solutions for clues on how to characterize more accurately the nature of relevant inputs.

Some blind and deaf children learn what they ''should'' not. There is still a widespread belief that the initial inputs for learning a concept, the primitive data upon which the concept is built, must be in the domain of the target concept, for example, visual concepts require exposure to visual data, auditory skills require auditory inputs. If so, the congenitally deaf should be at risk for acquiring language and the congenitally blind should be at risk for learning the meaning of visual terms, ones about seeing, looking, being blind, and the like. This way of characterizing the requirements that initial inputs must meet has a long and distinguished history. For example, when John Locke discussed the implications for blindness for his empiricist theory of concept learning, he concluded that blind children would not develop certain kinds of knowledge—this because they could not receive the requisite foundational inputs, sensations generated by light.

As a reminder, Locke assumed that concepts are built up by associations that are based on those primitive sense data that fall on functioning senses. The assumption that uninterpreted sense data have a privileged status is still very much with us. Many continue to hold that children learn the meaning of words by seeing someone point to objects and actions in the context in which a novel label is uttered. The assumption is that pertinent sensations from the target item, the spoken word, and the setting are generated close together in time and/or space, the consequence of which is that all can be associated together. Repeated exposure to such pairings of the sound sequence and other patterns of sensory data lead to the strengthening of associations between these. With the buildup of such associations, the sound sequence begins to take on, or stand for, a meaning, one that represents the object or events responsible for the sensory data that generated the sense data (see Gelman & Cohen, 1988, for a further discussion of this issue).

Presumably, the function of pointing in this account is to single out the pattern of visual input that should be associated with the sound of a given word. If so, blind children should have more trouble learning language than sighted children; they cannot receive that set of relevant sensations that have to do with pointing. In addition, they should be especially at risk when it comes to learning vocabulary terms of sight like LOOK, SEE, BLIND, SHOW. Knowledge of objects should be limited to those features that are defined haptically and/or aurally. Although it might seem reasonable to predict that the blind will fail to learn the meaning of visual terms, the prediction is wrong.

Landau and Gleitman (1985) found that blind children's acquisition of syntax, early vocabulary, and the functional uses of language can be remarkably like that of normal, sighted children. They offer compelling demonstrations that Kelli (one of their congenitally blind subjects) knew, at least by the time she was a preschooler, that sighted people can see. For example, Kelli would hold up an object when told to "let mommy see the car" and hide an object when told to "make it so mommy can't see X." She also turned around when asked to "let me see your back," not when asked to "let me see your front."

Kelli surely had to learn the meaning of SEE. She was not born knowing the English correspondence to this particular sound, any more than a Spanish child is born knowing that *si* means "yes." But her learning could not have taken the course that association theorists ever since Locke have assumed it must. Landau and Gleitman (1985) suggest that learning of such words occurred, in part, because Kelli *listened* to how the language she had started to learn was used by others. By listening to the way novel verbs were used in sentences, she was able to use her existing knowledge of syntax and semantics in order to construct guesses about the meaning of the visual terms. Consider how this might have happened.

To start, Landau and Gleitman (1985) note that LOOK is an agentive verb and SEE a nonagentive verb. Clauses that start with IN ORDER TO, or what are known as purposive clauses, are limited to being complements of agentive verbs. Speakers of English know they can say "John looked into the room in order to learn who was there." They also know that they cannot say "John saw into the room in order to learn who was there," presumably because they have implicit knowledge of the difference between the syntactic principles governing the difference between agentive and nonagentive verbs. There are other features about these verbs that bear on the Landau and Gleitman argument, features we leave to the reader to explore further. We turn to the points one can make with this example.

Novice learners can and do use inputs that do not fit our preconceptions of what is relevant. Had Landau and Gleitman not been willing to take seriously the possibility that the definition of relevant inputs need not be what we think it is, we might not yet know that knowledge of syntax can feed the learning of verb meanings in all language learners (Landau & Gleitman, 1985). The fact that visual concepts *can* develop in the absence of a functioning visual system highlights the need for us to reexamine assumptions regarding what counts as the foundational data for concept acquisition. We need to look for an alternative account of what the building blocks of experience are, to reconsider how one *describes* what counts as relevant inputs. Clues as to how to proceed are embedded in the previous example.

As soon as one allows that the rules of verb use can themselves serve to define relevant inputs for different concepts, one makes a move to a structural description of the required environment. No longer are the data best described in terms of what is seen by the eyes, let alone sensed or taken in at an uninterpreted sensory level. Instead, the data are better described in terms of the principles that serve to organize the very representations the novice uses in a given learning setting. Inputs are relevant if they are structured in a way that is consistent with the organization of the principles that will assimilate them. Language learning in the deaf offers converging evidence for these conclusions.

Until recently, it was broadly assumed that the deaf do not develop a language of their own. During the past 20 years linguists and psycholinguists have helped revolutionize our views on this matter. It is now known that the language of the deaf, one that makes use of our manual as opposed to spoken skills, is indeed a language, rich in structure for syntax, morphology, and phonetics (perhaps we should say "manetics"). American Sign Language is not a finger-spelling translation of English. Instead, it has its own different rules of syntax and morphology (see Klima & Bellugi, 1979; Suppalla, 1987). Of interest for this paper are Johnson and Newport's (1988) data on language acquisition in second generation congenitally deaf children, who, unlike their parents, were allowed to start learning to sign as soon as they showed any interest in language learning.

The deaf parents of the deaf children in question were raised in the oralist tradition and consequently were not exposed to sign until they went to schools for the deaf. Even then, they did not receive instruction in sign. In-class emphasis was on learning to speak. Nevertheless, learning of sign occurred—in the corridors, on the playing fields, in the dorms and cafeterias, and so on. Newport and her colleagues report that when the children of these same individuals are allowed to start signing as toddlers in their home, presumably with their parents serving as models, they end up with a deeper mastery of the target language than do their parents. For example, when their parents are more likely to use frozen signs, they are more likely to take apart such complex signs and decompose them into linguistically meaningful units. The result is that they are also better able to generate novel items and acquire more advanced rules of syntax.

We have seen that our assumptions about the kind of data that many take to be relevant for first language acquisition may not mesh with the learner's assumptions. The expert's idea that the deaf cannot and do not acquire language is very much tied to a particular theory of learning. Throughout the lengthy period that we have believed that languages must be spoken, and therefore that sign language was not a language, deaf communities have presented evidence to the contrary. Yet only recently have language experts recognized the import of these data. Given our own constructivist inclinations to apply our own theories, there is no guarantee that we will avoid similar errors in the future. Similarly, it is always possible that the novice will take as relevant data that we either think are irrelevant or fail to notice. In this sense then, the novice might be said to be more expert at defining relevant inputs than are those who have already mastered the domain—a sobering thought indeed.

Constructivist theory of mind: Empiricist laws of learning? Many theorists in the field of cognitive development say they prefer some variant of a nonassociationist model. Still, it is not hard to point to many among the same set who, surely unintentionally, work with one or another variant of an associationist theory of environment, for example, those who focus on that aspect of the Vygotskian account that assigns adult caretakers a privileged status with respect to the job of knowledge transmission. In this particular interpretation of Vygotsky, adults are not only the keepers and users of knowledge about concepts, social matters, culture, and so on, they are also the best transmitters of this pool of knowledge. But this cannot be true, at least not all the time.

We have just seen that many an expert linguist and psychologist failed to discover the relevant inputs for learning about the meaning of verbs. Similarly, experts in other areas have made recommendations that are consistent with their theory of learning, seemingly to ignore alternatives that might make sense. For example, there used to be math textbooks that taught the number facts $2 + 3 = 5$ and $3 + 2 = 5$ at widely separated intervals. The rationale was that this minimized the possibility that children's learning would suffer from the competing and interfering associations to common elements. Given a constructivist view of relevant inputs, the preceding number facts are far from interfering. They are structurally extremely similar.

Other associationist assumptions penetrate our intellectual unconscious about the conditions for learning, including that the young learn what we know simply because they are repeatedly exposed to the right environment. This explanation is a straightforward paraphrase of a fundamental associative law of learning, the law of frequency that states that the more often a given stimulus is presented, the more novices form association networks based on the input. However, in its unmodified form, this law cannot be a constructivist law of learning. The learner need not attend to the stimulation emanating from the object. And the learner could misinterpret the stimulation, even if she does attend to it. In either case, across trials, the data set may be common according to some objective standard. Nevertheless, it need not be common for the learner. If so, one might say that there are no repeated trials and hence no inputs that are more frequent than others. In the extreme, it is possible that each encounter with the "objectively" defined input is actually a different one for the subject.

Another way of putting the foregoing is to say that if both the empiricist and constructivist accounts of learning have a law of frequency, the law *must* work in different ways or exists for different reasons in the two cases. In the absence of the nature of such a law of learning within a constructivist framework, we run the risk of mixing together an empiricist account of learning with a constructivist account of the mind. In fact, if a sequence of inputs is structurally related, there is no need for the exact same ones to be repeated over time. Ones that form an equivalence class because they share a structural definition might well be interchangeable, as for example are $2 + 3$ and $3 + 2$.

Why the seeming tendency to fall back on associationist ideas about the way to nurture and advance cognitive development? Some of the tendency is surely due to the absence of a clear alternative. Given our everyday constructivist tendencies, we are bound to make implicit use of whatever theory we do have. Further factors might reinforce this tendency. Historically, the associationist theory of mind has been closely tied to the democratic political view that anyone's mental repertoire can be nurtured if given the right opportunities. The match between a commitment to equal opportunity and the goals of educators makes understandable our implicit use of an empiricist theory of environment. It is a piece of our cultural unconscious and therefore is used without awareness. It is as if it never occurs to us to ask whether there are other theories of the environment that are also consistent with our political and educational goals. Farfetched? We think not. In what follows we show that there has been a strong tendency within the field of cognitive development to accept as given the associationist definition of what are the first relevant data. Since this holds for the important traditional theories of cognitive development, it is no surprise that similar themes penetrate the rules for developing educational materials.

Implications for Theories of Cognitive Development and Learning

The major developmental theories, be they due to Bruner, Piaget, Vygotsky, or Werner, all share the premise that relevant inputs for cognitive development proceed from first being sensory to later being abstract—from the sensorimotor to the perceptual or concrete to the abstract or logical levels. Different terms are used by different theorists but all converge on the same conclusion. A similar description of the stimulus is assumed by those who construct educational materials and offer teachers guidelines. The theme is that one must first let children interact with "concrete materials" and not burden them with the purely symbolic or representation level; they are not ready to move beyond the perceptual. We are beginning to see evidence that challenges these deeply entrenched assumptions. There are now cases where the initial or early relevant inputs for cognitive development do not fit the rule that learning in the young proceeds necessarily from the sensory to the perceptual to the abstract. What has been taken as given is beginning to look more like an assumption that is tied to a given theoretical characterization of input primitives.

Learning About Objects

One standard account of how infants come to know objects is that they gradually build up associations based on the sensations garnered from exposure to the object. Objects that share a common color, substance, shape, texture, and so on generate sensations that are more proximate to each other than not, and hence ones that are most likely to be associated. Over time, the infant (or any novice learner) accrues a sufficiently rich associative store from which to induce the concept of the target object. Similarly, the ability to find an object, even when it is partially occluded, derives from common or similar sensory associations. For example, those parts that share a color or shape should be taken as the parts that go together. Although the

Piagetian account does not treat associations as a foundational mental ability, it does share with associationism the notion that the concept of an object is built up as more and more sensorimotor schemes are coordinated, that perception is first two dimensional, and that perception precedes conception.

An alternative to both the associationist and Piagetian accounts has been developed by Spelke and her collaborators. Spelke (1988) proposes that infants begin with the assumption that their environment is three dimensional and composed of things that occupy space, persist, move as units independently of one another, and maintain their coherence and boundaries as they move. Two principles of object perception follow: Two surfaces will be perceived as part of the same object if they touch each other, and two surfaces that move together at the same time and speed along parallel paths in three-dimensional space—even if their connection is concealed—will be perceived as surfaces of a single object. Together these principles would allow infants to learn which surfaces of a partially concealed object belong together.

Spelke's principles for defining the initially relevant data are stated in relational or structural terms, not in terms of separate bits of sensory data. It is not because Spelke denies infants the ability to sense these attributes; the idea is that these are just not the kind of data first used. Rather, her account reverses the definition of what kind of inputs are foundational and what kind of data are noticed later. In particular, Spelke suggests that the patterns of light that generate the sensations of color, brightness, and so on are only used after infants *first* sort the environment into things. Once noticed, infants' tendencies to explore things leads them to notice and learn details about these different things. We note that an account like this is better able to explain the fact that infants do not necessarily treat objects with different colors and textures on each surface as different objects (Kellman & Spelke, 1983). If infants see these two surfaces moving together in parallel, they are more likely to assume they belong to the same single object. Similarly, if two objects that are held, one in each hand, and connected by a *not-visible* moving rod, infants will treat the display as if the two objects are in fact parts of a single object (Spelke, 1990).

Spelke's idea is that infants first pick out objects on the basis of patterns of data that are related to the nature of three-dimensional object perception. For her, foundational inputs should be characterized in terms of *coordinated patterns* of inputs as opposed to points of sensations. These in turn are related to the definition of what is relevant as now specified by abstract principles of perception, and possibly cognition, not in terms of particular sensors that are ready to receive sensations from a given distal stimulus (Spelke, 1988).

Keeping Track of and Using Numbers at an Early Age

The possibility that infants do not treat punctate patches of light, sound waves, pressure, and so on as the primitive sources of data fits with findings that show that infants respond in *numerically* relevant ways when shown representations of a *set* of objects. In one experiment, six- to eight-month-old infants were shown a series of heterogeneous three-item displays. On each trial each item varied in shape, color, position on a screen, and so on. Similarly, item kind and a variety of surface variables of the items changed across trials. These displays were rich in sensory input potential. Yet infants did not fixate on these variations in sensory information. Instead, they habituated to the class of three-item displays, as evidenced by the fact that they only recovered their interest in looking at displays when the number of items contained in these changed (Starkey, Spelke, & Gelman, 1983, 1990; Starkey, Gelman, & Spelke, 1985).

Infants' tendencies to respond in numerically relevant ways are robust enough to serve investigators who "ask" them other questions. For example, Kesterbaum, Termine, and Spelke (1987) have shown that infants do not always perceive two objects when adults do. When two objects of the same kind that vary only in color are side by side, so that they are touching and in perfect alignment, infants see but one object; we see two objects. It is only when the objects are spatially separated that the two objects are perceived as two items by the infant.

There is an exceedingly popular and resilient belief that number-relevant responses in infants are controlled by a low-level general purpose perceptual mechanism (e.g., Shipley & Shepperson, 1990), as opposed to, say, principles of counting. The idea is that the data do not reveal a sensitivity to number-relevant dimensions but rather more primitive stimulus qualities, perhaps like brightness, intensity, and so on. An example of such an account is offered by Moore, Benenson, Reznick, Peterson, and Kagan (1987) for Starkey et al.'s (1983) finding that infants prefer to look at that slide of a pair that contains the same number of pictures as the number of drumbeat sounds they hear (two or three) at the same time. Moore et al. start with their finding that infants in their task responded intermodally to the pair of stimuli that differed in number. They go on to say that this "failure to replicate" Starkey et al. rules out a number-based account of both studies. They suggest that infants in their study responded on the basis of relative differences in intensity levels. Perhaps, but the same kind of explanation does not work for the Starkey et al. data because the displays within each of the two-element and three-element classes of stimuli were intentionally selected to vary in color, size, and so on. Therefore, there could not be a common intensity that characterized all of the two-item and none of the three-item displays, or vice versa (see also Starkey et al., 1990).

The Moore et al. (1987) account takes particular sensory attributes as primitive. Like Spelke, we do not. Instead we appeal to a more relational account of the relevant data. By allowing infants a principle that is akin to a principle of one–one correspondence, we give them the wherewithal to detect either the presence *or* absence of a *correspondence* between the sets of items (no matter what their sensory characteristics) and end up with one account of both the Starkey et al. and Moore et al. data. Why infants respond intermodally to a correspondence in the former set of studies and a lack of correspondence in the latter set is not answered by this account. However, this is a different kind of question, one that awaits the answer as to why infants sometimes respond intermodally to matches and sometimes to differences for a wide range of input types (Spelke, 1990).

If we allow that infants use an implicit principle of numerical correspondence, we achieve an account of their interest in, as well as attention to, inputs that are numerically relevant. The idea is that infants, like older children and adults, are motivated to apply their structures and will if the environment offers them an opportunity to do so. We also begin to zero in on the characteristics of relevant and irrelevant inputs for such nascent structures. For example, to apply a one–one principle, one simply must have two collections of entities. Otherwise, it does not matter what the entities are, including whether they are in the visual domain or not, that is, whether they project light that the retina can detect, how big they are, how bright they are individually or as a collection against a given background, what visual angle they subtend, and so on. Such characteristics are all irrelevant, *when it comes to matters of number*. We return to consider other findings that support the conclusion that infants can respond in numerically relevant ways in the section that discusses the nature of the preschooler's understanding in this domain.

Learning About Novel Instances in a Category

Despite differences in the way Bruner, Piaget, Vygotsky, and Werner discuss concept formation, they all share one theme: Young children's categories are formed first on the basis of the visible or audible or touchable surface similarities between items, for example, shape, color, size, sound, texture, and so on. Related to this conclusion is the idea that young children do not apply abstract classification structures when organizing their knowledge about objects. These conclusions have had a long staying power, most likely because they are grounded on robust and readily replicated findings (see Gelman & Baillargeon, 1983, for a review of much of the classical data). Once again, however, we challenge the fusing of results with a particular account and turn to scrutinize the belief that learning about categories necessarily starts with a focus on the sensory, that young children lack the conceptual competence to organize inputs according to hierarchies, or that young children cannot form inductions from abstract inputs. Research by S. Gelman and Markman (1986) on induction in children provides one line of pertinent data. Our own work on the role of causal principles in the development of an understanding of the animate and inanimate distinction provides a second and converging line of evidence.

S. Gelman and Markman (1986) taught four-year-olds new information about two objects and then tested to see whether perceptual characteristics as opposed to category membership determined transfer to a novel item. For example, in one study they pointed to a line drawing of a flamingo and a bat and said "this bird eats X and this bat eats Y." Ambiguous test items, for example, a gull that looks more like a bat but is an instance of the category *bird*, were used to determine whether children generalize on the basis of surface similarities or common category membership. Children's responses to test questions such as "What does this eat?" revealed a reliable tendency to generalize on the basis of category membership more than surface similarity.

Information about the category could hardly have served as a basis of generalization if the children were not inclined to interpret their environment in terms of at least some categories. That is, they must have had some conceptual competence for category structures. Evidence is accumulating that young children have considerable knowledge about a variety of category differences, including the animate-inanimate distinction (e.g., Bullock, 1985; Gelman, Spelke, & Meck, 1983; Keil, 1989; Richards & Siegler, 1986). Massey and Gelman's (1988) results serve the present discussion especially well. When the preschool-aged children in their study were asked to answer whether the item depicted in a photograph could move itself up and down a hill, items that shared surface similarity were not treated the same way. For example, unfamiliar statues of mammal-like animals were not treated as were unfamiliar mammals. Instead they were responded to in the same way that the children responded to unfamiliar wheeled objects and rigid, complex inanimate objects. Of particular interest is that unfamiliar nonmammalian animals were treated like the unfamiliar mammals, items they did not look like at all.

Of course, the children had to respond to something about the pictures. Subsequent analyses showed they used their ideas about core differences between animates and inanimates, including how they move, what they are made from, what kinds of part-whole structures they share, whether or not they can communicate, and so on, to guide their inspection and interpretation of the photographs (Gelman, 1990). Statues could not go by themselves because they were too shiny, needed a push, had no feet (even if there were feet represented in the picture), and so on. Animals could go by themselves because they were running, had feet (even when none were shown in the picture), and so on.

Inferences About Insides

Studies that ask young children about the *insides* of objects provide another important line of evidence as to whether the young are limited to using the elementary sense data given by the surface of an object. What should happen when young children try to answer when asked what is on the inside of both animate and inanimate objects? In neither case is there any reason to think they can see the insides and therefore they should not be able to offer sensible answers if they are restricted to using direct sensory data. Studies by Gelman and Meck (in Gelman, 1990) present the relevant findings.

In the Gelman and Meck studies, children between the ages of three and five years were asked to think about a series of animate (person, cat, elephant, mouse, bird) and inanimate (doll, puppet, ball, rock) items. No photographs or replicas were presented; children were simply told to think about these as they were asked in turn what was on the outside and inside of each one.

When asked the *outside* question about people, children had a strong tendency to talk about parts on the face and/or head (1.5 such answers per child). Figure 2.1 shows that questions about the *outsides* of dolls were more likely to elicit the same bias to talk about the face and parts on the face than were the outside questions for the other animate items. This result sets the stage for us to evaluate the proposal that

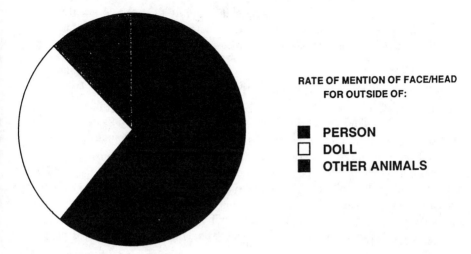

RATE OF MENTION OF FACE/HEAD
FOR OUTSIDE OF:

■ PERSON
☐ DOLL
■ OTHER ANIMALS

Figure 2.1. Tendency of children to say that inanimates (doll, all other relevant items) look like a person on the outside

the young children generalize on the basis of whether objects look alike on their surfaces. For example, did the children tell us that a doll and a puppet each have the same thing(s) on their respective insides as do people? Or did they, instead, treat questions about the insides of dolls and puppets more like ones about the insides of other inanimate objects, even if these did not look alike on the surface?

None of the children in any of the age groups volunteered that puppets and dolls have the same insides as do people. In contrast, despite the notable surface differences between an elephant, a bird, and a person, these same children told us that all had (at least) blood, bones, and food inside. The older the child, the more they told us of other organs on the insides of these target animate items, especially when they were answering about humans.

The blood, bones, and organs pattern of answers to the inside questions for animates was notably different from the one obtained for the inside questions about puppets and dolls. Now "insides" talk was about material (e.g., paper, cotton, fabric, stuff) "nothing" or known physical mechanisms (e.g., batteries, strings, etc.). Further, whereas the inside answers across animate types were relatively homogeneous, answers across inanimate types were decidedly heterogeneous. Children who knew something about the object in question knew to answer about the specific material or mechanism that might be inside that object. When they did not, they often answered in ways that suggested they thought the same features characterized the insides and outsides, for example, when they said steel (patterns) was on both the outside and inside of a ball or that cotton was on both the inside and outside of a doll.

These findings are reinforced by additional studies appearing in the literature (S. Gelman & Wellman, 1991; Markman, 1989). More and more it begins to look like we may have underestimated the young child's ability to reason abstractly and to form inductions from nonsensory, nonconcrete data. We return to this conclusion in the final section on our work on fractions.

Implicit Knowledge About Number Goes to School

In our discussion of how to characterize inputs within a constructivist account of learning, we introduced evidence of infants attending to number-relevant inputs. Other studies add weight to these findings. Strauss and Curtis (1984) have shown that infants respond to numerical orderings and Sophian and Adams (1987) have demonstrated that infants keep track of the numerical effects resulting from addition and subtraction. Such findings support our idea that early skeletons of domain-specific principles are available to support interest in and learning about number. So does the fact that young children enter school with a principled understanding of counting and its relationship to adding and subtracting (within a limited range of integers).

By about four or five years of age, children are able to count in principled ways, invent solutions to novel counting problems, detect errors in counting trails generated by others, and make up counting algorithms to solve simple addition and subtraction problems, at least for a limited range of numbers. (For reviews see Fuson, 1988; Resnick, 1988; Gelman & Greeno, 1989). It is not just preschool children who are able to take advantage of their environment to develop their skeletal knowledge of numbers. All over the world, both young children and nonschooled adults use counting algorithms to solve arithmetic problems. These are often made up and resemble those that schooled children invent.

Whether schooled or unschooled, individuals have strong tendencies to decompose natural numbers into manageable or known components, to count when adding or subtracting, and to use repeated addition (or subtraction) to solve "multiplication" (or "division") problems. These multiplication and division solutions are used both before and after children have been taught more standard multiplication and division algorithms in school. They are also used by unschooled adults and children in a variety of settings and cultures (e.g., Carraher, Carraher, & Schliemann, 1985; Ginsburg, 1977; Groen & Resnick, 1977; Lave, 1988; Resnick, 1986; Saxe, 1988; Saxe, Guberman, & Gearhart, 1987; Starkey & Gelman, 1982).

Some of the algorithms invented by older children and unschooled adults are more complex than those used by preschool children. Still, as Resnick (1986) notes in her analysis of these, all use principles of counting and addition (or subtraction) with the positive integers. An example from her own work illustrates this. Pitt (7 yrs–7 mos) said that he solved "two times three" as follows: ". . *two threes* . . . *one three is three, one more equals six.*" Similarly, schooled and unschooled individuals in Africa and Latin America use a combination of number decomposition moves and repeated additions (or subtractions) to solve the multiplication problems presented by investigators. Young children are also less able to work with large numbers; otherwise, it is hard to distinguish their invented, out-of-school solutions from those generated by older children and adults (Carraher et al., 1985; Saxe, 1988). Lave, Murtaugh, and de la Rocha's (1984) work with shoppers in a California supermarket provides an especially compelling documentation of how everyday "intuitive" solutions for determining unit prices are preferred over any taught in school.

This widespread invention of algorithms that are based on counting and/or repeated addition (subtraction) algorithms provides further support for our conclusion that a universal set of implicit principles governs the acquisition of initial mathematical concepts (Gelman, 1982; Gelman & Meck, 1986). A skeletal set of counting principles, in conjunction with some principles of addition and subtraction, promotes the uptake of mathematical data that are relevant to these principles. The skeletal principles provide the a priori structure necessary for learners to notice, assimilate, and store relevant data in an organized manner (Gelman, 1990; Gelman & Greeno, 1989).

The obvious question is whether this kind of knowledge provides a ready base upon which to achieve the goals of mathematics teachers—to teach mathematics. On the assumption that learners will be inclined to apply their initial theory about numbers to the novel inputs offered in schools, it is not clear that the knowledge they bring to the setting will support the correct interpretation of some kinds of data presented in math classes. To illustrate why, we consider some of our work on how kindergarten, first-grade, and second-grade children interpret commonly used teaching materials, so common in fact that it might be hard to believe they are misinterpreted. We will see that although preinstructional assumptions about the nature of numbers may serve many in their everyday interactions, they may nevertheless interfere with the learning of mathematics taught in school, even the seemingly simple concept of a fraction.

Learning About Fractions Might Be Hard, Despite Repeated Exposure to "Relevant" Inputs

From early on, children are repeatedly exposed to inputs that are assumed to be relevant for learning that fractions are kinds of numbers. These include the number line, fractional parts and wholes of circles, squares, rectangles, and triangles, as well as the numeric and written forms of ½, ¼, and ⅓. If decimal notation is introduced it is in the context of lessons about money. Visitors to American classrooms for Kindergarten, Grade 1, and Grade 2 children will see the number line as well as parts and wholes of shapes on the classroom's walls and blackboards more often than they will find symbolic forms of fractions in textbooks and notebooks. The former are frequently described by educators as concrete, the latter as abstract (cf. previous discussion on this distinction).

Although written fractions involve abstract symbols (be these numerals or words), the number line and part–whole shape items are *not* concrete in the usual sense. They too are representations of number in this context. On their own, they afford many other interpretations, for example, a line, a pie, a circle, round, and so on. If they are truly concrete materials, there is no reason to assume that the child will get the intended interpretations, let alone think of these in terms of fractional numbers. For this reason, it is important to ask how young children actually interpret such common classroom props. What mathematical concepts do they think these stand for?

Although there are principles that both guide and structure early learning about counting, this could be a mixed blessing. Whatever the mathematical prowess of the young child, further learning often requires that one transcend the principles that guided early learning. Much of mathematics involves operations and entities other than counting and the addition and subtraction of the counting numbers (or the positive integers). When it comes time to go beyond the early knowledge that is built upon the counting principles, continued adherence to these principles could yield misinterpretations of inputs designed to foster new learning. Given a constructivist mind, this seems likely if the data are not relevant (from the expert's viewpoint) to the count numbers. To illustrate why, we need not go too deeply into mathematics. The idea that a fraction is a noncounting number, but nevertheless a number, will serve our purposes—especially since it seems to be a watershed in elementary school mathematics learning (e.g., Carpenter, Corbitt, Kepner, Lindquist, & Reys, 1980).

One can characterize the way numbers are first thought about as follows: *Numbers are what you get when you count things and combine or take apart counts and/or their cardinal representations.* If this is a true characterization, what should happen when a child with this theory (be it implicit or explicit) attempts to assimilate common classroom inputs for learning about fractions? One cannot count things to get the answer to "Which is more ½ or ¼; 1.5 or 1.0?" Similarly, number lines are not simple representations of whole numbers. Young children might know that one can take apart a circle and a rectangle and get two "halves" on both occasions and still not appreciate why each of these halves can be represented with the written expression ½. The interpretation of the latter might be assimilated to the idea that such marks on paper must be about whole numbers.

In the absence of implicit principles for dealing with fractions, young learners might "overgeneralize" their counting principles and produce a distorted assimilation of the instructional materials on fractions. For their theory cannot handle such data veridically; it lacks principles that can recognize the input for what it is. This is because fractions are numbers generated by the division of two numerosities; *they are not count-numbers.* Since there is no reason to presume that the requisite principles for dealing with such entities are available when they are introduced, there is every reason to expect young children to err in their interpretation of data designed to teach them about fractions.

Studies have found children in the middle- and high-school grades make systematic errors with rational numbers (e.g., Behr, Washsmuth, Post, & Lesh, 1984; Hiebert & Wearne, 1986; Kerslake, 1986; Nesher & Peled, 1986). We know of none that have targeted children in their first few years of school, presumably because early math instruction does not focus on this topic. We thought it was especially important to focus on young children. If still younger children do bring with them the idea that numbers are what one gets when one counts things, they might start building, at an early age, erroneous representations of data meant to exemplify alternative notions of what numbers are about. These representations could, in turn, stand in the way of children's correct interpretation of later lesson plans on fractions, no matter how frequently they are presented.

As indicated, children in the United States in Kindergarten, Grade 1, and Grade 2 encounter fraction-relevant material and receive some instruction about fractions. Since we interviewed a sample from each grade at the end of their school year, even the kindergarten children had experienced at least the number line and the various symbolic forms (spoken terms, written words, and written numeric expressions) for $\frac{1}{2}$, $\frac{1}{4}$, and $\frac{1}{3}$. Some also were introduced to appropriately labeled and marked measuring cups in cooking class. The children in the first and second grades had more experiences like these, both in terms of classroom presentations and testing opportunities. Therefore, although their curricula did not delve into the conceptual and arithmetic characteristics of fractions as numbers, the children were offered some relevant data about the nature of fractions. How do these children interpret such offerings?

Fractions in the early grades

Some details about the study. The kindergarten ($N = 16$, mean age 5 years–9 mos), first grade ($N = 12$, mean age 6 yrs–9 mos), and a second grade ($N = 12$, mean age 7 yrs–9 mos) children who participated in the study attended one of three schools in the Greater Philadelphia area, all of which drew from middle-class samples. We had signed permission from the parents to interview the children in a quiet room away from their classrooms. The interviews were conducted on three different days. The first and second days of the interview were separated by at least two days (but not more than a week). In almost all cases the third day of the interview could occur anywhere between one and two months after the second.

The study involved a pretest, a five-phase placement interview, and a follow-up battery of arithmetic items. The sequence of the placement phases was designed to provide more and more task-relevant information without giving specific answers. Brown and Reeve (1987) recommend the use of such progressively more explicitly "hinting" in order to bring out whatever competence a child might have. Our own work confirms their view that such hints serve to limit misunderstanding about the task and therefore false negative attributions by an investigator (see also Gelman, 1978; Gelman & Meck, 1986). The items for the first two phases of our placement sequence were presented without hints so as to allow us to obtain some baseline data. Each successive phase after these introduced more and more relevant mathematical information and offered more detailed mathematical descriptions about the props in the task. This meant that we provided successively more hints about the nature of the task as we moved to the use of more and more explicit mathematical language.

The pretest questions and interactions familiarized children with "our special number line." When children came into the room, they saw "The Count," a puppet from the American televised program *Sesame Street*, sitting in the middle of the table alongside the folded-up number line. They were told that The Count had come to visit them at school because he wanted to learn new things about numbers.

To start the pretest, a child was shown, one at a time, displays of 1½, ½, 1¼, ¼, and ⅓ circles and asked "how much" (or "how many" since children offered this alternative) were present. If a child could not name 1½ or 1¼, the experimenter pointed to the whole circle and said, "This is one circle." Then, while pointing to a part of a circle (½ or ¼), she asked "What's this?" The part was correctly identified for children who could not answer on their own. After this introduction to relevant terms, the experimenter unfolded her "special number line" schematized in Figure 2.2A. The line was intentionally long (4′4″) so as to give the impression that it went on and on in both directions. Instead of using numerals to represent the cardinal values for successive integers, we used a line that had sets of *N* circles (4.75″ in diameter) where the integers should have been. At first a child saw

Figure 2.2. Schematic representations of the "Special Number Line" as seen by a child at the start of pretesting (A) and during placement trials (B)

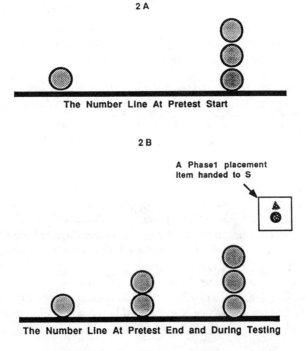

2 A

The Number Line At Pretest Start

2 B

A Phase1 placement
Item handed to S

The Number Line At Pretest End and During Testing

representations of 1 and 3; it was his task to take a set of two circles and place it where it should go, to answer what number would come after one and before three.

The pretest continued with talk about the ordering relations between the whole numbers, for example, "Is 4 more than 3, less than 3, or the same as 3; is 2 more than 1, less than 1 or the same as 1?" If necessary, feedback was provided since we wanted to encourage children to think of ordering numerical values. Then, to end the pretest, children were told, "The number line shows the numbers in order." To show us that they knew "how our number line works," they were then asked to place sets of N (1, 2, 3, or 4) small circles (ones much smaller than those on the line) "where they belong."

The pretest phase was followed on the same day by some of the phases of a five-phase fraction placement sequence and related test items. A sample fraction placement trial is shown in Figure 2.2A. On such trials a child's task was to put each test display below the point on the line "where it belonged" and then explain why it went there. No hints were provided for any of the test items used during either of the first two placement phases. In Phase 1, test displays contained 1½, 1⅓, and 1¼ circles. The second phase test displays contained ½, ⅓, and ¼ of a circle. Once Phase 2 was done, children were asked how the test items for that phase were the same or different. Although no hints were provided for the test items used during the first two phases, if children erred on either 1½ in Phase 1 or ½ in Phase 2, these items were repeated at the end of their respective testing periods, and the children were asked whether the numerical value represented was equal to, more than, or less than a whole number value.

The experimenter started Phase 3 by placing ½ circle between the positions for 0 and 1, and saying "we can put one half between zero and one because it is more than zero and less than one." A similar trial followed with a display with 1½ circles. Finally, the child was told, "We can count ½, 1, 1½, 2." Then the child was asked to place the test items (2½, 1¼, ⅓) and explain their placement. The experimenter did *not* verbalize the corresponding numerical values for these test items. The experimenter resumed talking about number at the end of the Phase 3 part of the placement interview. No props were used for this. A child was simply asked whether there were numbers between 1 and 2 (or 0 and 1), and if so how many there were. If a child said that there were no numbers between the named integers, the experimenter went on to task if 1½ (or ½) was such a number. The opportunity to count by rote and solve *verbally* presented arithmetic problems ended the interview for the first day.

Phase 4, which occurred at least two days, and as much as a week, after the previous placement phase, started with a brief reminder about the "special number line." For all subsequent test and demonstration items, the experimenter now used the terms that corresponded to the numerical values instantiated by the displays when she presented these. Children were questioned extensively about the ordering relations of the values represented by the described test items as well as the ordered positions the corresponding stimuli should assume on the number line. Phase 5 was much like Phase 4 and came right after it. These two phases differed mainly in terms of the display values presented.

The end of Phase 5 included some items designed to assess the extent to which our subjects interpreted the task as one that had something to do with counting things. A separate follow-up phase, a month to two later, yielded data on how the children read noninteger numerals when each was presented separately on a card. Finally, the design included some arithmetic items so that we could assess whether there is a relationship between our assessments of arithmetic skill and level of success on the fraction placement task. For example, we asked children to solve simple arithmetic problems with values of 0 and ½. (For more details, see Table 1 of Gelman, Cohen, & Hartnett, 1989.)

Some results

Kinds of baseline responses. Responses to the fraction placement target items were coded for each phase of the testing. Inspection of individual patterns of responding across Phases 1 and 2 (i.e., before hints were offered) revealed four patterns of baseline responding:

1. *Correct (at least 50%).* Children who used this baseline pattern of responding placed their items so as to integrate a metrically ordered positioning of the fractional parts and whole circles without feedback and did so on at least 3 of their total (6) Phase 1 and 2 test trials.
2. *Parts Alone Rank Ordered.* Some children neglected any whole circles in a display and responded as if they simply rank ordered the relative sizes of the parts. For example, one child placed 1¼ at "1," 1⅓ at "2," and 1½ between "2" and "3." Such responses map relative amount of area to relative length without regard to the size of the interval between successive points on the number line.
3. *Whole Number Placements.* Children assigned to this baseline category used counting strategies, either to count the number of separable parts and place accordingly, for example, 1½ circles at "2" and all of ½, ⅓, and ¼ circles at "1," or to ignore the fractions of a circle and simply count the remaining whole circles to place the former stimuli at either "1" or "0."
4. *Others.* All remaining response patterns were coded in this category. For Phases 1 and 2 these included those where children placed successive test displays from left to right, put each test item at a different position without any concern for order, or generated sequences that we could not decode. Once the experimenter began to show children where to put displays containing one half of a circle (during Phase 3), some started to mimic her. Mimics simply placed nearly all displays that had *any* parts on them halfway between two whole number positions. That is, they even placed displays containing ⅓ and ¼ at half-way points between successive instantiations of whole numbers.

The effect of hinting. Only 25% of the children responded according to baseline placement pattern (a), that is, correctly on at least 50% of their Phase 1 and Phase 2 test trials. A full 44.5% used counting strategies. A small number of the remaining children chose to ignore the whole circles when they encountered a combination of a part and one or more wholes. For such stimuli they simply rank ordered their relative size along three different points on the number line. Finally, there were a group of children who interpreted the task in nonnumerical ways, for example, they placed each successive test item further and further along the line.

Given these qualitatively different ways the children first interpreted the number line task, it is possible that the different baseline groups would likewise interpret the hints that followed in very different ways. Figure 2.3 shows that, depending on which baseline pattern a child started out with, the hints had opposite effects. If children started out being correct on at least 50% of their baseline test trials, they benefited from the hints. In contrast, if children started out as counters or in any of the other groups, they did not. Instead, they actually tended to get worse over trials. One reason for the deterioration in their performance has to do with their tendency to mimic the experimenter's demonstrations with halves. Given a hint that they

Figure 2.3. Differential effect of hinting as a function of children's baseline placement abilities as assessed during Phases 1 and 2

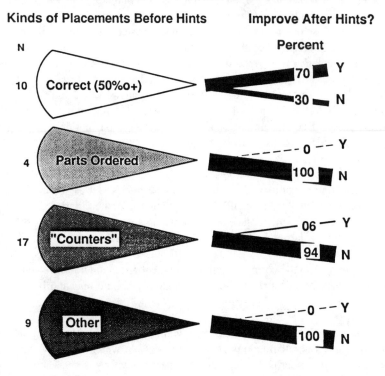

went between whole number places, mimickers placed all items with fractions of a circle on them at the *same* place trial after trial, that is, a halfway point, or some other constant point between two whole numbers.

The data shown in Figure 2.3 summarize the two main findings reported thus far. First, young children do have a strong bias to interpret the positions on a number line as if they represent whole numbers, a decidedly wrong conception. Second, didactic hints from experts had a differential effect depending on how well children did according to the baseline assessment. Those who tended to share out interpretation of the representations involved benefited from talk about fractions, ordering relations, and the like. Those who did not start out this way did not benefit. If anything, our inputs served to depress their performance levels, possibly because our talk offered children a clue that they were to do something else but no assimilable clues as to what to do. In other words, their conceptions stood in the way of their interpreting the inputs we hoped would help them.

The latter finding shows that most children in our study ran their initial theory of number roughshod over the inputs that are commonly used to introduce conceptions of fractions. This suggestion is supported by further results of the study. For example, we asked children to read aloud what ½ and ¼ said when each was printed on a card. Although the vast majority of the children could "point to the half" (our request), only those children who met the correct baseline placement criteria came within any range of accuracy when asked to read the numeral representations of the fractions. These children said things like "a half, one fourth" or "one and a half" (which is wrong), "one fourth," and so on in response to our request that they read the fractions. Children in the other three baseline groups had a terrible time reading these in mathematically correct ways; they offered a variety of novel answers, including "1 and 2"; "1 and 4" or "1 line 2," "1 line 4"; or "1, 2" and "1, 4" or "1 plus 2" and "1 plus 4." Some even offered the answers of 3 and 5, the sum of the two numerals, or 12 and 14, a totally unexpected interpretation of the two numerals in the fraction. In fact, only 5% of all of the children in the three noncorrect baseline groups read the fractions correctly.

Reading, comparing, and adding. Similarly tendencies to assimilate the input to the idea that representational materials are to be interpreted as if they are about whole numbers comes from results for the "which is more" items. Those in the three "incorrect" baseline placement groups had a reliable bias to select the reciprocals with the larger denominators as more for both the ¼ vs. ½ and ⅟₅₆ vs. ⅟₇₆ pairs of numerals ($x^2_1 = 11.27$, $p < .001$ and 8.06, $p < .01$, respectively). Although children in the correct baseline placement group did not have such a bias, they did not get the items right either. They simply had no bias and performed at chance levels.

Summing up. In sum, our guess that young children would interpret inputs designed to teach about fractions as yet more data to which to apply their initial theory of what a number is, the idea that numbers are what you get when you count entities, was supported. Simply making these materials available on a repeatable basis does not suffice to lead children to treat them as items that can be interpreted in a new way. In fact, reports by other investigators lead to the conclusion that additional schooling may serve mainly to provide yet more grist for this first theory of number and thereby increase the number of misunderstandings or misconceptions children end up with in their mathematics classes.

These findings merge with ones from related research with older children in the higher elementary grades. Here too students have a tendency to inappropriately generalize what they learn about the integers to other numbers. For example, they seem to believe that they can assume that the product that results when one multiplies two numbers is always larger than either of the original numbers—even when the numbers are fractions (e.g., Greer, 1987; Hart, 1981). Although this principle is valid for the *addition* of positive rationals, it is not for their multiplication. In fact, many secondary school students lack a mathematical understanding of division and multiplication (e.g., Fischbein, Deri, Nello, & Marino, 1985; Vergnaud, 1983), leading one to wonder how they could possibly understand that fractions are noninteger numbers. Findings like these make it clear that it is not only the young child's spontaneous theory of number that is exceedingly robust. It seems that a very large number of children continue to interpret inputs about fractions as if these were examples of integer numbers.

A Suggestion: To Learn Mathematics Is to Learn the Language and Structure of Mathematics

Despite the foregoing, we should not loose track of an equally important set of results from the studies already cited. Some children do rather well, that is, some children move on to more advanced mathematical interpretations given the opportunity to do so. How? Are there any clues to turn to either from research or our discussion of a constructivist theory of learning? We think there may be.

Recall that children's ability to correctly interpret one representational format of number, for example, our number line, went hand in hand with their ability to work correctly with the symbolic representations of the entities, operations, and principles of arithmetic. A similar result obtains in a subsequent questionnaire study we did with children in Grades 2 through 8 (Gelman, Cohen, & Hartnett, 1989). Many in this group responded incorrectly, much as did the young children who erred in our first study. However, some children in this second study were well on their way to a principled understanding of fractions as numbers. The data in Table 2.1 serve to illustrate.

Table 2.1 presents data from two grade levels as well as two ability levels. Children in the gifted classes in the school system visited are assigned to this track early on (sometimes Grade 2) on the basis of overall test scores. Therefore they may or may not have unusual mathematical talents. It is noteworthy that many of the answers offered by children in both the regular fourth- and seventh-grade classes can be characterized as tautological. In contrast, the gifted fourth-grade pupils

Table 2.1. Samples of Written Answers to "Why Are There Two Numbers in a Fraction?"

Grade and Subject Number

Regular 4th and 5th Grade

1. "Because if there weren't 2 numbers then you couldn't have a fraction."
2. "It is two numbers"
3. "Can't explain"
4. "To be equivalent."
5. "Because a fraction is a part of something. Not the hole thing."
6. "Because you have to hav a denomonator and a numarator"
7. "1 for one certain color on the thing 4 for all the things in the group"

Gifted 4th and 5th Grade

6. "4 is how many piecies and 1 is how many you got"
8. "the bottom one is how many in the whole and the top one is how many are left a in the whole."
9. "The denmunator is the hole, the numirator is how many peices you have of the hole"
10. ". . . one of the numbers stand for how many thimes something is divided up into and the other how many are taken."

Regular 7th Grade

11. "Because they wanted it that way."
12. "1/4 1 explains how many you have. 4 explains how many there are"
13. "1 shows you how many you have an the other shows you how many are there"
14. "Because 1 number is how many of something you have and how many there are in a whole."
16. "Because It Broke in to fractions I GUESS"
17. "Because"
18. "because it is a portion of a number"
20. "you need a numberator & denominator"
21. "the top one explain how many of the Bottom one there are"
24. "It is less than one whole"
25. "to show both halfs"
26. "Because it shows how many items you have out of a given amount of numbers."

provided rather acceptable answers to our novel question. These same children also outperformed their grade-level peers and the regular seventh-grade children on other items as well. Whatever the locus of the gifted effect, it is clear that these children are able to read and write about mathematical entities in at least a quasi-principled, if not principled way—even though we know they were not taught the answer to this particular question.

The latter finding fits with one previously presented on the relationship between level of mathematical understanding and language use—that they are positively correlated. Could it be that the dictum that "one only understands something well (i.e., explicitly) if one can talk or write about it clearly" is based on a pedagogical principle after all? Might it be that the engine that drives development in those children who do move on to learn more mathematics is decorated with material from the relevant language—that the way to characterize the learning that does take place in some children is to think of it as something akin to second language learning? If so, it occurs to us that we could be erring in putting off the teaching of such matters when it comes to the teaching of mathematics and science. One cannot be a fluent user of any language without an opportunity to master both the vocabulary and syntax of the domain in question. And it is at least common wisdom that immersion opportunities are better able to support inductions than are those that introduce a language bit by bit over many years.

True, to move in this direction would mean to go against the tide, the strong commitment to the view that we should start with the concrete. But, since there is nothing concrete about the language and principles of mathematics, it is not clear what it means to do this. Blocks or rods on their own are not mathematical objects, any more than they are props for a physics experiment. To become mathematical, they have to be interpreted, and not necessarily in the same way as they have to be interpreted, and not necessarily in the same way as they have to be interpreted in a physics experiment. They might be a representation of a given number in a mathematical setting and devices for balancing in a physics context. In other words, given the settings involved, physical items do not on their own afford their interpretations. Labels, concepts, symbols, and the like serve this purpose. And to the extent that these labels are understood, the object themselves become representations or entities within the domain in question. Sticks are number lines because they represent number; blocks are entities in a balance experiment because of their physical characteristics. In short, objects "out there" have to be interpreted by the mind if they are to stand for mathematical terms or concepts. Withholding such descriptions might amount to withholding data that are relevant. Similarly withholding information about mathematical operations and the relations between them might amount to withholding the data needed to develop new skeletal structures to which to assimilate new data.

The emerging data line in preschoolers shows that they can reach inductions from abstract inputs. Still, the hard work remains, this being to characterize the form of inputs that might succeed given the constructivist inclinations of the child, one who we already knows has a sufficiently robust theory of number that she might resist any talk about different ways of thinking about numbers, be it couched in the language of mathematics or not. But one thing seems clear A failure to try to structure input shortchanges children. For they do not even get the database necessary for the correct induction. Perhaps we owe it to the children to try to offer data designed to provide structured inputs and the related structures to which to assimilate these. The idea is not that we fill blackboards full of symbols, but rather that we insist on talking about the kind of things we teach in ways that bring out the relevant mathematical structures and how these relate to the kinds of mathematical entities pupils encounter. Lampert's (1986) work on the teaching of multiplication offers us one kind of existence proof that this can be done and can be effective. Math class dialogues between the Japanese teacher and his first-grade pupils offer an example of another kind (Stigler, 1988).

Even if we adopt the preliminary ideas in this section and proceed to develop suitable materials, we are well advised to proceed with caution. For no matter how consistent the recommendations may be with the kind of constructivist learning principles I have been trying to develop, there is one bold fact to remember. In the end, the children will determine whether we are right. They may treat our new ideas about relevant inputs as they have treated ones that come before—not consistent with either how they interpret the data or how they actually induce new principles. Or they may approximate a shared interpretation of some inputs and reject others. In other words, they must always remain our final source of validation and input as to how to tinker with, alter, or even change their curriculum.

For those who think that this caution is far from an optimistic way to end this chapter, we have but one rejoinder. In our efforts to develop physics materials for a museum for young children, we failed at first. After watching the children, we changed the exhibit and made some progress, but not the kind we wanted. A third trip to the drawing boards followed. This time we succeeded, that is, we ended up with an exhibit in which children talked about physics-relevant things to do. It is noteworthy that here too we had to introduce relevant talk—in this case, talk that pertains to scientific experimenting (Gelman, Massey, & McManus, 1989).

References

Behr, M. J., Washsmuth, I., Post, T. R., & Lesh, R. (1984). Order and equivalence: A clinical teaching experiment. *Journal for Research in Mathematics Education, 15*(5), 323–341.

Brown, A., & Reeve, R. A. (1987). Bandwidths of competence. The role of supportive contexts in learning and development. In L. S. Liben & D. H. Feldman (Eds.), *Development and learning: Conflict or congruence*. Hillsdale, NJ: Lawrence Erlbaum Associates, Inc.

Bullock, M. (1985). Animism in childhood thinking: A new look at an old question. *Developmental Psychology, 21*, 217–225.

Carey, S. (1986). Acquisition of scientific knowledge: The problem of reorganization. *American Psychologist, 41*(10), 1123–1130.

Carpenter, T. P., Corbitt, M. K., Kepner, H. S., Jr., Lindquist, M., & Reys, R. E. (1980). National assessment: Prospective of student's mastery of basic skills. In M. Lindquist (Ed.), *Selected issues in mathematics education*. Berkeley, CA: McCutchen.

Carraher, T. N., Carraher, D. W., & Schlieman, A. D. (1985). Mathematics in the street and in school. *British Journal of Developmental Psychology, 3*, 21–29.

Feldman, H., & Gelman, R. (1987). Otitis media and cognitive development. In J. F. Kavanagh (Ed.), *Otitis media and child development* (pp. 27–41). Parkton, MD: York Press.

Fischbein, E., Deri, M., Nello, M., & Marino, M. (1985). The role of implicit models in solving problems in multiplication and division. *Journal of Research in Mathematics Education, 16*, 3–17.

Fuson, K. C. (1988). *Children's counting and concepts of number*. New York: Springer-Verlag.

Gelman, R. (1978). Cognitive development. *Annual Review of Psychology, 29*, 297–332.

Gelman, R. (1982). Basic numerical abilities. In R. J. Sternberg (Ed.), *Advances in the psychology of human intelligence* (Vol. 1, pp. 181–205). Hillsdale, NJ: Lawrence Erlbaum Associates, Inc.

Gelman, R. (1990). First principles organize attention to relevant data and the acquisition of numerical and causal concepts. *Cognitive Science, 14*, 96–106.

Gelman, R., & Baillargeon, R. (1983). A review of some Piagetian concepts. In J. H. Flavell & E. M. Markman (Eds.), *Cognitive development* (pp. 169–230). New York: Wiley.

Gelman, R., & Brown, A. L. (1986). Changing views of cognitive competence in the young. In N. Smelser & D. Gerstein (Eds.), *Discoveries and trends in behavioral and social science* (pp. 175–207). Commission on Behavioral and Social Sciences and Education. Washington, DC: NRC Press.

Gelman, R., & Cohen, M. (1988). Qualitative differences in the way Down's Syndrome and normal children solve a novel counting problem. In L. Nadel (Ed.), *The psychobiology of Down's Syndrome* (pp. 2–99). Cambridge, MA: MIT Press/Bradford Books.

Gelman, R., Cohen, M., & Hartnett, P. (1989). To know mathematics is to go beyond the belief that "Fractions are not numbers." (Report No. CSRP-90.5). Los Angeles, CA: UCLA Cognitive Science.

Gelman, R., & Greeno, J. (1989). On the nature of competence: Principles for understanding in a domain. In L. B. Resnick (Ed.), *Knowing and learning: Essays in honor of Robert Glaser* (pp. 125–186). Hillsdale, NJ: Lawrence Erlbaum Associates, Inc.

Gelman, R., Massey, C., & McManus, M. (1989). Characteristics supporting environments for cognitive development: Learning from children in a museum. In J. M. Levine & L. B. Resnick (Eds.), *Socially shared cognition.* Washington, DC: American Psychological Association.

Gelman, R., & Meck, E. (1986). The notion of principle: The case of counting. In J. Hiebert (Ed.), *The relationship between procedural and conceptual competence* (pp. 29–57). Hillsdale, NJ: Lawrence Erlbaum Associates, Inc.

Gelman, R., Spelke, E., & Meck, E. (1983). What preschoolers know about animate and inanimate objects. In D. Rogers & J. A. Sloboda (Eds.), *The acquisition of symbolic skills* (pp. 297–326). London: Plenum.

Gelman, S., & Markman, E. (1986). Categories and induction in young children. *Cognition, 23,* 183–209.

Gelman, S., & Wellman, H. M. (1991). Insides and essences: Early understandings of the nonobvious. *Cognition, 38,* 213–244.

Ginsburg, H. P. (1977). *Children's arithmetic.* New York: Van Nostrand.

Glaser, R. (1987). Teaching expert novices. *Educational Researcher, 16,* 5.

Greer, B. (1987). Nonconservation of multiplication and division involving decimals. *Journal for Research in Mathematics Education, 18,* 37–45.

Groen, G., & Resnick, L. B. (1977). Can preschool children invent addition algorithms? *Journal of Educational Psychology, 69,* 645–652.

Hart, K. (1981). *Children's understanding of mathematics.* London: John Murrary.

Hiebert, J., & Wearne, D. (1986). Procedures over concepts: The acquisition of decimal number knowledge. In J. Hiebert (Ed.), *Conceptual and procedural knowledge: The case of mathematics.* Hillsdale, NJ: Lawrence Erlbaum Associates, Inc.

Johnson, J. S., & Newport, E. L. (1989). Critical period effects in second language learning: The influence of maturational state on the acquisition of English as a second language. *Cognitive Psychology, 21,* 60–90.

Keil, F. (1989). *Concepts, word meanings and cognitive development.* Cambridge: MIT Press.

Kellman, P., & Spelke, E. (1983). Perception of partly occluded objects in infancy. *Child Development, 57,* 72–86.

Kerslake, D. (1986). *Fractions: Children's strategies and errors. A report of the strategies and errors in the secondary mathematics project.* Windson, England: Nfer-Nelson.

Kesterbaum, R., Termine, N., & Spelke, E. S. (1987). Perception of objects and object boundaries by three-month-old infants. *British Journal of Developmental Psychology, 5,* 367–383.

Klima, E. S., & Bellugi, U. (1979). *The signs of language.* Cambridge, MA: Harvard University Press.

Lampert, M. (1986). Knowing, doing and teaching multiplication. *Cognition and Instruction, 3,* 305–342.

Landau, B., & Gleitman, L. (1985). *Language and experience: Evidence from the blind child.* Cambridge, MA: Harvard University Press.

Lave, J. (1988). *Cognition in practice: Mind, mathematics and culture in everyday life.* New York: Cambridge University Press.

Lave, J., Murtaugh, M., & de la Rocha, O. (1984). Dialectice of arithmetic in grocery shopping. In B. Rogoff & J. Lave (Eds.), *Everyday cognition: Its development in social context* (pp. 67–94). Cambridge, MA: Harvard University Press.

Markman, E. M. (1989). *Categorization and naming in children.* Cambridge, MA: MIT/Bradford Press.

Massey, C., & Gelman, R. (1988). Preschoolers decide whether pictured unfamiliar objects can move themselves. *Developmental Psychology, 24,* 307–317.

Moore, D., Benenson, J., Reznick, S., Peerson, M., & Kagan, J. (1987). Effect of auditory numerical information on infants' looking behavior: Contradictory evidence. *Developmental Psychology, 23,* 665–670.

Nesher, P., & Peled, I. (1986). Shift in reasoning. *Educational Studies in Mathematics, 17,* 67–79.

Resnick, L. B. (1986). The development of mathematical intuition. In M. Perlmutter (Ed.), *Perspectives on intellectual development: The Minnesota Symposia on Child Psychology* (Vol. 19, pp. 159–194). Hillsdale, NJ: Lawrence Erlbaum Associates, Inc.

Resnick, L. B. (1988). Learning in school and out. *Educational Researcher, 16,* 13–20.

Richards, D. D., & Siegler, R. S. (1986). Children's understandings of the attributes of life. *Journal of Experimental Child Psychology, 42,* 1–22.

Saxe, G. B. (1988). Candy selling and math learning. *Educational Research, 17,* 14–21.

Saxe, G. B., Guberman, S. R., & Gearhart, M. (1987). Social processes in early development. *Monographs of the Society for the Research in Child Development, 52* (Serial No. 216).

Shipley, E., & Shepperson, B. (1990). Countable entities: Developmental challenges. *Cognition, 34,* 109–136.

Sophian, C., & Adams, N. (1987). Infants' understanding of numerical transformations. *British Journal of Developmental Psychology, 5,* 257–264.

Spelke, E. (1988). Where perceiving ends and thinking begins: The apprehension of objects in infancy. In A. Yonas (Ed.), *Perceptual development in infancy. Minnesota Symposium on child Psychology* (Vol. 20). Hillsdale, NJ: Lawrence Erlbaum Associates, Inc.

Spelke, E. (1990). Principles of object perception. *Cognitive Psychology, 14,* 29–56.

Starkey, P., & Gelman, R. (1982). The development of addition and subtraction abilities prior to formal schooling in arithmetic. In T. P. Carpenter, J. M. Moser, & T. A. Romberg (Eds.), *Cognitive development: Vol 3. Handbook of child development* (pp. 99–116). New York: Wiley.

Starkey, P., Gelman, R., & Spelke, E. S. (1985). Response to Davis, Albert, & Baron's detection of number or numerousness by human infants. *Science, 228,* 1222–1223.

Starkey, P., Spelke, E. S., & Gelman, R. (1983). Detection of intermodal correspondence by human infants. *Science, 222,* 179–181.

Starkey, P., Spelke, E. S., & Gelman, R. (1990). Numerical abstraction by human infants. *Cognition, 34,* 97–127.

Stigler, J. W. (1988). The use of verbal explanation in Japanese and American classrooms. *The Arithmetic Journal, 36*(2), 27–29.

Strauss, M. S., & Curtis, L. E. (1984). Development of numerical concepts in infancy. In C. Sophian (Ed.), *Origins of cognitive skills* (pp. 131–155). Hillsdale, NJ: Lawrence Erlbaum Associates, Inc.

Suppalla, T. (1987). *Structure and acquisition of verbs of motion and location in American Sign Language.* Cambridge, MA: MIT/Bradford.

Vergnaud, G. A. (1983). Multiplicative structures. In R. Lesh & M. Landau (Eds.), *Acquisition of mathematics concepts and processes* (pp. 128–175). New York: Academic Press.

3

Representation and Misrepresentation: On the Beginnings of Symbolization in Young Children

David R. Olson

Ontario Institute
for Studies
in Education

Robin Campbell

University
of Stirling

The relationship between explicit and implicit knowledge may be approached by means of an inquiry into the relation between symbols, their users, and the things they represent. This is particularly the case for symbols that represent not only things in the world but also one's self, including one's talk, action, and epistemic states. The role of symbols in making knowledge explicit may be illustrated by saying that an average typist knows how to reach out to press the letter "K" on the typewriter but lacks explicit knowledge of the location of the letter "K." He may not be able, for example, to fill in the letter names on a diagram of a keyboard or name the keys adjacent to the letter "K." To do the latter, he would have to have explicit knowledge or belief about the key's location. What is involved in making the habitual "knowledge" explicit is representing that "knowledge" in a symbolic code such as language or diagrams. So the route from implicit knowledge to explicit knowledge is that of symbolization.

At the turn of the century, Charles Sanders Peirce advanced the notion that symbols were mediating structures between subjects and their experience, this "thirdness" creating the capacity for reflective and conscious thought. While behavior may be adjusted to the world without implicating thought or symbols—by means of implicit knowledge—explicit knowledge and conscious thought depend upon the availability of symbols. The development of thought, then, is a matter of the acquisition of symbolic means for representing oneself and the world. In more recent times, Goodman (1978) and Bruner (1973, 1986) have argued that the structure of cognition and consciousness is a matter of the structure of symbols available for representational purposes. This is the perspective adopted herein.

In this chapter we lay out the basic principles that appear to be involved in the acquisition of symbolic competence in children and the implications of that competence for thought.

This chapter is one of several that grew out of discussions that took place during Robin Campbell's stay at the University of Toronto in 1986–1987 and in the spring of 1989. We are grateful to Janet Astington for her suggestions on this topic. The authors gratefully acknowledge the support of the Spencer Foundation, SSHRC, and the Ontario Ministry of Education through its Block Transfer Grant to OISE.

Piaget (1962) was among the first to show that the beginnings of symbolization were to be found in pretend play in which one object was allowed to stand for, or to stand in for, another object. The importance of pretense has become even more obvious in recent research on children's acquisition of a "theory of mind" and children's understanding that their own and others' actions may be explained and predicted on the basis of beliefs, desires, and intentions (Astington, Harris, & Olson, 1988). Even prior to this development, children have a reasonable degree of implicit knowledge about the world: They know what to expect in particular situations, where to look for displaced objects, and what the consequences of action are. But when they are about two years old, they begin to pretend play. They begin to flap their arms as if they were trying to fly, they start to play tea party and to pretend to drink from empty glasses, to have invisible friends, and to use one object, say a bench, to "represent" or symbolize another object, say a horse.

It is possible to overstate the regularity of the onset of pretense and the uniformity of its expression. Malvestuto-Filice (1986) found that while two-year-olds could readily pretend to drink from an empty glass, when presented with a filled glass, they simply drank it down. It was some three or four years before they could "pretend" to drink from a filled glass. Furthermore, the richness of symbolic play that we see in Western cultures does not exist everywhere. Scollon and Scollon (1981) report that pretend play is particularly prominent in children who are exposed to literate narratives that involve the "fictionalizing" of the self, whereas it was virtually absent in children from traditional Alaskan Athabaskan communities. Other observers of non-Western cultures have reported that symbolic play does not exist at all in the cultures they have studied or that it exists only in very stereotypic forms and makes up a much smaller proportion of children's activity (Ariel & Sever, 1980; Feitelson, 1977; LeVine & LeVine, 1963; Smilansky, 1968; Smith, 1977).

What makes such pretense possible? Piaget's (1962) view was that pretend play involves a predominance of assimilation over accommodation, that is, the assimilation of an object to a schema and the resulting activation of the schema without the reciprocal modification in the schema in response to the new object. Indeed, pretend play can occur even when no stimulus is present to activate a schema, the activation being internally generated. The beginning of this "massive assimilation" was the beginning of one side of representation—the other side being the accommodation of the subject to an object, through imitation, to form a signifier. Signifier, a sign, plus the ability to activate the schema normally associated with an object, the signified, produced the first true symbol. The process of letting some object or sign stand for or signify some other object Piaget referred to as representation; the signifier is a symbol for the signified. Put simply, a bench could serve to symbolize, and thereby represent, a horse.

What makes assimilation without accommodation and accommodation without assimilation possible, Piaget never explained. Leslie (1987, 1988) has suggested an appropriate mechanism in his analysis of pretend play. Pretense, he argued, depends upon the developing child's new ability to represent, not the world, which, according to Leslie (as well as Fodor, 1975, and others), she has been doing for some time, but to represent her representations in the form of *metarepresentations*. Metarepresentations are created from primary representations by means of "decoupling" them from their normal input and output functions. Leslie advanced this notion to account for the feature that Piaget left unexplained, namely, how schema for objects, say horses, remain undistorted by the child's assimilating a bench into that schema when the child pretends that a bench is a horse. It does so by detaching the representation from its normal function, allowing the child to operate on the metarepresentation. The original representation remains undistorted. These metarepresentations are then subject to embedding in higher order structures and thereby have a form similar to that which would be expressed in English by the sentence "I pretend this bench is a horse."

Once decoupled from their ordinary representational functions, metarepresentations lose the semantic functions usually associated with ordinary representations and are characterizable in terms of deviant reference, deviant existence, and deviant truth—properties usually associated with opaque or intentional contexts. Thus of our bench–horse the child may meaningfully say "The horse is standing still" even if there is no horse to refer to, to predicate its motionlessness to, or for that predication to be true of (Leslie, 1987).

Now these properties of reference, existence, and truth are properties of representations, that is, of symbols. Deviant truth, existence, and reference are similarly properties of symbols. Hence, we can paraphrase Leslie's point about metarepresentation in terms of symbols. With Leslie, we could say that although children have known something about both horses and benches for some time, what is new is that the child, for the first time, *symbolizes* the horse by means of a bench. The bench becomes a symbol for the horse.

Talk of the children's achievement in terms of learning to use symbols rather than as acquiring metarepresentations preserves Leslie's point about isolating ordinary representations from metarepresentations or what we would prefer to distinguish as objects from symbols, but it has some additional advantages. First, it avoids the attribution to young infants of primary "representations" expressed in a "language of thought" that have been present essentially from birth (Leslie, 1987, p. 417; Olson & Campbell, 1993). We can allow the possibility that when children learn to symbolize, they are for the first time learning that one thing can represent another. On this view, symbols are children's first true representations. It leaves unspecified, as indeed it should given our almost complete absence of knowledge, how prelinguistic children and lower animals cognize the world (see Olson, 1988; Olson & Astington, 1987, for further discussion of this point).

This gambit has a second advantage. Because Leslie considers the beginnings of pretense as an indication of the onset of metarepresentation—metarepresentations having the properties previously mentioned, namely, deviant reference, existence, and truth—he is at a loss to explain cognitive achievements, such as children's understanding of false belief (Wimmer & Perner, 1983) and their understanding of the difference between appearance and reality (Flavell, 1986). He describes them simply as disguised versions of the pretend task even if they are known to be solved by children only two to three years later than the onset of pretense. If we analyze children's pretense in terms of the beginnings of symbolization, we can see that while this is a crucial first step, there are two equally significant achievements that children make before they are able to understand, and hence to ascribe to themselves and others, false beliefs.

Third, describing the beginnings of pretend play in terms of children's understanding of symbols rather than as acquiring metarepresentations allows us to reserve the concept of metarepresentation for those cases in which it is more seriously needed, namely, for concepts, including truth and falsity, that are genuinely metarepresentational. Truth is a predicate that takes representations as one of its arguments. We return to this point later.

And finally, to take representations to be symbols and to see pretense as dependent upon children's learning to use symbols allows us to entertain the possibility that in learning to use a symbol the child is learning the concept of symbol. If symbols are not recognized as symbols, they are not symbols at all. It is this recognition that prevents the pretending child from confusing benches with horses. The bench is a symbol for a horse (just as a line drawing may be) and the child knows that it is a symbol. Further, concepts are "bearers" of consciousness and are critical to the analysis of children's "awareness" of mental states. In learning to symbolize, then, the primary achievement is the concept of a symbol. "Symbolize" would be a two-place predicate relating a signifier—a mark or an object, for example, a bench—and a thing or class of things represented—for example, a horse, thus:

symbolize (bench, horse)   that is, symbolize (signifier, signified)

which may be expressed as "The bench symbolizes a horse."

If the main achievement of this period is the understanding that one object or event can stand for and symbolize another object, there is no reason why children's understanding of physical objects serving as symbols, such as a bench standing for a horse, is any different from their understanding that a word can stand for an object. It is tempting to think that words, unlike objects such as benches, have no independent prior significance and may therefore be easier to understand than other symbolic objects. But it appears that children's understanding that "things have names"—that words have a declarative naming function in addition to a pragmatic function, that pictures can represent objects and the like—develops at close to the same time. Baron-Cohen, Leslie, and Frith's (1985) claim that autistic children learn a language and yet fail to engage in pretense may be counter to this claim. However, if they use language pragmatically and if they fail to note that "things have names," then it may not be a counterargument.

Children's first symbols, we suggest, are just that; they are not, for example, beliefs. They are symbols for real, known objects and events. Dolls represent, that is, symbolize, people or animals, toy cars represent cars, benches represent horses, and so on. But they represent what is known as semantic knowledge—children's implicit knowledge about themselves and the world—rather than episodic knowledge, that is, autobiographical, time-dated knowledge of particulars.

This point requires some expansion. It has been assumed in empiricist theories, at least since the time of John Locke (1690/1989), that symbols first represent individuals or particulars by associating signs with things, similarities between these particulars leading to symbols that represent classes of objects. On this view, the child's first meaning for "dog" is the particular dog pointed to, and then by generalization, to the class of dogs. But an examination of children's first understandings of representations such as photographs and drawings suggests that this is not the case. Young children will identify themselves in photos, for example, as "a baby," rather than as Jennifer. And children's drawings of a particular object, say a pencil, placed in front of them will come out as a pencil drawing (Olson & Bialystok, 1983). Counter to the empiricist assumption then, if we approach cognitive growth as symbolic growth, the first symbols represent not particular objects but generalized meanings. The symbol, by definition, is a relation between a form, the bench, and a meaning, the child's knowledge of a horse. Children's first symbols, then, we suggest, represent the child's generic knowledge of objects and events. Symbols are relations between signs and meanings, not between signs and referents.

Once the child understands that symbols stand for meanings, the child is set for a second major achievement, a second stage in using symbols. It occurs when the child comes to see that a symbol may be used to represent a particular thing or situation. This is what permits the representation to be true or false of that thing or situation. The difference between the first understanding of symbols and the second understanding is the difference between a drawing of a face and a drawing of a particular face, a picture versus a portrait. Put another way, at the first stage, the child does not see the bench as a representation of Nelly, the family horse; it is just "a horse." A doll house represents "a house"—the generalized house; at the second stage, the child may see that same doll house as a representation of a particular house. Symbols acquire reference.

DeLoache (1987) has shown that although children know how to play with a doll house when they are about two years old, they have to be at least three years old to understand that a doll house may be a representation of a particular real house. She reports that shown the location of a hidden object in the doll house, the child of three can, for the first time, derive the location of the hidden object in the real house. The representation, that is, the symbol, at first only a representation of a meaning, "a" house, now comes to be a representation of "the" particular house.

These two achievements, first learning to use symbols to express a meaning, the second to learn how to use these meanings to represent particulars, constitute the heart of the symbolization process. DeLoache's view is that whereas two-year-olds understand conventional representations, such as words, only the three-year-olds have abstracted the concept of representation sufficiently to allow a novel model to represent a new state of affairs.

Perner (1991, p. 86) has denied that DeLoache's subjects, at age 3, manifest such metarepresentational abilities. We choose a middle ground. Three-year-olds, for the first time, grasp that the model represents not just a house but actually refers to and therefore symbolizes a particular house. What they fail to grasp at this point is not "representation" but "misrepresentation," that is, the concept of falsity.

Forguson and Gopnik (1988) have made a similar point in their discussion of the difference between pretend play and the false-belief tasks, suggesting that the crucial factor is that the child must come to see that real things can be represented too, that is, that a representation can represent a real state of affairs. Put in our terms, in pretense, symbols represent "meanings"; what DeLoache's task requires is the use of symbols to represent real, that is, particular, events. In our view, children understand symbols as representations all along; the bench symbolizes a horse, but it is not a representation of a particular horse. The doll house represented a house all along; that is what invites a particular form of play. What DeLoache's subjects discover at three is that a symbol represents not their general semantic knowledge of a house but rather that semantic knowledge can be about or *refer* to a particular real house.

Just how they allow a symbol to represent a particular situation is our next concern. It could be argued that they could elaborate the second argument of the representational scheme by changing the symbolic relation from the signifier representing *a* horse to representing *the* horse. We suggest rather that the child may, in fact, be acquiring a predicate for relating a symbol to a state of affairs. Candidate predicates may be such things as *refers to, is similar to,* or *looks like.* The resulting metarepresentational scheme would simply embed the earlier structure in a higher order relation:

refers to (symbol (signifier, signified), situation)

which would be translated something like "This object, which symbolizes a house, refers to the real house over there."

This representation has an additional advantage. It makes clear that, for the first time, children distinguish the *meaning* of the symbol from its *reference*. Pretend play allows for no such distinction.

The third, equally crucial, step will be taken approximately a year later. Wimmer and Perner (1983) in Austria were the first to show that if children are introduced to a protagonist who is shown to have grounds for holding a false belief and are then asked what that protagonist will do, children under three believe that the action will be premised on the true state of affairs rather than on the protagonist's false belief. By four, they understand the possibility of someone's holding and acting on a false belief. Gopnik and Astington (1988) showed that the understanding worked both ways; if children could not understand false beliefs in others, they could not ascribe them to themselves either. The symmetry of the relation suggests that the children have acquired a new concept that can be applied both to themselves and others. What is that concept?

Our suggestion is that when they are about four years old, children come to understand that a representation may *misrepresent* a real situation. The symbol can now be seen not only as a symbol, something the children could do at two, nor as a representation of a particular situation, something the children could do at three, but also as a misrepresentation of that thing or situation. It is only at this stage that children can understand the possibility of a false belief. They discover or understand the possibility of misrepresentation. False belief is a mismatch between the meaning of the symbol and the object the symbol refers to. Perner (1988) makes the same point by saying that the content of the representation differs from the referent of the representation (p. 158).

What is involved in understanding misrepresentation? Only certain types of symbols permit misrepresentation. The visual arts and the plastic arts, it is generally assumed, do not make statements and consequently cannot be true or false. Moore's bulges and hollows represent "woman," not misrepresent her, even if the sculpture does not clearly resemble its object. Similarly, a bench may be used to represent a horse, not to misrepresent a horse. A map, on the other hand, or a statement may represent a state of affairs or misrepresent that state of affairs. The crucial feature, of course, is that those representations may be true or false. What children acquire at this age is a concept or predicate that permits them to *judge* their representations as true or false. The children acquire, we suggest, concepts of true and false. What makes the acquisition of a concept of truth possible remains a moot question that has been addressed elsewhere (Olson, 1989). We leave open whether this predicate is or is not a natural predicate; it could be mentalese. But we are suspicious of predicates that are not predicates of a natural language (see Jackendoff, 1985; Olson & Bialystok, 1983; Olson & Campbell, 1993).

These may not be the first truly metarepresentational concepts that children acquire. They may learn to ascribe a property such as "good" to a drawing; a circle is a good symbol for a head whereas a straight line is not. "Good" in this context would be a metarepresentational term. And if the previous analysis of the DeLoache task is correct, they have already acquired a metarepresentational predicate such as "refers to." But the concepts of true and false are concepts that are fundamental to judgments about propositions, whether expressed in sentences or entertained as beliefs. "True" and "false" are predicates that mark judgments about the relation of a proposition—a symbol string—and a state of affairs, thus:

false (refers to (symbol (signifier, signified), situation))

which may be expressed as "This object which symbolizes a doll house is true of that particular doll house." Or in the false belief case, "This representation is false of that particular state of affairs."

Again, the symbol string has a meaning and that meaning refers to a state of affairs, the proposition being judged as true or false.

Children's understanding of false belief is a major achievement, then, because it involves the child's understanding of misrepresentation, misrepresentation being dependent upon concepts of truth and falsity. Perner's (1988) analysis of the false belief task is close, if not identical, to that advanced herein. He argues that what is crucial is that the child must "explicitly model . . . the semantic relationship between belief and world" (p. 155) and again that the child must represent "Mary as misrepresenting the real situation" (p. 144). But he thinks of this as representing the representing relation without indicating how that is represented. If by "representing the representing relation" he means representing the proposition as false, then our two views are equivalent. But he also says that the crucial factor is mapping the representation back into the world, a view that leads him to believe that children can remember their own and others' false beliefs; they just cannot succeed in mapping them into a prediction for action in the real world (p. 144). Subsequent research by Gopnik and Astington (1988), Harris, Johnson, and Harris (1987), and Wellman and Bartsch (1988) has shown that this is not the case; children's difficulty is not just in mapping their representations into a real state of affairs but rather a more general difficulty in *judging a representation as false*. The fundamental notions, then, are those of symbol, representation, and truth/falsity. Beliefs are states ascribed to people who entertain propositions, false beliefs to those who entertain false propositions. The recognition of beliefs as beliefs requires a concept of belief in the sense that the concept of belief is nothing more than the concept that a representation may be true or false. The concept of belief, therefore, may reduce to the concepts of symbol, and truth/falsity. It is even possible that the predicate "thought" could be reduced to some modal + say, for example, "could have said" or "would have said if asked." Symbols are representations; truth and falsity are metarepresentational concepts.

Second, Perner's account leaves unclear how the false belief task is related to the appearance-reality task studied by Flavell and his colleagues. It has been established by empirical means that the appearance-reality task is equivalent to the false-belief task (Flavell, 1988; Gopnik & Astington, 1988) at least in some cultures. A theory of the false-belief task, if general, should serve to explain the appearance-reality task as well. If children's difficulty is in understanding misrepresentations, and if the appearance task is seen as a question about misrepresentation, the equivalence between the tasks is clear; the appearance of the object misrepresents the object's true nature; it is false of the object's true identity.

Misrepresentation is a complex issue. The claim made here is not that the child for the first time encounters or endures misrepresentations; after all, babies suck pencils and fingers, perhaps taking them to be a nipple and later reject them because they are not. Rather, the claim is that the child comes to understand misrepresentation. The distinction is between rejecting a false representation and judging (recognizing) a representation as false. Children as young as two years of age can reject a false representation. If you show children a picture of a car and say "Truck," they reply, "No, car" (Pea, 1980). From this, most writers have inferred that children understand that utterances may be true or false, that is, that they understand truth-functions, including truth-functional negation. Further, as this judgment is a judgment about a sentence, the utterance, "No, ball," is taken to be a metalinguistic judgment (Pea, 1980). Macnamara (1986) goes further, arguing that the predicate *is true* is presupposed in learning a name (p. 106).

However, the child's response may more correctly be viewed as a simple rejection of the utterance, analogous to rejection of an offer, which children master even earlier. It is metalinguistic only in the sense that the negative response rejects the statement rather than rejecting the world. However, what is still missing is the child's ability to represent the sentence as false. The distinction, as in the misrepresentational case, is between rejecting a false sentence and representing the sentence as false. Only the latter requires the concepts of truth and falsity. Children's ability to represent sentences as false occurs somewhat later, the precise onset depending on the nature of the propositions but roughly in the period between the fourth and sixth years (Astington & Olson, 1983; Olson, 1987).

So we have a series of stages in the understanding of symbols. First, young children realize the possibility of symbolizing, that is, representing one thing by means of another. In learning to symbolize, children learn the concept that one thing can stand for, symbolize, or represent another thing or class of things. Next, children understand that a symbol may refer, that is, be used to represent a particular concrete, specific object or event. And third, they begin to understand the possibility that a representation may be true or false of the thing it is a representation of. It is only at this third stage, when children have acquired the metarepresentational concepts of true and false, that they can be said to have an adult-like concept of belief.

If a concept of belief depends upon the acquisition of a set of symbols for representing generic events, then a further set of symbols for relating those symbols to particular events, and still further symbols for representing representations as true or false, it seems that there is wide scope for the rise of cultural diversity. Thus it may be the case that some language groups may dispense with the predicate "false," and hence, with the Western concept of belief. Thus it is entirely plausible that some social groups may characterize themselves and others in terms of knowing or not knowing the states of the world but not of entertaining false beliefs. It becomes important to treat beliefs as different from simple knowing or not knowing something only when one is attempting to trick or otherwise deceive someone. For younger children it may be quite adequate to characterize them as knowing or not knowing something. The putative false beliefs they may be holding may be of no interest to them and may exist purely in the mind of the ascriber. (Even teachers view children as knowing or not knowing rather than as holding deviant beliefs that may be modified by appropriate arguments.) Hence, the cultural conventions for interpreting the behavior and talk of others in terms of beliefs, rather than in terms of reality, is an interesting, and open question (Duranti, 1985; McCormick, 1994).

Perner (1988) has made a similar point by distinguishing correctness from truth. Distinguishing the two, however, is not a simple matter. Agree–disagree judgments can serve most of the functions that truth–falsity judgments do. To disentangle them requires that the subject see that negative claims can be true, for example, "It's true that the man has no hat." These judgments are managed by five- or six-year-olds

(Astington & Olson, 1993). Simpler tests may involve the child's willingness to report statements the child knows to be false. Deliberate lying and false belief tasks would seem to be promising candidates (Peskin, 1992).

It is not without significance that the properties of propositions, including truth and falsity, are identical to those of minds. Saying and thinking, as many philosophers have noted, are two sides of the same coin. Truth of a proposition, like meaning of a sentence, is a semantic notion, premised on the existence of symbols.

We can now state more clearly the relation between the hypothesis offered here and those advanced by other theorists of false belief. Forguson and Gopnik suggested that what is acquired is an understanding that real things can be represented too. The distinction is between representing fictions and representing "reals." Our suggestion is that the achievement is the distinction between two reals, the general and the particular; the bench represents *a* horse and *the* horse. A representation of "a horse" is general and is captured in the notion of meaning or, in the cognitive literature, of semantic memory. A representation of *the* horse is a perceptual event referred to. Judgments of true and false become possible when the child is capable of representing both "a horse" and "the horse" at the same time and relating them.

This theory also diverges somewhat from that held by Leslie. Metarepresentations are, in our view, not merely decoupled from real objects and applied to other events. Rather, metarepresentations are higher order predicates, such as true and false, which relate lower order schemes. Perner's discussion of "representing the representational process" as mentioned earlier, is similar to that offered here.

To summarize. Symbolization, we have argued, is central to the origins of self-conscious, reflective thought. Symbolization is a matter of using explicit forms, whether sounds, marks, or objects, to represent meanings, these meanings being the accumulated implicit semantic knowledge that people have acquired through experience. Once symbols are available, they may be used for explicitly representing particular events in the world. Explication is equivalent to symbolization.

The uses of symbols and representations in education may be clarified somewhat by appealing to the previous analysis. Symbols are essential to any form of thought. So, clearly, a primary educational concern is that of teaching children alternative representations of themselves and the world. In educational discourse, this important perspective frequently gets confused by the educational attempt to simply "teach" symbolization. What is overlooked is that the child has to have some implicit knowledge that is to serve as the object of that symbolization.

Consider the teaching of grammar. Decades, indeed centuries, of students have been subjected to the teaching of grammar, often to little avail. Part of the difficulty is that grammar is taught as a formal body of knowledge that children are expected to learn. As long as teaching was treated as the route to learning, this seemed like a perfectly straightforward process. However, if we think of this learning in terms of symbolization, it becomes clear that children's speaking abilities, that is, their implicit knowledge of the language, is the implicit knowledge that is to be represented in the symbol system that we call the explicit grammar. Learning grammar, then, is a matter of learning a metalanguage, a language that takes for its content the speaking practices of the children. Grammar can be taught successfully only by showing the child how a formal symbol system, the explicit grammar, can serve as a representation of the child's implicit knowledge. If that implicit knowledge is not in place, and accessible in the form of intuition, the explicit grammar is impossible to learn.

Now consider the analogous case in the learning of mathematics. Numbers, at first, represent objects in the world: Numbers are about, symbolize, or represent collections and individuals in those collections. When we now try to teach the "rules" of mathematics, analogous to the "rules" of grammar, we are teaching the child a metalanguage, a way of talking about the implicit knowledge of number. If those intuitions, that is, the implicit knowledge, are not available, it is essentially impossible to learn the metalanguage, that is, the rules of the number system, successfully. Nor is it possible to learn other metarepresentations of number such as a number line. Part of the difficulty would perhaps be overcome if teachers, and in turn students, understood that numbers, which represent the world, must be distinguished from the "grammar," that is, the rules of mathematics, that constitutes a metalanguage for talking about number.

Such examples simply illustrate but do not exhaust the kinds of issues that arise if one begins to think of symbols standing for meanings and then thinking of how those meanings may be used to represent particular events in the world. The problems that arise in both developing psychological theories and in extrapolating to educational practice is a certain blindness to the relation of symbols to the things they represent. We must, as Korzybski (1958) urged almost a half-century ago, not confuse the map with the territory.

References

Ariel, S., & Sever, I. (1980). Play in the desert and play in the town: On play activities of Bedouin Arab children. In H. B. Schwartzman (Ed.), *Play and culture*. New York: Leisure Press.

Astington, J. W., Harris, P. L., & Olson, D. R. (Eds.). (1988). *Developing theories of mind*. Cambridge: Cambridge University Press.

Astington, J. W., & Olson, D. R. (1993, June). *Children's comprehension of true negation*. Paper presented at the annual meeting of the Canadian Psychological Association, Quebec City, PQ.

Baron-Cohen, S., Leslie, A., & Frith, U. (1985). Does the autistic child have a "theory of mind"? *Cognition, 21*, 37–46.

Bruner, J. S. (1973). The growth of representational processes in childhood. In J. M. Anglin (Ed.), *Beyond the information given* (pp. 313–324). New York: W. W. Norton.

Bruner, J. S. (1986). *Actual minds, possible worlds*. Cambridge, MA: Harvard University Press.

DeLoache, J. (1987). Rapid change in the symbolic functioning of very young children. *Science, 238*, 1556–1557.

Duranti, A. (1985). Famous theories and local theories: The Samoans and Wittgenstein. *Quarterly Newsletter of the Laboratory of Comparative Human Cognition, 7*, 46–51.

Feitelson, D. (1977). Cross-cultural studies of representational play. In B. Tizard & D. Harvey (Eds.), *Biology of play* (pp. 6–14). Philadelphia: Lippincott.

Flavell, J. H. (1986). The development of children's knowledge about the appearance-reality distinction. *American Psychologist, 41*, 418–425.

Flavell, J. (1988). The development of children's knowledge about the mind: From cognitive connections to mental representations. In J. W. Astington, P. L. Harris, & D. R. Olson (Eds.), *Developing theories of mind* (pp. 244–267). Cambridge: Cambridge University Press.

Fodor, J. (1975). *The language of thought.* Cambridge, MA: Harvard University Press.

Forguson, L., & Gopnik, A. (1988). The ontogeny of common sense. In J. W. Astington, P. L. Harris, & D. R. Olson (Eds.), *Developing theories of mind* (pp. 226–243). Cambridge: Cambridge University Press.

Goodman, N. (1978). *Ways of worldmaking.* Indianapolis: Hackett.

Gopnik, A., & Astington, J. (1988). Children's understanding of representational change and its relation to the understanding of false belief and the appearance-reality distinction. *Child Development, 59*(1), 26–37.

Harris, L., Johnson, C. N., & Harris, P. L. (1987). *Understanding false belief by young children.* Unpublished manuscript, University of Oxford, Oxford, England.

Jackendoff, R. (1985). *Semantics and cognition.* Cambridge, MA: Bradford Books/MIT Press.

Korzybski, A. (1958). *Science and sanity* (4th ed.). Lakeville, CT: The International Non-Aristotelian Library Publishing Company.

Leslie, A. (1987). Pretense and representation: The origins of "theory of mind." *Psychological Review, 94*(4), 412–426.

Leslie, A. (1988). Some implications of pretense of mechanisms underlying the child's theory of mind. In J. W. Astington, P. L. Harris, & D. R. Olson (Eds.), *Developing theories of mind* (pp. 19–46). Cambridge: Cambridge University Press.

LeVine, R., & LeVine, B. (1963). Nyansongo: A Gusii community in Kenya. In B. Whiting (Ed.), *Six cultures: Studies of child rearing* (pp. 15–54). New York: Wiley.

Locke, J. (1989). *Some thoughts concerning education* (J. W. Yolton & J. S. Yolton, Eds.). Oxford: Clarendon Press. (Original work published 1690)

Macnamara, J. (1986). *A border dispute: The place of logic in psychology.* Cambridge, MA: Bradford Books/MIT Press.

Malvestuto-Filice, G. (1986, June). *Children's understanding of concepts of pretense.* Paper presented at the annual meeting of the Canadian Psychological Association, Toronto, Canada.

McCormick, P. (1994). *Children's understanding of mind: A case for cultural diversity.* Unpublished Ph.D. thesis, University of Toronto.

Olson, D. R. (1987). Thinking about logic. A review of J. Macnamara's *A border dispute: The place of logic in psychology. Canadian Journal of Psychology, 41*(3), 392–398.

Olson, D. R. (1988). On the origins of beliefs and other intentional states in children. In J. W. Astington, P. L. Harris, & D. R. Olson (Eds.), *Developing theories of mind* (pp. 414–426). Cambridge: Cambridge University Press.

Olson, D. R. (1989). Making up your mind. *Canadian Psychology, 30*(4), 617–627.

Olson, D. R., & Astington, J. W. (1987). Seeing and knowing: On the ascription of mental states to young children. *Canadian Journal of Psychology, 41*(4), 399–411.

Olson, D. R., & Bialystok, E. (1983). *Spatial cognition: The structure and development of the mental representation of spatial relations.* Hillsdale, NJ: Erlbaum.

Olson, D. R., & Campbell, R. (1993). Constructing representations. In C. Pratt & A. F. Garton (Eds.), *Systems of representation in children: Development and use* (pp. 11–26). Chichester: Wiley.

Pea, R. (1980). The development of negation in early child language. In D. Olson (Ed.), *The social foundations of language and thought* (pp. 156–186). New York: Norton.

Peirce, C. S. (1935–1963). *The collected works of C. S. Peirce* (Vols. 1–8) (C. Hartshorne & P. Weiss, Eds.). Cambridge, MA: Harvard University Press/Belknap.

Perner, J. (1988). Developing semantics for theories of mind: From propositional attitudes to mental representation. In J. W. Astington, P. L. Harris, & D. R. Olson (Eds.), *Developing theories of mind* (pp. 141–172). Cambridge: Cambridge University Press.

Perner, J. (1991). *Understanding the representational mind.* Cambridge, MA: Bradford Books/MIT Press.

Peskin, J. (1992). Ruse and representations: On children's ability to conceal information. *Developmental Psychology, 28*(1), 84–89.

Piaget, J. (1962). *Play, dreams, and imitation in childhood* (C. Gattegno & F. M. Hodgson, Trans.). New York: Norton.

Scollon, R., & Scollon, S. B. K. (1981). *Narrative, literacy and face in interethnic communication.* Norwood, NJ: Ablex.

Smilansky, S. (1968). *The effects of sociodramatic play on disadvantaged preschool children.* New York: Wiley.

Smith, P. K. (1977). Social and fantasy play in young children. In B. Tizard & D. Harvey (Eds.), *Biology of play* (pp. 123–145). Philadelphia: Lippincott.

Wellman, H., & Bartsch, K. (1988). *Young children's reasoning about beliefs.* University of Michigan, Ann Arbor, Mimeo.

Wimmer, H., & Perner, J. (1983). Beliefs about beliefs: Representation and constraining function of wrong beliefs in young children's understanding of deception. *Cognition, 13*, 103–128.

4
Tacit Models

Efraim Fischbein
Tel-Aviv University

Representations and Models

Representation is rather a vague notion. It refers to a large variety of mental and physical entities like symbols, concepts, models, images, diagrams, and so on. What all these have in common is that they are related to certain objects that they may replace in our cognitive activities.

Kaput distinguishes four interaction types of representation: (a) cognitive and perceptual representations, (b) explanatory representations involving models, (c) representation within mathematics, and (d) external symbolic representation (Kaput, 1987, p. 23). Kaput's classification attempt gives an idea of how complex the notion of representation is. It is certain that representations play a fundamental role in all kinds of reasoning.

In our opinion a fundamental distinction should be made to put some order in that domain. We suggest distinguishing two essentially different types of representation: symbols and models.

Let us consider, for example, the letters P_1, P_2 and l_1, l_2. Let us declare that they are the symbols of some mental objects called points (P_1 and P_2) and lines (l_1 and l_2). We do not know what the original objects look like. P_1, P_2 and l_1, l_2 are symbols. There is a one-to-one correspondence between them and the original objects.

Could these symbols be used in order to discover some properties of the represented objects, or some relations between them? Certainly not. Pure symbols are representations that cannot produce any information by themselves.

The situation is totally different with models. Let us represent the mathematical notions, points and lines, by pictures—small spots for points and fine strips of ink for lines. In this case, we may discover a number of properties expressed as theorems. Two points determine a line; two different lines determine a point; if two lines have two points in common they have an infinity of points in common.

The basic difference between a pure symbol and a model is that models are structured representations, while pure symbols are not. By the word *structured*, I intend to emphasize that a model always has an inner structure like a material object, with defined relationships between its elements. A number of symbols may play the role of a model if they are organized in a certain structure. It is due to its structure that the model may correspond to a certain original and replace it in certain conditions.

Let us consider a different, artificial example. Let us assume that in order to motivate children to learn arithmetic, one has decided to represent the first 20 natural numbers by some interesting images. One is a dog, two is a cat, three is a mouse, four is a sheep, five is a flower, six is a bird, and so on. All these are symbols, but they do not constitute a model of something, because there is not any defined structure that would correspond to the properties and operations of the set of natural numbers.

Let us try to define more specifically the term *model*. Given two systems A and B, B may be considered a model of A if, on the basis of a certain isomorphism between A and B, a description or a solution produced in terms of A may be reflected consistently in terms of B and vice versa. Our artificial example with images representing numbers does not constitute a model because no problem with natural numbers can be solved using combinations of images. In fact, no such combinations have been defined in our example. If one asks how much is $2 + 3$ and one translates the problem in terms of the conventional symbols, one gets a cat and a mouse. But a combination between a cat and a mouse does not produce *by itself* a flower. A model must possess a certain autonomy; otherwise it cannot be used to solve a problem put first in terms of the original.

It is different when using the number line for representing numbers and operations with them. After defining a unit segment, the computation $2 + 3$ may be made by counting on the number line a segment of two and a segment of three. The result is imposed by the model—a segment of five units.

A set of symbols may be used to produce a model only by conferring on it a certain internal structure. This implies the existence of a number of defined relationships between the respective symbols.

Categories of Models

A first rough dichotomy distinguishes abstract and intuitive models. An abstract model consists usually of symbols organized in a certain structure. Mathematical or logical formulae are examples of abstract models. In order to describe the relationship between time and space in the case of a falling body, we use the formula $S = \frac{1}{2}gt^2$. This is a model because using the formula we may predict the space traveled by the falling body in a certain interval of time. The problem put in terms of real phenomena (space, time) is solved by operating on the formula. The result obtained by calculation has a definite meaning in practical terms. An enormous advantage of mathematics is that it permits the construction of a practically infinite number of models that may be manipulated mentally for solving practical problems. This may sound trivial, but, in fact, it raises fundamental philosophical problems, first of all because the elaboration of mathematics is, in principle, a process that may be accomplished without referring to reality.

Intuitive models are of a sensorial kind. An atom is represented by a center—the nucleus—surrounded by moving particles. An electrical current may be represented by a fluid flowing through a narrow pipe. Studying the laws of the fluid, we may deduce certain laws governing the electrical current (Law of Ohm $U = IR$). A small spot is an intuitive model for a point, and a narrow strip of ink, drawn on a piece of paper, is a model for a line. A graph representing a function is an intuitive model of that function.

As a matter of fact, intuitive models are, very often, not simple, direct representations of certain realities. Vectorial magnitudes—like forces or velocities—are represented by oriented line segments. The line segment does not simply mirror sensorially the original magnitude. The "mirroring" process is based on a number of conventions that have to be explicitly formulated. Such conventions may be of an abstract nature. The intuitive representation may be in fact governed by conceptual constraints. A graph representing the motion of a falling body is not the direct image of the falling process. It is the intuitive representation of the function $\frac{1}{2}gt^2$ which, in turn, is the abstract model of the original reality. Very often sensorial models are related to the original indirectly, through an intervening conceptual representation. It is important to mention this aspect not only for psychological reasons but also for didactical purposes. It has been found out that students tend to forget that the relation between the model and the original is very often mediated by intervening conceptual structures. As a consequence they interpret the model in an erroneous manner. For instance they may consider that the shape of a graph representing a motion reproduces the trajectory of the motion (for details see Janvier, 1981).

A second dichotomy distinguishes between implicit (or tacit) and explicit models.

An implicit model influences the reasoning strategies and decisions of an individual from "behind the scenes," that is, without the individual's being aware of that influence. When using terms like *short-term memory*, we are generally not aware of the fact that adjectives like "short" and "long" are, in fact, of spatial origin. The tacit model here is a line segment that may be shorter or longer. Terms like *deep structure, surface structure, subconscious* and *subliminal* are also of spatial origin. What we have in mind in these last examples is a kind of building with two levels. Certainly, nothing like this exists in the psychological world.

Explicit models are those of which we are aware. A diagram or a graph are generally used consciously in mathematics or in physics. In statistics one uses histograms, in geography one uses maps, and so on. All these are examples of explicit models. Explicit models are usually under a conceptual control, while tacit models are not.

A third dichotomy may distinguish analogical and paradigmatic models.

In the case of analogies, we deal with two distinct systems, one of which is the original, the other is the model. The atom structure is represented by the image of a planetary system. There is a certain analogy between living bodies and self-controlled machines. There is a certain analogy between a social group and a living organism.

A paradigmatic model is an exemplar or a subclass of a certain class, which plays the role of a model for the whole class. When we think of numbers, we usually have natural numbers in mind. When using the term *animal*, people refer tacitly to familiar mammals like dogs, cats, and horses and not, for instance, to insects. Children asked about the meaning of the term *liquid* answer frequently: It is a "water."

Paradigmatic models play an essential role in the way in which we define and apply intuitively the concepts we use. It is difficult to accept intuitively that fog consists of liquid particles or smoke of solid particles because liquids and solids are usually represented by substances having totally different properties.

It is important to emphasize that the formal definition and the practically used definition (when identifying elements of a class) frequently do not coincide, because the practical definition is imposed by a certain paradigmatic model—with its inherent limitations.

The dichotomies previously mentioned do not represent clear-cut disjunctions. Things are relatively complex and absolute classifications are not possible.

Tacit Models

I want to concentrate now on tacit models and distinguish some typical situations:

1. Sometimes the individual may be completely unaware of the presence of a certain model which, in fact, influences his reasoning process.
2. There are situations in which a certain originally explicit model may become tacit. It continues to influence the individual's way of reasoning even after it had become obsolete (considering the newly acquired knowledge). For instance, children learn, initially, to define multiplication as repeated addition. Later on, they learn to generalize and formalize the concept of multiplication and to apply it to numbers for which repeated addition may not hold anymore. Nevertheless, the repeated addition model may continue to exert an impact on the individual's solving decisions, even in such situations in which the model does not apply anymore.
3. Finally, there are also situations in which a model, as such, is used consciously, but the individual is not aware of all the implications the model may have for her ways of reasoning.

Absence of Awareness of the Model and of Its Influence

In research carried out a number of years ago, the following question was asked: "Three resistors, R_1, R_2, R_3, are connected in series (see Figure 4.1). An amperemeter measures the current successively in points A_1, A_2, A_3. What will indicate the amperemeter in these three different points?" This question—among others—has been addressed to high school pupils who had already taken a course in electricity. All of them were successful students. Despite this, most of them answered that the amperemeter will indicate that the current diminishes. "Each of the resistors contributes to the reduction of the current," explained one of the pupils. He was then asked to define I. He answered: "The number of electrons which pass through a transversal section in a time unit" (Fischbein et al., 1963, p. 376).

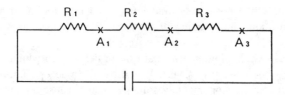

Figure 4.1.

One has, then, to consider, two models in this case. One is the learned electron model that should have led the student to conclude that the current does not diminish successively when passing through the three resistors: The number of electrons per unit of surface remains the same. The second is a hypothetical construct, a tacit model that was decisive for the student's reaction. The electrical current is identified with a kind of fluid and the resistors with obstacles. The intensity of the current is reduced by the successive obstacles. In order to justify their conclusion, the students referred to the law at Ohm, $V = IR$, from which we deduce $I = V/R$. With I being inversely proportional with R, it follows that by adding resistors one reduces the current. Under the influence of their tacit model, the students forgot that the intensity of the current is determined by the total resistance of the circuit and that it remains the same along the entire circuit.

We have here an example of a tacit model, conflicting tacitly with an explicit model. The tacit model is able to annihilate the influence of the explicit model; moreover, the individual is ready to invent an ad hoc justification for his incorrect conclusion, apparently in accordance with his conceptual knowledge. This is a very spread phenomenon.

Let us consider a second example referring to tacit models whose origin and influence remain unconscious: the concept of impetus. The impetus theory was developed during the Middle Ages, and it was, to a certain extent, a continuation of the Aristotelian theory of motion. The main idea of that theory is that a launched object continues to move after losing contact with the mover because a certain force has been impressed on it (see Franklin, 1978). That view has been contradicted by the Newtonian concept of inertia: A body tends to conserve its state of rest or uniform motion, unless it is compelled to change that state by forces impressed upon it.

In research carried out more recently, we have identified two versions of the impetus theory in high school students.

One version has been called the Marchian type (Franciscus de Marchia, ca. 1320, cf. Franklin, 1978, p. 203). In this version, the subject considers that an object set in motion by a mover continues to move because it has received a certain quantum of force (impetus) impressed on it. When the quantum of force has been used up, the object stops moving.

In the Buridan type of motion (Buridan, 1300–1358, cf. Franklin, 1978, p. 204), the impetus is considered of permanent nature and, consequently, the object will stop moving only if a certain cause intervenes.

In both conceptions, that of de Marchia and that of Buridan, the continuation of motion is determined by a kind of force impressed on the object. The launched object receives from the mover an impetus that sustains the motion.

Various authors have found that students, even after taking courses in mechanics, keep thinking in terms of the impetus theory (Viennot, 1978; Clement, 1982; McCloskey, 1983; McCloskey, Washburn, & Felch, 1983; Green, McCloskey, & Caramazza, 1985).

Here is a fragment of a protocol taken from a recent research of ours (Fischbein, Stavy, & Ma-Naim, 1987, p. 9, unpublished):

> *S:* A (launched) ball will continue the motion when its force is finished.
> *E:* Why?
> *S:* Because it will not have any more force to continue and will stop.
> *E:* What is pushing it forward?
> *S:* There is an internal force pushing it. (Alon, grade 10)

The hypothetical tacit model, in this case, is a kind of fuel or energy capital that sustains the motion but is consumed by the motion itself. When that "capital of force" is completely consumed, the motion stops. The model is very resistant. It remains active even after the student has taken a course in mechanics and has learned the principle of inertia.

One may assume that this model is inspired by our terrestrial life: In our concrete experience, after losing contact with the mover, a body keeps moving only a limited time, if a force does not intervene. Friction and gravitation, in fact, stop the motion. Inertia is a theoretical concept corresponding to ideal conditions.

Tacit, intuitive models seem, then, to exert a strong influence on our reasoning processes. Their strength is probably due to their empirical origin. They correspond to our practical experience. The theoretical interpretations, accepted by the scientific community are based on logical coherence. It seems that, at least in certain circumstances, an empirically based model has a stronger impact on our ways of reasoning than a conceptual one.

A third, well-known example refers to the notion of heat and temperature.

Temperature is a property that expresses the state of agitation of particles, that is, temperature is related to the kinetic energy of these particles.

Heat refers to the interactions between systems. It is the difference between temperatures that determines the transfer of heat, and this, in fact, represents an alteration of the internal energies of the systems.

As investigations have shown, children tend to interpret the transfer of heat as a transfer of some substance.

During an interview, a pupil explained that a whole metal rod gets hot when heated only at one end "because the heat keeps moving from one point of the rod to the next until the whole rod is hot" (cf. Erickson & Tiberghien, 1985, p. 58). What this subject seems to have in mind is a kind of substance that travels only *in one direction* from a hot zone to a cold one. The idea of an interaction of systems in which the state of internal energy is changed is a subtle one and has no intuitive basis.

This very common model reminds us of the caloric theory of the 18th and 19th centuries, according to which heat was represented as a subtle, weightless fluid capable of penetrating all material body (cf. Erickson & Tiberghien, 1985, p. 53).

Sometimes this type of model becomes explicit: "Heat is warm air"; "heat is a warming fluid or solid," claim some of the subjects (cf. Erickson & Tiberghien, 1985, p. 56).

Learned Models That Become Tacit

In the course of the instructional process, one uses various models in order to help students better understand the taught concepts. At higher levels, such models may become obsolete, that is, they may not continue to correspond to more accurate definitions or to the formal, scientific, understanding of the concept. For instance, for a child, the concept of number is, initially, connected only with the set representation of numbers. A certain number is represented by a collection of objects and the child learns to identify, implicitly, the common property of all the sets having the same cardinal as a number. Consequently, in the child's initial experience a number is a natural number. Later on the child learns about decimals, negative numbers, irrational numbers, and imaginary numbers.

The initial collection model does not correspond any more to these new types of numbers. Nevertheless, the collection model may continue, in certain circumstances, to act tacitly and to distort or to block the assimilation of the respective concepts.

Let me consider another example, referring to elementary arithmetical operations, specifically multiplication and division. *Formally*, multiplication is a commutative operation. *Formally*, 3×5 and 5×3 have exactly the same meaning. But in a practical context, things are different. The two numbers may get different roles. Five boxes with three pencils in each, and three boxes with five pencils in each constitute two different situations, although the total number of pencils is the same.

If one says "three times five," the number "three" is in this case the operator and "five" the operand. If one says "five times three," the role of the two numbers changes. As long as we deal with natural numbers, the whole story is not relevant. But when decimals are introduced certain difficulties may appear. Let us consider the following two examples:

1. 1 liter of juice costs \$2. What would be the price of 3 liters?
2. 1 liter of juice costs \$2. What will be the price of 0.75 liter?

In the first problem, one has to multiply 3×2 and in the second 0.75×2. The two problems have, mathematically, the same structure. Nevertheless, the second is more difficult. We do not refer to the computation. We are referring to the choice of the operation.

A first possible explanation would be that of the presence of the decimal is the source of the difficulty.

But let us consider the following two problems from research carried out some years ago in Italy:

1. For one cake you need 1.25 "etti" of sugar. How much sugar to you need for 15 cakes?
2. For a 2 kilo of cake you use 15 g. of yeast. How much do you use for 1.25 kilos of cake?

The term *etti* is very familiar to Italian pupils, and it means 100 grams.

The subjects were only asked to indicate the operation and *not* to perform the computation (Fischbein, Deri, Nello, & Marino, 1985, p. 9).

Both problems are solved by the multiplication: 15×1.25.

Three grade levels were considered: 5, 7, and 9. With the first problem the percentages of correct answers were, respectively, 84, 91, 94. With the second problem, the percentages of correct answers were 54, 38, 46. Many pupils did not answer at all to the second problem.

The difference between the two problems is that in the first case the operator is a whole number, while in the second case the operator is a decimal.

What is the explanation of these findings? We have offered the following theory: The initial model used in school for multiplication is repeated addition. According to this model one has to distinguish an operator and an operand. Five times three means $3 + 3 + 3 + 3 + 3$, while three times five means $5 + 5 + 5$. If the operator is a whole number things are intuitively fully acceptable according to the repeated additional model—even if the operand is a decimal. For instance 3 times 0.65 means $0.65 + 0.65 + 0.65$. But if the operator is a decimal, the operation has no intuitive meaning. The operation 0.65 times 3 cannot be translated in terms of repeated addition. The same with 15×1.25. The multiplication 1.25 times 15 has no intuitive meaning. The main finding of the research we are referring to was that even ninth grade students (and, in fact, even adults) were facing the same kind of difficulty as the younger subjects. The ninth grade students had already learned to generalize and formalize the concept of multiplication, extending it to rational and real numbers. Nevertheless, the repeated addition model continues to exert a tacit influence on their capacity of solving multiplication problems. The older students obtained even worse results than the younger ones. Certainly, they were not aware that the primitive repeated addition model blocked the correct answer.

Similar findings have been obtained with division problems. In this case, the hypothetical primitive models are those of partitive and quotative division. In the case of the partitive division, the operator (the divisor) should be a whole number in order to fit the intuitive constraints of the model. Dividing a certain magnitude into 3,4,5 and so on fragments has an intuitive meaning. But dividing a magnitude into

1.25 or 0.65 fragments has no intuitive meaning. Let us consider two problems from the same research.

1. Five friends together bought 0.75 kg of chocolate. How much does each one get?
2. I spent 900 lire for 0.75 etti of cocoa. What is the price of one etto?

In both problems, there is a decimal number. But in the first, the operator is a whole number while in the second problem it is the operator that has the decimal.

For the first problem the percentages of correct answers were respectively 85, 77, 83. For the second problem the percentages of correct answers were 22, 25, and 40 (Fischbein et al. 1985, pp. 9–12).

As in the case of multiplication, division also remains attached to certain tacit, primitive models, which influence the solution decision. If the numbers used in a problem do not correspond to the constraints imposed by the model, the subjects (even adolescents and adults) are facing difficulties in finding the right answer.

Conscious Models Tacitly Influencing the Solution Decisions

In many situations, the individual may be aware that she is using a certain representation for her abstract concepts. She may be convinced that she is in full control of the influence of the model, but, nevertheless, the tacit influence of the model may exceed the controlled influence.

In geometry, one uses drawings for representing geometrical concepts. A point has no dimensions, but it is represented by a small spot. A line is unidimensional but it is represented by a fine ink strip. The mathematician—and even the student—knows that the mathematical objects are ideal ones and that the drawings are only representations of them. As a matter of fact, these models are very useful. It would be difficult—if not impossible—as we already said, to produce mathematical theorems only by way of deduction, using pure symbols and formal definitions. To a great extent, the correspondence between the mathematical concepts and their material models acts very well. By drawing points as small spots and straight lines as fine ink strips, one may correctly find that two points determine a straight line, that two straight lines may have in common one point or an infinity of points, that a line segment is the shortest way between two points, and so on.

But the modeling capacity of the drawings is limited. In the domain of infinity the correspondence may not hold anymore.

Let us compare the sets of points of two line segments *AB* and *CD* having different lengths (Figure 4.2).

Two opposite, both intuitively based, answers may come into mind. On one hand, one tends to affirm that the two sets are equivalent because both sets are infinite. On the other hand, the longer segment seems to contain more points. *AB* may be made to coincide with *EF* and then one has the additional segments *CE* and *FD*. The conflict is produced by the fact that one continues to use, tacitly, the

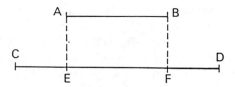

Figure 4.2.

pictorial representation of points and lines. There are, certainly, more small spots in *CD* and in *AB*. With regard to mathematical points, only formal arguments may decide about the equivalence or nonequivalence of infinite sets.

The difficulty is still more acute if one compares a one-dimensional with a bidimensional set (the set of points of a segment with the set of points of a square). We have asked this question to students belonging to different grades (5 to 9). About three-quarters of the subjects answered that the two sets were not equivalent (Fischbein, Tirosh, & Hess, 1979, p. 21). Even mathematicians in the time of Cantor could not accept the equivalence of these two sets. Despite the fact that one knows that the mathematical point has no dimensions, one continues to be influenced, tacitly, by the pictorial model of it. It is practically impossible to neutralize that influence at the intuitive level.

Until Weierstrass, mathematicians were convinced that a continuous real function must certainly have derivatives at some points at least. It was Weierstrass who first presented a famous counterexample of a continuous function defined over reals that has no derivatives at all (cf. Wilder, 1965, p. 201). The idea that a continuous function must have derivatives is, in fact, based tacitly on the graph model of functions. A *drawn* curve must have tangents at least in some of its points. But in fact, not every function is graphically representable. Mathematicians did not take into account the fact that the graph is only a visual, geometrical model of a function. It is a very useful model but we are not admitted to transfer *all* the properties of the model (the graph) to the original (in this case the function).

Tacit and Explicit Models

Is there a clear-cut distinction between tacit and explicit models? In our opinion there is no intrinsic difference between the two categories of models. Our hypothesis is that there is rather a continuum from unconscious models to conscious models through semiconscious ones. Explicit models may become implicit as an effect of routine or if their explicit use may contradict newly learned principles. We have seen that the repeated addition model for multiplication becomes obsolete after the student has learned to generalize the concept of multiplication for decimal and irrational numbers. Nevertheless, the model continues to influence the students solving decisions "from behind the scenes."

The individual may become aware of his tacit models—or of the tacit influence of his models—by an analytical effort. This may happen spontaneously or as an effect of external help. A child who affirms that the "heat is a kind of warm air" becomes aware of this initially implicit model when asked to explain the phenomenon of transfer of heat. A child who is asked to explain what he means by the term *liquid* says that it is "a kind of water." His implicit paradigmatic model (water) for liquids become conscious as an effect of the question put to him. Otherwise he simply identifies various liquids as liquids without resorting consciously to any definition or model.

A student who accepts that ABCD (Figure 4.3) is a rectangle but does not accept that it is a parallelogram has in mind the paradigmatic model of an oblique parallelogram. It is this type of image that is generally used for parallelograms in the classroom in order to avoid the association of other uncommon properties (like right angles) with the general concept. In this case, we have a rather semiconscious model in the sense that the student consciously connects oblicity with the concept of parallelogram, but he is not aware of the fact that he has, in fact, restricted implicitly his definition to that subcategory of parallelograms.

In our opinion, the problem has to be attacked by metacognitive means. The knowledge of the formal definition of parallelograms has to be refreshed: According to their formal definition, rectangles *are* parallelograms. The didactical and psychological difficulty here is that one has to rely only on formal definitions and not on paradigmatic models while, in fact, *our need for an intuitive support remains always very high.*

In the teaching of science and mathematics, this problem arises frequently: The student needs an intuitive support for the abstract concepts that are taught. Such an intuitive support is offered by the teacher or is consciously or unconsciously produced by the learner herself. There is almost never an absolute correspondence between the concept controlled by the formal definition and the concept controlled tacitly by analogies or paradigmatic models. In principle, the student has to give up her primitive models and rely only on formal definitions but this would risk destroying the productivity of her reasoning processes.

I see the solution only in resorting to metacognitive procedures. The *students should be helped to consider consciously all the implications of the formal definitions taught and to try to apply them to particular cases,* especially those known by the teacher to produce certain difficulties.

Figure 4.3.

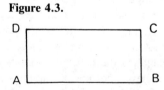

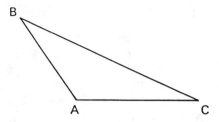

Figure 4.4.

Hershkowitz and Vinner (1982) have shown that only 32% of their subjects correctly draw the altitude in a triangle having an obtuse angle (Figure 4.4). In contrast, 74% of the students gave correct answers for isosceles triangles. Their tacit paradigmatic model for the concept of altitude of a triangle was then related to isosceles triangles. This implies that the teacher has to return to the formal definition of altitude and check for all those types of triangles that remained *outside* the paradigmatically based definition. It may be supposed that, as an effect, instead of one paradigm the student will acquire several paradigms supporting intuitively the correct use of the formal definition.

The primitive representation of force is associated with the image of an individual acting upon an object, trying to push or to pull it. This becomes the general, tacit, paradigmatic model for the concept of force. Consequently, force becomes associated with motion and with the feeling of effort. It is, then, difficult to admit that friction is a force, that an object resting on a table is not only pulled downward by gravitation but also pushed upwards by the table. There is no primitive, intuitive support for such notions. Consequently it is recommendable to reveal in the classroom the original tacit restricted intuitive meaning of the notion of force and to help students broaden their intuitive background by analyzing the implications of the corresponding formal knowledge (mainly the three laws of Newton). Usually the student learns the Newtonian mechanics formally, but care is not taken to render explicit the intuitive constraints imposed by the initial model and their effect on the interpretation of the formal concepts. The paradigmatic resources have to be systematically enriched in order to fit, as much as possible, the conceptual requirements.

Generally, one of the main reasons it is so difficult to accept the three laws of Newton is just the intuitive, primitive model of force. The first law contradicts the idea that motion is the result of an applied force. The second law affirms that acceleration is proportional to force, while, intuitively, one considers that velocity is proportional to force (a force is necessary to maintain a constant velocity). The third law contradicts the primitive idea that motionless objects, being unable of an effort, cannot be the origin of a force.

Common Properties of Tacit Models

Tacit models have in common a number of properties. As a matter of fact, these properties may be identified also in explicit, intuitive models; but in the case of tacit models, their impact on the reasoning process is more striking.

First, a tacit model is usually a spatial representation of a concept or a relationship. When we refer to an "amount of energy," we have tacitly in mind something like the amount of a liquid in a vessel. When we refer to the order of numbers, we imagine that order in a spatial way. The intersection and union of concepts are represented—both tacitly and explictly—as spatial relationships.

Second, we tend to substantialize the representation of phenomena. Time can either be lived directly, intensively, as pure quality or represented as a measurable quantity and then a spatial representation must tacitly or explicitly intervene (Bergson, 1921).

A geometrical point, and a geometrical line become objects in our representation. Heat and electricity are modeled as fluids, and, thus, it becomes possible to represent their conduction through various conductors or their transfer from one system to another.

Third, let me mention the manipulative nature of an intuitive model. In order to be able to represent the particular dynamics of the original, the model should not be a rigid reality. We should be able *to work* with it. The graphs, the fluids, the mechanical representations of psychological phenomena, and so on are subject to modifications, to processes having a practical meaning. The "repression" of a feeling is a mechanical metaphor for a phenomenon for which we have no better term in English. Vectors can be easily manipulated.

Electrons are represented as tiny objects that can be manipulated mentally. The repeated addition model for multiplication and the partitive and the quotative models for division have a practical, manipulatory nature. Three times five means 5 + 5 + 5, and this operation is easily understandable because it has a behavioral, manipulatory meaning. The three diagrams for combinatory analysis are useful not only because they represent spatial displays of possible combinations, but also because they have a manipulatory, constructive character.

Fourth, we tend to produce or to choose models that would be, as much as possible, familiar representations. A model is easily accessible and the results of its manipulations are easily predictable (and these are conditions of good models) if the model belongs to a system that is familiar to us. This is true for both analogical and paradigmatic models. A child would say that a liquid is "a water" because water is the most familiar liquid. A student would tacitly imagine an electrical current as a fluid instead of the electronic model because the fluid representation is more familiar—it belongs to a more familiar domain than the flow of electrons.

This natural tendency toward familiar realities for representing abstract, complex, unaccessible phenomena is probably stronger for tacit than for explicit models.

A force is tacitly represented in relation with the human actions of pulling or pushing, which are very familiar. In addition these actions offer also a subjective complement, the sensation of effort which is also very familiar. The same individual will resort explicitly to the learned vector representation of force, but it happens frequently that the tacit model is, finally, decisive in controlling the student's answers. For instance, a subject is asked to change the trajectory of a moving body in order to hit a certain target. The subject applies a force to the moving body oriented directly to the target, ignoring the existing motion (di Sessa, 1983). In fact, the subject makes his decision not according to the vectorial representation of force and motion but considering only his subjective feeling of a force pushing the object toward the target.

Generally speaking, one may affirm that spontaneous tacit models are usually better integrated than explicit learned ones in the individual's reasoning schemata because they are automatically produced or chosen to fit these schemata.

As we already mentioned, these properties—spatiality, substantiality, manipulativeness, familiarity—are more striking and influential in tacit models, just because of the absence of a direct, conscious control on them.

In our opinion, the success of an instructional process depends, to a great extent, on the knowledge we have about the tacit models that influence the students' interpretations and solving strategies.

References

Bergson, H. (1921). *Essai sur les données immédiates de la conscience*. Paris: Alcan.

Clement, J. (1982, January) Students' preconceptions in introductory mechanics. *American Journal of Physics*, 50 (1), 66–71.

diSessa, A. A. (1983). Phenomenology and the evolution of intuition. In D. Gentner & A. Stevens (Eds.), *Mental models* (pp. 15–33). Hillsdale, NJ: Lawrence Erlbaum Associates, Inc.

Erickson, G., & Tiberghien, A. (1985). Heat and temperature. In R. Driver, E. Gesne, & A. Tiberghien (Eds.), *Children's ideas in science* (pp. 82–84.) Philadelphia, Open University Press.

Fischbein, E., Deri, M., Nello, M. S., & Marino, S. M. (Eds.). (1985). The role of implicit models in solving verbal problems in multiplication and division. *Journal for Research in Mathematics Education, 16*(1), 3–17.

Fischbein, E., Hangea, N., Popescu, I., Radulescu, L., Turcanu, E., & Zamfir, E. (1963). Rolul modelelor in insusirea notiunilor de electricitate de catre elevi. *Revista de Psihologie, 3*, IX, 353–385.

Fischbein, E., Stavy, R., & Ma-Naim, H. (1987). *Factors affecting the naive impetus theory in high school students*. Unpublished manuscript, Tel-Aviv University, School of Education, Tel-Aviv, Israel.

Fischbein, E., Tirosh, D., & Hess, P. (1979). The intuition of infinity. *Educational Studies in Mathematics, 10*, 3–40.

Franklin, A. (1978, April). Inertia in the Middle Ages. *The Physics Teacher*, pp. 201–208.

Green, B. F., McCloskey, M., & Caramazza, A. (1985). The relation of knowledge to problem solving, with examples from kinematics. In S. F. Chipman, J. W. Segal, & R. Glaser (Eds.), *Thinking, learning and skills* (Vol. II, pp. 127–139). Hillsdale, NJ: Lawrence Erlbaum Associates, Inc.

Hershkowitz, R., & Vinner, S. (1982). Basic geometric concepts—definitions and images. In *Proceedings of the Sixth International Conference for the Psychology of Mathematics Education*, pp. 18–22. A. Vermandel (Ed.), Antwerpen: Universitaire Instellig.

Janvier, C. (1981). Use of situations in mathematics education. *Educational Studies in Mathematics, 12*, 113–122.

Kaput, J. J. (1987). Representation systems in mathematics. In C. Janvier (Ed.), *Problems of representation in the teaching and learning of mathematics* (pp. 19–26). Hillsdale, NJ: Lawrence Erlbaum Associates, Inc.

McCloskey, M. (1983). Naive theories of motion. In D. Gentner & A. L. Stevens (Eds.), *Mental models* (pp. 299–323). Hillsdale, NJ: Lawrence Erlbaum Associates, Inc.

McCloskey, M., Washburn, A., & Felch, L. (1983). Intuitive physics: The straight-down belief and its origin. *Journal of Experimental Psychology: Learning, Memory and Cognition, 9*, 636–649.

Viennot, L., (1978). Le raisonnement spontanée en dynamique elémentaire. *Revue Française de Pédagogie, 45*, 16–24.

Wilder, R. L. (1965). *Introduction to the foundations of mathematics.* New York: John Wiley.

5

Implicit and Explicit Knowledge: The Case of Multiplication and Division

Dina Tirosh
Tel-Aviv University

Anna O. Graeber
University of Maryland

Students' mathematical and scientific concepts have been the focus of numerous studies in recent years. These investigations stem from the realization that students build their own conceptions and that these conceptions are not always adequate. If learning is the result of interaction between what the student is taught and his existing concepts, then understanding these concepts is essential for improving science and mathematics education.

One of the widely researched topics in mathematics education is children's and adolescents' concepts of arithmetical operations, especially their skills and thinking processes about addition and subtraction. Recently attention has turned to students' conceptions of multiplication and division. These studies have focused on computational skills, understandings of the operations, and performance in solving multiplication and division word problems.

Several authors have shown that many children and adolescents have difficulty selecting the operation needed to solve multiplication and division word problems. These difficulties have been attributed to the type of word problem, complexity of the language, familiarity with the context, and the order in which the data appear.

Bell, Swan, and Taylor (1981), Hart (1981), Greer and Mangan (1986), Owens (1987), and Sowder (1986) showed that children and adolescents find word problems with decimals considerably more difficult to solve than those with whole numbers. They noted that when children were presented with a series of word problems with the same content, the operation they chose to solve a problem varied with the nature of the given numbers (e.g., whole numbers versus decimal fractions). For instance, when 12- to 15-year-old pupils were asked to write an expression to solve the problem: "The cost of one gallon of petrol is \$1.20. What is the cost of 0.22 gallons of petrol?," the most common answer was $1.20 \div 0.22$. However, when asked to find the cost of 5 gallons of petrol if one gallon cost \$2, the pupils answered correctly: $2 * 5$. Interviews with the pupils revealed that they did not consider it incongruous for the required operation to change when the numbers changed (Bell et al., 1981). Greer (1987) has labeled this phenomenon "non-conservation of operation."

Several researchers have suggested sources for these difficulties. Bell (1982) argued that children frequently attribute the observed properties of operations with whole numbers to operations with all numbers. For example, their experience with whole numbers teaches them that multiplication always makes bigger. Consequently, when the context of a problem suggests that the answer is smaller than one of the given numbers in a multiplication word problem (as in the case of the 0.22 gallons of gasoline problem previously cited), the students have difficulty selecting multiplication as an appropriate operation.

Another possible source of difficulty is children's conceptions of rational numbers, a topic widely investigated in recent years. Behr, Wachsmuth, Post, and Lesh (1984), Carpenter, Corbitt, Kepner, Linquist, and Reys (1981), Hiebert and Wearne (1986), and Kieren (1980), among others, showed that many children and adults have fundamental misconceptions about the nature and use of rational numbers. Behr et al. (1984) and Nesher and Peled (1986) found that learners' previous knowledge about whole numbers interfered with their understanding of rational numbers. Kerslake (1986) observed that many children found it difficult to accept that a rational number is a number and do not realize that the use of rational numbers involves an extension of the number system. She suggests that the introduction of operations with fractions before children have grasped the idea that rational numbers are numbers and before they have made a major adjustment in the meaning of number is a source of confusion and low performance in solving word problems involving rational numbers.

Fischbein, Deri, Nello, and Marino (1985) developed a theory to account for some misconceptions students hold about the operations. The main thesis of this theory is that each arithmetical operation remains linked to an implicit model that imposes its own constraints on the operation. These constraints do not always match those of the formal mathematical operation. The identification of the operation required to solve a simple word problem is influenced by the implicit models. The implicit model, which dominates the learner's reasoning, may prompt her to resolve the conflict by choosing an expression that does not match the problem but does satisfy the constraints of the implicit model.

Fischbein et al. (1985) argued that the implicit model associated with multiplication is repeated addition, in which a number of equivalent collections are put together. This interpretation does not view multiplication as commutative. One factor, the magnitude of each collection, is an operand; the other factor, the number of equivalent collections, is an operator. Thus a repeated addition model confines one to problems with whole number operators and, with the exception of the cases of 0 and 1 as operators, to problems where the product is greater than either factor.

Two implicit models are associated with division: a primitive partitive and a primitive measurement model. In using the primitive partitive model of division, an object or collection of objects is divided into a given whole number of equal parts or subcollections. This model imposes three constraints: The divisor "must" be a whole number; the divisor "must" be less than the dividend; and the quotient "must" be less that the dividend. In using the primitive measurement model, one seeks to determine how many times a given quantity is contained in a larger quantity. The only constraint implied by the primitive measurement model is that the divisor "must" be less than the dividend.

Studies by Bell, Fischbein, and Greer (1984), Fischbein et al. (1985), Greer (1987), Greer and Mangan (1986), Verschaffel, De Corte, and Van Coillie (1988) demonstrated that some of the difficulties children and adolescents encounter in solving verbal multiplication and division problems do indeed seem to stem from the influence of the implicit models. Research has confirmed that preservice teachers' difficulties are similar to children's difficulties in selecting the operation needed to solve word problems involving decimals (Graeber, Tirosh, & Glover, 1989; Greer & Mangan, 1986). Thus research in mathematics education should further explore preservice teachers' conceptions of the operations and should find and share ways to help students overcome the debilitating influence of the primitive models. This chapter deals with such attempts.

Preservice Teachers' Conceptions of Multiplication and Division (Experiment 1)

Our early studies addressed three main questions:

1. Do the implicit models of multiplication and division influence preservice teachers' performance in solving multiplication and division word problems?
2. What explicit beliefs do preservice teachers hold about multiplication and division?
3. How do preservice teachers perform on computational exercises that are counterexamples to the beliefs imposed by the implicit models?

Method

Subjects. The subjects were 136 college preservice elementary teachers enrolled in mathematics content or mathematics method courses in a large university in the southeastern United States. Students typically entered the two-quarter mathematics methods course as juniors, after having completed at least the first of two quarters of the mathematics content courses.

Instruments. Each subject completed the following three paper-and-pencil instruments:

Writing expressions for word problems. Various forms of this instrument were prepared to assess the influence that specific constraints of the implicit models had on preservice teachers' thinking about multiplication and division. Each form included 16 word problems, of which 13 were multiplication and division problems. It is important to note that all the multiplication problems were asymmetrical, that is, problems in which the two quantities multiplied played a psychologically different role in the problem situation. The division problems were of the measurement or partitive type. The influence of the implicit models on other types of multiplication and division problems, such as area problems, was not assessed in this study.

Each form included numerical data that conformed to the implicit models and problems with data that conflicted with the constraints of the primitive models (e.g., a decimal operator, divisor smaller than the dividend, and a decimal divisor). The subjects were asked to write an expression in the form of ''a number, an operation, and a number'' that would lead to the solution of the problem but not to perform the actual operation.

Statements of belief. Subjects were asked to label as ''True'' or ''False'' each of the following seven statements related to the constraints of the primitive models of multiplication and division and to provide a noncomputational justification for each response.

1. In a multiplication problem, the product is greater than either factor.
2. The product of .45 × 90 is less than 90.
3. In a division problem, the divisor can be larger than the dividend.
4. In a division problem, the divisor must be a whole number.
5. The quotient for the problem 60/.65 is greater than 60.
6. The quotient for the problem 70 ÷ ½ is less than 70.
7. In a division problem, the quotient must be less than the dividend.

Computation with decimal numbers. Subjects were asked to compute products or quotients of examples (e.g., 3.2 × 5.14, .38 × 5.14, .75) 3.75, and 15) 5) that violate the beliefs associated with the implicit models. This test was designed to determine whether or not the preservice teachers' performance on these computational tasks was consistent with their beliefs about the operations.

Procedure. The preservice teachers completed the ''statements-of-beliefs'' and the ''computations-with-decimal-numbers'' instruments during a regular class meeting. They completed the ''writing-expressions-for-word-problems'' instrument in a subsequent class. Three or four weeks later, the authors conducted 30–50-minute individual interviews with 71 of the preservice teachers. The interviews were designed to obtain more information about preservice teachers' conceptions of multiplication and division. They were given a number of word problems similar to those they missed on the ''writing-expressions-for-word-problems'' instrument and asked to tell which expression would solve the problem and to explain their logic in selecting the operation.

Results

Influence of implicit models on performance in solving word problems. The preservice teachers' performance in writing expressions for word problems suggested that many of them were influenced by the misconceptions associated with the implicit models. The effect of the repeated addition model of multiplication became evident when their performance on problems with whole number operators was

Table 5.1. Sample of Responses to Multiplication Problems

Problem	Percent Correct	Percent (most common error)
For one cake you need 2.25 grams of spice. How much spice do you need for 15 cakes?	99	
For one kilogram of meatloaf you use 15 grams of salt. How much salt do you need for 1.25 kilograms of meatloaf?	72	12 (1.25 ÷ 15)
One kilogram of detergent is used in making 15 kilograms of soap. How much soap can be made from .75 kilograms of detergent?	59	17 (15 ÷ .75)

compared with their performance on similar problems with noninteger operators. The data, a sample of which is shown in Table 5.1, indicate that word problems with noninteger operators, especially operators less than one, proved troublesome.

The most common erroneous response to a multiplication problem that included a decimal operator less than one was a division expression. The context of these problems suggests that the answer ought to be less than the given operand. The interviews lent support to the assumption that the incorrect expressions resulted from misconceptions: in order to obtain a larger result multiply, to get a smaller result divide. These misconceptions are consistent with the constraints imposed by the repeated addition model.

In solving division word problems, the preservice teachers were more successful in writing expressions for problems that conformed to the implicit models than for those that violated the models. Problems with a whole number divisor greater than a whole number dividend resulted in a high percent of incorrect responses. Typically these incorrect responses were division expressions in which the role of the divisor and the dividend were reversed (see Table 5.2). This indicates the influence of the constraint of both the primitive models of division, "the dividend must be greater than the divisor." The influence of this constraint is most clearly seen when comparing the preservice teachers' responses to word problems that are similar in context and contain similar numerical data but differ in the roles the numbers play.

Division by a positive decimal divisor less than one violates "the divisor must be a whole number" and "the quotient must be less than the dividend" constraints of the primitive partitive model. Preservice teachers were more successful in writing expressions for word problems that involved division by a whole number greater than the dividend than for word problems that involved division by a decimal. Partitive problems with decimal divisors proved to be extremely difficult: The success rate in these problems was 54%. Interviews indicated that the constraints associated with the partitive models influenced the teachers' responses even when they solved measurement-type problems with decimal divisors. Thus, 32% of the preservice teachers incorrectly wrote the expression .65 × 5 for the measurement problem, "Girls club cookies are packed .65 pounds to a box. How many boxes can be filled with 5 pounds of cookies?" During interviews, a number of the preservice

Table 5.2. Sample of Responses to Division Problems

Problem	Percent Correct	Percent (most common error)
Partitive Problem		
The Yale desk encyclopedia is shipped three copies to a box. If 3 of the copies weigh 13 pounds, how much does each copy weigh?	90	
Necklaces are shipped 13 to a box. If 13 of the necklaces weigh 3 pounds, how much does each necklace weigh?	42	56 (13:3)
Measurement Problems		
A paperhanger needs 3 rolls of paper to do a room. How many similar rooms can the paperhanger do with 13 rolls of the same wallpaper?	95	
A paperhanger needs 13 rolls of wallpaper to finish a job. How much of the job was done with 3 rolls of wallpaper?	32	65 (13:3)

teachers explained that they rejected division as the appropriate operation because they knew the answer ought to be larger than five. Interviewees from among the 8% who wrote the incorrect expression .65 ÷ 5 claimed that "the divisor cannot be a decimal." These commonly voiced beliefs, "division always makes smaller" and "the divisor must be a whole number," are only constraints of the primitive partitive model.

During interviews, the influence of "the divisor must be a whole number" constraint of the partitive model was observed even among those who wrote correct expressions for division word problems involving decimal dividends smaller than whole number divisors. Some of these preservice teachers reported that they first reversed the role of the divisor and the dividend to get a dividend greater than the divisor. However, they were then confronted with decimal divisors and reverted to the "correct" answer. Thus, it seems that the faulty rule, "the divisor must be a whole number," has greater strength than the faulty rule about the relative size of the divisor and the dividend.

Of the two models of division, the partitive model appears to dominate the measurement model. This is inferred from the subjects' higher success rate on partitive problems than on measurement problems. Moreover, when asked what division meant, most of the subjects were able to provide only a partitive interpretation of division.

These data indicate that when faced with word problems containing numerical data that conflict with the constraints of the primitive models, any of the preservice teachers wrote expressions that did not match the problem but did match the constraints of the implicit models. Thus, it seems that preservice teachers' performance in solving asymmetrical multiplication word problems and measurement and partitive division word problems was heavily influenced by the repeated addition model of multiplication and by the primitive partitive model of division.

Explicit beliefs about multiplication and division. The majority of the preservice teachers responded correctly to six of the seven statements about the two operations (see Table 5.3). Only the statement, "The quotient must be less than the dividend," deviated from the pattern, with 52% of the preservice teachers incorrectly agreeing with it.

The preservice teachers' justifications for both correct and incorrect statements can be placed in three categories:

- *Reliance on the domain of whole numbers.* For example, about 40% of the preservice teachers relied on specific examples from the domain of whole numbers, justifying the falsity of "the product is always greater than either factor" statement by citing cases of 0 or 1 as factors.
- *The dominance of the implicit models of the operations.* For example, 50% of the preservice teachers' faulty responses to the statement, "In a multiplication problem, the product is greater than either factor," were based on a description of multiplication as repeated addition.
- *Procedural knowledge about the operations.* In responding to the statement "the divisor must be a whole number," 12% of the students argued that "even if you have a decimal number for a divisor, it must be changed to a whole number." On the other hand 14% of the students who responded correctly to this statement specifically mentioned the need to "move the decimal" point.

Procedural knowledge (e.g., change the decimal divisor to a whole number) appears to be translated into beliefs about operations (you cannot divide by a decimal) and is used like conceptual knowledge to justify responses such as "The divisor must be a whole number."

Preservice teachers' computational skills. Table 5.4 shows the high rate of success the preservice teachers had with the four computational exercises. Eighty-

Table 5.3. Responses to Statements About Multiplication and Division

Statements	Percent Correct
In a multiplication problem, the product is greater than either factor	85
The product of .45 × 90 is less than 90	90
In a division problem, the divisor can be larger than the dividend	87
In a division problem, the divisor must be a whole number	80
The quotient for 60 ÷ 65 is greater than 60	62
The quotient for 70 ÷ 1/2 is less than 70	60
In a division problem, the quotient must be less than the dividend	45

Table 5.4. Success on Multiplication and Division Computation

Item	Percent Correct
3.2 × 5.14	93
.38 × 5.14	91
.75)3.75	87
15)5	89

six percent of the subjects computed all the examples correctly and none computed all incorrectly. Thus, most of the preservice teachers were able to correctly compute examples that violated the beliefs associated with the implicit models.

Inconsistencies in beliefs about the operations. A review of the data from the studies described here reveals discrepancies between preservice teachers' implicit and explicit knowledge about multiplication and division. The preservice teachers' responses in writing expressions to multiplication and division word problems and the justifications they offered in describing their selection of an operation for a word problem are assumed to reveal their implicit knowledge about the operations. Their responses to statements about multiplication and division and their performance on computational examples reveal their explicit knowledge. The apparent inconsistencies are classified into four main categories.

1. Inconsistencies between explicit and implicit beliefs
   - Eight-five percent argued that in a multiplication problem the product is *not* always greater than either factor. Yet, 40–45% indicated that you find the cost of .75 of a bolt by dividing the cost of the whole bolt by .75 because you want an answer less than the cost of the whole bolt.
   - Eighty-seven percent argued that the divisor can be greater than the dividend. However, about 50% indicated that you find the answer for "12 friends shared 5 pounds of cookies, how many pounds did each get?" with the expression 12 ÷ 5.

2. Inconsistencies between implicit beliefs and computational skills
   - Eighty-nine percent correctly computed 15) 5.0. However, about 50% indicated that you find the answer for "12 friends shared 5 pounds of cookies, how many pounds did each get?" with the expression 12 ÷ 5.
   - Ninety-one percent correctly computed .38 × 5.14. In contrast, the average percent correct on word problems with a decimal operator less than one was 50%.

3. Inconsistencies between explicit beliefs and computational skills
   - Eighty-seven percent correctly computed .75) 3.75 as 5. In contrast, only 45% correctly identified the statement "the quotient must be smaller than the dividend" as false.
   - Sixteen percent of the preservice teachers incorrectly agreed with the state-

ment: "In a division problem, the divisor must be a whole number" and yet these same subjects correctly computed the example $.75 \overline{)\,3.75}$.

4. Inconsistencies among explicit beliefs about the operations

   - Forty-five percent argued that the product in multiplication is not always greater than either factor and yet agreed that the quotient must be less than the dividend. This is true despite the fact that these same preservice teachers' written justifications and oral comments during interviews show that they recognized multiplication and division as inverse operations.

   - Thirty-six percent correctly agreed that the quotient must be less than the dividend and yet correctly identified the relative size of the quotient and dividend for $60/.65$ or $70 \div \frac{1}{2}$.

   - Sixteen percent incorrectly argued that the divisor must be a whole number and yet correctly identified the relative size of the quotient and dividend for $60/.65$ or $70 \div \frac{1}{2}$.

Substantial discrepancies exist between the students' explicit knowledge about multiplication and division and the implicit knowledge evidenced in their selection of these operations to solve word problems. Similar differences were found between the subjects' computational skill and their implicit beliefs. Some may ascribe these inconsistencies to the fact that different types of knowledge (explicit, implicit) are being compared. More vexing, however, are the discrepancies among the preservice teachers' responses to explicit statements about the operations.

Conclusions and Discussion

This inquiry sheds light on preservice teachers' conceptions of multiplication and division. They prove to be quite successful at computing multiplication and division examples involving decimals, and they generally hold adequate explicit beliefs about the operations. However, their performance in solving multiplication and division word problems involving decimals is rather poor and reflects the influence of the constraints of the implicit models. Thus, implicit models exert a stronger influence on preservice teachers' word-problem solving skills than do their explicit beliefs about multiplication and division.

The discrepancies found among preservice teachers' performance in solving word problems, their performance on computational examples, and their professed explicitly held beliefs indicate that they had not integrated *all* their knowledge and skills about multiplication and division. However, their implicit beliefs, considered alone, appear to be well integrated and are consistently explained by the primitive models of multiplication and division.

It is noteworthy that the difficulties faced by the preservice teachers are similar to those faced by children solving these problems. This lends further weight to the importance of working with preservice teachers on their conceptions in an attempt to prevent a vicious learning–teaching–learning cycle. Preservice teachers must be given an education that will help them overcome their misconceptions about the operations, sharpen their awareness of the impact of the implicit models on their thinking, and teach them to develop efficient strategies to monitor and control the impact of the models on their and their students' thinking. Special attention should be paid to integrating their knowledge about the operations.

The difficulty in getting students to reconstruct their knowledge about scientific and mathematical concepts is recognized by many researchers (Clement, 1982; Driver, Guesne, & Tiberghien, 1985; Owens, 1987; Sowder, 1986). Drawing from learning theories on the difference between acquiring and reconstructing knowledge, the acquisition of information consistent with the students' existing knowledge appears easier than acquisition that requires conceptual change or reorganization. The case of preservice teachers' conceptions of multiplication and division is not only a matter of acquisition of new information, but also one of changing existing conceptions and reorganizing knowledge. The changes needed in preservice teachers' understanding of multiplication and division with decimals may be particularly difficult to achieve since their implicit knowledge seems so consistent and well integrated with itself. Further, the curricular emphasis on computation does not challenge their understanding of the operations. The preservice teachers' good facility with computational tasks provides them with many experiences of success. Thus, there is a lack of some conditions that are assumed to be necessary for motivating learners to change their conceptions.

Overcoming Preservice Teachers' Misconceptions About Multiplication and Division

The rest of this chapter describes two small-scale, short-term interventions aimed at helping preservice teachers reconstruct their knowledge about division. In the first study, the conflict teaching method was used to help preservice teachers overcome their explicitly held misconception about the relative size of the dividend and the quotient. The second study involved an interactive computer program developed to increase the preservice teachers' awareness of the sources of their difficulty in solving division word problems with a divisor greater than the dividend and to help improve their performance on these problems.

The subjects in the study were drawn from the same preservice elementary teacher population and the instruments used in the two studies were similar. In both studies the subjects were elementary preservice teachers enrolled in one of the mathematics content or method courses in a large university in the southeastern United States. A pretest and posttest form of three different instruments was used. They were essentially the same instruments as those used in the study previously described ("writing an expression for word problems," "statements of beliefs," and "computation with decimal numbers"). The posttest form of each instrument was similar, but not identical, to the pretest.

Exploring the Conflict Teaching Method (Experiment 2)

The conflict teaching method is based on Piaget's (1976) notion of cognitive conflict, which suggests that significant cognitive progress is made through a three-stage process involving equilibrium: (a) cognitive equilibrium at a lower developmental stage, (b) cognitive disequilibrium induced by an awareness of contradiction in data, and (c) cognitive equilibrium at a higher developmental stage as a result of reconceptualizing in a way that resolves the original conflict. Piaget argued that when a child is able to see a previously unnoticed problematic aspect of a concept, he is likely to feel uncomfortable with that concept. He attempts to return to a new state of equilibrium by seeking to fit this newly noticed aspect of the concept into his own existing schema. The "cognitive teaching" approach, developed by Swan (1983), was designed to involve students in discussion of, and reflection on, their errors and misconceptions. One intent of this approach was to help learners become aware that their conceptions were inadequate and in need of modification.

Underlying this approach is the assumption that a necessary stage in this process is the learner's realization of the inherent conflict between two elements in a situation. One way to create this realization is by increasing the learner's awareness of inconsistencies in her own thinking. It was assumed that raising a preservice teacher's awareness of inconsistencies in her own thinking about multiplication and division would create a feeling that "something is wrong." This feeling could motivate one to search for a resolution and acquire a new conceptualization that resolves the conflict. We attempted to raise a cognitive conflict in the preservice teachers' minds by challenging the widely held misconception, "The quotient must be less than the dividend," with the result of a division computation example with a decimal divisor less than one.

The main goals of this study were

1. To assess the extent to which the preservice teachers realize the inconsistency between their stated misconception and the correct result of their computation of division examples with decimals less than one.
2. To determine the efficacy of this approach in helping preservice teachers abandon this misconception and replace it with an accurate belief about the size of the dividend and the quotient. In other words, would the method change their explicit belief?
3. To study the influence of this method on preservice teachers' performance in solving division word problems that are related to this misconception. That is, what is the influence of this method on their implicit beliefs?

Procedure. The three pretest instruments were administered to one male and 57 female preservice elementary teachers at the beginning of the academic quarter. Researchers then conducted individual interviews with the 21 preservice teachers who correctly computed $3.75 \div .75$, but had incorrectly agreed with the written statement: "The quotient must be less than the dividend." In all of the interviews the preservice teachers were asked: (a) What does division mean to you?; (b) are there any restrictions on the divisor, dividend, or quotient (can any kind of number play any of these roles?); and (c) are there any restriction on the relative size of the dividend and the quotient? Preservice teachers who responded correctly to each of the questions during the interview were asked if they knew why they had previously responded differently to the question about the relative size of the dividend and the quotient. Preserve teachers who during the interview again expressed the notion that the quotient must be less than the dividend were orally asked, "What is four divided by five-tenths?" If necessary, they were then encouraged to make an observation about their calculation and their previously expressed belief.

All interviews were audiorecorded and transcribed. A minimum of three weeks elapsed between the interview and the administration of the posttest instruments.

Results

Realization of conflict. Of the 21 preservice teachers interviewed, six indicated uncertainty about their previous statements concerning the relative size of the dividend and the quotient at the beginning of the interview and expressed their need to check it. These preservice teachers wrote counterexamples, such as 4 ÷ ½, rephrased their statement of belief, and explained their previous incorrect response by arguing that they had thought only about whole numbers.

The 15 preservice teachers who stated, with certainty, that the quotient must be less than the dividend were asked to calculate examples like 4 ÷ .5. Following this calculation, three immediately rephrased their belief, and four did so after a second prompt such as: "What was the answer to the original problem? Does this answer, 8, suggest anything to you?" Eight preservice teachers did not notice a contradiction, stating they were not sure if the quotient to the original example, .5 ÷ 4, was ⁸⁄₁₀ or 8. An example of one such conversation follows:

I: You said that the quotient is always less than the dividend.
S: Yes.
I: So now I'll ask you to solve the problem 4 ÷ .5.
S: [writes .5) 4] I'll move the decimal here to the right, add a zero to the 4, and I'll get 8.
I: What would the answer to 4 ÷ .5 be?
S: Eight or .8? I don't know.

These eight preservice teachers were then asked to calculate 4 ÷ ½. After calculating, three realized the contradiction, and the remaining five incorrectly argued that 4 divided by ½ is 2. These five were then asked to try and use the measurement interpretation to calculate 4 divided by ½. To help them with this task, the interviewer modeled the measurement interpretation of division using whole numbers (e.g., If I write 8 ÷ 2, it can mean: How many twos are there in eight?). The subjects were then encouraged to apply this interpretation to the problem 4 ÷ .5; all were able to apply the interpretation. Given one or more cues and prompts (e.g., "What does it tell you about division?" or "Look at the dividend and the quotient."), four of them realized a conflict.

One preservice teacher did not experience a conflict. At different times during the interview, she stated that ".5 equals ½" and, incorrectly, that "4 ÷ .5 is .8 and 4 ÷ ½ = 2." Her comments reflected her conviction that mathematics is a series of meaningless rules. For her .5 and ½ were not different symbols representing the same quantity but completely different mathematical entities obeying different rules.

Changes in explicit beliefs. Table 5.5 shows that the preservice teachers did considerably better on all three belief statements in the posttest. The types of knowledge students used in justifying their conclusions about the beliefs statements concerning the relative size of the dividend and quotient changed from pretest to posttest. The majority of justifications written on the pretest suggested that the preservice teachers used the primitive partitive model of division or procedural knowledge about the division algorithm. Whenever possible they calculated. Posttest justifications of the first statement included counterexamples or general statements, such as "If the divisor is a decimal less than one, then the quotient is greater than the dividend." Many preservice teachers used the measurement interpretation of division to justify the second and the third statements. A typical response was: "60 ÷ ¼ means how many quarters are there in 60. There are 4 quarters in one, therefore there are more than 60 quarters in 60."

Changes in implicit beliefs. The preservice teachers' performance in writing expressions for word problems improved dramatically from pretest to posttest. On the pretest, 33% of the responses to the multiplication problems with a positive operator less than one were correct, and 64% of the answers to division problems with decimal divisor less than one were correct. On the posttest, 64% of the former and 98% of the latter were correct.

The change in overall performance was not a result of drastic improvement by a few. In fact, 14 of the 21 preservice teachers improved their performance, and the remaining seven, including the preservice teacher who did not experience a conflict in the interviews, wrote exactly the same number of correct expressions on the posttest as they had on the pretest. Furthermore, a comparison of the responses to the two tests showed that the improvement was consistent with progress in overcoming the misconception that division always makes smaller. For example, 10 of the 14 incorrect expressions written in the pretest for the first multiplication word problem were division expressions. Since the content of the problem suggested that the answer was less than the operand, it is reasonable to hypothesize that the belief

Table 5.5. Responses to Statements About Division on Pretest and Posttest

Statements	Pretest	Posttest
Quotient is less than dividend	0	—
Dividend must be greater than quotient	—	20
10 ÷ .65 is greater than 10	8	—
70 ÷ .35 is greater than 70	—	20
70 + 1/2 is less than 70	9	—
60 ÷ 1/4 is less than 60	—	19

Note—Dash indicates item not administered; $n = 21$.

that division always makes smaller influenced their responses. On the posttest, only five of the preservice teachers wrote a division expression for a similar word problem.

Conclusions and discussion. The results suggest that the conflict teaching approach was quite effective in helping preservice teachers overcome their explicitly held misconception and form more accurate conceptions about division. Although the issue of choice of operation was not dealt with directly, performance in writing expressions for word problems improved considerably. The fact that some posttest errors could still be attributed to the misconception seems to confirm that awareness of misconceptions is not a sufficient condition for better conceptualization and improved performance (Flavell, 1977).

A surprisingly large number of preservice teachers were ready to change the result of the correct computational example and not their explicit misconception. One possible explanation is that this misconception is very strongly rooted in learners' minds and so resistant to change that they were willing to "adjust" their correct computational skills so as not to contradict their belief. It is possible that they had only an instrumental understanding of the division algorithm.

Some students had difficulty realizing a conflict since they were not convinced that the quotient of the original problem was the same as the quotient obtained after "the decimal points were moved." In fact, given a division example with a decimal divisor less than one (e.g., $.5\overline{)4}$) the final algorithmic form $(5\overline{)40})$ does indeed present a quotient less than the dividend and may even reinforce the belief that the quotient is always less than the dividend. In this case, lack of a meaningful interpretation of the division algorithm apparently reduced both the desire and the likelihood of finding a means to resolve the conflict by overcoming the misconception. Thus, when trying to bring a student to realize a conflict, care must be taken that the student is highly confident in the knowledge to be used as a trigger. If he is not confident in that knowledge, he may adjust his fragile knowledge and maintain his misconception.

The only misconception about division held explicitly by a large portion of the preservice teachers was the one about the relative size of the dividend. However, other misconceptions about the operations seemed to be held implicitly by a sizable portion of them. Many investigators agree that awareness of misconceptions is necessary to overcome them. According to these researchers, the implicit/explicit nature of the misconception has a crucial effect on the instructional path chosen to help learners overcome the debilitating effects of the misconceptions (Fischbein, 1987; Strauss, 1987; Strike & Posner, 1985). Explicitly held ones, such as "the quotient must be less than the dividend," require a situation in which the beliefs are challenged. Implicitly held beliefs, such as "the divisor must be a whole number," or "the product is greater than either factor," first requires making the preservice teachers aware of their behavior and the likely implicit beliefs responsible for it. One way to accomplish this task is to give preservice teachers a series of word problems to solve, to draw their attention to systematic mistakes they make, and help them find the reason underlying their inadequate performance. Exploring the extent to which this method helped preservice teachers become aware of their implicit misconceptions was one of the main goals of our third experiment.

Exploring Estimation and Diagrams in a Computer Environment (Experiment 3)

As previously mentioned, a substantial number of preservice teachers encounter difficulty in solving word problems with whole number divisors greater than whole number dividends. This difficulty seems to arise from their implicit belief that "the dividend must be greater that the divisor." In this study we explored the potential of an computer instructional program designed to (a) increase the preservice teachers' awareness of their misconception and (b) provide them with strategies to improve their performance in solving these division word problems.

Two types of computer programs were developed: a tutorial program and a drill and practice program designed as a control treatment. The tutorial program was developed after interviews revealed that the majority of preservice teachers accepted diagrams and estimations as appropriate means to visualize the problems and assess the correctness of their answers. Thus, it was assumed that a tutoring computer program that implements the diagrams and the estimation strategies might help preservice teachers improve their performance in solving word problems. The drill and practice program gives the learner immediate feedback about whether responses are right or wrong and provides opportunities to correct the latter.

Procedure
The three pretest instruments were administered to 59 preservice elementary teachers at the beginning of an academic quarter. For this experiment the write-an-expression-for-a-word-problem instrument was revised to include 13 division problems, four multiplication problems, two subtraction problems, and one addition problem. Six of the division problems had a divisor larger than the dividend. The 32 subjects who were included in the study reversed the role of the divisor and the dividend in answering two or more of these six word problems. Sixteen of these subjects were assigned to a tutorial program and sixteen to a drill and practice computer program. In assigning these subjects to one of two treatment groups every attempt was made to balance the groups with respect to (a) number of correct responses to division problems with the divisor greater than the dividend, (b) number of correct responses to the remaining seven division problems, (c) number of correct responses to the nondivision word problems, (d) performance on the computation-with-decimal-numbers instrument, and (e) students' reactions to the beliefs statement, "In a division problem, the divisor must be larger than the dividend." Immediately after their experience with a computer program, they were interviewed to see if they could identify the reasons they were assigned to work with a computer program. Three weeks later, the subjects were given another form of the three instruments used in the pretest.

Tutoring computer program. This program presented eight division word problems one by one. The problems included four with a divisor greater than the dividend and four with a divisor smaller than the dividend. For each problem, three sets of cues were available: (a) a diagram that illustrated the word problem, (b) a question that required the student to estimate if the answer was greater than or less than one, and (c) a question about the relative size of the divisor and the dividend. The preservice teachers received these cues in the order just listed. Clues were only provided upon the student's request or in response to an incorrect answer. The sequence of cues was terminated when the student gave a correct response and indicated with certainty that the answer was correct. If the student finished the set of cues without giving the correct response, the correct response and rationale were provided. After completing the work on each of the four problems with the divisor greater than the dividend, the student was shown a statement about the relative size of the dividend, divisor, and the quotient of that problem.

The drill and practice computer program. This computer program included the same problems used in the tutorial program. Again the problems were presented on the screen one at a time. The subject had three opportunities to provide the expression needed to solve a problem. After each trial the subject got an immediate response about the correctness of the answer. If the subject gave incorrect answers in each of the three trials, the correct answer was provided. No reference was made to the relative size of the divisor and the dividend.

Results
Most of the students in both the tutorial and the drill and practice groups were able to respond correctly to division problems when assistance or feedback was available. Eleven of the 16 preservice teachers in the tutoring group and 13 of the 16 in the drill group wrote fewer reversed expressions on the delayed posttest than on the pretest. The number of expressions for which the role of the divisor and dividend were reversed decreased from 44 on the pretest to 23 on the posttest in the tutoring group and from 41 to 18 in the drill group.

After the treatment, 10 of the 16 subjects assigned to the tutorial program attributed their poor performance on the pretest to their tendency to divide by the smaller number, and only four of the students in the drill program made such an attribution. The remaining 12 subjects in the drill and practice program attributed their assignment to the treatment to careless errors.

Three weeks after instruction, all the students from the tutorial group gave a correct response to the statement about the relative size of the divisor and the dividend, whereas two students from the drill group still claimed incorrectly that the dividend must always be greater than the divisor.

Conclusions and Discussion
The results show that the two computer programs were equally effective in improving the preservice teachers' performance in writing expressions for division word

problems with divisors greater than the dividends. However, the tutorial program was more effective than the drill and practice program in increasing the preservice teachers' awareness of their tendency to divide by the smaller number. The tutorial program was also apparently more effective in helping preservice teachers change their explicit misconception about the relative size of the dividend and the divisor.

The subjects in the drill and practice group, who apparently were not aware of their tendency to divide by the smaller number, were just as successful in writing expressions for division word problems as the students in the tutorial group, who did identify their misconception. This might suggest that the awareness of their misconception did not play a *major* role in improving their performance in solving division word problems. This conclusion might be premature, since in this study the delayed posttest was administered only three weeks after the treatment. It is also possible that those who did become aware of their misconceptions might retain their learning for a longer period of time. Another interpretation of the results of this study is that the experience of solving word problems that violated the constraints was by itself a powerful means of changing implicit knowledge. These are, of course, hypotheses in need of testing.

Moreover, it is crucial that preservice teachers become knowledgeable about possible misconceptions their future students may hold. Thus, it is not enough to help the preservice teachers improve their own performance. It is equally important to increase their awareness of common misconceptions and lead them to the point where they can consciously monitor their own and their students' thinking.

General Conclusions and Educational Implications

Our experiments have shown that a substantial portion of preservice elementary teachers hold inadequate implicit beliefs about multiplication and division. These beliefs are rarely reflected in their performance on computation tasks. Even explicitly stated probes about the operations may not elicit the faulty conceptions that nevertheless seem to influence their performance in solving multiplication and division word problems. Thus, a careful diagnosis of preservice teachers' conceptions of multiplication and division must include examination of their ability to solve word problems as well as individual interviews aimed at exposing their conceptions.

The studies described here reveal three main sources for the misconceptions exhibited by the preservice teachers: reliance on examples from the domain of whole numbers, dominance of the implicit models, and an instrumental understanding of the computational procedures. Since the implicit models for these operations are true in the domain of whole numbers and a number of them are supported by the procedures for operating with whole numbers, the usual curricular sequence nurtures the associated misconceptions. This may be reflected in the fact that the preservice teachers appeared to have implicit knowledge that was firmly established (well integrated), whereas their explicit knowledge was frequently contradictory and fragile.

The sources of the misconceptions suggest two global strategies the curriculum might employ to lessen the influence of these misconceptions: (a) The early curriculum might be revised to provide more models that can be applied not only to whole numbers but also to rational numbers, and (b) the transition from the whole number domain to the rational number domain might contrast the properties of operations in the two domains. In order to accomplish such changes, teachers must be able to recognize the common misconceptions, know how to help students control their influence, and be able to monitor their own and their students' misconceptions.

This chapter also reported on initial explorations of two strategies that can be used to help preservice elementary teachers become aware of and control the influence of two specific misconceptions about division. Other strategies that theory suggests for helping learners overcome misconceptions about multiplication and division are

- Present models of the operations that apply to a wide range of numbers: for example, the area model of multiplication and the measurement interpretation of division. Using these models first with whole numbers and then with decimals may give the learner more confidence in them and their results.
- Develop their concept of rational numbers. This may be done in a number of ways: by presenting the history of the development of the concept of rational numbers; emphasizing the difficulties that mathematicians experience in accepting the rational numbers as numbers and the sources of these difficulties; presenting different interpretations of rational numbers; discussing the isomorphism between the different notation (decimal, common fraction) of rational numbers.
- Emphasize the similarities and differences between the properties of the operations in the two domains. This may be accomplished by contrasting operations involving whole numbers with those involving rational numbers less than one and by discussing the "gains and losses" that result from this extension. Emphasis should be given to discussion of all the misconceptions associated with the primitive models, their relationships, and roots.
- Present multiplication and division as formal, abstract mathematical operations by emphasizing that (a) multiplication and division are binary operations and (b) the models are not isomorphic to the operations and therefore impose some irrelevant constraints on the operations.
- Emphasize conceptual understanding of the operations by using estimation and even mental arithmetic to find solutions to simple multiplication and division exercises involving decimals.
- Study patterns such as $24 \div 24$, $24 \div 12$, $24 \div 6$, $24 \div 4$, $24 \div 2$, $24 \div 1$, $24 \div .5$, $24 \div .25$ to help the learners accept a quotient that is greater than the dividend or a product less than one or more factors.

These and many other suggestions for improving learners' understanding of multiplication and division have been proffered on theoretical grounds. Hart (1989, Foreword) has noted that

Mathematics educators can be identified by their enthusiasm for mathematics and for the abundance of their "good ideas" on how to make others like/use/succeed in mathematics. This enthusiasm without evidence on effectiveness may be a disservice to teachers and children. We need copious research in classrooms to validate what are now firmly and fervently held beliefs before we start putting new "good ideas" into the schools.

Our work exploring two strategies for helping preservice teachers reinforces the view that the implementation of strategies that seem obvious from a theoretical perspective may have unanticipated ramifications. For example, theory clearly suggests that learners who are not aware of their misconceptions are less likely to apply them than are learners who are aware of their misconceptions. The results of our study suggest that awareness of misconceptions may not be sufficient for changing behavior. Perhaps it is also essential for learners to have experience with techniques for monitoring the debilitating effects of the primitive models. This is one example of a case where application of theory leads to new insights into what is needed to improve instruction.

The apparent success of the drill and practice computer program suggests that experience in solving word problems that violate the constraints of the primitive models helps improve performance in solving such word problems. Recent studies indicate that students' opportunities for solving word problems with numerical data that violate the constraints of the primitive models are very limited (Graeber & Baker, 1991, 1992). These findings raise the recurring question, "What is the role experience plays in forming conceptions and overcoming misconceptions?" Other issues that need further research include: Is explicit awareness of a misconception a necessary stage in controlling the influence of the misconception? and, How, if at all, should intervention strategies designed to impact explicit as opposed to implicit misconceptions differ?

References

Behr, M., Wachsmuth, I., Post, T., & Lesh, R. (1984). Order and equivalence of rational numbers: A clinical teaching experiment. *Journal for Research in Mathematics Education, 15*, 323–341.

Bell, A. W. (1982). Diagnosing students misconceptions. *Australian Mathematics Teacher, 38*, 6–10.

Bell, A., Fischbein, E., & Greer, B. (1984). Choice of operation in verbal arithmetic problems: The effects of number size, problem structure and content. *Education Studies in Mathematics, 15*, 129–147.

Bell, A., Swan, M., & Taylor, G. (1981). Choice of operation in verbal problems with decimal numbers. *Educational Studies in Mathematics, 12*, 399–420.

Carpenter, T. C., Corbitt, M. K., Kepner, H. S., Lindquist, M. N., & Reys, R. E. (1981). Decimals: Results and implications from national assessment. *Arithmetic Teacher, 28*, 34–37.

Clement, J. (1982). Students' perceptions in introductory mechanics. *American Journal of Physics, 50*, 151–169.

Driver, R., Guesne, E., & Tiberghien, A. (1985). (Eds.). *Children's ideas in science*. Milton Keynes, England: Open University Press.

Fischbein, E. (1987). *Intuition in science and mathematics*. Dordrecht, Holland: Reidel.

Fischbein, E., Deri, M., Nello, M., & Marino, M. (1985). The role of implicit models in solving problems in multiplication and division. *Journal of Research in Mathematics Education, 16*, 3–17.

Flavell, J. (1977). *Cognitive development*. Englewood Cliffs, NJ: Prentice Hall.

Graeber, A., & Baker, K. (1991). Curriculum materials and misconceptions concerning multiplication and division. *Focus on Learning Problems in Mathematics, 13*, 25–38.

Graeber, A., & Baker, K. (1992). Little into big is the way it always is. *Arithmetic Teacher, 39*, 18–21.

Graeber, A., Tirosh, D., & Glover, R. (1989). Preservice teachers' misconceptions in solving verbal problems in multiplication and division. *Journal for Research in Mathematics Education, 16*, 3–17.

Greer, B. (1987). Nonconservation of multiplication and division involving decimals. *Journal for Research in Mathematics Education, 18*, 37–45.

Greer, B., & Mangan, C. (1986). Choice of operations: From 10-year-old to students teachers. In *Proceedings of the Tenth International Group for the Psychology of Mathematics Education* (pp. 27–32), London, England.

Hart, K. (1981). *Children's understanding of mathematics: (11–16)*. London: John Murray.

Hart, K. (1989). Foreword. In B. Greer & G. Mulhern (Eds.), *New directions in mathematics education*. London: Routledge.

Hiebert, J., & Wearne, D. (1986). Procedures over concepts: The acquisition of decimal number knowledge. In J. Hiebert (Ed.), *Conceptual and procedural knowledge: The case of mathematics* (pp. 199–223). Hillsdale, NJ: Lawrence Erlbaum Associates, Inc.

Kerslake, D. (1986). *Fractions: Children's strategies and errors. A report of the strategies and errors in secondary mathematics project*. Windsor, England: Nfer-Nelson.

Kieren, T. E. (1980). Knowing rational numbers: Ideas and symbols. In M. M. Lindquist (Ed.), *Selected issues in mathematics education* (pp. 69–81). Berkeley, CA: McCutchan.

Nesher, P., & Peled, I. (1986). Shifts in reasoning. *Educational Studies in Mathematics, 17*, 67–79.

Owens, D. T. (1987). Decimal multiplication in grade seven. In J. C. Bergeron, N. Herscovics, & C. Kieren (Eds.), *Proceedings of the Eleventh International Conference for the Psychology of Mathematics Education* (Vol. 2, pp. 423–429). Montreal, Canada.

Piaget, J. (1976). *The grasp of consciousness: Action and concept in young child*. Cambridge, MA: Harvard University Press.

Sowder, L. (1986). Strategies children use in solving problems. *Proceedings of the Tenth International Conference for the Psychology of Mathematics Education* (pp. 469–474), London, England.

Strauss, S. (1987). Educational-developmental psychology and school learning. In L. Liben (Ed.), *Development and learning: Convergence of conflict*. Hillsdale, NJ: Lawrence Erlbaum Associates, Inc.

Strike, K., & Posner, G. (1985). A conceptual change view of learning and understanding. In L. West & A. Pines (Eds.), *Cognitive structure and conceptual change* (pp. 211–230). Orlando, FL: Academic Press.

Swan, M. (1983). *Teaching decimal place value: A comparative study of ''conflict'' and ''positive only'' approaches*. Nottingham, England: Shell Centre for Mathematical Education, University of Nottingham.

Verschaffel, L., De Corte, E., & Van Coillie, V. (1988). Specifying the multiplier effect on children's solutions of simple multiplication word problem. In A. Borbas (Ed.), *Proceedings of the Twelfth International Conference for the Psychology of Mathematics Education* (Vol. 2, pp. 617–624), Weszprem, Hungary.

6

Children's Construction of Meaning for Arithmetical Words: A Curriculum Problem

Leslie P. Steffe
University of Georgia

In the context of a curriculum improvement study conducted by the Center for the Learning and Teaching of Elementary Subjects at Michigan State University, I was asked to review a mathematics textbook series that is widely used in the United States. One of my purposes for doing the review was to search for indicators that the authors based their learning materials regarding number on a theory of how children construct the number sequence. The results of my search served as an inspiration for writing this chapter and led me to recall an experience as a participant in developing a mathematics curriculum for elementary school when I was at the University of Wisconsin. The interesting thing was that we mounted a concomitant research program in which curriculum and theory development were to mutually overlap, each providing problems and insights for the other. It should be no surprise that our attempts to articulate the two activities fell far short of my expectations. This earlier experience led me to forgo curriculum development and to concentrate on child studies in an attempt to formulate viable models of children's mathematical concepts and operations. At the time, I believed that such models were desperately needed in mathematics education because our curriculum development efforts were based on how we adults understood mathematics.

How we organized the curriculum for the numbers through twelve was almost the same as did the authors of the textbook series I reviewed in the curriculum improvement study. In the more recent textbook series, given a model set (a pictorial display), the children are to learn the relation "as many as" by drawing lines between the pictorial items and the items of several other (usually three) pictorial displays. In the case of "one" through "four," the children are expected to look at a pictorial display of perceptual items and learn to recognize the display

This paper was written for the Conference on Implicit and Explicit Knowledge in Science and Mathematics held at Tel Aviv University, Tel Aviv, Israel, in October 1988. The research on which the paper is based was supported by the National Science Foundation under Grant No. SED 80-16562; the Department of Mathematics Education and the Institute for Behavioral Research of the University of Georgia. All opinions and findings are those of the author and are not necessarily representative of the sponsoring agencies.

I would like to thank Dr. Iris Levin and Dr. Dina Tirosh for their insightful comments and criticisms on an earlier draft of this paper. Any inadequacies that remain are my responsibility.

by saying a number word and then, based on the relation "as many as," know that four is the number of any other set equivalent to the model set. To develop meaning for "five" through "twelve," the relation "one more than" is used. By imagining putting one more perceptual item with a pictorial display of five items, the children are to learn the meaning for "six," and so on. The "one more than" activities are correlated with counting perceptual items—to find "how many" birds are in a picture of birds, the children are to count the birds—and counting is the only difference in how we and the authors of the more recent textbook series organized the work on the numbers through twelve.

This approach to number is based on cardinal number theory, where a cardinal number is taken to be an object that is assigned to each set in such a way that equivalent sets, and equivalent sets only, have the same object corresponding to them (Hausdorff, 1962, p. 28). In my work with children, I have found an "ordinal approach" to number to be more appropriate for reasons that are given later in the chapter. But this is not my essential point, because to base the curriculum on either of these two approaches is tantamount to basing the curriculum on how adults understand mathematics and on a view of the mathematics education of children as a process of transferring information, which is written in mathematics textbooks, to children without taking into account *children's mathematics*. The main thrust of my work, and I want it to be understood in this way, is to specify *numerical concepts and operations of children and make those the conceptual foundations of number in school mathematics*.

Children's Mathematics

Individuals who believe that mathematics is the way it is rather than the way human beings make it to be might reject my work out of hand because they may not believe that children's mathematics is a legitimate mathematics. I find this to be particularly unsettling, because in my way of thinking, the mathematical knowledge of the other must be taken as being relative to one's own frame of reference. It can be known through interpreting the language and actions of the other—by forming a possible conceptual model. These models are understood as springing from the conceptual operations that are available to the knower. They are nothing other than a constellation of available conceptual operations that are formed in organizing, or making sense of, experiential encounters with children. Such models constitute mathematics of children even though they are not taken to characterize how the mathematical knowledge of children really is. They are taken as a *fit* rather than a *match* (von Glasersfeld, 1983). So, to believe that the mathematics of children is not a legitimate mathematics is to essentially reject one's own mathematical concepts and operations.

Mathematics *for* a child consists of those mathematical concepts and operations that one hypothesizes the child might learn. These hypotheses might be formulated in such a way that they constitute a model something like what Vygotsky (1956) has called the child's zone of potential development—that which the child is capable of learning with the help of a teacher. But there are differences in my characterization of mathematics for children and Vygotsky's notion of a zone of potential development because mathematics *for* children is of the same basic nature as mathematics *of* children. I base mathematics for children on *experiential abstractions* from interactive communication with children. In the development of mathematics for children, at some point an adult makes hypotheses about what a child might learn based on past experience with the given child and without having tested how other children might alter a model of elements of the child's mathematical knowledge. But I would not call these hypotheses mathematics for children any more than I would consider my knowledge of calculus to be mathematics for, say, a 10-year-old. My choice is to think of mathematics *for* particular children to be mathematics *of* some other children.

Children's Mathematics and Solipsism

Because mathematics of and for children are concepts of the observer, it might seem that what I propose is nothing but solipsism—the theory that one's own knowledge is the only thing that can be known and verified. It has been interpreted in this way by at least two authors (Vergnaud, 1987; Wheeler, 1987). However, von Foerster (1984) has explicitly rejected solipsism.

> My arguments make, I understand, a most unpopular claim. One way of sweeping it under the rug is to dismiss it as just another attempt to rescue "solipsism," the view that this world is only in my imagination and the only reality is the imagining "I." Indeed, that was precisely what I was saying before, but I was talking only about a single organism. The situation is quite different when there are two, as I shall demonstrate. . . . [T]he solipsistic claim falls to pieces when besides me I invent another autonomous organism. (p. 59)

Children's mathematics *as I perceive it* is my invention. But, according to von Foerster's analysis, children's mathematics is not only in my imagination; for if I agree, say, that there is another organism not unlike myself, I have to agree that the other organism can insist that its mathematical reality is the sole mathematical reality and that everything else is in *its* imagination, including my own mathematical reality. However, I know that my mathematical reality is not simply a concoction of the other's imagination and so I have to accept the other's mathematical reality as being distinct from my own. However, having no direct access to the other's reality, the only way I can know it is to make a model of it.

So, we must come to know the mathematics of and for children through intensive and extensive experiential encounters, and "to know" means to make models of their evolving mathematical concepts and operations. I emphasize "evolving" because children's mathematics is not static; it is to be viewed as the mathematics children construct in experiential contexts. What I do in this chapter is discuss some of my current understandings of children's numerical knowledge and indicate how it is strikingly different from what appears in school mathematics textbooks.

The models I construct of children's evolving mathematical concepts and operations are based in part on what I observe in the context of actually teaching children. These teaching experiments are exploratory and are aimed at discovering what might go on in children's heads. The methodology of the teaching experiment (Cobb & Steffe, 1983; Hunting, 1983; Steffe, 1983; Thompson, 1982b) is derived from Piaget's clinical interview, but because it also involves experimentations with the ways and means of influencing children's knowledge, it is more than a clinical interview. The clinical interview is aimed at establishing where children are, but the teaching experiment is directed toward understanding the progress children make over extended periods of time where there is no intention of teaching a predetermined way of operating.

In the following discussions of children's meanings for number words, I present specimens of interactive communication between myself (or other researchers working with me) and individual children along with interpretations of the specimens. The interpretations are not based solely on the particular specimens, but on a sequence of teaching episodes. I cannot emphasize this important point enough, because a specimen represents only a small segment of a half-hour videotape of a teaching episode and over 60 of these videotapes exist for each child.

Brenda's Construction of Meanings for Number Words

Consider the following interchange with a six-year-old child, Brenda.[1] I presented her with a task where four of a collection of squares were covered by a cloth (three were visible) and told her that four of them were hidden and asked her to find how many there were in all. She first tried to raise the cloth to see the squares, but I asked her to try to find out without looking at the ones covered. She counted the three visible squares ("B" is used for "Brenda" and "T" is used for "teacher").

Protocol 1

B: 1–2–3 (touches each visible square in turn).

T: There are four here (taps the cloth).

B: (Lifts the cloth, revealing two squares) 4–5. (She touches each of these squares and puts the cloth back.)

T: OK, I will show you two of them (folds back the cloth to reveal two of the four covered squares). There are four here, you count them.

B: 1–2–3–4–5 (touches each visible square in turn).

T: There are two more here (taps the cloth).

B: (Attempts to lift the cloth, so T removes it.) 6–7 (touches the last two squares).

The meaning of "four" for Brenda is certainly at issue. Her attempt to lift the cloth indicates that she was aware of the hidden squares and intended to count the

---

[1] Brenda was a participant in a two-year teaching experiment carried out to study the construction of numerical knowledge by six 6-year-old children. The protocol is an excerpt from an interview held on October 21 of Brenda's first grade in school (Steffe & Cobb, 1988).

collection of squares. But her awareness of the hidden squares did not lead to counting.

Another interchange provides further insight into her possible meaning of number words. I covered six of a collection of marbles with my hand (three were visible) and asked Brenda to count all of the marbles after telling her that there were six under my hand. She first counted my five fingers saying "1–2–3–4–5" synchronous with touching each one and then counted the three visible marbles "6–7–8." After I then said that I had six marbles in my hand, Brenda said, "I don't see no six!"

Obviously, my concept of number differed from whatever meaning Brenda gave to "four" and "six." How could I possible understand what her meanings might be like? The "trick" is, as Cobb and Wheatley (1988) said, "to develop an understanding of children's mathematics so that their actions can be seen as rational and sensible. The focus of a conceptual analysis is therefore on children's meanings" (p. 2). But what would keep us from assuming Brenda had a concept of number (she did count perceptual items) and then try to imagine what we have to give up in, say, Hausdorff's cardinal number theory so that the remaining components would seem compatible with what Brenda does when solving tasks? This might seem to be a reasonable way to proceed, but I believe it is a particularly unfortunate choice.

Refusing to admit that human beings construct number and accepting that number is innate, as do Gelman and Gallistel (1978), can only delude us as mathematics educators. We can then assume that the numerical meanings of young children are not unlike ours. A corollary would be to teach Brenda as if her received meanings somehow fit her teacher's intended meanings—as if she can make numerical sense of what her teacher says about numbers in the way her teacher does or in the way the authors of the textbooks do.

Pluralities and Collections

My interpretation of Brenda's being unable to count perceptual items she could not see is based on von Glasersfeld's (1981) notion of a collection. Collections are experiential composite wholes composed of perceptual items. In von Glasersfeld's model, children early in life isolate co-occurring sensorimotor signals in the stream of experience by a process of unitizing—cutting discrete items out of the flow of experience. These discrete experiential items form the "things" from which object concepts are somehow abstracted. When a child can monitor using an object concept and tell the difference between using it once and more than once in an experiential situation, its repeated use produces a *plurality* of perceptual items. Let us say, for example, that a child recognizes a perceptual situation as an instantiation of the concept it has associated with the word "cup." The child may continue exploring its visual field, assimilating another combination of sensory signals, and then another. If the child keeps track that its concept of cup was repeatedly used, it could utter the word "cups." The cups would be bounded in the child's visual field if and when the child perceives the table on which they are arrayed as a background. In that case, the cups on the table form an experientially bounded plurality, or *collection*.

Von Glasersfeld's notion of collection is compatible with Piaget's (1937) model for the developmental process that results in the child's conception of objects as externalized, *permanent objects* that are considered to have an existence in their own space and time independent of the experiencing subject. Brenda could use her object concept associated with "marble" to recognize (assimilate) actual sensorimotor experiences as instances of the object. For Brenda to believe that there were marbles hidden, she would have to use her object concept to create a re-presentation[2] of a marble regardless of the absence or presence of perceptual signals. There was good indication that Brenda could use her object concept in both of these ways, as we would expect children six years of age to be able to do. She could create *figural* as well as *perceptual* items. But these figural items did not appear to be available to her as countable items.

Returning now to Brenda's meanings of "four" and "six," during our exchanges I would say *Brenda had no object concepts for the words*. I know from other interviews that Brenda could recognize triangular and linear arrangements of three items as "three" and any two items as "two" after seeing the arrangements only for a moment. When a square array of four dots was shown, however, she had to count the dots before she could say "four." There was no indication she could re-present an arrangement of four dots and count its re-presented elements.[3] Moreover, she did not recognize a row of four dots as "four" nor a domino five as "five." Without actually counting these arrangements, she could not say how many dots they contained. Her meanings of number words "four" and beyond had to be made by actually counting collections and did not exist independently of the counted collections. There were no *object concepts* for these words and they referred to the transitory experience of counting collections or to its results. She was aware of counting in much the same way she was of, say, skipping rope. Both were sensorimotor activities. Prior to skipping rope, three jumps would not be a meaning of "three." But if "1–2–3" were coordinated with jumps, that would be counting, and the experience would be a meaning of "three." Children like Brenda for whom collections must be available to establish units that can be counted are called *counters of perceptual unit items* (Steffe, von Glasersfeld, Richards, & Cobb, 1983). They know how to count but need a collection of marbles, beads, fingers, jumps of a rope, and so on in order to carry out the activity.

One of the first manifestations of independence from immediate perception in counting occurs when a collection of items can be counted even though it is not within the child's range of immediate perception or action. In this case, a child might attempt to count the items of a screened collection by coordinating the sequential production of visualized images of the perceptual items with the sequential production of number words. In this case, I would say the child counted figural unit items. When a child can count only perceptual unit items, I refer to their

---

[2] A re-presentation of a perceptual item is a re-creation of an experience of the item in its absence. No assumption is made concerning what aspect of a past experience is re-created.

[3] A re-presentation of a sensory pattern is a re-creation of the pattern without actual sensory material available.

counting scheme as *a perceptual counting scheme* and when they can count figural unit items as well, I refer to it as a *figurative counting scheme*.

Awareness of Plurality

The question remains why Brenda seemed to be aware of the hidden items but, crucially, could not count them. An *awareness of plurality* requires the production of a visualized image of a perceptual item along with its actual repetitions. It is an awareness of more than one perceptual unit item. The repetitions create a collection of perceptual *unit* items because the perceptual items are now considered from the point of view of their unitariness or wholeness. A *figural plurality* is the experiential results of repeatedly re-presenting a perceptual unit item in the absence of sensory material. When there is an experiential context that forms a boundary for the process of creating figural unit items, we might think of the figural unit items as a *figural collection*. In Brenda's case, the cloth and my hand formed such possible experiential contexts. But it is my belief that Brenda could not repeatedly re-present her object concepts and, hence, could not make figural collections.

If this was the case, as her inability to re-present a collection of two perceptual items seems to indicate (Steffe & Cobb, 1988, p. 99), then we still have to explain the sense in which she was aware of the hidden items. In the explanation, it is my assumption that for objects to exist for a child in space and time independently of the experiencing child, the child must be able to re-present the material in an object concept. Otherwise, there would be nothing in the child's awareness that could "exist." I take this to be the sense in which Brenda was aware of the hidden items.

An *awareness of figural plurality* requires the re-presentation of a perceptual unit item along with its *repeatability*. Given that Brenda could re-present a perceptual unit item but not a collection of two perceptual unit items, there is reason to believe that she did not repeatedly re-present a perceptual unit item—repeatability was not a property of her figural unit items. Creating figural collections must be more demanding for some children than we adults might expect it to be.

An awareness of plurality (perceptual or figural) should be thought of as being indispensable in activating counting, and a lack of counting figural unit items is an indication of an inability to make figural collections. How Brenda constructed figural collections is an interesting story to which I now turn.

Brenda's Use of Finger Patterns

The construction of figural collections involved finger patterns for Brenda. The following protocol is an excerpt from a teaching episode held with Brenda on March 19 of her first-grade year.

Protocol 2

T: (Displays four squares) See those?
B: (Nods her head "yes.")
T: (Hides the four squares and displays three squares) See those? (Hides the three squares)

B: (Simultaneously puts up four fingers) Four. (Closes her hand and sequentially puts up the same four fingers) 1–2–3–4 (continues sequentially putting up fingers on her other hand) 5–6–7.

Brenda now seemed to have constructed object concepts to which "four" and "three" referred. The act of simultaneously putting up four fingers while uttering "four" and then closing her hand and sequentially putting up the same four fingers while uttering "1–2–3–4" (counting) is a strong indication that Brenda re-presented the finger pattern and then counted the elements of the re-presented pattern. In other words, "four" could refer to a re-presented unitary whole comprising figural unit items that could be sequentially isolated and counted. The fingers of her figurative finger pattern were *countable figural unit items.*

It is especially significant that Brenda could coordinate the implementation of a finger pattern for "three" with her utterances "5–6–7." This shows that "three" referred to a re-presented finger pattern whose elements could be coordinated with any three number words in sequence. She made similar coordinations using finger patterns associated with "two," "four," and "five." Her ability to re-present these finger patterns and count them in a continuation of counting provides the necessary basis for considering them to be figural concepts of the involved number words. At no time did I observe Brenda constructing meaning for number words using the relation "one more than," a relation that she was yet to construct. Moreover, I found that she could establish a relation between two collections by counting the perceptual unit items of the collections or by physically pairing them one-to-one. But these relations were of the same nature as her transient meaning of number words and could not be used as foundational in constructing object concepts for number words.

Activation of counting. There is a fundamental issue suggested by protocol 2. Apart from Brenda's ability to re-present finger patterns, how can we explain that counting was now activated in protocol 2 when in protocol 1 it was not? I could detect nothing different in the social situation in the two protocols that would suggest that Brenda expected to count in protocol 2 but not in protocol 1. In fact, in protocol 1, I suggested to Brenda that she count, but no such suggestions were made in protocol 2.

The semantic connections that Brenda earlier established between perceptual finger patterns and the number words "two," "three," "four," and "five" were the results of counting. If a child counts the fingers of a finger pattern "1–2–3," connecting the counted finger pattern with the last word said is an act of pseudo-empirical abstraction (Piaget, 1980a). The counting activity can be curtailed because the pattern embodies its results. I think of the counting acts as being *recorded* in the finger pattern, having been introduced into the finger pattern by the child's activity. If a finger pattern is then isolated on some future occasion, the assimilation could lead to the activation of the records, which in turn activates the response "three" without intervening counting activity.

Reflecting on finger patterns. A finger pattern provides an opportunity for a child to construct the dual meaning of the result of counting—unitary and at the same time composite. The items of a finger pattern seem to co-occur in the child's perceptual field and the experiential pattern gives the child something to reflect on. Without this dual meaning, it would seem very implausible to me that a child would reflect on the results of counting and isolate a connection between the last word said when counting and the finger pattern. That Brenda did reflect on her perceptual finger patterns is clearly indicated in protocol 3 excerpted from a teaching episode held on the 10th of February.

Protocol 3

T: (Places three marbles in front of Brenda) How many marbles?
B: Three (immediately).
T: How many marbles do we have there (places four marbles in front of Brenda)?
B: (Touches each marble) 1–2–3–4.
T: (Places paper cups over the marbles) How many marbles do we have altogether?
B: (Stares straight ahead for about 25 seconds with her hands resting in her lap) I hope it's seven!
T: It's seven all right! How did you get that?
B: I counted on my fingers!

Reflection requires the reflecting subject to "hold an object still at a distance." During the 25 seconds that Brenda stared straight ahead, she displayed intense concentration and seemed to be aware of what she was doing with her fingers as they rested on her lap. She seemed to hold the finger patterns still in her tactual and kinesthetic fields and then count the elements of those patterns. Her perceptual finger patterns evidently provided her with composite wholes of which she was aware. The whole protocol indicates to me that *internalization* of her finger patterns was at least beginning.

Internalization of Finger Patterns

Internalization can lead to visualization in any sensory modality. It is the process that results in the ability to re-present a sensory item without the relevant sensory signals being available in actual perception or in the ability to re-enact a motor activity without the presence of the kinesthetic signals from actual physical movement. Staring straight ahead while counting indicates to me that Brenda re-presented the visual component of her finger patterns while creating sensory material in her kinesthetic and tactual fields. Using the visual records of her finger pattern in re-presentation while enacting the kinesthetic and tactual records serves in the internalization of the enacted records.

Establishing her finger patterns in her tactual and kinesthetic fields while visualizing them in her visual field indicates to me that Brenda was beginning to internalize the kinesthetic component involved in simultaneously putting up fingers. Likewise, counting her fingers while staring straight ahead indicates to me that she was beginning to internalize moving individual fingers when counting. Protocol 2 more or less indicates a completion of the internalization process and Brenda could now establish specific figural collections—her finger patterns. Her finger patterns were now *object concepts* connected to her number words "one" through "five," and she now had countable figural items available to count—her fingers.

Sequentially putting up fingers in protocol 2 indicates to me that *repeatability* was becoming a property of her figural items. Using her finger patterns circumvented the necessity of establishing repeatability as a property of more general figural unit items to create figural collections because she simultaneously put up fingers to establish a finger pattern. Nevertheless, the action that was introduced on the sensorimotor level by counting the fingers of her perceptual finger patterns and by the covert finger movements like those that must have occurred in protocol 3 was implicit in the re-presented finger patterns. It was made explicit when Brenda sequentially put up fingers synchronous with uttering number words to instantiate the finger patterns. Brenda *externalized* what had been previously *internalized*, and her sensorimotor finger patterns established by counting reflected her object concepts.

On May 5, Brenda's solution of a task indicates a more complete externalization of the motor acts implicit in her finger patterns. After the teacher presented the problem "You have 13 dolls and I have four dolls. How many dolls do we both have?" Brenda asked if she could count and then sequentially put up all 10 fingers, closed one hand, and sequentially put up three fingers for a second time while synchronously uttering "1–2– . . . –13." She now seemed to focus on the activity of counting rather than on her global perception of the items she had established by counting (i.e., a finger pattern). This gave Brenda greater generative power because she was no longer stymied when she ran out of fingers. In particular, Brenda recounted three fingers when she established the collection of 13 fingers. As this collection could not be bounded by scanning visually, I infer that it was bounded by the beginning and end of the activity she performed while creating it. This is important because it indicates that she transcended visual perception in establishing the result of counting. This led to the establishment of sophisticated finger patterns.

Sophisticated Finger Patterns

A second issue that emerges from protocol 2 is whether her finger patterns were now numerical rather than only figurative.[4] One indication of their figurative nature was their specificity. "Four," for example, referred to the four fingers of either of her hands excluding her thumbs and "five" referred only to an open hand. In protocol 3, "three" referred to a finger pattern she completed on her remaining hand after completing a finger pattern for "four" using the index, middle, ring, and little fingers of her other hand. She did not use her thumb and two fingers of her

---

[4] A numerical finger pattern is created by applying the unitizing operation to a figurative finger pattern. Numerical finger patterns have a property of mobility and are not limited to specific finger patterns.

remaining hand to complete a finger pattern for "three"—she did not split her finger pattern for "three" between two hands.

A second indication that her finger patterns were figurative rather than numerical was the necessity for Brenda to create an experiential meaning as well as a figurative meaning for number words, as we see in protocols 4 and 5. Brenda had established perceptual finger patterns for the number words "six" through "ten" prior to March 19, the time of protocol 2. She constructed these finger patterns along with sophisticated finger patterns for the number words "eleven" through "fifteen" as figurative concepts by November 7 of her second-grade year. These sophisticated finger patterns were a complete surprise to me.

Protocol 4

T: (Covers eleven marbles with a cloth and then places three more on top of the cloth) Now there are three more.

B: Eleven (simultaneously puts up five fingers on her left hand and one on her right hand to indicate "eleven"). 1–2–3 (sequentially puts up three of her remaining fingers) fourteen!

The patterns for "eleven" through "fifteen" involved taking an open hand as an abbreviated finger pattern for "ten." To clarify the status of Brenda's sophisticated finger patterns, I asked her to close her eyes when solving a task involving "eight" and "five."

Protocol 5

B: 1–2–3–4–5–6–7–8 (sequentially puts up five fingers on her left hand and three on her right hand). 1–2 (sequentially puts up her remaining two fingers) 3–4–5 (sequentially wiggles three fingers of her left hand) thirteen!

Brenda said "thirteen" without her open right hand and three fingers of her left hand being in her visual field. This suggests to me that her results of operating were recognized in her tactual and kinesthetic fields using an internalized finger pattern for "thirteen"—an open hand and three fingers. Whether this finger pattern was to be called "eight" or "thirteen" was determined by context. These sophisticated finger patterns confirm that Brenda was indeed aware of the results of counting to "thirteen" by sequentially putting up thirteen fingers, as I described earlier.

Dual Meanings of Number Words

Brenda's finger patterns led to dual meanings of number words through "fifteen" by the first of February of her second year in school. In protocol 6, Brenda counted to find "fifteen plus nine."

Protocol 6

B: 1–2–3– . . . –15 (simultaneously puts up ten fingers) 16–17– . . . –24 (sequentially folds down nine fingers).

To give meaning to "fifteen," Brenda could simply utter the appropriate counting word sequence[5] or else put up ten fingers. In either case, she created an experiential meaning for "fifteen." Nevertheless, she had made progress because she had curtailed the coordinations involved in counting. This is what I call *counting verbal unit items.*

There was no indication during the two-year duration of the teaching experiment that Brenda *interiorized* her finger patterns, creating numerical finger patterns. So I now turn to exploring the meanings of number words for Jason, another participant in the same teaching experiment, in part to illustrate what I mean by the interiorization of patterns.

Jason's Construction of Meanings for Arithmetical Words

Before exploring interiorization, there is another issue that I left implicit in the discussion of figural collections in Brenda's case that I now make explicit. The issue is "Can a child make figural collections using perceptual collections whose elements are not arranged in a pattern by the child and take their elements as countable?" To investigate the issue, I offer the following exchange with Jason. The protocol is excerpted from an interview that occurred on October 16 of Jason's first grade in school.

Protocol 7

T: (Presents two cloths that Jason takes as covering squares) There are six here and five here. How many squares are there altogether?

J: (Sequentially moves fingers on his left hand, moving his index finger twice) 1–2–3–4–5–6. (Continues sequentially moving fingers on his left hand) 7–8 (middle and ring finger) 9–10 (index and middle finger) 11–12 (moving no fingers).

This was the first time that I had worked with Jason, so I had no previous influence whatsoever on how he responded to my question. Jason had not established finger patterns as meanings of number words at this time in the teaching experiment expect for "two" and "ten." In fact, it was not until December 3 of the same school year that I observed Jason use a finger pattern for "three."

Jason's Meaning for "Five" and "Six"

Given that Jason had no finger pattern connected to "six," the interpretation of the first part of his counting episode becomes interesting. Did he have an object concept associated with "six" other than a finger pattern, or is there another way to explain his behavior? My choice is to attribute an awareness of a figural plurality of squares to him and an intention to count them. Given that he wanted to count, a lack of perceptual material to instantiate his concept, square, to make countable items could

---

[5] A counting word sequence is a number word sequence whose lexical items signify countable items.

leave him in a state of activation, searching for something to count. It seems reasonable to me that Jason would "call up" records of his past counting acts in his search if "six" referred to counting the squares. That Jason was successful indicates to me that at least the auditory records of his past counting acts were *internalized*—they could be re-presented in the absence of actual sensorimotor material.

Figurative number word sequence. The "image of the standard number word sequence" refers to a more or less permanent record of the kinesthetic or auditory aspect of saying number words in the standard order (Steffe et al., 1983, p. 26). When these records can be used in re-presentation, the number word sequence is internalized and I call it "figurative." Activating the image of the standard number word sequence can in turn activate instantiating the records, which means number words in sequence starting from "one." Being in a state of activation but having no squares in his visual field to count, Jason generated the sensorimotor items of putting up fingers as countable items.

To explain where the motor acts of putting up fingers came from, we have to look to when Jason counted perceptual unit items in other counting episodes. An *act of counting a perceptual unit item* is the more or less co-occurrence of uttering a counting word and instantiating an object concept, where the co-occurrence is often experientially determined by a guiding motor act—a finger movement. In that his intention was to count the squares and given that there was no perceptual material he could use to make a square, he enacted the guiding motor acts his number words signified and took *them* as countable items. Focusing attention on the guiding motor act between uttering a number word and instantiating an object concept when the there is no perceptual material that can be used in instantiation is what I mean by substituting a motor act for a figural unit item in counting.

So, I can see no reason to believe that Jason needed an object concept of "six" in order to count as he did, and it was not a necessary part of my explanation. I do believe that "six" referred to a figural plurality, but there was no necessity that he could "see" six individual figural unit items that appeared to co-occur in some pattern. The counting meaning of "six" alleviated that necessity. However, an internalized counting word sequence was essential for the search of something to count to be completed and for counting to be successfully actualized to create an experiential meaning for "six."

The explanation of the first part of Jason's counting episode is what I mean by a *counter of motor unit items.* After Brenda became able to sequentially put up fingers when counting to "thirteen," I also call her a counter of motor unit items because I believe by that time she became aware of a *figural plurality of fingers.* This is a more restricted meaning of being a counter of motor unit items than I explained in the case of Jason. Jason, in contrast to Brenda, could use almost any of his object concepts in creating figural pluralities and an awareness of these figural pluralities in part activated counting.

Jason's continuation of counting. I turn now to the second part of Jason's counting episode because it is so delightfully consistent with my explanation of the first part. After uttering "six" and putting up his index finger, he continued on uttering "7–8" while putting up his middle and ring fingers and then returned to putting up his index finger and his middle finger while uttering "9–10." At this point he seemed to be "lost in counting" and went on uttering two more number words "11–12." He seemed to not use an object concept connected to "five" to keep track of continuing to count beyond "six." His counting behavior indicates to me that he intended to count all of the hidden items, and separating his continuation of counting from the first part further indicates to me that he was aware of an experiential separation in the items he was counting. An awareness of the second part coupled with a counting meaning for "five" activated his continuation.[6] He used his two-pattern in an attempt to keep track of his continuation of counting *but he did not monitor his use of the pattern, creating a pattern for "five" as a result of his activity.*

Monitoring a Continuation of Counting

It is interesting to speculate whether Jason's awareness of figural plurality was indicative of a number concept. In other words, should we consider Jason's result of counting to "six" to be an instantiation of a numerical concept for "six"? Although a counterargument has been presented, it is certainly a possible interpretation and I can imagine someone making it because there was a time when I interpreted equivalent counting behavior in that way (Steffe, Richards, & von Glasersfeld, 1979). Since that time I have become aware of a more essential criterion for imputing numerical concepts to a child. Had Jason monitored his continuation of counting, creating a concept for "five" on the spot, then I would be willing to attribute the operations to him that are necessary for children to make numbers.

On March 18 during Jason's first grade in school, he did monitor a continuation of counting in such a way that indicated to me that he was in control of his actions in the counting episode. As early as January of his first grade in school, he had established linear and domino patterns for the number words through "six" as figurative concepts. Jason's teacher presented him with a "missing items" task, which he interpreted in his own way.

Protocol 8

T: (Places a cloth in front of Jason) See those chocolate cookies under there (the teacher and Jason were only pretending)? Put the number on the cloth that shows how many you would like to put under the cloth. (Jason puts "8" on top of the cloth; the teacher lifts an adjacent cloth) See those chocolate cookies under there?

---

[6] Why a continuation of counting was activated rather than "1–2–3–4–5" can be understood if one thinks of Jason's figural collection of squares as being experientially separated. In this case, his intention could be to count all of the experientially separated squares starting with "one" and continuing until he counted all of them.

J: Uh huh (no).

T: Well, let's put some under there. Now, there are ten cookies under both cloths (places the numeral "10" immediately above both cloths). How many are under here (the adjacent cloth)?

T: (Touches the cloth with the numeral "8" on it eight times) 1–2–3–4–5–6–7–8. (Continues touching the other cloth as if it hid ten cookies) 9–10–11–12 (completes a row of four points of contact and then continues touching the cloth immediately beneath the completed row) 13–14–15—16. (Looks up at the teacher while saying "sixteen" and then continues touching the cloth immediately beneath the two completed rows, continuing to look at the teacher) 17—18 (touches the cloth emphatically when saying "eighteen" indicating that he was done).

The crucial indicator that Jason monitored his continuation of counting is that he looked intently at the cloth he took as covering ten "cookies" as he completed two rows of four and then changed from looking intently at the cloth in order to recognize the successive patterns to looking at his teacher. This indicates that he reflected on his counting activity and "took stock" of where he was as he was counting. He did not seek nor did he receive nonverbal cues that would indicate to him when to stop counting. He behaved in such a way that I have to attribute to him the operations necessary to create numerical patterns on the spot.

Jason could make numerical finger patterns as well as numerical spatial patterns. In the same teaching episode, his teacher placed "8" on one cloth as in protocol 7 and "12" above both cloths. Jason sequentially put up fingers synchronous with uttering "1–2–3–4–5–6–7–8" and then continued, putting up two remaining fingers on his right hand (his thumb and little finger) while uttering "9–10" and then moved his index and middle finger of his right hand while uttering "11–12." Upon the completion of counting, he was left with two open hands. Nevertheless, after about five seconds, he said "four!" He obviously separated his first eight counting acts from those he subsequently performed to count to "twelve" in a review of the results of counting and recognized a finger pattern—four. As there were no explicit perceptual records in his visual field, such recognition requires reflection. I infer that he reviewed the records of his continuation of counting using his unitizing operation. In this way, he created what I call numerical finger patterns. This was a remarkable achievement for Jason at this time in the teaching experiment and constituted the first time I observed him solving a missing items task "correctly." I never observed Brenda monitor her continuations of counting in the way Jason did. I have to stress that Jason *independently* monitored his counting activity without suggestion. Nevertheless, the processes Jason used to establish meaning for "ten" are not even close to those implied by the relation "one more than," which he was yet to construct.

Figurative counting schemes revisited. I can now make the notion of a figurative counting scheme a little more explicit. I have already said that when a child can create and count the items of a figurative collection, his counting scheme is a figurative scheme. Figurative counting schemes include those cases in which the child can create and count motor acts as did Jason or can simply utter counting words in sequence. In the latter case, the child has created an internalized sequence of counting acts. The involved number word sequence is internalized as well as the kinesthetic, visual, and auditory aspects of counting. Because the kinesthetic aspect is also internalized, the child can utter number words in sequence with no other accompanying motor acts, where the number words signify other countable items. In these cases (counting motor and verbal unit items), the experience of counting is bounded by its beginning and end, and this experience constitutes the meaning of the last number word said when counting. There was certainly no indication in protocols 2, 3, and 6 for Brenda and protocol 7 for Jason that these children took the items of the figurative patterns or collections as one thing prior to counting because they always started to count from "one."[7] There also was no indication in the protocols that the children took the items of the counted collection as one thing.

Interiorization of the Counting Scheme

When Jason was producing a pattern consisting of the records of his points of contact of his finger on a cloth in protocol 8, he had to establish what pattern he produced after each touch because there were no visible traces of his points of contact. The act of simply recognizing a row of dots by saying a number word does not require an intentional monitoring of the activity that produces the pattern. In producing the patterns, he had to recreate his acts of counting for the simple reason that there were no visual traces of counting. I have diagrammed the situation in Figure 6.1 after Jason had counted "9–10," when it was his intention to continue to count until completing a pattern for "ten."

Re-presentation alone is not sufficient to explain Jason's monitoring behavior because in protocols 2, 3, 6, and 7, Brenda and Jason could use figurative patterns to keep track of a continuation of counting but could not create patterns when intentionally monitoring counting. I did not observe Brenda create a pattern in the activity of continuing to count at any time I taught her over the two years of the teaching experiment.

To monitor counting activity intentionally as did Jason in protocol 8, there must be an explicit awareness of a figurative pattern, which is to say the child must reflect on the figurative pattern. To explain how Jason was explicitly aware of the figurative patterns he used to take stock of where he was after completing each counting act, my hypothesis is that he applied his unitizing operation to the elements of the figurative patterns. "Running through" or reprocessing the elements of the patterns strips the figurative counting acts of their sensorimotor quality and creates a sequence of abstract unit items that contain records of the counting acts (abstract discreteness). The sequence of abstract unit items is what I call a numerical pattern or composite—a pair of interiorized counting acts. The concept that Jason finally

---

[7] Toward the last part of the teaching experiment, Brenda did "count on" in some situations, but her behavior only indicated pseudo–counting on—counting on beyond a pattern—because she did not independently produce counting on nor did she ever independently solve a "missing items" task.

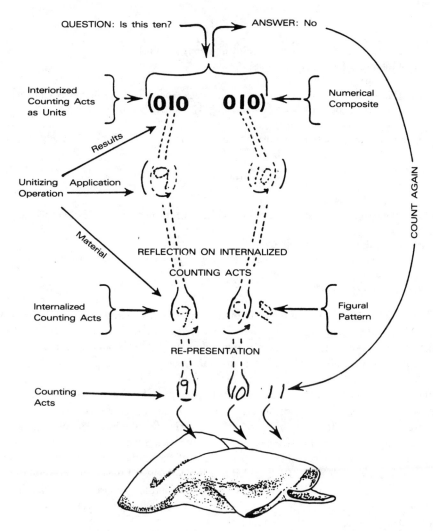

NOTE: Numerals rather than number words are used to simplify the figure.

↳ Denotes pointing acts.

Figure 6.1. Jason's initial interiorization of counting

created for "ten" was, in my model, a numerical pattern that contained the records of counting "9–10–11–12–13–14–15–16–17–18."

A reorganization of Jason's counting scheme. By May 21 of Jason's first grade in school, he could use his counting scheme in ways that were previously not possible.

Protocol 9

T: (After Jason places 16 poker chips in a cup) Take out four.

J: (Takes out four)

T: How many are left in there?

J: (Places his hands on his lap and concentrates on manipulating the poker chips; the teacher cannot see what Jason is doing) There's twelve in there.

T: Tell me how you did that!

J: (Places the poker chips on the table one at a time) 16–15–14–13—there's twelve in there.

Protocol 10

J: (Puts 14 checkers into a cup)

T: (Puts more checkers into another cup) Altogether there are twenty. How many are in here?

J: I was thinking there was six!

T: Ok. (Takes three out and pours the rest into Jason's cup, which contains fourteen) There are seventeen in there. How many did I put in?

J: 15–16–17—three!

The change in Jason's use of his counting scheme implies an underlying reorganization of the scheme. Because I had never observed him use it in these ways prior to this teaching episode, it is not too much to say that his counting scheme had undergone a metamorphosis and was now an interiorized scheme.

An interiorized counting act is an abstract unit item that contains records of an internalized counting act. It too can be re-presented by re-presenting what the records point to. So, an interiorized sequence of counting acts is a sequence of abstract unit items that contain records of the internalized sequence of counting acts that served as material in its construction. I call such an interiorized sequence of counting acts a *number sequence*. In the case of the initial construction, "initial number sequence" is used. By a *verbal number sequence*, I mean a re-presentation or re-enactment of a number sequence using the auditory records—an operative counting word sequence. The lexical items of a verbal number sequence symbolize abstract unit items as well as counting acts.

From Jason's perspective, he still had only one counting word sequence. Nevertheless, he could certainly use it differently now that it had been interiorized. From protocols 9 and 10, I infer that Jason's number words could symbolize initial segments of his verbal number sequence. "Sixteen," for example, seemed to symbolize the verbal number sequence starting with "sixteen" and proceeding down to "one." He partitioned this sequence into "16–15–14–13" and "12" by counting backward, where "twelve" symbolized the rest of the sequence. The inference is strengthened by Jason's taking counting to "fourteen" as a given when he counted up to "seventeen." Moreover, he made an uncannily accurate estimate of the numerosity[8] of the checkers placed with the original fourteen. I infer that his

---

[8] The numerosity of a composite unit can be formed by instantiating a number sequence in an experiential context.

estimate "six" referred to the counting acts he would perform were he to start counting with "fourteen" and proceed on to "twenty."

Monitoring as feedback. The accommodation of Jason's counting scheme that engendered his reorganization of counting was monitoring a continuation of counting (cf. protocol 8). To explain what I mean by monitoring, I refer again to Figure 6.1. Application of the unitizing operation to re-presented counting acts—"9, 10" in the figure—disembeds the involved counting acts from the rest of the internalized counting scheme and records them at the level of interiorization. Jason, intending to continue on counting—could now take the interiorized counting acts as belonging to the items he was counting, to the *countable* items. The application of the unitizing operation thus made it possible for the counted items to feed back into the countable items, and this is what I mean by monitoring counting in this case. Simply put, the child reconstitutes the counted items as countable items. Jason's goal to continue on counting ten times sustained this feedback system until the goal was reached. That Jason knew when he had reached "ten" is confirmation that he reconstituted his counted items as being countable.

I do not believe that Jason "double counted" in the sense of saying "9" is one; etc. Being involved in counting, Jason created two four patterns (numerical patterns) and he knew that two four patterns make an eight pattern. This was intuitive because it was based on figurative patterns, a level below where he was operating. That two four patterns make an eight pattern was implicit in his operating as was the completion of a pattern for "ten." Using figurative patterns, "ten" referred to two four patterns and a two pattern. The numerical patterns, being a focus of his attention, were explicit.

Autoregulation of monitoring. The metamorphosis of his counting scheme (cf. protocols 9 and 10) can be explained by *autoregulation of the monitoring activity.* I hypothesize that a perturbation was created by part of his counting word sequence being recorded at the level of interiorization and the rest of it being only internalized. It existed on two levels. I further hypothesize that this perturbation was neutralized by autoregulation of the monitoring activity. There are no assumptions made about how many times the unitizing operation was reapplied or how many adjacent number words might have served as material for a particular application. The only assumption that I make is that the unitizing operation was reapplied enough times to interiorize his figurative number word sequence. The completion of the interiorization process was indicated when Jason used his verbal number sequence in assimilation and solution of missing items tasks in protocols 9 and 10.

The counting scheme as a numerical concept. Jason's number words through the teens now symbolized initial segments of his verbal number sequence. These symbolized segments in turn symbolized sequences of abstract unit items as well as the activity and results of counting from, say, "one" up to and including "sixteen." In protocol 10, for example, Jason took "sixteen" as symbolizing the numerosity of any sequence of perceptual unit items he could create and count using his verbal number sequence. He could also re-present the symbolized initial segment in either the forward or backward direction.

An initial number sequence should be thought of as an elaborated numerical pattern. To use it means to instantiate the records that compose it, or more simply, to count. When counting, the child is aware of the counting acts inside of the beginning and end of counting. After counting, the child is aware of what is inside of the boundaries of counting but does not take the bounded results of counting as one thing, although it is a connected activity for the child. A lexical item of the initial number sequence symbolizes these operations and, as an item of a sequence, it refers to the lexical items up to and including the given lexical item.

An *extensive* meaning of "sixteen" was provided by the symbolized initial segment of Jason's verbal number sequence, and the counting acts symbolized by this initial segment constituted an *intensive* meaning of "sixteen" (Thompson, 1982a). Because of the symbolizing function of his number words, it could be said that, from Jason's perspective, the meaning of number words was an intention to act (Van Engen, 1949). The possibility of acting provided a dynamic quality to Jason's numerical meanings, and it was a source of his confidence that he could solve a wide variety of numerical problems. We can see how important these possibilities were in protocols 9 and 10.[9]

I regard Jason's initial number sequence as a numerical counting scheme. As activity, counting fits Piaget's (1980b) characterization of scheme: "All action that is repeatable or generalized through application to new objects engenders . . . a "scheme" (p. 24). But to view counting as simply activity provides no insight into why children count nor what the result of the activity might be for children. Toward such an end, von Glasersfeld (1980) separated Piaget's notion of scheme into three parts. First is the child's recognition of an experiential situation as one that has been experienced before; second is the specific activity the child has come to associate with the situation; and third is the result that the child has come to expect of the activity in the situation. Von Glasersfeld's emphasis on experiential situations is clarified by a comment Piaget (1964) once made about a stimulus in a critique of associationism:

A stimulus is really a stimulus only when it is assimilated into a structure and it is this structure which sets off the response. Consequently, it is not an exaggeration to say that the response is there first. (p. 15)

---

[9] Jason's extensive and intensive meanings of number words are more compatible with ordinal number theory than with cardinal number theory. However, I would not say that "sixteen" referred to an ordinal number if what is meant by that term is an object that is assigned to each well-ordered set in such a way that similar sets, and similar sets only, have the same object corresponding to them (Hausdorff, 1962, p. 65). Although there are many points of difference, Jason's *numerical concepts* as I have modeled them were not unlike ordinal numbers. An important feature of these numerical concepts was that he *focused on the constituent unit items* of the composite units he made rather than on the composite units as one thing.

After Jason's counting scheme was interiorized, it definitely was not an exaggeration to say that his initial number sequence contained counting. A number word, say "sixteen," had been involved in the process of interiorization of counting and it therefore could *symbolize* the operations that were involved in that process and their result—a sequence of abstract unit items that contained the records of counting. So, the activity of counting had become an aspect of the first part of his counting scheme.

Engendering and metamorphic accommodations. The interiorization of the counting scheme also emerged in the context of patterns in the cases of Tyrone and Scenetra, Jason's cohorts in the teaching experiments. Figurative concepts of number words seemed to play a crucial role in the construction of the initial number sequence for all three children. In retrospect, it is not surprising that interiorization of the counting scheme emerged in the context of figurative patterns, because a pattern provides children with an experiential unity whose elements seem to co-occur—an immediate apprehension of plurality and unity.

Alone, however, figurative concepts of number words would never propel a child forward into the realm of number. It takes reprocessing them using the unitizing operation to create numerical patterns. But without perturbations being induced in the use of their counting scheme, I cannot imagine how children would construct an initial number sequence. For example, before Tyrone reorganized counting, he lost track of counting over a cloth covering the second hidden portion of a collection because he did not recognize touching the cloth five times with his finger. He started over again without suggestion from his teacher and monitored the nonvisual records of his counting acts, creating a pattern for "five" on the spot (Steffe, 1988, p. 153). This was a solid indication that he was aware of an uncertainty in the results of counting.

Scenetra used her unitizing operation in the context of patterns to neutralize perturbations she experienced in assimilation. In the context of finding how many squares were in a collection, where five were hidden and six were visible, Scenetra counted the visible squares and then tried to use her perceptual finger patterns. Not having enough fingers created a perturbation she neutralized by changing her scheme of operating from finger patterns to counting. I inferred that she reprocessed visible squares that she had previously counted using her unitizing operation because, in her words, she "put them in my head" and counted on from "six" five more times. The independence she exemplified in switching from one scheme to another indicates a deliberate choice and reflection on her actions. I believe both her choice and reflection were made possible by her creating numerical composites using her figurative patterns (Steffe, 1988, p. 178).

Although I have not provided a protocol for it, Jason also reinitialized his counting scheme as the result of a perturbation (Steffe & Cobb, 1988). In protocol 8, he monitored his counting acts; and in the counting activity immediately following protocol 8, he reviewed his records of past counting activity. In fact, all three children could monitor their current counting actions or review their past counting actions. These modifications turned out to be *engendering accommodations.*[10] *The metamorphic accommodations*[11] to which they lead in the cases of Tyrone and Scenetra were manifest by January 8 and March 5, respectively. These were the dates I first observed reorganizations in the two children's counting schemes that were on a par with reorganizations Jason made in protocols 9 and 10.

The Period of the Initial Number Sequence

One of the most significant but surprising results of the teaching experiment was that approximately eight months elapsed before any of the three children used their initial number sequence in such a way that indicated another fundamental reorganization. During this period, a novel use of the unitizing operation appeared that is called the *uniting operation*. This operation has been identified by Menninger (1969) in a study of the cultural history of numbers. Menninger commented that in two as unity, "we experience the very essence of number more intensely than in other numbers, that essence being to bind many together into one, to equate plurality and unity" (p. 13). This is compatible with Brouwer's (1913, p. 85) analysis of the basal intuition of mathematics as being the bare "two-oneness."

The issue of whether two is a property of two perceptual items is critical. According to Menninger, two cannot be a property of two perceptual items because it cannot be a property of a single perceptual item and, thus, two cannot be found in nature. Rather, it takes an operation of the mind that binds distinct unitary items together into a unity and two can be a property of that composite unity.

> The intellect . . . does not find numbers but makes them; it considers different things, each distinct in itself; and intentionally unites them in thought. (Caramuel, 1977, p. 44; trans. by E. von Glasersfeld)

To make a unit of units, a child can reprocess a collection of perceptual unit items using the unitizing operation and then reprocess those results using the uniting operation as indicated by Caramuel. From here on, when I say that a child uses the uniting operation, I refer to this process. The material of operating, however, does not have to be a collection of perceptual unit items. It could be, say, re-presented counting acts. In some cases, reprocessing a collection of perceptual unit items is symbolized. In other cases, a child might re-present the material of a sequence of abstract unit items that were created in the past by using the unitizing operation. In these cases, I say that the involved sequence of abstract unit items are taken as a given by the child. This can occur especially in the case of the initial number sequence because a lexical item of the sequence can symbolize counting as well as the verbal number sequence of which it is the last element.

---

[10] A functional accommodation of a counting scheme is a modification of the scheme that occurs in the context of using the scheme. An engendering accommodation is a functional accommodation that is self-initiated, involves using conceptual elements external as well as internal to the scheme, leads to further accommodations, and involves or leads to a structural reorganization of the scheme.

[11] A metamorphic accommodation of a counting scheme is a modification of the scheme that occurs independently but not in any particular application of the scheme.

Adding and subtracting schemes. Toward the last part of the period of the initial number sequence, the children often took the experiential results of counting as material of application of their uniting operation. Moreover, they constructed adding and subtracting schemes using their initial number sequence. Protocol 11 is excerpted from a teaching episode on December 14 of Jason's second grade.

Protocol 11

T: (Places "17 − 8" in front of Jason) What would that be?
J: 17–16–15–14–13–12–11–10 (in synchrony with putting up fingers) That would be (pauses)—nine!

It would be very unlikely that Jason would say "nine" without taking the results of counting as one thing. Although he could be *trained* to do that, the independent way in which he said "nine" along with that fact that he did say it indicates to me that he took the results of counting as one thing—as material of his uniting operation. He could then "rise above" his activity and "see" his verbal number sequence 17, 16, . . ., 2, 1 as being separated into two parts—into {17, 16, . . ., 10}[12] and into the other part which was symbolized by "nine."

It is interesting to speculate on what went on before Jason counted in protocol 11—on his subtraction concept. I look to Jason's subtracting acts (his counting acts) for insight because they were not simply connected to "17 − 8" as an appropriate movement in square dancing is to "do-si-do." Based on his counting acts, his subtraction concept seems to be best understood as a sequence of possible actions—interiorized actions—that he isolated in the past when he used his counting scheme. Although I do not trace the construction of his subtraction concept, we do see its initial form in protocol 9.[13] There, he counted backward only after he physically removed the four poker chips to find where he was before he counted the four he removed. Counting backward would not have been activated by expressions like "16 − 4." It did provide a possible experience for the necessary abstractions in constructing a subtraction concept. In contrast, in protocol 11, "17 − 8" symbolized subtracting actions.

So, rather than physically remove 8 items from a collection of 17, he used the elements of a numerical finger pattern as symbolizing the items being removed. Using this concept of "eight," he counted "17," then "16," and so on "off from" the backward verbal number sequence. The lexical items of his verbal number sequence were his countable items and he "counted" them by recording each word

---

[12] I use braces to indicate that Jason took the results of counting as one thing, which is to say that he took his finger pattern as one thing.

[13] It is understandable why Jason said "16–15–14–13" to find how many poker chips remained under the cloth in protocol 9 because he had just counted to "sixteen" to place sixteen poker chips in the cup. Experientially, he was at the "end'" of the verbal number sequence that now symbolized counting the chips. Any chip could correspond to "sixteen" because that word symbolized a counting act. He uttered the four counting words backward to find where he was in counting before he counted the four visible chips.

said by putting up a finger. Putting up a finger carried the force of uttering a number word of the sequence "1–2–. . .–8." Functionally, he was double counting but he could not yet explicitly double count. What would be explicit later was now only implicit. Taking the results of counting—the elements of a counted finger pattern—as one thing certainly constituted a reinteriorization of part of his counting scheme as well as an accommodation of counting to reach his goal.[14] After counting, he had a solid basis for establishing numerical connections among the three principal number words.

Before counting, Jason's intention seemed to be to separate the backward segment of his verbal number sequence symbolized by "17" into two parts, the first consisting of eight lexical items and the second an an initial segment of yet unknown numerosity. But I take this goal to be only implicit in his actions. In other words, I do not think he consciously made plans prior to counting. It just appeared to him as the thing to do without knowing why or without having alternatives. The "goal" I alluded to previously was created by the activation of his program of subtracting actions and his anticipation of what the result would be. Carrying out the actions was one way he could satisfy his goal. It is worth noting that his estimate "six" shows that he could anticipate what the results of counting would be if it were to be carried out, which indicates awareness of results of counting but not necessarily of why he counted as he did.

Whatever the terms *addition, subtraction,* and *missing addend* might mean to us as adults, the three children interpreted our problem situations in terms of their initial number sequences—as counting problems. Counting was symbolized by arithmetical words. For example, it could be the intention of the children to count to "twenty-one," say, to find how many of a collection of 21 blocks were hidden. If the children counted the visible items, they could apply the uniting operation to the counted items and then continue to count to "twenty-one," whereupon they could once again apply the uniting operation to their records of continuing to count, creating a numerical whole whose numerosity could be established. These are what I call *sequential uniting operations.* If the children were simply told how many items were visible, that number word could symbolize an uniting operation and they could in this case again continue to count. This symbolizing function of number words permitted the children to appear to be able to perform more sophisticated operations than sequential uniting operations. It is important to note that sequential uniting operations were carried out during rather than before problem solution. In this sense, the children were in the process of constructing more sophisticated addition and subtraction schemes than I have explained.

The major insight that the children could at most make sequential uniting operations in activity provides a powerful explanation for certain observations that are not otherwise explicable. For example, not one of the three children could

---

[14] A procedural accommodation is a functional accommodation that involves a modification of the activity of counting or a novel way to view the results of counting. A procedural accommodation might be an engendering accommodation.

strategically find the pairs of numbers whose sum was, say, ten. They could find certain pairs, but they could not use a given pair to generate the next pair. And this was a general characteristic because the children solved each situation independently of prior related situations. Also, they could not understand subtraction as the inversion of addition nor could they construct a meaning of "ten" as one ten prior to acting. This restriction in their meaning of "ten" prohibited them from constructing counting by ten as an anticipatory scheme and from using this scheme to establish how many units of ten could be made using a particular number sequence or collection. For example, they could not independently count by ten, keeping track of how many times they counted, to find how many units of ten could be made from 59 blocks. They learned linguistic rules in their classroom for separating "59" into "five tens and nine ones," but that was unrelated to their number sequence.

The Explicitly and Tacitly Nested Number Sequences
On March 29 of Jason's second grade in school, the way Jason could solve problems changed dramatically. One strategy was to estimate the missing addend, add the estimate to the first addend, and check the result to see if it was the sum.

Protocol 12

T: (Places the expression "27 + _____ = 36" in front of Jason) We have twenty-seven and some more and that is thirty-six.

J: Twenty-seven—(pause of about 20 seconds). Let me see—(another pause)—twenty-seven plus seven—it's nine more!

T: That's really good! Is there another way to solve that one?

J: Uh-uh (no).

T: Could you do it by counting backwards?

J: (Sequentially puts up fingers) 36–35– . . . –27. Nine.

Jason seemed to view 27 as a number in its own right, as well as a part of 36 because he did not simply make an estimate and quit. Rather, after he made an estimate, he saw it as a possibility rather than as the answer. After estimating the missing number to be 7, he added it to 27, continued to 36, and then added the continuation to 7. These operations indicate that he used the units the numerals referred to as one thing, as well as composites. Moreover, 27 and 36 were related, in that 27 was a part that he had disembedded from 36. These claims are confirmed by the ease with which he counted from 36 down to 27. The teacher also tried his best to present "36 − 9 = _____" as a novel task immediately afterward.

Protocol 13

T: I am going to give you another one. This time we are going to have something to take away (presents the sentence).

J: (Immediately) Twenty-seven.

T: How did you know?

J: Because we just did it!

Jason clearly viewed subtraction as the inversion of addition. In fact, the two problems involved identical parts of the same whole, and he merely had to recover the known missing part. Addition and subtraction were now explainable as reversible part–while operations. "Thirty-six" referred to {1, 2, 3, . . ., 36}, where the braces are used to connote a *unit* containing a number sequence. "Twenty-seven" referred to a segment of thirty-six—to {1, 2, 3, 4, . . ., 27}, and it was Jason's intention to find the numerosity of the remainder of this segment in thirty-six—{28, 29, 30, 31, . . ., 36}. I believe he could disembed the two parts of thirty-six from thirty-six while leaving them in thirty-six (he did not destroy the whole by focusing his attention on the parts). Thirty-six was still "there" beside the parts (it was at least symbolized by "36"). In establishing the numerosity of the remainder, he could move back and forth between the parts and the whole, establishing new parts and combining them with the old parts to yield partial wholes. These operations provided him with great flexibility and were a complex form of the operations he had to carry out to understand that twenty-seven was the answer to "36 − 9 = _____" without counting.

When comparing Jason's methods of operating with numerical symbols in protocol 13 with his methods in protocols 9 and 10, it is as if he were a different child. His number sequence had undergone another metamorphosis. It is quite complex to explain because there was an intermediate step when he still operated sequentially. I call his number sequence in protocols 12 and 13 his *explicitly nested number sequence* because any word of the sequence symbolized a corresponding initial segment that he saw in two ways—as a composite and as a unit. A second critical characteristic was that he could, at one and the same time, view the composite unit as part of the sequence as well as a number in its own right. His number sequence was now *graduated*.

The tacitly nested number sequence. The initial number sequences were not inclusive in the sense that one is included in two, two is included in three, three is included in four, and so on, as Piaget's model of the development of number would have us believe (Sinclair, 1971). The initial number sequence is just that for children—a sequence. The children were yet to construct *nested* number sequences. A number word was yet to symbolize the number sequence up to and including that number word as one thing. It could symbolize the individual number words in sequence, but it was yet to symbolize a unit containing that sequence. The children still had not constructed a "one more than" relation. They could isolate the number words following and preceding a given number word, but a relation of precedence and "one more than" are quite different because the latter implies order with inclusion, whereas the former implies order without inclusion.

To explain how the children may have constructed a nested number sequence, I turn to the sequential uniting operations that I illustrated in protocol 11. They exemplify the emergence of the uniting operation in the context of the initial number sequence. The technique of hiding part of a collection of items and then asking the children to find how many were hidden contributed to the application of the uniting operation to segments of the initial number sequence. However, performing sequential uniting operations is not the same thing as having these operations symbolized. In fact, the difference is profound. For example, after Scenetra constructed the tacitly nested number sequence, she independently made a choice between using counting-down-to and counting-off-from the first time she was observed using the former to solve a subtractive situation,[15] and we had not worked on counting-down-to in subtraction with her. The solution episode was quite dramatic and occurred in the same way for Tyrone. His use of counting-down-to to solve a subtraction situation was a surprise because we had not worked with him in solving a subtraction situation in that way.

There was reason to believe that Jason reorganized his initial number sequence by February 22 of his second grade, about two months after the teaching episode of protocol 11. We can see the progress Jason made in protocols 14 and 15 excerpted from a teaching experiment on February 15 of his second grade. Just before protocol 14, Jason had counted-on to solve "19 + 6 = _____."

Protocol 14

T: (Makes "19 + 6 = 25" using felt numerals) OK, Jason, can you find any more numbers that make twenty-five?

J: Twenty plus five.

T: Any more?

J: Eighteen plus seven!

Jason then proceeded to say the appropriate expressions to "thirteen plus twelve" after being asked by the teacher each time. The most striking feature of his behavior was the seemingly effortless way in which he generated an appropriate sequence of expressions. This is one of the first times he was observed using a strategy to generate possible addends whose sum was a fixed number. It is called a local compensation strategy because Jason used known sums to generate other sums by adding and subtracting one, starting with a sum he had just found. The second noticeable advance was that Jason could coordinate two number sequences.

Protocol 15

T: (Makes "31 + 6 = 37" using felt numerals) Can you think of some other problems which are like that one, but where you keep thirty-one the same?

J: No, I can't.

T: What would it be if it was seven instead of six?

---

[15] Scenetra solved "48 − 37 = _____." by ticking off fingers synchronous with uttering "47–46–45–44–43–42–41–40–39–38–37" and then said "eleven," recognizing the resulting finger pattern. Immediately afterwards, she solved "53 − 12 = _____." by ticking off fingers synchronous with uttering "52–51–. . .–42." She passed over her thumb without saying "forty-two," a simple error in coordination.

J: Thirty-one plus seven equals thirty-eight.
T: Can you tell me some more?
J: Thirty-one plus nine is forty, ..., thirty-one plus fifteen is forty-six.
T: How far do you think you could keep going like that?
J: 'Till one hundred.

The strategies that Jason was capable of using while he was in the period of his initial number sequence were not iterative. By December 14 of his second grade, he could find the sum of nine and eight by using eighteen as the sum of nine and nine and decreasing it by one, but he did not iterate the strategy. Iterative strategies did not emerge until February 15. In fact, I did not observe him use any strategy until December 14 of his second grade.

To explain his shift to iterative strategies requires postulation of a new use of the uniting operation—progressive uniting operations. He could now take the results of using his uniting operation as material of its application. As a consequence, a number word was now a symbol for a unit containing a number sequence from one up to and including that number word (or any other segment of a number sequence of specific numerosity indicated by the number word).

In protocol 15, Jason could create new unit items by performing a counting act and unite them with what preceded. For the first time, Jason's counting activity could be described as did Sinclair (1971) when explaining Piaget's model of the construction of number. In effect, Jason doubled counted "7 is 38, 8 is 39, 9 is 40, ..., 15 is 46," where the constant addend "31" was understood. I take Jason's words of the two involved number sequences as being his symbols for the progressive uniting operations that he could carry out. "Seven," for example, could be united with the counting acts implied by "six," but I can see no reason to believe that was actually done by Jason as he counted.

Autoregulation as a process of construction. Autoregulation can be used to explain how procedural accommodations like those illustrated in protocol 11 could lead to reorganization of the initial number sequence. In protocol 11, Jason's concept for "eight" had been activated and served as a template for monitoring his further activity. The coordinated sensory signals generated by uttering a number word and the act of putting up a finger fed back into his template and he could combine them into discrete experiential items, one after the other, until he filled the slots that constituted his numerical finger pattern. Without this feedback, there would be no possibility for me to explain how Jason reorganized his counting scheme.

When Jason united the elements of his experiential finger pattern together into a unitary whole, this left the experiential finger pattern "behind" and created an abstract unit comprising a sequence of "slots" that contained the records of the experiential finger pattern. Because it was his numerical finger pattern that had been instantiated (his template had been "externalized" because of the feedback), this amounted to a modification in his concept for "eight." The word could now refer to what I call an "abstract composite unit."

There is no reason to believe that Jason took his finger pattern associated with "15–16–17" in protocol 10 as material for his uniting operation because he could simply recognize the finger pattern as "three." In protocol 11, however, a deliberate act was necessary to extract himself from the experience of creating a finger pattern because he had to take that activity as having been completed in order to focus his attention on the remaining number sequence. He had to "rise above" his experience of the finger pattern and focus his attention on the next lexical item in the backward sequence. Because this item ("nine") symbolized what was not spoken, there was a necessary element of reflection on what he was doing.

This might seem to be enough to reorganize his initial number sequence. But we have to remember that the involved number words were "17–16–. . .–10," and they were involved in the context of his finger pattern. He had created a novel object concept for "eight" that contained these number words. "Eight" still referred to an initial segment of his initial number sequence. In so far as this initial segment was implicit in his instantiated finger pattern for "eight,"he now had constructed an abstract composite unit for "eight" whose elements contained coordinated records of two segments of his verbal number sequence.

This is a reinteriorization of a segment of the initial number sequence, but the reinteriorization was not at a new level. It was still at the same level as the initial number sequence because the numerical composite for eight was first instantiated in experience and then the experiential results of operating were reprocessed, which does constitute a reinteriorization but not at a new level. What I mean can be understood by formulating a possible way of operating that Jason may have used. Had Jason, after counting "17, 16," re-presented the two counting acts and then took the re-presented results as one thing, this would have reinteriorized the two counting acts at a new level and would have involved monitoring counting backward as I have already explained earlier. This provides the child with a possibility of constructing novel operations—progressive uniting operations. For example, after taking "17, 16" as counted items, if Jason re-presented these two counted items and then applied the uniting operation to them, this would create a unit of two countable items. Then uttering "15" (regardless of whether it is coordinated with putting up a finger) and re-presenting the three lexical items involves re-presenting the unit containing the records of saying "17, 16" and applying the uniting operation to what is in re-presentation. This creates the possibility of the child seeing "17, 16, 15" in two ways—as a unit containing records of the three items, where the first two contain records of belonging to a unit created as a result of prior operating. These are records of progressive uniting operations created in operating. To create progressive uniting operations, the child operates on re-presented elements of the initial number sequence using the uniting operation.

Continuing until counting eight times creates a novel number sequence "1, 2, 3, 4, 5, 6, 7, 8" that contains the records of progressive uniting operations at a level of interiorization "above" the initial number sequence. This is a recurrence of the disembedding operation that engendered the initial number sequence, but in a more sophisticated form. Double counting and progressive uniting operations are introduced as novelties. These novelties engender the tacitly nested number sequence, a sequence of abstract unit items that contain records of counting acts, but with the additional feature that when the auditory records are used in re-presentation, the lexical items of the verbal number sequence symbolize progressive uniting operations.

As before, it is not plausible that a child would complete the construction of the tacitly nested number sequence in the context of solving problems such as the those I have previously described. I do not know how many such problem solutions it might take for a child to create a partial number sequence at a level superior to the initial number sequence and a feedback system from the initial number sequence to that partial sequence that is strong enough to sustain autoregulation of the disembedding operation until the process of reinteriorization is completed. But that is what it takes to construct the tacitly nested number sequence.

During the approximately two-month period between December 14 and February 22, there were opportunities for Jason to solve problems in the way I have described (cf. Steffe, 1988, p. 209). Moreover, the process a child uses when solving a problem can only be inferred, so it is possible that reinteriorization of the initial number sequence occurred when I least expected it as a teacher. Although I have no estimate of how many or which problems Jason may have solved, there were apparently enough to sustain the type of perturbations that I have explained and to activate autoregulation of the application of the uniting operation to re-presentations of his initial number sequence. Without appealing to autoregulation to complete the reinteriorization of his initial number sequence that had been initiated in experiential contexts, I could not explain the underlying reorganizations that led to his counting behavior in protocols 14 and 15.

The Explicitly Nested Number Sequence

Jason's period of the tacitly nested number sequence was preparatory for the emergence of the explicitly nested number sequence illustrated in protocol 12. Experiential episodes like those illustrated in protocols 14 and 15 can only encourage the child to apply the uniting operation to figurative segments of the tacitly nested number sequence, creating a unit that contains such segments. This again seemed to lead to an internal reorganization of Jason's number sequence. The new operations allow a child to operate in a way that is no longer sequential. A number word can now symbolize a unit that contains a tacitly nested sequence. The symbolized sequential operations can be carried out, of course, but the child finds new power in leaving them unexpressed.

An important result is that the inclusion relation that was implicit in the tacitly nested number sequence is now made explicit. The child can "see" the inclusion relation in the reorganized number sequence because it is symbolized by the sequence and can therefore intentionally disembed a segment of the explicitly nested number sequence from its inclusion in the containing sequence and treat it as a unit in its own right. The child can also perform these operations using units for which there is no explicit symbol (like the remainder of 27 in 36). Moreover, the child can replace what was extracted, which is another way of saying the child does not destroy the records of the original number sequence by performing these operations. They can now have two number sequences side-by-side and understand that one of them can be included in the other, whereas before they could only coordinate two different number sequences. These sophisticated, reversible part–whole operations are critical to the mathematical progress of the child.

Final Comments

Uses of "Implicit" and "Explicit"

The words *implicit* and *explicit* were used in several ways in the chapter that can be made more general. First, I spoke of Brenda's finger movements as being implicit in her figurative finger patterns and of the movements being made explicit when she sequentially put up fingers when counting (cf. p. 140). I also said that Jason's counting acts "1, 2, 3, 4, 5, 6, 7, 8" were implicit in his numerical finger pattern associated with "eight" and could be made explicit by counting (cf. p. 159). More generally, I would say that Jason's counting acts were implicit in a sequence of abstract unit items. Applying the unitizing operation to sensorimotor or figurative items "strips" them of their sensorimotor material. Because there are records of the sensorimotor material that was "left behind" by the stripping action, what the records point to are implicit in the unit pattern that was "lifted" from the antecedent items. Although the discussion of Brenda's finger pattern did not involve the unitizing operation, it could be elaborated in that way.

On another occasion, I used "implicit" a little differently. When speaking of a subtracting scheme Jason had constructed, I spoke of a goal of the scheme as being implicit in his actions (cf. p. 154). There is definitely a stage in the construction of subtracting schemes and adding schemes where the schemes are interiorized and are available for use but where the child has no awareness of addition and subtraction as operations. In this case, if the child assimilates a situation using her subtracting scheme, the three parts of the scheme are used in assimilation rather than just the first part because all three parts are contained in (or are implicit in) the first part. In Jason's case, "17 − 8" could symbolize the *result of counting* because the activity was recorded in the sequence of abstract unit items symbolized. Being aware of the possible results of acting, or anticipating acting, means that the response of the scheme has been activated but not actualized. The state of activation (or goal) constitutes a perturbation that can be neutralized by acting, and this is why I said that the goal was implicit in Jason's subtracting actions. It could not be separated from the scheme; rather, it was made possible by the functioning scheme. For a goal to be explicit, it would have to refer to no particular activity, as exemplified by Protocol 12. There, the assimilating part–whole operations were sufficient for Jason to create a goal without there being a particular way of operating.

Third, there was Jason's implicit use of figurative patterns for "ten" in protocol 8. He organized his counting activity into two sequences of four abstract unit items (two numerical patterns) and then a pair of abstract unit items. It was because he organized his counting activity in this way that I said the figurative pattern was implicit in his operating (cf. p. 149). The pattern for "ten" was active throughout his counting activity and provided a template he used to organize the activity. He was "inside" of the pattern, reprocessing its material into numerical subpatterns. This use of a "within stage" structure in the creation of novelties that led to vertical reorganization can be contrasted with the following use of the terms.

Fourth, I identified five stages of the counting scheme. In each stage, the products of operating in a preceding stage are made explicit in the current stage in the sense that they can be now taken as material of operating (they were used as material of reprocessing that led to a stage shift). As previously noted, when children are in the stage of the initial number sequence, counting-off-from in subtraction is a method of subtracting for the children, but they have no awareness of why they subtract in that way or why it works. After constructing the tacitly nested number sequence, the children can make decisions concerning whether to count-down-to or to count-off-from when doing a subtraction problem, and they can say why they operate as they do. But the "subtrahend" and the "difference" they create by subtracting are results that they will take as material of further operating when they construct the explicitly nested number sequence. At that stage, the children can use both of these parts and put them "back together" to form the minuend. This new power of operating permits the construction of the inversion between addition and subtraction, but the part-to-whole operations are yet to become material of operating.

Finally, I commented that double counting was implicit in Jason's counting acts and that the counting acts carried the force of double counting (cf. p. 154). Moreover, I commented that the inclusion relation was implicit in the tacitly nested number sequence (cf. p. 160). This is a different use of the term than in the fourth case because there, for the operations involved in double counting to be implicit, the child would have to be able to double count—"four is one, five is two, etc." If I wanted to say that double counting was implicit for the child in the fourth sense of using the term, I would have to be able to make the inference that the child could double count and that he was aware of the results of double counting but could not use those results as material for further operating. The child would know how to double count and would be aware of double counting in that way. But he would not be aware of the structure of operating. This might seem to be confusing, but when I said that the counting acts carried the force of double counting, the comment was made from the perspective of that part of my mathematical knowledge that did not include Jason's mathematical knowledge. My analysis of "implicit" and "explicit" in the first four cases are from the point of view of the actor only—that part of my mathematical knowledge that does include the child's mathematical knowledge.

When the knowledge of two people enters into consideration, the terms *explicit* and *implicit* take on new meaning. As observer, I say that double counting is *implicit* if the child puts up fingers to make records of counting backward even though the child cannot double count. The child's behavior *fits* my concept of double counting in that *I can see* coordinations the child makes, because putting up a finger when saying "sixteen" functions as a double count. The child's finger pattern for "eight" serves as an "automatic" counting device and makes the functional coordination possible. So, when the child is able to function as, if he were using operations that are not available to him, I as observer call those operations implicit. This may seem to be only semantics, but it is an important distinction because what an observer can "see" in the way a child currently functions may be a forerunner of novelties the child constructs in subsequent stages.

The distinction between what is implicit or explicit in one frame of reference versus two frames of reference is made from the point of view of the observer. Nevertheless, one can make *within-model* distinctions as well as *between-model* distinctions. For example, from the perspective of *within-model* distinctions, the initial number sequence is a reorganization of the figurative counting scheme and the tacitly nested number sequence is a reorganization of the initial number sequence. From that perspective, we have to ask whether any number sequence is what Fischbein (1987) calls a primary intuition because novelties are introduced in the constructive process that have no natural roots, if "natural roots" is interpreted to mean roots in sensory experience. Double counting, for example, is introduced by the operating child through reprocessing re-presented segments of the initial number sequence using the unitizing operation. In other words, it is introduced by the child through operating on the products of past operating.

The initial number sequence is also constructed by the child through autoregulation of using the unitizing operation, so it too has no "natural roots." Because it is the first mathematical concept, my only conclusion is that none of mathematics can be categorized as a primary intuition if we speak from the point of view of the actor. From that point of view, if there is any part of mathematics that one would want to call intuitive, and that is certainly the case, it seems to me that it would be at least a secondary intuition. Mathematics *has no natural roots* but is introduced as a novelty by the operating organism.

It is also important to note that while children are in a given learning stage of the counting scheme, they perform operations that engender the next stage. The products of operating in a given stage prepare the way for the next stage, but a reorganization is required to achieve the next stage. So, even in this very elementary case, children reorganize their counting scheme as they achieve a new stage. The entire counting scheme is reorganized rather than pieces of it, which is what Fischbein takes as being necessary for a secondary intuition. The reorganization that leads to the explicitly nested number sequence is the fourth, so it might be called a fourth order intuition rather than a secondary intuition.

There is no necessity for anyone to construct mathematics, even the initial number sequence. But the observation that almost all human beings do construct elementary mathematical concepts and operations does make it reasonable to make a distinction between something like primary and secondary intuitions. I believe this distinction is based on two frames of reference—Fischbein's knowledge of mathematics (and physics) that does not include the mathematics of children and his knowledge of the mathematics of children. This is a fundamental and essential distinction that is especially important when considering what the mathematics of schooling might be.

Experiencing Uncertainties

The question of how a child might become aware of an uncertainty in the results of operating is central to formulating a theory of cognitive constructions. Some progress can be made on the question in the particular case of Tyrone that I mentioned (cf. p. 151). Tyrone was yet to construct numerical patterns, but he had constructed figurative patterns as meanings of the number words through "five." His counting scheme was a figurative scheme and, like Jason, he was a counter of motor unit items. Given a collection of items to count where the items were hidden by two screens, one hiding seven and the other five, Tyrone tried to count the items beginning with "one." He characteristically pointed to the screen hiding the seven items synchronous with uttering the first seven number words and then continued on, pointing to the second screen synchronous with uttering "8, 9, ..." Tyrone's points of contact formed a row, but there were no visible traces and hence no visual pattern that was obvious to the observer. Nevertheless, "five" had meaning for Tyrone in that he could visualize a domino five pattern upon hearing the word spoken and this pattern served in goal setting—count five more times. But he could not stop counting at a specific counting act to fulfill his goal for the simple reason that the figurative pattern was not used in keeping track of counting nor could it be used to recognize five counting acts. Nevertheless, it was an active goal. So, because there was no feedback from the results of counting to the goal that activated counting, the goal could not be satisfied by performing the activity. This creates an uncertainty in knowing when to stop counting. In fact, it led to Tyrone's reinitializing his counting scheme and using his unitizing operation to reprocess re-presented results of counting in the creation of a feedback system.

Children's Mathematics and Education

Teaching experiments. Children's mathematics consists of the mathematical schemes of children that can function reliably and effectively and how those schemes might be modified as they are used. The methodology of the teaching experiment was developed for the explicit purpose of isolating those schemes and their modifications. A teaching experiment, even a two-year teaching experiment, usually is not taken to replace the overall educational experiences of children in mathematics. Rather, the goal is to study the mathematical operations of children, and the teaching episodes constitute occasions for observation. The researchers do not assume that there is a causal relation between what transpires in the teaching episodes and what the child learns. Quite the contrary, the teaching experiment is conducted in the context of the ongoing school program in mathematics and the changes that are observed in teaching episodes might well be a result of what transpired in the child's mathematics classroom. The teaching episodes are supplementary to the school mathematics program and so become a window on the mathematical operations children construct outside as well as within teaching episodes.

Because a teaching experiment consists of a sequence of teaching episodes, it is possible to observe modifications children make in their schemes. The goal is to learn the mathematics of children, and this is why it is essential to be a participant in children's cognitive constructions. Piaget (1964) isolated experience as one crucial factor of intellectual development, and this applies to researchers who aim at acquiring knowledge concerning children's conceptual structures and their evolution. My intention is to maximize my experience and reflection on that experience because the mathematical knowledge of children is always and inevitably seen in terms of my own frame of reference and can therefore be known only in terms of my own concepts and operations. There is no other way known to me that a viable theory of children's cognitive constructions in mathematics can be formulated.

A theory of cognitive constructions will always be relative to those who do the constructing. Researchers who build up a theory of children's mathematics can of course never discover what the children's "real" knowledge is in an ontological sense. What we can and must try to do is to build a model that is compatible with our observations of children; and because we assume, as scientists do, that there is some regularity in our experiential world, we can reach a point of relative closure after which we may feel justified to project the model into the future and to make predictions about further experiences with children. The "generality" of the models that are constructed relies on the theoretical constructs that are used in the conceptual analyses that comprise model building and on the powers of reasoning and insights of the model builders. But having something to explain is an essential part of building cognitive models—one must construct something like primary intuitions—and that is why theory and observation are mutually supporting.

The mathematics of schooling. There is always the question concerning the total educational experiences of children in mathematics and how the models constructed in a teaching experiment can contribute to those experiences. Personally, I can see no viable alternative to making children's mathematics the mathematics of schooling. To do less seems to me to continue to appeal to mathematics as we adults know it for the mathematics of schooling, a practice that trivializes the mathematics that children do construct.

For example, children's number sequences in a given culture cannot be taken as being imbued with all of their cultural meaning, if for no other reason than the operations that they symbolize can be quite different among children to say nothing of the differences between children and adults. It is quite significant that the verbal number sequence was built up long before a mature system of written numerals became established.

> Our researches thus far have shown us that the laws that govern early numerals, ordering and grouping, do not in fact correspond to the rule of the sequence, which is stepwise gradation. Hence, the writing of numerals is not merely the representation of the number-word sequence. (Menninger, 1969, p. 53)

Menninger's observation that Roman and Indo-European number sequences differ only in minor details, but that their systems of numeration differ radically, demonstrates the independence of verbal and written systems. It also provides a perspective on why there can be an unresolved tension between children's verbal number sequences and written numerals.

Whatever those numerical operations are that are available to children, they are initially symbolized by their verbal number sequences. Because of the way arithmetic is taught, these verbal number sequences often do not serve as a basis for children's constructing the written system. The current "place value" approach to teaching number sequences used by most school mathematics programs serves as an example. Although logically impeccable, this cardinal approach puts great demands on the children's uniting operation. After making one ten, the children are to make one ten and one more (a progressive uniting operation) and name that "eleven," and continue on until making two tens. They are then to take these two tens together as a unit to form a composite unit involving three ranks. They are to "see" twenty as a unit containing two units each of which contains ten units. To give meaning to "twenty" as "two tens," they have to unpack the containing unit into two tens and to further unpack the two tens and apprehend those singleton units as "twenty," because that was involved in establishing the two tens. This unit composition and decomposition is very demanding because it involves making a unit of units of units.

Children who have only constructed the initial number sequence must *make* a unit of units in activity and cannot take the resulting abstract composite unit as a given in further operating. So, we can see the large gap between the operations available to these children and what is demanded of them in the school program to work with "twenty." These children view "twenty" in terms of the intensive and extensive meanings that I have outlined *for units of one*. To organize these two meanings into a unit of units of units as I have just described is not possible for these children in their immediate future. The situation is only a little better for children whose number words symbolize part–whole operations because they are also yet to construct a unit of units of units. They can find how many tens are in, say, 100 by counting by tens, but they have to actually perform the activity to find that result. Prior to counting, they do not view 100 blocks, say, as being already partitioned into so many abstract composite units of ten. They can construct these partitioning operations, but that is another learning stage beyond the five I have already identified.

So, the results of teaching experiments can have fundamental importance for teaching mathematics in the elementary school if the mathematics of concern consists of children's mathematics. Given that this mathematics has been and will continue to be isolated in the interactive mathematical communication between adults and children (as well as among children) in learning environments, my hope is that it will be taken seriously by other mathematics educators as they strive to build educational programs in mathematics that are harmonious with children's ways and means of operating.

References

Brouwer, L. E. J. (1913). Intuitionism and formalism. *Bulletin of the American Mathematical Society*, *20*, 81–96.

Caramuel, J. (1977). Meditatio prooemialis, mathesis biceps. In A. Parea, P. Soriano, & P. Terzi (Eds.), *L'aritmetica binaria e le altre aritmetiche di Giovanni Caramuel, Vescovo di Vigevano*. Vigevano, Italy: Academia Tiberina. (Original work published 1670)

Cobb, P., & Steffe, L. P. (1983). The constructivist researcher as teacher and model builder. *Journal for Research in Mathematics Education*, *14*, 83–94.

Cobb, P., & Wheatley, G. (1988). Children's initial understandings of ten. *Focus on Learning Problems in Mathematics*, *10* (3), 1–28.

Fischbein, E. (1987). *Intuition in science and mathematics*. Dordrecht, Holland: D. Reidel.

Gelman, R., & Gallistel, C. R. (1978). *The child's understanding of number*. Cambridge: Harvard University Press.

Hausdorff, F. (1962). *Set theory*. New York: Chelsea.

Hunting, R. (1983). Emerging methodologies for understanding internal processes governing children's mathematical behavior. *The Australian Journal of Education*, *27*(1), 45–61.

Menninger, K. (1969). *Number words and number symbols: A cultural history of numbers*. Cambridge: The MIT Press.

Piaget, J. (1937). *La construction du reel chez l'enfant*. Neuchatel: Delachaux et Niestle.

Piaget, J. (1964). Development and learning. In R. E. Ripple, V. N. Rockcastle (Eds.), *Piaget rediscovered: A report of the conference on cognitive studies and curriculum development* (pp. 7–29). Ithaca: Cornell University Press.

Piaget, J. (1980a). *Adaptation and intelligence: Organic selection and phenocopy*. Chicago: University of Chicago Press.

Piaget, J. (1980b). The psychogenesis of knowledge and its epistemological significance. In M. Piattelli-Palmarini (Ed.), *Language and learning: The debate between Jean Piaget and Noam Chomsky* (pp. 23–34). Cambridge: Harvard University Press.

Sinclair, H. (1971). Number and measurement. In M. F. Rosskopf, L. P. Steffe, & S. Taback (Eds.), *Piagetian cognitive development research and mathematical education* (pp. 149–159). Washington, DC: NCTM.

Steffe, L. P. (1983). The teaching experiment in a constructivist research program. In M. Zweng, T. Green, J. Kilpatrick, H. Pollak, & M. Suydam (Eds.), Proceedings of the forth international congress on mathematical education (pp. 469–471). Boston: Birkhauser.

Steffe, L. P. (1988). Lexical and syntactical meanings: Tyrone, Scenetra and Jason. In L. P. Steffe & P. Cobb (Eds.), *Construction of arithmetical meanings and strategies* (pp. 148–221). New York: Springer Verlag.

Steffe, L. P. & Cobb, P. (with E. von Glasersfeld). (1988). *Construction of arithmetical meanings and strategies*. New York: Springer Verlag.

Steffe, L. P., Richards, J., & von Glasersfeld, E. (1979). Experimental models for the child's acquisition of counting and of addition and subtraction. In K. Fuson & W. E. Geeslin (Eds.), *Explorations in the modeling of the learning of mathematics* (pp. 27–44). Columbus: ERIC Clearinghouse for Science, Mathematics, and Environmental Education.

Steffe, L. P., von Glasersfeld, E., Richards, J., & Cobb, P. (1983). *Children's counting types: Philosophy, theory, and application*. New York: Praeger Scientific.

Thompson, P. (1982a). A theoretical framework for understanding young children's concepts of whole number numeration. *Dissertation Abstracts International*, *43*, 1868A.

Thompson, P. (1982b). Were lions to speak, we wouldn't understand. *Journal of Mathematical Behavior*, *3*(2), 145–165.

Van Engen, H. (1949). An analysis of meaning in arithmetic. *Elementary School Journal*, *49*, 321–329, 395–400.

Vergnaud, G. (1987). About constructivism. In J. C. Bergeron, N. Herscovics, & C. Kieran (Eds.), *Psychology of mathematics education: PME-XI* (pp. 42–54). Montreal, Canada.

von Foerster, H. (1984). On constructing a reality. In P. Watzlawick (Ed.), *The invented reality: How do we know what we believe we know?* London: W. W. Norton.

von Glasersfeld, E. (1980). The concept of equilibration in a constructivist theory of knowledge. In F. Benseler, P. M. Hejl, & W. K. Kock (Eds.), *Autopoiesis, communication, and society* (pp. 75–85). Frankfurt: Campus Verlag.

von Glasersfeld, E. (1981). An attentional model for the conceptual construction of units and number. *Journal for Research in Mathematics Education, 12,* 83–94.

von Glasersfeld, E. (1983). Learning as constructive activity. In J. C. Bergeron & N. Herscovics (Eds.), *Proceedings of the Fifth Annual Meeting of the North American Chapter of the International Group for the Psychology of Mathematics Education.* PME-NA, Montreal, Canada.

Vygotsky, L. S. (1934/1956). Leaning and mental development at school age. In A. N. Leontiev & A. R. Luria (Eds.), *Selected psychological works* (pp. 438–452), Moscow.

Wheeler, D. (1987). The world of mathematics: Dream, myth, or reality? In J. C. Bergeron, N. Herscovics, & C. Kierean (Eds.), *Psychology of mathematics education: PME-XI* (pp. 55–66). Montreal, Canada.

7

Literacy Development: Construction and Reconstruction

Emilia Ferreiro

Centro de Investigaciones y Estudios Avanzados (CINVESTAV)—Mexico

The difficulties children face and try to overcome in their efforts to become the owners of the socially constituted writing system could hardly be understood if we do not question the deeply rooted idea that an alphabetical writing system consists basically of a way of coding phonic units into graphic ones. It is only when we consider the alphabetical writing system as being primarily a *representational system* (as *any* writing system is) that we can understand that many of the difficulties children face are indeed legitimate problems, and we can start to recognize that the solutions they elaborate are, in fact, original constructions.

Children's difficulties are not primarily linked to the arbitrariness of the symbols utilized.[1] The construction of any kind of representational system (I will speak here only about *systems of representation*, not about isolate conventional representations) requires, first of all, making a clear distinction within all the elements, properties, and relations identified in the object, among those that will be kept in the representation and those that will be left aside, even though they are recognized as being important. This step is not characterized by arbitrariness. Arbitrariness appears only afterwards, when it becomes necessary to choose the particular shapes, forms, colors, distances, and so on that will represent the elements, properties, or relationships distinguished in the real object.

In all our research on developmental literacy, we have been able to show that children look for an answer to a very general question: the nature of the link between the real object (i.e., language, as they know it) and its representation (as it is assimilated by them during their development) (cf. Ferreiro, 1984, 1985, 1986, 1988; Ferreiro & Teberosky, 1982).

No representation could be identical to the piece of reality it intends to represent. If it were identical, it would not be a representation but another instance of the same kind of reality. As a consequence, a convenient representation should combine two seemingly incompatible conditions: It must retain some of the properties and relations of the real object but, at the same time, it must necessarily leave aside

---

[1] The arbitrariness of the system can be neither its ultimate legitimation nor the principal learning difficulty, because prior to learning that a given arbitrary representation could be substituted by anyone else, children may approach the task to understand such a system by searching for nonarbitrary reasons (as they in fact do).

some of its recognized properties and relations. To ask "what is represented by a writing system?" is a legitimate question. It cannot be answered by simply saying "it represents language," because the link between "language" and this particular kind of representation (the alphabetical writing system) is neither direct nor obvious. The complex nature of linguistic symbols leaves the door open to a variety of ways to conceive a convenient representation for language and, in fact, many different solutions have been given historically.

Once a convenient representational system has been constructed, it is easy to conceive other derivative systems, taking the original one as the starting point and changing the way to represent the *already distinguished* elements, properties, and relationships. I submit that only in this last case are we really engaging in a coding activity when searching for a *new code for a formerly existing representational system.*[2] The important difference between both activities (constructing a representational system and constructing a new code) lies in this fact: In order to construct a new code we take the already established units, properties, and relationships as *given*, without questioning them. On the other hand, to construct a representational system one is bound to analyze the piece of reality to be represented. Historically speaking, the construction of such representational systems has been carried out through extended periods of time before they become socially validated. The history of writing is the history of one of the most powerful representational systems created by humanity.

It may be argued that *constructing* a representation is one thing, whereas *accepting* a representation already built up and culturally validated is quite another matter. The point in question is not to deny the difference but rather that such a difference does not consist in an opposition between an *active* process and a *receptive* one. In the case of other socially constructed objects (the standard meter, for instance), we know that it is not enough to provide the learner with the directions for use (cf. Piaget, Inhelder, & Szeminska, 1948): Children need to reconstruct some of the *basic operations* that constitute it. (This *does not* mean, of course, to recapitulate the historical pathway.) The same seems to apply to other socially constituted systems of marks, such as the graphic representation of numbers (cf. Sinclair, Bamberger, Ferreiro, Frey-Streiff, & Sinclair, 1988), although we do not yet have as much data concerning the comprehension of the written symbols of "graphic arithmetics" as we have data concerning written language.

Once all this has been said, we may now turn to the question of what is the school asking children to do when approaching the task of learning how to read and write. Children are treated as if their task were merely a coding task, as if all they needed to do was distinguish the sound units (phones) and match them to the graphic units (letters). All the exceptions (which are indeed more than a few!) are avoided at the

---

[2] For instance, the construction of a Morse code is the construction of a new code for the alphabetical representation of natural languages: Every graphic configuration in the first system (i.e., the letters) is transformed in a sequence of dots and lines; a one-to-one correspondence is established between both sets; "new letters" are not added nor are "old distinctions" missed.

beginning because the system is treated as if it were characterized by a perfect one-to-one correspondence. Children are supposed to acquire a particular skill, not to understand a particular type of representation.

The presuppositions underlying this kind of pedagogic attitude are clear enough. In the first place, once a particular writing system has been socially adopted and convalidated, it seems so "natural" to the members of the society that any other solution appears to be "unnatural." So, the alphabetical writing system is not conceived anymore as *a particular solution* to the problem of language representation, but as *the* solution (all the others being merely attempts to do it). Second, there is another presupposition rooted in the traditional view that a mechanical phase must precede the intelligent use of it. This conception was applied traditionally to arithmetics (learning by rote the multiplication tables, for instance), but nowadays it is difficult to find researchers (and even teachers) who rationally maintain this kind of approach. Thanks mainly to the pioneering work of Piaget, it is now widely recognized that learning mathematics implies developing some of the most powerful categories of logical thinking. However, in the field of reading and writing it was only very recently that learning became conceived as being from the very beginning a matter of thinking rather than a process starting with the learning of "the mechanics of the code" in order to proceed afterward (but only afterward) to an intelligent use of the code.

Even though the school reduces the alphabetical writing system to a code and, as a consequence, its learning boils down to a technical matter, children—usually by themselves—are approaching the task from another standpoint. Some of the questions that guide their search could be formulated in the following question, "What is the relationship between these particular marks and language?" Some way or another children who grow in literate environments may reach the conclusion that these marks have the property of eliciting language, but this is not enough to reach the conclusion that these marks in fact stand for the language they already know how to speak. Even when children reach the conclusion that these special marks stand for language, new problems arise—precisely the ones linked to the construction of a representational system. For instance, do the differences between the marks stand for differences between the signifiers themselves or rather between the meanings attached to them? Strings of sounds without meaning would not be communicative. Children are reluctant to pay exclusive attention to the sounds because they know that meaning cannot be disregarded as far as one likes to remain in a linguistic framework. And what about the properties, objects, and situations referred to? Are they relevant to constitute the representation as such? Children will discover progressively that many aspects of language, so important as the words themselves to convey the meaning of a message (intonation, for instance), are almost entirely disregarded by the representation. They will discover that differences in strings of sounds are put on the first place but also that the system is far from being consistent in its way of treating differences in sound. They need to deal with particularities of the graphic display that are not inherent to the main principles of an alphabetical writing system. Such is the case, for instance, of empty spaces that are not related to voice stops but are used to indicate word boundaries, a category of speech that children have certainly dealt with at the oral level, but that they will need to revise because writing itself will oblige the learner to adopt a new definition of what a word is.

While children are approaching written language as a conceptual task, the school treats them merely as machines that are not so well prepared for the task of discriminating and associating forms with sounds. Children construct knowledge about the written language that has remained nonobservable[3] since researchers did not question the presuppositions that guide the traditional school approach—they did not question the deeply rooted idea that an alphabetical writing system consists basically of a way of coding phonic units into graphic ones. Children construct knowledge about the written language that also remains implicit in school environments where the teachers' approach prevents them from recognizing any growth in knowledge (not in skills) in their pupils.

Now, let us assume that researchers *and* teachers agree on recognizing that children build up "wonderful ideas" about the socially constituted writing system. They may recognize this without accepting that these ideas have anything to do with the "right ideas" needed to deal with an alphabetical writing system. In such a case, teachers *and* researchers may agree on the convenience of helping children become aware of their wonderful (but useless) ideas, in order to contribute to destroying them (the ideas, of course).

Here lies, in my opinion, one of the more common misconceptions: It is easy to accept that children have wonderful ideas, and even to collect and publish them as a collection of anecdotes. But these ideas—conceived merely as funny things—are in one way or another condemned in advance to the waste basket (as is childhood itself—it is a wonderful period of life, but it will be inescapably replaced by another period, no doubt less funny but surely more reliable). Following this conception, the wonderful ideas that precede (developmentally speaking) the "right ones" do not play any role in generating the next developmental set of ideas, except the role of precedence. But to precede does not necessarily mean to contribute to the next period. A chronological relation of precedence does not imply a relation of conditionality or one of causality.

It is important to point out that to adopt a constructivist view implies the acceptance that precedence is not enough. A researcher convinced of the usefulness of constructivism will search among the antecedents of such or such behavior the ones that may constitute real antecedents of the next period, trying to explain why the construction of a novelty could be realized taking as the starting point the previous construction. In this sense, earlier children's ideas could not be dismissed simply as being "wrong." Of course, among the "wonderful ideas" we need to distinguish those that are shared by many children (perhaps all children) and those

---

[3] In Piaget's theory all the *observables* are constructed; they depend on the assimilatory schema—in this case, the theoretical framework—that allow them to become observables. No one of them—at any developmental level, including scientific knowledge—is immediately "given."

that could be sustained by some children but do not express a kind of consensus among children at a given point in their development. Next, we need to distinguish among the ideas shared by many children those that constitute landmarks in development in the precise sense that they fulfill the function of making possible the next development. This function could be accomplished by ideas that in a certain sense "prefigurate" the "right ones," but *also* by ideas that will conflict with others. It is important to keep in mind that some of these ideas (that express, in fact, assimilatory schemas) are not wrong in themselves: Some of them could be right in a limited domain, becoming wrong only when overgeneralized; others need to be relativized; others—and this is particularly important in the case of literacy development—will be right if applied to other systems, not to the alphabetical one.

I would like to give two examples of these apparently wrong ideas that fulfill a special role in literacy development: the minimum quantity principle and the syllabic hypothesis.

The Minimum Quantity Principle

We have given this name to a requirement that children express very clearly in their writing productions and also (although with less force) in their interpretations of environmental print. This requirement could be expressed in the following terms: We need a given amount of letterlike forms (usually three) to have a written string that could receive a meaningful interpretation. Of course, children do not express this requirement in those terms. Their behaviors correspond to a wide range of spontaneous remarks and elicited answers. For instance, Gabriel (4 yrs–7 mos) was drawing letters—an activity that he himself differentiated from the activity of writing. He wrote three different letters, looked at the result, and said aloud: "With all of this it can already say something . . .!" (In Spanish: "Con todo esto ya puede decir algo . . .!"). When we present a set of written cards asking children to sort the ones that are "good for reading," Spanish-speaking children reject those with few letters (one or two) saying that "con sólo dos no se puede leer," while French-speaking children say "on ne peut pas lire avec seulement deux," and English-speaking children say "has to have more letters," "has to have lots of letters." (Data obtained with Italian-speaking children are similar; cf. Ferreiro, 1988; Freeman & Whitesell, 1985; Pontecorvo & Zucc02hermaglio, 1988.)

The importance of this requirement lies in two facts: In the first place, it is never taught (neither formally nor informally) because in the languages mentioned, there are many written common words with one or two letters; in the second place, this requirement is repeatedly disconfirmed by data coming from environmental print (where there many written common words appear with one or two letters).

What is the function fulfilled by such a requirement, so strongly kept by children during a relatively long period of their literacy development? Why do they continue to keep it in spite of disconfirming evidence and in spite of a lack of confirmation from literate persons of their environment? One of the functions of the minimum quantity requirement is to keep a distinction between the elements used to write (the letters) and a meaningful piece of writing. A letter is an isolatable element without meaning; a written noun or word is a string of letters. In order to have a string one needs more than one element. Two is enough for some children but not for all of them. With three elements (i.e., with three letters) we reach consensus: All children agree that this is the ideal minimum amount.

What could be the origin of the numerical value of the minimum quantity requirement? Children who use this requirement never count in front of a piece of writing. When dealing with strings of three, four, or more elements, they immediately considered them as being "interpretable," without a previous counting. Preliminary data from our current research seem to indicate that the "magic number three" is related to the quantitative (but nonnumeric) evaluations of countable sets of small elements. Three could function as the frontier between "few" and "many." Languages such as Spanish or English do not have a precise common term between "many" and "few" to refer to a quantity that is "just enough." (There is such a term in French: "*Juste assez*" is a common term that refers precisely to the frontier between few and many). Asking four- and five-year-old children to evaluate sets composed of small objects (that were constructed initially by one-to-one correspondence and were then transformed by addition or subtraction of elements), we find that some children use a verbal dichotomy; others utilize many diminutive forms that apply to the way to be "few" (*poquitito* or *poquititito* can roughly be translated as "very little" or "very very little"; the suffix form -*ito* can be reiterated as many times necessary). There are other types of verbal solutions that we will not deal with here. The only important point is that each individual child seems to have an internal evaluation of the frontier between "few" and "many" and also that she seems to be rather consistent in the way to apply verbal labels to the sets (taking into account, however, that changes introduced by addition are not necessarily treated as symmetrical to those introduced by subtraction of elements).

It seems then, that we need to distinguish between (a) the minimum quantity requirement, that fulfill the function of keeping the distinction between the elements that compose a totality and the totality itself (i.e., just one particular case of a very general cognitive problem: the distinction between the parts and the totality; (b) the *numeric* value assigned to this requirement, that apparently is related to other types of problems, in particular to the quantitative (but nonnumeric) evaluations of small sets. In both cases we are in front of general cognitive solutions elaborated to deal with general problems—not just specific literacy problems.

I would say that this is not very surprising. As any constructivist developmental psychologist knows, when we find, in a given domain, some kind of idea that is sustained by children against all kind of contradictory evidence, it is seldom the case that this idea would be restrained to the particular domain on which we were focusing.

This does not mean that all principles or requirements children build up in literacy development are nonspecific in nature. Next we analyze a kind of problem that, although having certain general aspects, receives a peculiar definition in written language domains.

Now, it is useful to point out that in later periods in literacy development, particularly when children start to understand that letter strings have a particular relationship with the sound pattern of the word (i.e., the beginning of the phonetization period[4]), the minimum quantity requirement fulfills the function of introducing new and unexpected conflicts. One of the most common conflicts in this period arises with the written representation of monosyllabic or bisyllabic words: According to the syllabic hypothesis (one letter = one syllable), these words must be written with only one or two letters; but children still keep alive the idea that a letter and a written word are two different things, so one or two letters are not enough to obtain a *meaningful string*. So, thanks to the minimum quantity requirement we see children looking for ways to add "pieces of sound" to the monosyllabic or bisyllabic words. This is very often accomplished in Spanish by two procedures that help the children keep their hypotheses: to give the diminutive of a given word or to obtain two syllables by duplication of the intermediate vowel. To give the diminutive of a given word generally means, in Spanish, to add one or more syllables to the word [for instance: bar-qui-to (little boat) instead of bar-co (boat); pan-ci-to or pa-ne-ci-to (little bread) instead of pan (bread)]. Most of the monosyllabic words that are related to common objects present a definite string composed of consonant–vowel–consonant; this way of composition allows the following procedure: In order to obtain a bisyllabic word you may repeat the vowel, one as the final part of the first syllable and the other as the initial part of the second syllable [for instance pa-an instead of pan (bread); ma-ar instead of mar (sea); pe-ez instead of pez (fish), etc.]. However, these procedures cannot be applied to all the situations. Children repeatedly face the need to add more letters that cannot be justified by the syllabic hypothesis. In this sense, the minimum quantity requirement helps children understand that they need to go "beyond the syllable" in order to find in the oral word enough "pieces of sound" to put in correspondence with the minimum quantity of letters required.[5]

The Construction of the Syllabic Hypothesis

Before starting their syllabic period in literacy development, children are able to make syllabic decomposition of a word at the oral level (at least in a task that implies making a stop before each one of the "oral pieces" of a given word). However, this "know-how" at the oral level seems to need a reconstruction in order

---

[4] In languages with a strong syllabic structure such as Spanish the phonetization period starts with the search of a one-to-one correspondence between syllables and letters.

[5] Pontecorvo and Zucchermagliio (1988) write: "In our data, we found that all children who were writing syllabically . . . have, with mono- or bisyllabic words, a conflict between the hypothesis of minimum quantity and the syllabic hypothesis."

to be applied to writing situations. Not yet conclusive but indeed very suggestive evidence comes from a research work of Sofia Vernon (1986). She employed the following technique. She selected a group of four- to five-year-old children who were at the most evolved period of presyllabic development (showing quantitative control of their written productions—minimum and maximum number of graphemes; intra- and interrelational qualitative differentiations[6]). She asked those children to write a set of words (belonging to the same conceptual field) having different number of syllables. But instead of allowing them to write the word at once, she interrupted the writing, asking the child "what does it say" with one, two, three letters (etc.) until reaching the number of letters children required.

Employing this technique she found various types of responses. The most interesting are the following:

1.   Children are not able to interpret the parts as such. With only one letter "it doesn't say anything" (minimum quantity requirement); with two or three letters "it says" the whole word; however, the word has not yet the status of a "complete" piece of writing.

Example: Itzel [starting to write triciclo (tricycle) she writes an O]

What does it say?	Nothing (she adds another letter: O r)
What does it say?	Triciclo
It is enough?	No
Does it need anything more?	Yes (she adds another letter: O r F)
What does it say?	Triciclo
It is enough?	Yes.

2.   Children hesitate between saying the first (syllabic) part of a word or the entire word as such when the writing is still unfinished.

Example: Pablo. [He starts to write barco (boat) with O]

What does it say?	Barco, bar
Do you need any more letters?	(He adds another letter: O t)
What does it say?	Barco
It is ready now?	No
What does it say?	Bar, barco
Do you need more?	Yes (He adds another: O t ∃)
	Barco.

3.   Children get to distinguish the beginning of a word (the first syllable) and the whole. To an "incomplete" string of letters they attribute the first syllable; as the addition of letters does not change the "incompleteness" of the string, they continue to say the same syllable until reaching the required amount of letters.

---

[6] Cf. Ferreiro, 1988, for a precise definition of these technical terms.

Example: Lupita. [She starts to write barco *(boat)]*

Q	ba
QI	ba
QIꓱ	ba
QIꓱI	ba
QIꓱIE	ba
QIꓱIEA	barco!

4. These are answers that are very close to the preceding ones. The difference lies in an incipient awareness of the fact that an addition of letters implies a change in the sound. However, instead of answering with some kind of "sound incrementation" (quantitative variation), these children make qualitative variations on the initial syllable.

Example: Vladimir. (He starts to write tortilla*)*

∩	tor
∩I	tor
∩Iꓱ	tar
∩IꓱN	tir
∩IꓱNI	tor
∩IꓱNIO	tortilla

5. Children start finding a quantitative correspondence: More letters imply more sounds. But they are not able to make a correct anticipation, so they usually write more letters than needed. This forces them to adjust the uttered parts of these "additional" writing pieces. Three main procedures are used to obtain such adjustments: vocalic changes, the introduction of consonants with a "neutral" value, and the passage to the diminutive of the word.

Example: Karla [She starts to write avion *(airplane)]*

L	a-vi
LA	avío
LAR	a-vi-o
LΛRO	a-vü-o (ü = French /y/)
LAROL	a-vü-oon
LAROLO	a-vi-on, avión

Example: Angiu [She starts to write tamarindo*]*

E	ta
EM	ta-ma
EMI	ta-ma-rin
EMII	ta-ma-rin-m
EMIIM	ta-ma-rin-m-m
EMIIMO	ta-ma-rin-m-m-m
EMIIMOO	tamarindo

6. The most evolved answers are those provided by children who make consistent efforts to keep the quantitative correspondence under control: An increase in the number of letters is followed by an increase in the number of uttered syllables, even when this adjustment is not exactly one syllable per letter.

*Example: Rodrigo (He starts to write **tamarindo**)*

I	ta
Ib	ta-ma
IbF	ta-ma-rindo

It must be remembered that all these answers come from children who have no difficulty in making a syllabic decomposition of the word at the oral level. It seems, then, that the syllabic hypothesis—constructed at a given moment to explain the relationship between a whole (the written word) and its parts (the constitutive letters)—does not result in a mere application of a previous "know-how" at the oral level. The evidence suggests that children need to rediscover (reconstruct) the syllable in order to elaborate a new "theory" about the writing system.

Implicit and Explicit Knowledge in Educational and Psychological Domains

Now, let us take the two examples just briefly mentioned in order to analyze their pedagogical implications. We may ask some questions and provide some tentative answers.

Are children aware of the fact that the minimum quantity requirement is not useful in dealing with an alphabetical writing system? If not, is it useful to make them aware of this inadequacy, hoping that they will abandon such a requirement?

Accepting that this requirement helps them keep the distinction between elements and totalities, we can answer that the inadequacy of this internal requirement to some of the characteristics of external print is not the main point. At the beginning of the phonetization period, children are trying to understand what kind of segmentation of utterances fits with the socially convalidated way of writing. It is not sufficient to inform them that letters stand for phonemes.[7]

If we agree with the previous analyses, according to which the minimum quantity principle has an intrinsic rationality and a positive role to play in development—because of the introduction of conflicts that need to be overcome—then we cannot treat such a requirement as being simply "a wrong idea." Instead, we can stimulate children to face situations in which this principle seems to be contradicted; we can provoke multiple confrontations between the way such or such an utterance could be represented and the conventional way to do it.

Does it help to make children aware of the fact that only an analysis of utterances

---

[7] It is neither sufficient nor adequate because phonemes are abstract entities that cannot be shown directly. Consonant phonemes cannot be physically realized independently. In addition, a particular realization of a phoneme is only a *particular realization*; we cannot present a given phoneme as such.

in terms of their ultimate sound constituents is useful to deal with an alphabetical writing system? What is the necessity of waiting until children discover first a kind of rigorous syllabic correspondence in order to abandon it afterward? Would it be more useful to prevent children from exploring such "blind alleys," helping them to find more quickly the "right roads"?

Piaget used to say that everything we teach children prevents them from inventing or discovering it. It is, of course, an expression that opens the way to many misunderstandings. It does not mean that teaching is useless nor that it is better to wait until children discover all by themselves. It does mean that explicit teaching is useful only when it helps children go by themselves over the necessary steps to become convinced of the soundness or appropriateness of such or such a solution. Nothing is easier than taking a ready-made piece of knowledge and repeating it as being the truth. Nothing is more difficult than giving the proof of such a truth. To let children discover the right solution to a given problem is to help them (not only to let them) face all the difficulties of the problem, to try multiple solutions, to evaluate them and then to decide what is the best one given the data that are to be taken into account.

In this sense I emphasize the usefulness of having a general theoretical account of the significance of implicit knowledge that children bring with them when approaching the task of learning how to read and write.

This notwithstanding, I am not so convinced of the usefulness of the dichotomy of implicit/explicit knowledge in psychological research. In the present state of the discussion, the implicit/explicit dichotomy conveys the meaning of an heterogeneous amount of other dichotomies: for instance, unconscious vs. conscious (or available to awareness); idiosyncratic vs. shared (or expressed through socially shared symbols); intuitive vs. organized; based on images vs. symbols; nonsystematic vs. organized; "common sense" (socially shared) vs. scientific; what is meant (intended meaning) vs. what is said (literal meaning); and so on. It seems to me very hard to find a common denominator throughout these varieties of meanings. In addition, and taking into account that because we are dealing with cognitive development we are also obliged to deal with temporal variables, what kind of relation could be established between what is implicit at T1 and what is implicit (or explicit) at T2? Is it possible for an explicit knowledge at time T1 to become implicit at T2? Is it possible the other way around? Could we consider the transit from implicit to explicit knowledge as consisting only in expressing in symbols what was already implicit? Is it not a much more complex process involving modifications in the knowledge as such? Should we not conceive that transit as a real reconstruction? It is possible that we were facing conflicting demands coming from psychological research and from pedagogical research. It is possible that pedagogical research needs to deal more and more with the problem of knowledge constructed outside school settings vs. knowledge explicitly taught in school settings. The relationships between both types of knowledge could (perhaps) be expressed through the implicit/explicit dichotomy. Psychological research dealing with developmentally constructed knowledge needs (perhaps) other types of theoretical constructions.

References

Ferreiro, E., & Teberosky, A. (1982). *Literacy before schooling*. Exeter, N. H. and London: Heinemann. (Spanish original: *Los sistemas de escritura en el desarrollo del niño*. Mexico: Siglo XXI Editores, 1979. 9a.ed. 1988)

Ferreiro, E. (1984). The underlying logic of literacy development. In H. Goelman, A. Oberg, & F. Smith (Eds.), *Awakening to literacy* (pp. 154–173). Exeter, NH: Heinemann.

Ferreiro, E. (1985). Literacy development: A psychogenetic perspective. In D. Olson, N. Torrance, & A. Hildyard (Eds.), *Literacy, language and learning* (pp. 217–228). New York: Cambridge. University Press.

Ferreiro, E. (1986). The interplay between information and assimilation in beginning literacy. In W. Teale & E. Sulzby (Eds.), *Emergent literacy* (pp. 15–49). Norwood, NJ: Ablex.

Ferreiro, E. (1988). L'écriture avant la lettre. In H. Sinclair (Eds.), *La production de notations chez le jeune enfant* (pp. 17–70). Paris: Presses Universitaires de France.

Freeman, Y., & Whitesell, L. (1985). What preschoolers already know about print. *Educational Horizons, 64* (1), 22–24.

Piaget, J., Inhelder, B., & Szeminska, A. (1948). *La géométrie spontanée de l'enfant*. Paris: Presses Universitaires de France.

Pontecorvo, C., & Zucchermaglio, C. (1988). Modes of differentiation in children's writing construction. *European Journal of Psychology of Education, 3* (4), 371–384.

Sinclair, H., Bamberger, J., Ferreiro, E., Frey-Streiff, M., & Sinclair, A. (1988). *La production de notations chez le jeune enfant—Langage, nombre, rythmes et mélodies*. Paris: Presses Universitaires de France.

Vernon, S. (1986). *El proceso de construcción de la correspondencia sonora en la escritura (En la transición entre los períodos pre-silábicos y el silábico)*. Master's thesis. Mexico: CINVESTAV. (miméo)

8

Everyday Concepts and Formal Concepts: Do Children Distinguish Between Linear and Rotational Speeds?

Iris Levin

Tel Aviv University

Rami Gardosh

Mental Health Clinic
Health Center, Kiryat Shmona

Although teaching and learning are sequential processes, the structure of the knowledge in the majority of domains is not organized temporally. Hence, the sequence chosen for instruction is not determined by the knowledge structure per se. Rather, it is decided upon, intuitively, by taking into account the presumed convenience of the learner. For instance, reading is taught in Hebrew with a voweling system of diacritic marks. Later, these marks are omitted since they are considered redundant and are hardly ever included in a regular Hebrew text. While there is a widespread consensus among educators and laypeople in Israel that only fluent Hebrew readers can read a Hebrew text without diacritic marks, some teachers are convinced that these marks only complicate the information processing involved in learning to decode Hebrew. They claim that diacritic marks should be introduced only at a later stage, as part of the teaching of formal Hebrew grammar. The common resolution of this venerable debate (see Levy, 1943), much like that of similar ones in education, is to apply "common sense" uncritically to determine what seems to be "easy" or "difficult." No account is taken of the cognitive properties of the child or of the child's prior knowledge in literacy. This prior knowledge may be very different, and at times much richer, than is supposed (Levin & Tolchinsky-Landsmann, 1989; Tolchinsky-Landsmann & Levin, 1986).

In the last decade or so, developmental psychologists interested in education have proposed that children's prior knowledge in a domain should be taken into consideration when designing a curriculum (e.g., Strauss, 1991). Ignoring the knowledge brought by the child into the classroom does not suppress its effect on the learning process. At times this knowledge may interfere with the child's assimilation of the formal knowledge taught in school (Halloun & Hestenes, 1985a, 1985b). At other times, the educational process could have been easer or richer had

This chapter is based on Working Paper no. 79 of the Tel Aviv Study Group on Human Development and Education. We wish to thank Ruma Falk, Jonathan Berg, Ruth Stavi, and Dina Tirosh for their insightful and constructive comments on a previous version of this chapter. Thanks are also extended to the participants of the workshop, whose discussion led us to reconsider and reexamine many issues raised in our original presentation. The study reported was supported by the Fund for Basic Research of the Tel Aviv University, grant number 651-591.

the prior knowledge of the child been respected rather than ignored (Ferreiro & Teberosky, 1982).

If we wish to take prior knowledge into account, we must first uncover it. One way to find out about such knowledge is to analyze the meaning of everyday concepts that children are exposed to outside of school. As a rule there are major differences between the scientific or textbook meaning of a concept and its everyday meaning. Ponder the different meanings of "force" on the street and in the textbook (Clement, 1977; Viennot, 1979; Watts, 1983). Thus, science learning involves applying familiar concepts to new meanings, sometimes with features contradicting the old. This situation is further complicated by the abundant use of metaphorical language in daily speech.

The present chapter describes an attempt to investigate the interaction between everyday concepts and the formal concepts taught in school. To do so we chose to examine the concept of *speed*. We first analyzed the way people commonly use the terms "speed," "fast," and "slow" and compared this to be meaning attributed to these concepts in textbooks. Thus, we came to the conclusion that the everyday meaning of speed is broader and less differentiated. We then sought to examine the interaction between children's presumed prior everyday concept and the confined and more specific concept taught in school. If schooling does not change the prior structures of many students, as is known to be the case in other scientific domains where misconceptions often persist despite formal instruction (Halloun & Hestenes, 1985a, 1985b), the question remains as to whether the distinction between the everyday concept and the formal concept taught in school actually interferes with schooling. Interference can be expected, particularly if the child is unaware of the different meanings attached to the same concept in school and out.

The Concept of Speed in School

In the Israeli school, the child learns about speed in math and physics classes. In math, speed is introduced in the sixth grade (11 years old) and, in physics, in the ninth grade (14 years old). Within the two frameworks it is encountered again for several weeks virtually each year until the end of high school (18 years old). During these years, speed is presented as distance traveled per unit time and is defined by the formula: $V = S/T$. The paradigm of motion to which this formula is applied in math lessons is of a limited nature: The way is always linear; speed is symbolized by a single value; and whenever the speed of an object changes, the change is always abrupt, shifting from one single speed to another; and most importantly for our purposes, the speed is always linear, defined in terms of linear distance per unit time. While the paradigm of motion and speed does not change in math lessons from one year to the next, it is used to solve progressively more complicated algebra problems.

Speed has a richer meaning in physics lessons. In the tenth and eleventh grades (15–16 years old), the meaning of speed is somewhat expanded and includes average and instantaneous speed, constant acceleration, Newton's laws, the distinction between speed and velocity, and vectorial addition of linear velocities. In the eleventh grade children who study an advanced program in physics are also introduced to rotational motion. They learn the concept of angular speed, its relation to linear speed, and how to transform one speed into the other by means of the formula $V = w \times r$. For our purposes, however, it is important to note that the majority of students are only exposed to the concept of speed within the limited linear framework, as though "speed" were identical to "linear speed."

This is the case not only in Israel but also in many school systems around the world. The reason could be that people tend to believe, rather intuitively, that angular speed is generally speaking more difficult to grasp. This intuition may be associated with the related belief that linear distance is an easier concept than angles or angular distance. These ideas, though "commonsensical" enough, are not based on analysis of children's conceptions of speed, exhibited both prior to and during their school years. What do we know about children's developing concept of speed? This is our next question.

Children's Concept of Speed: Experimental Evidence

As early as four to five months of age, human infants can distinguish between different rates of visual and auditory change (Bertenthal, Bradbury, & Kramer, 1989; Kaufmann, Stucki, & Kaufmann-Hayoz, 1985; Lewkowicz, 1985, 1989; Marcell & Allen, 1982; Spelke, 1976, 1979) and can even coordinate the speed of their hand with that of a moving object when reaching for an object (von Hofsten, 1980, 1983; von Hofsten & Lindhagen, 1979). Toddlers show fine discriminations among different levels of speed (Carpenter & Carpenter, 1958), and young school-children's adjustment of hand to the speed of a moving object is already similar to that of adults (Bairstow, 1987a, 1987b, 1989). Furthermore, at an early age children already talk about "fast" and "slow" and often deliberately manipulate speed—for example, when playing with their toy cars. Kindergartners and young schoolchildren are aware of relations of speed, distance, and time, and of speed and rate (Gatehouse & Frankie, 1980; Montangero, 1985; Siegler & Richards, 1979; Wilkening, 1981, 1982). Schoolage children also acknowledge measures of speed indicated by the speedometer in real cars. Hence, when motion problems are introduced in class, speed is by no means a vacant notion for the child. Our main question, though, is whether or at what age children distinguish between linear and rotational speed.

The assumption that at an early age speed is conceptualized only within a linear framework is accepted by all researchers. Piaget (1946/1970) and other researchers using tasks calling for the comparison of two synchronous motions (Acredolo & Schmid, 1981; Al Fakhri, 1977; Lovell, Kellett, & Moorehouse, 1962; Siegler & Richards, 1979; Tanaka, 1971; Za'rour & Khuri, 1977) assumed either implicitly or explicitly that the only framework that children develop for the conception of speed is the linear one. In other words, from a certain age on, children understand speed to mean the relation between linear distance and time. Consequently, most of the tasks constructed by Piaget and others involved linear motions. Moreover, whenever rotational motions were presented, the researchers defined responses based on linear speed as the only correct answers.

The linear concept of speed was characterized by Piaget, and by others who adopted his stage model, as acquired by children in the "concrete operational" stage. Younger children were claimed to judge speed "intuitively" according to cues other than distance and time. The main cues in use were said to be those of passing and points of arrival. For instance, when two cars traveled in the same direction, the car that passed the other was judged by young children to be going faster. Similarly, children attributed a higher speed to the car that stopped farther ahead. The use of these cues to judge speed decreased gradually with age and by the age of about seven or eight it gave way to the conventional reliance on linear distance and duration.

To illustrate children's use of the cue of passing they were shown, for instance, two cars running on parallel tracks, with one passing the other. From a very young age children could tell that the passing car was faster. However, until the age of seven or eight they generally failed to identify the faster car when the vehicles went into tunnels, so that the moment of passing was concealed. The impact of points of arrival on children's speed judgments was shown, for example, by children's responses to two cars traveling side by side, one on a linear and the other on a zigzag track. Until the aforementioned age children tended to conclude that the cars that stopped side by side were going at the same speed, despite the salient difference in the distance they traversed.

Starting with Piaget (1946/1970), concentric motions were used in a few studies (Lovell et al., 1962; Tanaka, 1971). In these studies, young children who were observed judged two objects to be going at the same speed when the objects were traveling on parallel concentric tracks, with neither passing each other and both stopping side by side. With age, there was an increase in the number of children who related speed to distance and time and judged correctly that the external object was faster.

However, it should be noted that the "same speed" judgment could also have stemmed from judging speed in rotational terms. Since the objects completed the same number of circles, or covered the same angular distance per time unit, their rotational speed is indeed the same. Piaget (1946/1970) raised this possibility but dismissed it. He explained his position thus: "Should these subjects be credited with intuition of angular or rotational speed, which in effect remains constant? Certainly not, first because older children change their opinion and in particular because these same subjects often come to consider the object traveling round the small circle as being faster, which is enough to indicate how primitive their conception of speed still is" (p. 144).

In summary, the literature suggests that the only framework children develop is the linear one. The acquisition of the rotational framework is supposedly acquired as a result of schooling at the end of high school or at the university level.

The Everyday Concept of Speed

Our analysis of the everyday use of the terms "speed," "fast," and "slow" led us to believe that the everyday concept of speed might not be limited to its linear version alone. Moreover, it is not limited only to the change in space with time. We propose that the meaning of speed in everyday communication is that of a relation between time and any change, the change often being measured by the amount of invested effort or the amount of output. Different kinds of change are relevant in different contexts. Imagine two children competing in building towers with blocks. One child works impulsively with fast movements so that his blocks tend to fall. He succeeds in building several towers in the allotted time. The other child, working slowly and carefully, constructs more towers in the same time. The question of which of the two children worked faster can commonly be answered in either of the two possible ways depending on the kind of change with time that is chosen as relevant by the responder. If the child's "style" is of interest, then the first child can be said to have worked faster; if the child's success in building towers is under consideration, then it is the second child who has worked faster.

Clearly, different kinds of motions call for a different output to be chosen as the relevant change. The relevant output of a car is different from that of a record. While a car proceeds, more or less linearly, a record rotates. Hence, its speed is "naturally" decided upon by the number of rotations it completes per time unit. Though the edge of the record covers a linear distance and thus moves at a certain linear speed, this speed is not as relevant to the operation of the record player as is its angular speed. In the same vein, for the passenger the relevant output of a car is its linear progression. Hence, people commonly refer to a car's linear speed, though its speed can be (and actually often is) measured by the rotational speed of its wheels.

While we argue that adults' everyday meaning of speed is broad, we also suggest that the formal definition of speed for many adults is limited to linear speed. This formal definition is acquired through pronounced curriculum in school, where speed is typically introduced in spatial and linear terms alone. The amount of nonspatial output per time, which in everyday communication is also referred to as speed, is labeled in school curriculum by a different term—rate. Rate means amount of output per unit time and is used in math problems that call for the coordination of time–rate–output in contexts such as workers' completing a job or water pipes' filling a pool. We believe that people are often unaware of the discrepancies between their everyday and curriculum-based concepts of speed. Thus, our aim in this study was to examine whether children at different ages distinguish between linear and rotational meanings of speed. We used questions that did not confound the use of rotational speed with that of overtaking and arrival points. Instead of asking for a comparison between two circular motions, we asked children to relate to the speed of two different kinds of objects: those that proceed naturally on linear tracks (e.g., an ant) and those that move rotationally (e.g., a drill).

Method

Subjects

A total of 200 subjects participated in the study. Forty subjects equally divided by sex were recruited from each of five age groups: third, fifth, seventh, and ninth graders and university students. They participated in the experiment during the last quarter of the school year. The mean ages in years and months, and their ranges, from the youngest to the oldest group were: 9 yrs (8 yrs–4 mos—9 yrs–9 mos), 11 yrs (10 yrs–4 mos—11 yrs–10 mos), 13 yrs–1 mo (12 yrs–4 mos—14 yrs), 15 yrs–2 mos (14 yrs–9 mos—15 yrs–7 mos) and 23 yrs–7 mos (19 yrs–4 mos—34 yrs–2 mos).

The school children (third to ninth graders) were selected from a number of kibbutzim. This particular population was selected for convenience, since the interviewer lives on a kibbutz. The kibbutz movement is known to value education and to devote substantial resources to schooling. All children in each class contacted participated in the study, except for a very few who were left over after the required sample was completed.

The curricula and books used in math and physics in kibbutzim are the same as those in Israeli cities. The educational outcomes are considered comparable to those of the urban schools in middle to middle-high SES neighborhoods. Most of the children in the kibbutzim finish high school and cope successfully with the national matriculation exams. The proportion of kibbutz members who graduate from institutions of higher education such as universities, paramedical departments, and teachers' colleges, is about 1.7 times higher than the comparable proportion among the Israeli population (Gamson, 1977; Greenbaum & Kugelmass, 1980; Israeli Central Bureau of Statistics, 1988; Levitan, 1977; Noy, 1977).

The university students were recruited from the Faculties of Humanities and Social Studies in the departments of education, psychology, political sciences and general studies at Tel Aviv University. They were taking introductory courses in psychology and chose to participate in this study as part of their course require-ments. A few of them came from kibbutzim.

None of the university students had participated in a math or physics course at the university level. Only four of them had studied the advanced program in physics in high school and took an advanced matriculation exam in physics. All the rest either took the lowest level of matriculation in physics, or took no matriculation exam in this subject. Consequently, our sample as a whole had been formally taught about speed in its linear meaning only. This level of physics education is typical of university students in the aforementioned departments.

Interview

The data were collected in semistructured interviews carried out by one of the authors (R.G.). The interviews were quite elaborate and lasted from about 20 minutes to an hour. They were taperecorded and transcribed verbatim.

Only one section of the interview will be reported herewith, that which dealt with the distinction between linear and rotational speed. This section consisted of three parts. The first part was related to the speed of five familiar objects. Two of the objects represented linear motions—an ant and a car—and three represented rotational motions—a mixer, a drill, and a record. Within each motion type, there were objects whose speeds are conventionally referred to in terms of an appropriate measure: a car (KPH, i.e., kilometers per hour or MPH, i.e., mileage per hour) and a record (RPM, i.e., rotations per minute), and those whose speeds are rarely if ever measured either in school or on the street: an ant, a drill, and a mixer. The objects were never shown to subjects, only talked about. The participants were asked to determine (a) the speed of each of the objects and (b) how they could tell the speed. If they seemed to have trouble with these questions, they were encouraged to invent a way to determine the speed of the object involved.

The second part referred to transformations. Subjects were asked to compare the speed of objects that move linearly (e.g., an ant) with that of objects that rotate (e.g., a mixer). They had to decide which one was faster and explain how they could tell. The purpose was to examine the ability of subjects at different ages to come up with a way to transform one speed into another.

The third part related to the formulae for linear and angular speeds. First, subjects were asked the meaning of these terms. Whether or not they could provide an answer, they were encouraged to invent a way to formulate the speed of a linear object—a car—and of a rotational object—a record. Here we were looking for them to provide the mathematical relation between speed, time, and distance.

To encourage the interviewee to provide as rich and advanced knowledge as possible, nonleading questions were employed when it was believed that the subject could add valuable information. For the same purpose, a free and supportive atmosphere was maintained.

To give an idea of the nature of the interview, the translation of a part dealing with the speed of a mixer from a session with a seventh grader follows.

E: What is the speed of a mixer?
S: Don't know.
E: Try and guess.
S: Can I say the speed in . . . (long pause).
E: Whatever seems logical to you.
S: Fa-s-t (hesitantly).
E: Fa-s-t . . . (somewhat unsure what is meant).
S: Fast, but fast relative to something; relative to a car which goes fast the mixer is slow; relative to . . . (long pause).
E: How do we know the speed of a mixer?
S: I imagine there is a way to measure it. I don't know . . .
E: Invent something . . . Let's pretend you are sent to the kitchen in order to come back with an answer to the question: "What is the speed of a mixer?" What would you do?

S: To measure . . . To define the speed of a mixer . . . To say how much?
E: To say exactly what the speed of a mixer is.
S: Perhaps . . . How many rotations it makes in a certain time.
E: Yes . . . ? (encouragingly)
S: And . . . and . . . I don't know . . . To divide it . . . also.
E: To divide by what? What to divide?
S: One by the other. To divide the number of rotations by the time . . . it takes it.

Results

Speed of objects

To analyze the distinction between the speeds applied to linear and to rotational motions, a coding system was constructed to categorize the responses. The overall reliability of coding was quite high, $K = 0.87$, employing the formula suggested by Bishop, Feinberg, and Holland (1975), which takes into account the marginal frequencies. The computation of K was based on the independent coding of 20 interviews carried out by the two authors. The interviews were randomly selected from all cells of the design to represent equally all grade and sex groups. The reliabilities computed for each of the objects separately were 0.83, 0.81, 0.77, 0.72, 0.79 for ant, mixer, drill, record, and car, respectively.

The responses were classified into four major categories: (a) preformal, (b) linear, (c) rotational, and (d) both linear and rotational, or transformational. Explanations of the categories along with examples translated from our data follow:

1. Preformal responses consisting primarily of five types of answers:
    a. *Tautological responses, based on what we might call "eye testimony."*
       Example for a mixer: "I watch those things that mix and see if they mix slowly or if they mix quickly . . . and if it mixes slowly I know it is slow" (third grader).
    b. *Responses referring to a single dimension—time, distance, or some other output—without relating time to output or distance.*
       Example for an ant: "I would check on a watch for how many seconds it walks . . . how much time it takes to go . . . all day long" (third grader).
    c. *Ordinal responses, based on comparison with some other object or with expectations.*
       Example for an ant: "It is fast relative to us . . . Because it is tiny and when you take one step it must go a lot . . . It is fast relative to its size" (seventh grader).
    d. *Responses referring to nonspatial outcome in relation to time.*
       Example for a drill: "Let's say it makes a hole in an hour" (third grader).
    e. *Other.*
       Example for an ant: "An ant is fast because it is diligent" (third grader).

While these responses may be of different levels, they were all considered preformal. The formal meaning of speed was confined to the meaning that relates distance to time.

2. Linear responses referring to linear distance and time and consisting primarily of three types of responses:

   a. *Measuring the time taken to cover a certain linear distance.*

      Example for an ant: "We can take a ruler and measure time . . . When it gets, let's say, to the end of the ruler, I could stop the time, and see how much time it took it (to go) thirty centimeters" (seventh grader).

   b. *Measuring the linear distance covered in a certain length of time.*

      Example for an ant: "Let's say I prepare some kind of a stick and I mark the centimeters on it. I measure, let's say, a minute and see how many (centimeters) it went" (fifth grader).

   c. *Dividing linear distance by time.*

      Example for a car: "Measuring the distance it traversed and dividing it by the time it took" (university student).

3. Rotational responses referring to rotations and time and consisting primarily of three types of answers, parallel to those of linear responses:

   a. *Measuring the time taken to complete a rotation, or a number of rotations.*

      Example for a mixer: "You measure how much time it takes for a rotation" (third grader).

      Example for a record: "It completes a rotation in 2 seconds. You mark a line on the record and till it comes back to the point it started from, I measure with a stop watch" (seventh grader).

   b. *Measuring the number of rotations completed in a certain length of time.*

      Example for a drill: "This thing rotates . . . and let's say it reaches an hour, then you stop it and see how many rotations (it completed)" (third grader).

      Example for a mixer: "You see how many rotations (it makes) in a minute. You count the rotations" (fifth grader).

   c. *Dividing number of rotations by time.*

      Example for a record: "To try and take, you know, twenty seconds . . . whatever . . . thirty seconds . . . and to measure the number of rotations, and to divide . . . the number of rotations by the time" (university student).

4. Both linear and rotational or transformational responses consisting mainly of linear and rotational responses as noted; otherwise, they consisted of two types of responses:

   a. *Number of rotations transformed into linear distance and related to time.*

      Example for a mixer: "Let's tie a certain string to it that will make a circle.

Let it [the mixer] rotate. Let's say that the length of the string is one meter . . . I measure how much time it takes to make a meter . . ." (ninth grader).

b. *Linear distance measured by rotations and related to time.*

Example for a car: "You count the speed of rotations completed by the wheels, I guess . . . So you simply count the number of rotations that the wheels made till the car covered a certain distance. You divide it by the time taken" (university student).

Since subjects could give explanations that fit more than one of these categories, we coded their overall performance according to the following rule. First, we assumed that the four response categories represented three levels. Preformal categories were considered lowest; mentioning both linear and rotational or transformational was taken as the highest level of performance; and either linear responses or rotational responses were placed at the intermediate level. This done, the child's best response for linear objects (the ant and the car) and for rotational objects (the mixer, the drill, and the record), as indexed by the level of explanation, was determined and used for the following analyses.

Table 8.1 presents the distribution of subjects according to the categories they used to describe the speed of linear and of rotational motions, by grade. The difference between categories used for linear and for rotational motions is clear and needs no statistical analysis. Linear motions were described by the majority in linear terms, and rotational motions in rotational terms. In contrast, almost no one described linear motions in rotational terms only or rotational motions in linear terms alone. To examine the effect of motion type and grade on the use of linear and rotational speed, each child received a score of 1 on linear speed if he or she used it

Table 8.1. The Distribution of Subjects by Categories Used to Describe Speed and by Grade ($n = 200$)

	Linear Motions Grade				University Students	Total
	Third	Fifth	Seventh	Ninth		
Preformal	11	3	0	0	0	14
Linear	26	35	39	39	38	177
Rotational	1	0	0	0	0	1
Transformational	2	2	1	1	2	8

	Rotational Motions Grade				University Students	Total
	Third	Fifth	Seventh	Ninth		
Preformal	16	5	5	0	0	26
Linear	0	0	0	0	1	1
Rotational	21	27	23	34	28	133
Transformational	3	8	12	6	11	40

at least once for linear objects. Similarly, a score of 1 was given to those who used a rotational speed at least once for rotational objects. A 2 (motion type: linear or rotational) by 5 (grade: third, fifth, seventh, ninth graders or university students) ANOVA, with repeated measures on the first factor, revealed a significant effect of motion type [$F_{(1,195)} = 12.94$, $p < .001$]; a significant effect of grade [$F_{(4,195)} = 12.67$, $p < .001$] and no significant interaction. In each grade, more children described linear motions by linear speed than rotational motions by rotational speed. Overall, 93% described linear objects by linear speed (4% of them also mentioning rotational speed), and 87% depicted rotational objects by rotational speed (23% using linear speed as well). Moreover, all the subjects who described the speed of rotational objects in rotational terms, also described the speed of linear motions in linear terms. In contrast, 7% of the 185 subjects who used linear speed for linearly moving objects failed to use rotational speed when appropriate. This marginal difference in the accessibility of the two terms of speed can perhaps be attributed to the exclusive use of linear speed in school.

The difference between grades was further examined by a post hoc analysis (Scheffe, $\alpha = .05$) carried out separately on the linear and the rotational motions. In both analyses, the youngest group, third graders, differed significantly from all the rest.

In summary, there is no indication that people conceive speed linearly only. On the contrary, a clear differentiation between the two frameworks was evidenced from the youngest age on.

Transformations

If children use different types of speed in dealing with linear and with rotational motions, do they recognize that one type of speed can be transformed into the other, so that the speed of the same object can be expressed in two ways? Can they generate such a transformation? These questions were addressed in the next section of the interview.

Subjects were asked to judge which of two of the aforementioned subjects was faster, and how they could tell. They were taken aback by questions such as: "Which is faster, an ant or a mixer?" and at times were amused by the apparent absurdity. When asked the first of these questions, whether an ant or a mixer was faster, 19% said that it was impossible to compare the two. However, after gentle prodding they did come up with an answer, and there was an impressive consensus in their judgments, with 88% saying that the mixer was faster.

Data on explanations were similar for all pairs composed of one linear and one rotational object. The following data refer to the comparison between the ant and the mixer. Explanations lent themselves to classification into six types. The types along with a sample of responses provided by our subjects, follow:

1. Tautological comparisons based on "eye testimony":

    Example: "According to the eye . . . I see the mixer revolving so very quickly and the ant going slowly" (seventh grader).

2. Reference to effort or output:

   Example: "The mixer works on electricity and the ant works on strength and it gets tired, a mixer doesn't" (seventh grader).

3. No integration: Reference to a single dimension, be it distance or time without integrating the two, or to distance and time in one case and to output and time in the other, without coordinating the two:

   Example: "To take about half a minute and see how far the ant goes and how much the mixer whips up" (ninth grader).

4. No coordination: Distance of the linear object is dealt with linearly, and of the rotational object rotationally. No attempt is made to coordinate the two.

   Example: "An ant takes more steps per second than a mixer makes rotations per second" (fifth grader).

5. Rotational transformation: Linear distance is transformed into rotations, and a direct comparison is drawn between the two durations or the number of rotations.

   Example: "We can prepare for the ant a certain circle, a certain path it cannot get out of, in the size of the circle of a mixer, and see who gets to the beginning of the circle, to the point they started from first" (third grader).

   Example: "If the ant walked in a circle like the mixer, and the mixer rotated in a circle, the ant would complete fewer circles in a minute than the mixer" (ninth grader).

6. Linear transformation: Rotations are transformed into linear distance, and a direct comparison drawn between the distances covered per time unit, the times taken to cover a distance, or the speeds.

   Example: "The revolution (of the mixer) is a certain distance. It's a circle, isn't it? I would open all the circles it makes and join them to a meter, to a distance . . ., and then I would see how much time it takes to go this distance and how much time the ant takes to go this distance" (seventh grader).

Reliability coefficients for the judgments and the explanations, based on the independent coding of the 20 selected interviews, were quite satisfactory: on judgments $K = 0.85$ and on explanations $K = 0.74$.

It was decided to view the different explanation types as constituting a scale of different levels. The responses were ordered according to the sequence in which they were previously presented with tautological responses considered lowest and linear or rotational transformation highest (no one mentioned both transformations). Since each subject could provide more than one explanation, it was decided that the representative explanation used for each subject would be the best explanation he or she provided. The distribution of subjects according to explanation and grade appears in Table 8.2.

Data in Table 8.2 show that the most prevalent explanation was on the highest level and involved linear transformation. Preformal comparisons of speed, relating to the "eye testimony" of the motions or to the effort invested and output derived,

Table 8.2. The Distribution of Subjects by Categories Used to Compare Speed of an Ant and a Mixer, by Grade ($n = 200$)

| | Grade | | | | University | |
	Third	Fifth	Seventh	Ninth	Students	Total
Tautological	18	13	9	1	2	43
Effort/output	11	6	5	1	0	23
No integration	2	3	2	5	3	15
No coordination	4	4	4	3	2	17
Rotational transformation	2	2	7	9	11	31
Linear transformation	1	10	10	21	22	64
Other	2	2	3	0	0	7

decreased with grade. These response types, however, still appeared among 35% of the seventh graders. Explanations that ignored the difference between rotational and linear distances, and compared numbers related to different units, appeared to an equally low extent at all grades. Hence, at no age group did subjects overlook the fact that they were dealing with different meanings of speed for different motions.

Transformations increased with grade. Each subject received a score of 1 if he or she provided either a linear or a rotational transformation when comparing the speed of an ant with that of a mixer. One way ANOVA revealed a significant increase with grade on the use of transformation [$F (4,195) = 22.29$, $p < .001$]. Post hoc analysis (Scheffe $\alpha = .05$) indicated that the increase was significant between the third and seventh grades, and between the seventh and ninth grades. From the seventh to the ninth grade, rotational speed is not dealt with in school, while linear speed is studied quite intensively.

We further examined whether there is a substantial gap between children's application of the two meanings of speed—linear and rotational—and their ability to transform one meaning into the other. Among the 163 subjects who mentioned linear speed for the ant and rotational speed for the mixer, only 55% transformed one speed into the other when asked to compare their speeds. Thus, using both frameworks did not guarantee the application of correct transformation for the purpose of comparing the speeds. In comparison, among the other 37 subjects who failed to use linear speed for the ant and/or rotational speed for the mixer, 16% unexpectedly transformed one speed into the other when comparing the speeds of these two objects. However, these 6 subjects (who constituted the 16% of 37) did apply speed both in the linear and the rotational meaning for objects other than the ant and/or the mixer. Hence, using both frameworks in measuring speeds seems to be a necessary but insufficient condition for the ability to transform one type of speed into the other. It should be mentioned that all of the children and the majority of adults (i.e., except for 4 university students) participating in our study had never been taught such a transformation in school.

Linear and Rotational Formulae for Speed

Our next analyses addressed the question of whether, or at what age, children are able to provide the formulae for linear and rotational speeds. We distinguished between familiarity with the terms "linear speed" and "rotational angular speed" and the ability to provide formal expressions of these terms. At the end of the experimental session, subjects were explicitly asked whether they recognized the terms "linear speed" and "rotational or angular speed." Only four of the university students answered in the affirmative. In fact their familiarity with the terms had been apparent throughout the interview. These subjects had taken the expanded program in physics in high school, while all the rest had not. The other subjects stated that they had no idea what the terms meant.

However, results were different when the subjects were asked to provide the formulae for calculating the speed of a car and of a record. Subjects who claimed not to know the answer to these questions were encouraged to invest a formula, again in an attempt to extract implicit knowledge. Since the linear formula of $V = S/T$ is taught from about the sixth grade, we expected subjects from that age on to provide a formula for speed, and that it be the linear formula only. We further expected that they would mention this formula for the car but not for the record. In the case of records, whose speed is mainly described in rotational terms, either no formula would be provided or the rotations would first be transformed into a linear distance, affording a linear formula, by older children and adults. Alternatively, it was possible that subjects who treated rotational motions in rotational terms, and knew the formula for linear speed from school, could invent a formula for angular speed.

For a subject to be said to have provided a formula, he or she had to mention three components: distance, time, and a mathematical operation connecting them, that is, multiplication or division. When the distance was linear the formula was considered linear, and when it consisted of rotations the formula was considered rotational. An incorrect formula contained the necessary components mentioned, but either the divisor and the dividend were reversed or the mathematical operation was the wrong one.

Reliability of formula coding was examined by the independent coding of the 20 selected interviews and found to be high: $K = .92$ and $K = .81$ for linear and rotational formulae, respectively. Following are the translations of four typical responses:

> Correct linear formula: "Let's divide the distance it traversed by the time" (seventh grader).
>
> Incorrect linear formula: "Time multiplied by distance is speed" (ninth grader).
>
> Correct rotational formula: "Number of rotations divided by time" (seventh grader).
>
> Incorrect rotational formula: "Number of rotations multiplied by time equals speed" (ninth grader).

Table 8.3 presents the distribution of subjects by grade according to the correct and incorrect formulae of linear and rotational speeds they provided for the car and for the record. A rather surprising finding is that children in the seventh and ninth grades, who are formally taught motion problems, provided correct and incorrect linear formulae to a similar extent. This result indicates that many children in this age range are confused as to what should be divided by what, or whether division or multiplication should be carried out. Only adults, university students, on the whole had no difficulty in producing the correct linear formula for a linear motion. In line with expectations, up to the seventh grade, the linear formula was never mentioned. From then on there was an increase in the use of the linear formula for linear motion.

Most of our subjects had never been introduced to the formula for rotational speed. As far as we could tell they had no idea that such a formula even existed. However, when encouraged to provide one on their own, 20% of the subjects came up with a relation between number of rotations and time, and 69% of them intuited the correct relation. Each subject received a score of 1 if he or she provided a correct linear formula for the speed of a car, and a score of 1 for a correct rotational formula for a record. A 2 (object: car or record) by 5 (grades) ANOVA, with repeated measures on the first factor, revealed a significant increase with grade in providing correct formulae [$F(4,195) = 12.33, p < .001$], a significantly higher provision of linear formula for car than rotational formula for record [$F (1,195) = 37.56, p <$

Table 8.3. The Distribution of Subjects According to the Formulae of Linear and Rotational Speed, by Grade ($n = 200$)

| | Car | | | | | |
| | | | Grade | | University | |
Formula	Third	Fifth	Seventh	Ninth	Students	Total
None	40	38	20	13	4	115
Linear incorrect	0	2	13	12	3	30
Linear correct	0	0	7	15	33	55

| | Record | | | | | |
| | | | Grade | | University | |
Formula	Third	Fifth	Seventh	Ninth	Students	Total
None	40	39	29	23	12	143
Linear incorrect	0	0	3	3	2	8
Linear correct	0	0	1	4	5	10
Rotational incorrect	0	1	4	6	1	12
Rotational correct	0	0	3	4	20	27

.001], and a significant interaction [F (4,195) = 8.94, $p < .001$]. Post hoc analysis (Scheffe, $\alpha = .05$) was carried out separately on the linear and on the rotational formulae. A significant difference was found between the seventh and the ninth grade, and between the ninth grade and university students, on the linear formula. On the rotational formula the only significant difference was found between university students and all the rest.

A most interesting finding is that the results regarding rotational formula for the record were similar in certain respects to those regarding linear formula for the car: Third and fifth graders never mentioned the correct rotational formula; seventh and ninth graders came up with correct and incorrect responses to a similarly low extent; and only university students were more correct than incorrect and significantly more correct than the rest. The major difference between the provision of the linear and the rotational formulae was in their frequency. The rotational formula was produced less often in each and every grade. In fact, 26 of the 27 subjects who provided a correct rotational formula were included among the 55 subjects who gave a correct linear formula. Thus, the provision of a linear formula seems to be a necessary but insufficient condition for the provision of a rotational formula.

The similarity between the two formulae in the results obtained is quite intriguing if we take into account the continuous instruction of the linear formula from the seventh grade on and the lack of any reference to the rotational formula in school, in the case of all but four of our subjects.

A low percentage of subjects (5%) provided a linear formula for the record, an answer that contradicts the conventional measure of speed for records and requires a rather awkward preliminary transformation of number of rotations to linear distance. This transformation is awkward because it overlooks the fact that the linear distance at the center of the record is different from that at the edge. Linear transformation also took the form of opening up the entire path that the needle covers. Such a transformation, though, may indicate that the subject treated the linear formula as the only possible formula for speed. It is revealing that this kind of response was so rare.

Conclusions: The Effect of Schooling on the Concept of Speed

How does schooling interact with the informal knowledge of speed brought to school? The answer to this question is not a simple one.

For most Israeli students, including all but four of our subjects, speed as presented in the pronounced curriculum in school has (inter alia) two characteristics: It is related to displacement in space and it is linear. Everyday conversation about speed conveys different characteristics: It is not necessarily related to spatial displacement, and when displacement is involved it is not necessarily linear. Furthermore, speed is introduced in school by a formula—a mathematical relation between two components: distance and time. In everyday communication the mathematical relation is hardly ever mentioned. However, the relation of speed to each of these components is often implied.

Our study analyzed the concept of speed by asking subjects to answer the question "What is the speed of . . ." It should be noted that this question is not a typical school-type question. As we have seen, in school problems, speed, distance, and time are denoted symbolically by numbers; and solutions are obtained by manipulating these numbers. No moving object is observed and children are never asked to relate a number of, say, a speed, to the perceptual impression of a motion. Moreover, the typical speed of an action is never considered. The actions depicted in motion problems are frequently of a type of which the child has no immediate experience, such as that of an airplane.

By asking the subjects this type of question, we oriented them to use their everyday knowledge concerning the motions of familiar objects. However, they could not make use of ready-made answers (i.e., the speed is such and such), except in the case of a car. For the objects whose speed is rarely measured (e.g., an ant or a drill), they could only generate their answers on the basis of estimations of time and distance. Thus, the question "What is the speed of . . ." required the use of formal knowledge about speed, its relation to distance per time, or the time taken to cover a particular distance. Thus, this simple question demanded the coordination of everyday knowledge with curriculum-based knowledge.

Our data suggest that schooling has an effect on the spatialization of speed. With age, children begin to treat speed as a more specific concept, relating it to spatial displacement rather than to amount of any change per time. Answers of the effort/output kind, which were included in the category of "preformal responses," were given almost only by third graders, who had not yet been introduced to motion problems in school.

It should be kept in mind, though, that our data do not suggest that speed in everyday conversation becomes exclusively spatial. On the contrary, we believe that people continue to communicate about speed as a broad and unanalyzed term related to effort/output and time. This broad concept of speed is reflected in general dictionaries. Webster (1981) defines speed as both "rate of motion" and "swiftness or rate of performance or action." Eben-Shushan (1966) adds examples of phrases addressing the speed of the army's progression, of grasping an issue, and of a march played by an orchestra.

Schooling seems to have no substantial effect on the linearization of speed. Our data suggest that for most pupils the fact that speed in the curriculum is identified with linear speed does not suppress the differentiation between linear and angular speed. The majority of subjects described each object by the speed relevant to its motion: Linear motions were described in linear terms, and rotational motions in rotational terms. Spontaneous attempts to transform rotational motions into linear, in order to afford the application of linear speed to rotational motions, were rare.

The differentiation between the two meanings of speed, which is evidenced by most children from the youngest group on, does not guarantee the ability to transform one type of speed into the other. Within each grade there were more children who used both rotational and linear speeds than children who were able to transform one type into the other. However, only a minority of children within each grade ignored the fact that they were being asked to compare two types of speed that could not be directly compared. Very few were satisfied with comparing, say, number of rotations to centimeters. This type of response was not popular at any age level. Rather, it seems to have been a last resort that a very few fell back on when they were unable to find an appropriate transformation.

When the subjects were asked to compare the speed of an object that moves linearly to the speed of a rotating object, transformations were, overall, the most prevalent response. Moreover, the transformation chosen was most often the more suitable one. Rotational transformation involved counting rotations that could have been covered by an object moving linearly. In contrast, linear transformation involved the linearization of a circular path and counting the conventional units of length, for example, centimeters of the distance covered. Linear transformation is more sensible since it leads to unequivocal results as long as a given unit of length is maintained. Rotational transformation, on the contrary, can produce different results depending on the radius chosen. There are no conventional radii equivalent to the conventional unit of length. Thus, the preference for linear transformation to rotational seems to us related not only to schooling, but also to cultural conventions at large.

These results taken together imply that although the concept of rotational speed is introduced in the eleventh grade and only to advanced students in physics, it may be employed by children as early as the third grade. Moreover, they are aware, some even in the fifth grade and the majority in the ninth, that there are at least two different types of speed, and they are able to carry out transformations between them. These results also indicate that children can intuitively characterize the speed of the same motion in two different ways.

The request to provide a formula to calculate the speed of a car or a record seemed to induce subjects to draw on curriculum-based knowledge. In our study a subject was said to have provided a formula only if he or she mentioned the mathematical relation between distance and time. Everyday conversation rarely involves the mathematical integration of distance and time in reference to speed, though the integration is perhaps grasped intuitively when speed is estimated (see Wilkening, 1981, 1982, for intuitive mathematical integration).

Data show that the formula was rarely provided by children younger than seventh graders. This may shed light on the particular effect of schooling. Although children relate to distance and time when considering speed even without learning to do so in school, they need the school's input to grasp that speed is measured by a mathematical relation (multiplication/division) between them.

It appears, however, that information provided only or mostly by the curriculum is not easy to grasp. The number of children who produced the wrong version of the formula was similar to the number who came up with the right one. Subjects frequently mixed up the divisor and dividend or reversed the mathematical operation. This finding indicates that for many the formula remains vacant information unrelated to what they know when pondering or visualizing real motions. They do know, however, what the components of the formula should be, and that the mathematical integration involved is multiplicative rather than additive.

In contrast to children, adults frequently provided the correct formula. This is to be expected, because after the ninth grade students continue to study the subject for another two or three years and are tested on it in the national matriculation exams. Their knowledge does not seem to be of a transient nature since most of them probably did not deal formally with this issue for some five years prior to the study. Israeli students enter the university in their mid-twenties, after several years of army service where the vast majority do not study physics.

The most interesting effect of schooling seems to be apparent in our results on the angular formula. Although most subjects were never taught about angular speed, 50% of the adults produced the relevant formula when considering the speed of a record. They probably "invented" the formula by applying the linear formula to the context of rotational motion. This could be viewed as a case of transfer of learning.

Educational Implications

The starting point in many areas of science education is the definition of concepts. Once concepts are defined, they are accepted as binding and general, providing the constraints for the domain at hand. This approach applies to the subject of motion problems as well. Once teachers or curriculum designers define speed as $V = S/T$, they believe that students accept the definition as valid and applicable to each and every motion. They may be right, but only superficially. Students may indeed assume, either explicitly or implicitly, that the linear definition of speed is always valid. But they may also be quite ready to ignore it when the definition leads them to conclusions that contradict other beliefs they hold in regard to speed. Our study implies that most children and adults do not accept the formal definition of linear speed as obligatory when other types of motion are concerned. This equivocal attitude toward the definition may result from the fact that it is vacant. In other words, the definition is taken as a formula relating symbols to each other, which serves as a useful tool for solving motion problems in school, but is somehow grasped as unrelated or not clearly related to motions experienced in the "real" world.

The gap between real motions and textbook motions is probably strengthened by the procedures used in solving motion problems. The preferred procedure here is to design a three-column table and fill it up with numbers designating speed, distance, and time. This procedure may give the impression that speed, distance, and time are in fact three distinct objects of thought. Such an impression is inconsistent with the experience of real motions in which the three dimensions are interwoven. This is not to say that the use of this procedure should be abandoned. It may indeed be helpful in dealing with motions on the symbolic level, but it can also take its toll.

We suggest that motion has at least two different kinds of representations. One is composed of symbols, be it words or signs, and the other of images and kinesthetic sensations of motion. These two kinds of representation are either never related to each other, or if related are grasped as connected by some unclear coding rule. The major discrepancy between the image and the symbol concerns speed, more so than time or distance. We tend to believe that the image and sensation of motion for most children and adults involve instantaneous speed that continuously undergoes gradual change. This image and sensation are inconsistent with the concept of speed presented in motion problems, where speed is often attributed a single value that refers to the motion in its totality. Moreover, while experienced speed changes from one instant to the next, the symbolic value of speed is computed through the relation of the entire distance to the entire time accumulated throughout the motion.

Curriculum designers and teachers are aware that speed is not a constant feature of a natural motion. They know that the often-used term "constant speed" stands for "average speed," though the two are not identical. The learner, however, may notice that speed is interchangeably referred to in motion problems as "the speed," "the constant speed," or "the average speed" and be perplexed as to how these three different terms serve exactly the same function in the formula. It is also plausible that many students ignore the use of different terms for speed and are never troubled by the question of their interrelations. Many may also be unaware of the discrepancy between their image of speed and the paradigm of motion in math problems. No matter whether the student ignores the discrepancies discussed or is perplexed by them, a gap is created between the scientific and the everyday meaning of motion, which may be detrimental to meaningful learning.

In a new, popular math book in Israel used mainly in the sixth grade (Gefner & Arnon, 1980), an attempt is made to explain the relation between "constant speed" and "average speed" in the following way:

Nisim: It is impossible to ride at a constant speed in a car on the road from Tel Aviv to Metula.
Yoram: When you say:
The car was going at an average speed of 80 kilometers per hour.
you mean:
Let us assume that the car was going at a constant speed of 80 kilometers each hour. (p. 46)

Although this explanation reveals an awareness of this problem, it does not seem to clarify it at all, particularly since the averaging procedure involved is not specified, and its comprehension cannot be taken for granted (Gorodetsky, Hoz, & Vinner, 1986).

We argue that the gap between the two representations of speed should be bridged. The most obvious way to do this would be to introduce real motions into the classroom and deal with them in terms of numbers. Computers could be of help in an elegant and painless manner, for two reasons. First, they can present dynamic rather than static displays, and second, changing a motion on a computer involves easier and more flexible procedures than doing so with concrete objects. Children could be asked, for example, to manipulate motions by changing the indices of their distance, time, or speed. They could be required to estimate indices of displayed motions. The programming of problems involving two or more related motions (e.g., the meeting of two vehicles traveling toward each other) could be a stage in learning to solve them.

Another bridge is required as well: one that could span the gap between the broad everyday notion of speed and the concept of speed taught in school. Nonlinear motions should be introduced earlier in school, and not only in advanced physics programs. This need not pose special difficulty because children intuitively construe rotational speed when dealing with rotational motions, as our study has clearly shown. Moreover, the complexity of angular speed, in the sense of number of rotations per time, is not particularly greater than that of linear speed. While angles, as such, may indeed be more difficult to grasp than linear distance, children in junior high school can already cope with them to some extent. Further, children could be led to distinguish between their everyday concept of speed, which is not necessarily spatial, and the school concept, which is confined to spatial progression.

On a more general level, we agree in principle with the popular idea that children should first be exposed to simple ideas, concepts, and procedures and only later built on these more complicated structures that better approximate scientific knowledge. However, the nature of simplification should be based on the learner's knowledge structure and cognitive abilities. We suspect that children know more than teachers imagine in very many areas. Hence, presenting them with overly simple ideas may create inconsistencies in their understanding of a domain and can lead them to grasp school-based knowledge as irrelevant to the solving of everyday problems. Furthermore, oversimplification can make the learning process more boring and dull than it need be. Tall (1989) expressed a similar concern in the following words: "We do students a disservice by organizing the curriculum so that they are presented only with simple ideas first and given too great an exposure to an environment which contains regularities which do not hold in general" (p. 44). Dealing with nonspatial and with rotational speed in the classroom could help make school more relevant to children's everyday purposes and ideas of motion.

References

Acredolo, C., & Schmid, J. (1981). The understanding of relative speeds, distances and durations of movement. *Developmental Psychology, 17*, 490–493.

Al Fakhri, S. (1977). The development of the concept of speed among Iraqi children. In P R Dasen (Ed.), *Piagetian psychology: Cross cultural contributions* (pp. 203–215). Gardner Press.

Bairstow, J. P. (1987a). Analysis of hand movement to moving targets. *Human Movement Science, 6*, 205–231.

Bairstow, J. P. (1987b). Hand movement to moving targets: Planning and adjustment of speed and direction. In A. Colley & J. Beech (Eds.), *Cognition and action in skilled behavior*. Amsterdam: North Holland.

Bairstow, J. P. (1989). Development of planning and control of hand movement to moving targets. *British Journal of Developmental Psychology, 7*, 29–42.

Bertenthal, B. I., Bradbury, A., & Kramer, S. J. (1989). *Velocity thresholds in 5-month-old infants.* Paper presented at the conference of the Society for Research in Child Development. Kansas City.

Bishop, Y., Feinberg, S., & Holland, P. (1975). *Discrete multivariate analysis* (pp. 395–397). Cambridge: MIT Press.

Carpenter, B., & Carpenter, J. T. (1958). The perception of movement by young chimpanzees and human children. *Journal of Comparative and Physiological Psychology, 51*, 782–784.

Clement, J. (1977). *Catalogue of students' conceptual models in physics. Section 1: Movement and force.* Mimeograph. Department of Physics and Astronomy, University of Massachusetts, Amherst.

Eben Shushan, A. (1966). *New dictionary.* Jerusalem: Kiryat Sefer. (Hebrew)

Ferreiro, E., & Teberosky, A. (1982). *Literacy before schooling.* New York: Heinemann.

Gamson, Z. M. (1977). The Kibbutz and higher education: Cultures in collision? *The Kibbutz, 5*, 63–83. (Hebrew)

Gatehouse, R. W., & Frankie, G. H. (1980). The development of auditory concept of speed. *The Journal of Genetic Psychology, 136*, 221–229

Gefner, O., & Arnon, I. (1980). *Simple fractions: Part 4. An Experimental Edition.* The Ministry of Education and Culture—The Center for Educational Television. (Hebrew)

Gorodetsky, M., Hoz, R., and Vinner, S. (1986). Hierarchical solution models at speed problems. *Science Education, 70*, 565–582.

Greenbaum, C. W., & Kugelmass, S. (1980). Human development and socialization in cross-cultural perspective: Issues arising from research in Israel. In N. Warren (Ed.), *Studies in cross-cultural psychology* (pp. 95–156). New York: Academic Press.

Halloun, I. B., & Hestenes, D. (1985a). The initial knowledge state of college physics students. *American Journal of Physics, 53*, 1043–1055.

Halloun, I. B., & Hestenes, D. (1985b). Common sense concepts about motion. *American Journal of Physics, 53*, 1056–1065.

Israeli Central Bureau of Statistics, Jerusalem. (1988). Survey of graduates of universities and post secondary education, 1984. *Special Series*, nos., *795, 820.*

Kaufmann, F., Stucki, M., & Kaufmann-Hayoz, R. (1985). Development of infants' sensitivity for slow and rapid motions. *Infants' Behavior and Development, 8*, 89–98.

Levin, I., & Tolchinsky-Landsmann, L. (1989). Becoming literate: Referential and phonetic strategies in early reading and writing. *International Journal of Behavioral Development, 12*, 369–384.

Levitan, U. (1977). Higher education in the Kibbutz—"Consumption or investment?" *The Kibbutz, 5*, 99–110. (Hebrew)

Levy, Y. (1943). Psychological bases of reading in Hebrew. *Education.* (Hebrew)

Lewkowicz, D. J. (1985). Bisensory response to temporal frequency in 4-month-old infants. *Developmental Psychology, 21*, 306–317.

Lewkowicz, D. J. (1989). The role of temporal factors in infant behavior and development. In I. Levin, & D. Zakay (Eds.), *Time and human cognition: A life span perspective* (pp. 9–62). Amsterdam: North Holland.

Lovell, K., Kellett, V. L., & Moorehouse, E. (1962). The growth of the concept of speed: A comparative study. *Journal of Child Psychology and Psychiatry, 3*, 101–110.

Marcell, M. M., & Allen T. W. (1982). *Auditory and visual discrimination of rhythmic sequences by young infants.* Paper presented at the American Psychological Association Convention. Washington, D.C.

Montangero, J. (1985). *Genetic epistemology: Yesterday and today.* New York: The Graduate School and University Center, City University of New York.

Noy, D. (1977). The change in attitudes towards higher education in the Kibbutz movement. *The Kibbutz, 5*, 51-62. (Hebrew)

Piaget, J. (1946/1970). *The child's conception of movement and speed* (G. E. T. Holloway & M. J. Mackenzie, Trans.). New York: Basic Books.

Siegler, R. S., & Richards, D. D. (1979). The development of time, speed and distance concepts. *Developmental Psychology, 15*, 288–298.

Spelke, E. S. (1976). Infants' intermodal perception of events. *Cognitive Psychology, 8,* 553–560.

Spelke, E. S. (1979). Perceiving bimodally specified events in infancy. *Developmental Psychology, 15,* 626–636.

Strauss, S. (1991). Towards a developmental model of instruction. In L. Tolchinsky-Landsmann (Ed.), *Culture, schooling, and psychological development* (pp. 112–135). Norwood, NJ: Ablex

Tall, D. (1989). *Inconsistencies in the learning of calculus and analysis.* Paper presented at the annual meeting of the National Council of Mathematics Teachers, Orlando, FL.

Tanaka, M. (1971). The development of the concept of speed. *Journal of Child Development, 7,* 1–11.

Tolchinsky-Landsmann, L., & Levin, I. (1986). Writing in preschoolers: An age-related analysis. *Applied Psycholinguistics* (special issue on *Psycholinguistics and Writing*), *6,* 319–339.

Viennot, L. (1979). Spontaneous reasoning in elementary dynamics. *European Journal of Science Education, 1,* 205–221.

Von Hofsten, C. (1980). Predictive reaching for moving objects by human infants. *Journal of Human Movement Studies, 5,* 160–178.

Von Hofsten, C. (1983). Catching skills in infancy. *Journal of Experimental Psychology: Human Perception and Performance, 9,* 75–85.

Von Hofsten, C., & Lindhagen, K. (1979). Observations on the development of reaching for moving targets. *Journal of Experimental Child Psychology, 28,* 158–173.

Watts, D. M. (1983). A study of school children's alternative frameworks of the concept of force. *European Journal of Science Education, 5,* 217–230.

Webster's (1981) *New collegiate dictionary.* Springfield, MA: G & C Merriam Company.

Wilkening, F. (1981). Integrating velocity, time and distance information: A developmental study. *Cognitive Psychology, 13,* 231–247.

Wilkening, R. (1982). Children's knowledge about time, distance and velocity interrelations. In W. J. Friedman (Ed.), *The developmental psychology of time* (pp. 87–112). New York: Academic Press.

Za'rour, I. G., & Khuri, A. G. (1977). The development of the concept of speed by Jordanian children in Amman. In P. R. Dasen (Ed.), *Piagetian psychology: Cross cultural contributions* (pp. 216–226). New York: Gardner Press.

9

Use of Physical Intuition and Imagistic Simulation in Expert Problem Solving

John Clement
University of Massachusetts

Introduction

Overview

It is quite natural to suppose that the knowledge used by experts in science is abstract and that the knowledge used by novices is concrete. This chapter discusses evidence from thinking-aloud case studies that indicates that part of the knowledge used by expert problem solvers consists of concrete physical intuitions rather than abstract verbal principles or equations. This evidence also indicates that the role of these intuitions is not restricted to a "start-up" role in a brief period at the beginning of the problem solution—in particular they can play the important role of anchoring assumptions that underpin explanations constituting the subject's central understanding of a system. The case study examples focus on a number of observable behaviors in transcripts, including imagery reports, depictive hand motions, and references to using intuition. In many cases, these co-occur with predictions or conclusions about the problem situation.

Hypothesized cognitive structures and processes that can account for these behavior patterns will be proposed. A current limitation of most theories concerning the use of imagery in thinking is the focus on images of objects rather than of actions. I will hypothesize the use of dynamic imagery in conjunction with perceptual motor schemas in order to account for cases where the subject appears to be "running an imagistic simulation" of an event on the basis of a physical intuition. In this model, new knowledge can be derived from an imagistic simulation that does not depend on inferences from chains of wordlike symbols. Evidence will also be presented indicating that imagistic simulation can be used to make knowledge that is implicit in a physical intuition more explicit. Thus the chapter attempts to outline an initial framework that describes basic relationships between physical intuitions, imagery, imagined actions, implicit knowledge, and mental simulation. The intuitions discussed here are very basic, involving only one or two causal relationships. Whereas a good deal of prior theoretical work in artificial intelligence has been done on complex forms of simulation involving inferences on chains of causes with many

This research was supported by National Science Foundation Grant NSF #MDR-8751398. Any opinions, findings, and conclusions or recommendations expressed in this publication are those of the author and do not necessarily reflect the views of the National Science Foundation.

links (e.g., de Kleer & Brown, 1983; Forbus, 1984), very little attention has been given to the nature of the underlying elemental simulations in humans involving a single causal relationship. Descriptions of processes involved in elemental mental simulations may provide a foundation for helping us understand more complex processes such as scientific explanation and thought experiments.

Concrete Versus Abstract Knowledge in Experts

Expert knowledge is commonly described as predominantly abstract. For example, Chi, Feltovich, and Glaser (1981) state that experts in physics use

> abstract physics principles to approach and solve a problem representation. (p. 121)
> The early stage of problem solving (the qualitative analysis) involves the activation and confirmation of an appropriate principle-oriented knowledge structure . . . [that] provides the general form that specific equations to be used for solution will take. (p. 149)

Here the authors are referring to principles such as energy conservation, which, although they can be expressed at a qualitative level, are highly abstract in the sense of being very general and nonconcrete, in addition to being strongly associated with mathematical expressions. Novices, on the other hand, "base their representation and approaches on the problem's literal features" (p. 121) and are "lacking abstracted solution methods" (p. 151). They also observe that experts classify homework problems on the basis of abstract principles, in contrast to novices, who tend to classify problems on the basis of concrete physical features.

This focus on abstract principles appears to conflict with some retrospective reports of scientists, such as the following one collected from Einstein by Hadamard:

> The words or the language . . . do not seem to play any role in my mechanism of thought. The . . . elements in thought are certain signs and more or less clear images which can be "voluntarily" reproduced and combined. . . . The desire to arrive finally at logically connected concepts is the emotional basis of this rather vague play . . . but . . . this combinatory play seems to be the essential feature in productive thought—before there is any connection with logical construction in words. . . . The above mentioned elements are, in my case, of visual and some of muscular type. (Hadamard, 1945, pp. 142–143)

Here Einstein appears to emphasize the role of concrete imagery in thought experiments rather than abstract logical principles in his most productive thinking. Although Einstein is undoubtedly making an honest and insightful statement here, one strength of the Chi study is that it is based on real-time observations of problem solving, including thinking-aloud data, rather than a retrospective self-analysis. This motivates the present study of expert thinking-aloud data that documents the use of concrete physical intuitions. Findings from this study argue that a predominant focus on abstract principles in expert thinking is not always appropriate and that concrete physical intuition schemas can play an important role as well. In the conclusion I discuss whether these two contrasting views are in any way reconcilable. Although concrete intuitive knowledge structures may be considered by some to be unsophisticated, I suggest that they can play a significant role in expert thought and provide the foundation for important kinds of explanation. diSessa (1983, 1985) has referred to such conceptions as phenomenological primitives. For example, one may believe that, in general, one must exert more force or effort to throw an object at a high speed than at a low speed. In this chapter I refer to such conceptions as "elemental physical intuitions." Studies in this area are also motivated by recent studies in the history of science on the important cognitive roles played by (a) actions involved in experimental practice (Gooding, 1990; Tweney, 1986) and (b) imagery (Miller, 1987; Nersessian, 1984; Nersessian & Greeno, 1990; Qin & Simon, 1990).

Outline of the Chapter

After describing data collection methods, I first present some examples of the use of physical intuition by expert problem solvers and identify some observable behaviors in transcripts, including reports of using intuition, depictive hand motions, and spontaneous reports of using imagery. Additional examples are then analyzed as I discuss specific topics under the following section headings: working definition for an elemental physical intuition; imagery reports and imagistic simulation; physical intuition schemas; implicit knowledge and physical intuitions; knowledge as action; and can physical intuitions and simulations play an important role in expert thought?

Data Collection Method

Ten subjects were asked to solve the "Spring Problem" shown in Figure 9.1. Subjects were told that the purpose of the interviews was to study problem-solving methods and were asked to think aloud as much as possible during the solution attempt. All were advanced doctoral students or professors in technical fields. By "expert problem solver" in this context, I mean a person who is an experienced problem solver in a technical field. Most subjects were not experts on the specific content domain of the theory of static forces in springs. Subjects were given instructions to solve the problem "in any way that you can" and were asked to give a rough estimate of confidence in their answer. Probes by the interviewer were kept to a minimum and usually consisted of a reminder to keep talking. Occasionally the interviewer would ask for clarification of an ambiguous report. All sessions discussed in this chapter were videotaped except subject S5, who was audiotaped. The correct answer to the spring problem is that the wide spring will stretch farther.

The subjects' solutions were up to 90 minutes long and contained a number of different types of nonformal reasoning. The main purpose of my account here is to document a set of examples of the use of physical intuition and to develop some initial hypothesized constructs for describing and classifying the underlying processes. I attempt to provide an in-depth view of the phenomena by concentrating on examples from the protocols of four subjects.

SPRING PROBLEM

A WEIGHT IS HUNG ON A SPRING. THE ORIGINAL SPRING IS
REPLACED WITH A SPRING:
    --MADE OF THE SAME KIND OF WIRE,
    --WITH THE SAME NUMBER OF COILS,
    --BUT WITH COILS THAT ARE TWICE AS WIDE IN DIAMETER.

WILL THE SPRING STRETCH FROM ITS NATURAL LENGTH, MORE, LESS, OR
THE SAME AMOUNT UNDER THE SAME WEIGHT? (ASSUME THE MASS OF THE
SPRING IS NEGLIGIBLE COMPARED TO THE MASS OF THE WEIGHT.)

WHY DO YOU THINK SO?

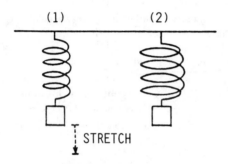

Figure 9.1. Spring Problem

It is important to distinguish between descriptions of the external observable behavior of the subject (such as a spontaneous reference to using intuition or imagery) and hypotheses about internal cognitive structures and processes. Therefore I begin with a discussion of some observable behaviors that suggest the use of physical intuition.

Initial Examples of Intuition

I first consider two of the simplest examples of a solution approach that appears to rely on the direct application of a physical intuition. The first is from the solution of an expert in mathematics and computer science referred to here as S2. The actual protocols for difficult problems are quite long; therefore, I present verbatim segments of protocols here. Numbers indicate the position of an excerpt in the protocol.

05 S2: I'm going to try to visualize it to imagine what would happen—uh, my guess would be that it [the larger spring] would stretch more—my guess is . . . a kind of a kinesthetic sense that somehow a bigger spring is looser. Umm, that's high uncertainty.

Here the subject refers to visualizing the spring; this is an example of what I call a spontaneous *imagery report*. He also refers to a "kinesthetic sense," indicating that he is thinking about muscle movements, or the sensation of muscular effort. Although the subject makes a definite prediction here, his certainty in this prediction is low.

Occasionally subjects provide evidence that an intuition is based on a specific set of experiences with physical phenomena. The following example comes from the solution of a research physicist, S1.

027   *S1:*   You don't have to know any formulas to see that it's;—Why would I bet that it's more? [the stretch of the wider spring] Not because I've analyzed the physics. Because when I sit there and see that spring, and now I take the same wire and make a big spring like that and put my weight on it, God almighty! Of course it goes way down. You know. How could it do otherwise?

028   *S1:*   So that's just a matter of almost uh—I've wound springs you know in the shop, and that's a seat-of-the-pants feeling I would trust beyond any of it. So if you asked how much will I bet uhh, on the answer that it stretches more than the same length, I would bet a thousand to one.

Here the subject indicates that he is very confident in his intuition. To counter the idea that physical intuitions are used only by those who lack more formal reasoning capabilities, it should be noted that this subject is a Nobel laureate in physics.

Intuition Reports
S1 refers to a "seat-of-the-pants feeling" as the source of his prediction. Both this and subject S2's excerpt contain an example of what I refer to as a physical *intuition report*, where the subjects report using an "intuition" or use terms that indicate they are proceeding primarily on the basis of a nonformal "feeling" or "sense" of what will happen to a physical system.

S1 later goes on to the more advanced problem of making a quantitative prediction for the amount of change in the stretch of the spring. However, for the original qualitative problem of concern in this chapter, he indicates that (a) he relies on a physical intuition to think about qualitative features of the problem; and (b) he trusts those intuitions in this case as much or more than his formal knowledge of physics for this problem. The subject's statement that he has wound springs in the lab provides evidence that the intuition is at least partly an abstraction from experience in manipulating physical objects. (Other subjects had had much less experience with springs, and for them the qualitative question of whether the wide spring stretches more was more challenging.)

Use of the term "physical intuition." In natural language the word "intuition" unfortunately has multiple meanings. Schon (1981) sorted through a number of these meanings and pointed to some common ambiguities, some of which stem from using the term to refer to both elemental knowledge structures and complex nonformal reasoning processes. Attempts to analyze a considerable number of expert protocols involving qualitative knowledge and reasoning have led me to the position that it is useful to separate these two meanings of the term. I will therefore avoid the latter use here, so that I will not use the term "physical intuition" for reasoning processes such as induction, analogical reasoning, or heuristic strategies for problem solving. Instead, I focus on elemental knowledge structures seen as basic units of knowledge. I call these "elemental physical intuitions." The two examples given so far appear to involve elemental physical intuitions. Fischbein (1987) surveys uses of intuition in mathematics. (Throughout the remainder of this chapter, when I use the term "intuition" I mean an elemental physical intuition.)

Theoretical Overview

With these initial examples in mind, here I give a preview of the theoretical concepts and general framework to be proposed. I hypothesize that the subjects possess knowledge structures called *elemental physical intuitions* that are concrete and self-evaluated, have modest generality, and stand without further explanation or justification. A physical intuition is thought of here as an expectation with the previously mentioned properties that is embodied in a *schema*. The word schema has been used for knowledge structures of many different sizes, and here I have in mind smaller structures that might, for example, embody one or two causal relationships.

Reports of using intuition are often accompanied by hand motions or reports of using imagery. The imagery reported is not just visual imagery but sometimes also kinesthetic and can involve imagined actions. In particular, many of the examples to be discussed in this chapter appear to involve perceptual motor or action schemas where subjects imagine acting on objects with their hands in order to simulate the effects of forces on a system. Presumably these intuitions have developed from prior experiences in acting on physical objects in the world.

An important observation is that imagery reports can co-occur with subjects' predictions about a system. I account for this observation by hypothesizing that subjects are running through an elemental *imagistic simulation* where a schema assimilates a mental image of a particular situation and operates in "dry run" mode to produce expectations about its behavior. I also propose that subjects can focus on features in such a simulation that were previously not consciously attended to, or not described, thereby converting implicit knowledge into explicit knowledge.

Elemental Intuitions as Knowledge Structures

In both transcript excerpts previously presented, the subject's expectations do not appear to follow from more elementary propositions; they themselves appear to be ideas for which the subject has no immediate justification or explanation. This suggests that the ideas are primitive or elemental, rather than built on other more elemental ideas. A third example occurs in the following excerpt from S3, who is an advanced Ph.D. candidate in computer science and has worked as an electrical engineer. Immediately after reading the problem, S3 proceeds as follows:

008   S3:   Well right off the bat I have no idea. Umm, and my first thought is that the length . . . of the coil spring being greater (traces circles in air with finger spiralling downward) and the strength of the metal being the same means that there's going to be kind of more leverage for bending [in the wider spring].

009   S3:   And that therefore it's going to hang further down. And that's pretty much strictly an intuition based on my familiarity with metal and with working with metal. . . . Let me just think through that . . .

010   S3:   (Draws long and short horizontal rods) . . . And my intuition about that is that if you took the same wire that was fastened on the left here [short horizontal rod] and doubled the length and hung some weight on it, that the same material uh, with some weight on it, would bend considerably farther . . .

019   S3:   It would seem that that means that um, that back in the original problem, the spring in picture 2 [the wider spring] is going to hang farther; it's going to be stretched more.

021   S3:   . . . and I have a confidence of about 75% . . .

022   S3:   . . . I have a great deal of confidence that Da [the displacement of the long rod] is greater than Db [the displacement of the short rod] in any case. I would say 100% confidence.

S3 generates the analogous case of bending long and short horizontal rods and decides that the longer one will bend more. The intuition reports in lines 009 and 010 suggest that he was using an elemental physical intuition to reach this conclusion. He then makes an inference by analogy that the wider spring will stretch more. As shown by the solid square in Figure 9.2, S3 has 100% confidence in this intuition that the long rod will bend more, but only 75% confidence in the validity of the analogy relation between the spring and rod cases. Thus, applying the elemental intuition to the rods and subsequently making inferences about the spring by analogy can be viewed as two separate processes.

Although it is very interesting that a conclusion from intuition can be transferred by analogy to another case, I want to focus in this chapter on the nature of elemental intuitions as knowledge structures, rather than on the separate issue of analogical

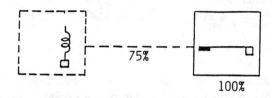

Figure 9.2. Confidence Levels for Elements of S3's Bending Rod Analogy

reasoning. The nature of spontaneous analogical reasoning and other nonformal reasoning strategies is a large issue in its own right (Clement 1982, 1986, 1988a, 1988b). Thus, for S3, I wish to focus on the right hand square only in Figure 9.2, that is, on the question of how an elemental intuition can be used directly on a given case, such as the bending rod, to obtain a prediction. In this case his intuition about the bending rod serves as an assumption on which his explanation is grounded—a basic assumption that is not further justified, but that is used as the basis for later inferences.

Observable Properties Associated with Physical Intuitions

On the basis of transcripts like those presented, one can point to a basic cluster of phenomena that suggests the existence of elemental physical intuitions as a type of natural cognitive structure. But how should one define the term "physical intuitions"? Are they nonabstract? Unconscious? Indescribable? Can they be taught, or should they be self-constructed? I will propose a definition after listing some observable properties from the transcripts.

> *Intuition reports.* In thinking about a physical system, subjects sometimes spontaneously report making a prediction based on an intuition. However, we cannot attach too much importance to a subject's use of the term, since, for one thing, its meaning in natural language is so broad and vague. Thus, this observation should probably be used only in conjunction with others.
>
> *Unexplained, unjustified.* Subjects speak of a physical intuition as a starting point without a need to have it be further justified or explained.
>
> *Modest generality.* The situation referred to by subjects is often more general than the memory of a specific incident. The terms they use refer to a broader class of phenomena. As diSessa (1983) points out, however, the degree of generality is not nearly so large as that of the concepts used in Newtonian mechanics.
>
> *Self-evaluated.* Subjects indicate that they are evaluating their confidence in an intuition based on criteria that are internal; they do not refer to an external authority as the source of support for the intuition.
>
> *Oriented to concrete objects.* Subjects usually speak of an intuition as referring directly to objects and physical phenomena, not to abstract equations.

One of the intended purposes of the body of case study data being presented here is to demonstrate the presence of these observable properties and to provide something like an initial "existence proof" for them.

Working Definition for an Elemental Physical Intuition

The foregoing observations form a foundation for the definition given below— basically a hypothesis proposing the existence of a particular type of internal knowledge structure. Of course, any definition is partly a matter of choice; the goal here is to construct a definition that will be as useful as possible in constructing an explanatory cognitive model.

diSessa refers to certain kinds of intuitions as "phenomenological primitives" and proposes some of their properties, based on interviews with physics students. Phenomenological primitives are "relatively minimal abstractions of simple common phenomena" that "stand without significant explanatory substructure or justification" (diSessa, 1983, p. 15). A physical intuition can be activated by a process of "recognition" that is left as a yet-to-be-explained process. He proposes that physics expertise is partially built on phenomenological primitives, but that these primitives have in many cases been modified, reorganized, and made more precise. I use the term "elemental physical intuition" here in a way that shares many of the features of a phenomenological primitive, including the following ones.

> *Knowledge structures.* Physical intuitions are knowledge structures that reside in long-term memory and can be activated to provide an interpretation of or an expectation about a physical phenomenon.
>
> *Elemental.* They are elemental in the sense that the subject does not feel a need to explain or justify them on other grounds.[1]
>
> *General.* As knowledge structures in long-term memory, physical intuitions assimilate a certain *range* of other representations such as members of a certain class of perceived objects. In this sense they are abstractions with a certain degree of generality, although naive intuitions are typically not nearly as general as scientific theories.

The observable behaviors of experts listed earlier provide some support for these features. In addition to the features identified by diSessa, I would also point to some other characteristics of physical intuitions that are supported:

> *Intrinsic or self-evaluated.* References to confidence levels indicate that a subject's level of belief in a particular physical intuition can be strong or weak. Thus, while some intuitions can carry low levels of confidence, an important point is that some can carry very high levels of confidence, even though they are not explained or justified further by empirical or rational means. These intuitions have something like the status of a self-evident truth for the subject.
>
> However, these references to confidence levels, whether high or low, also suggest that the subject's ideas are to some extent intrinsic. That is, strength of belief in a physical intuition is determined largely via internal criteria rather than being dependent on the evaluation of an authority. The idea "makes sense" to the subject to a certain extent. For example, the subject does not say

---

[1] It is possible that intuitions can be assembled into more complex structures, such as scientific models, involving several intuitions. Such structures will be referred to here as models grounded in intuition but not as elemental intuitions in themselves.

"I remember my physics teacher saying that . . ." but rather "I have a fairly strong feeling that . . ." Effectively, this criterion eliminates rote learning as a source of intuitions.

Concrete. The object-oriented examples discussed here suggest that an elemental physical intuition provides "direct" knowledge of the behavior of a physical object or system—knowledge that does not depend on a formal symbol system. This is in contrast to the use of a symbolic mathematical expression, which would be indirect in the sense that it would need to be reinterpreted to be applied to the physical system. As used here, elemental physical intuitions are knowledge about objects and manipulations of or relationships between them. They provide direct expectations about what will happen, rather than a symbolic result that must be interpreted. They may stand behind and be used in interpreting formal equations, but they are not themselves formal equations.

This definition of physical intuition involves some semantic choices, and the preceding features reflect some conscious decisions. For example, there is not a requirement that a physical intuition be entirely untutored. This allows for the possibility that the construction of intuitions can be fostered by certain experiences in school, making it possible to frame hypotheses such as: "By carrying out suggested experiments with pucks on a frictionless air table, students can develop intuitions about motion in a frictionless environment." Yet it was stipulated that physical intuitions must be self-evaluated. This rules out rote learning as a source of intuitions and captures the sense in which they are "natural" knowledge structures with intrinsic appeal.

Imagery Reports and Imagistic Simulation

In this section I present evidence indicating that the use of an intuition can involve dynamic imagery. Introspectively, we tend to associate intuition with the use of imagery. Yet there is a lack of discussion in the literature that relates the two. One source of difficulty here is that most discussions of imagery involve vision alone, whereas physical intuition often appears to involve imagining *actions* taken on objects as well. This raises an important question about the relationship between intuition, action, and imagery.

To anticipate, the view I propose here is that although imagery plays a role in physical intuition, elemental physical intuitions do not just consist of specific images. Rather, they involve a general schema, often an action oriented, perceptual motor schema accompanied by kinesthetic as well as visual imagery.

Imagery Reports

In the cases to be examined subjects spontaneously use terms like "imagining," "picturing," "hearing," a situation or "feeling what it's like to manipulate" a situation. I refer to such statements as *imagery reports*. These reports include several sensory modes, including kinesthetic imagery. In contrast to most of the literature on imagery, I am concerned here with *spontaneous* imagery reports where the interviewer does not ask the subject whether an image was used. (The interviewer was careful not to be the first to introduce terms such as "image" or "picture" in the interviews.)

Reports of imagery accompanied by a prediction. I have already presented one case containing an imagery report: the first example presented on p. 207 where S2 refers to "visualizing" the spring in order to think about it in transcript line 5. An important observation that can be made from this transcript is that an imagery report can co-occur with a subject's predictions about a system. As another example, later in his solution S2 is comparing short and long springs and says:

> 041 *S2:* I'm imagining that one applies a force closer and closer to the origin [top] of the spring, and . . . it hardly stretches at all.

Again we see the co-occurrence of an imagery report and a prediction. S2 provides a third example of this kind in the excerpt that follows. At this point he has decided that a twisting deformation in the wire is one of the consequences of stretching the spring. (Twisting of the wire and the resulting torsion do in fact play a predominant role in determining the behavior of a spring.) He is trying to decide what effect widening the spring will have on the twisting deformation by imagining himself twisting a straight horizontal rod:

> 137 *S2:* . . . If I have a longer rod, and I put a twist on it (moves hands as if twisting a rod, as shown in Figure 9.3), it seems to me—again physical intuition—that it will twist more. Uhh, I'm—I think I trust that intuition.
>
> 138 *1:* Can you stop thinking ahead and just think back on that; what that intuition is like?
>
> 139 *S2:* Oh, I have a kinesthetic intuition . . . I'm imagining holding something that has a certain twistyness to it and twisting it.
>
> 140 *1:* MmMm
>
> 141 *S2:* Like a bar of metal or something like that. Uhh, and it just seems to me as though it [a longer bar] would twist more.

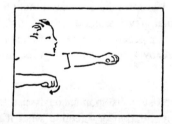

Figure 9.3. Hand Movement During Imagistic Simulation for S2 (Drawing is an exact tracing from photograph of video image.)

Here one can observe a number of the phenomena under discussion: occurrence of an imagery report (line 139) and a stated prediction (137, 139), intuition reports (137, 139), and depictive hand motions (137). In addition line 139 is an example of a *dynamic imagery report*, where the subject describes a situation in an imagery report as changing with time. Also, the fact that an imagery report co-occurs with an intuition report provides evidence that the use of physical intuition can involve imagery. The subject eventually uses this result as a basic assumption or starting point in order to make inferences about the spring.

Imagistic Simulation Processes

Having considered several examples of imagery reports, some accompanied by predictions, I can now offer some general hypotheses concerning the cognitive processes that accompany these statements. I begin by assuming that subjects giving imagery reports refer to an experience that has some of the characteristics of actually perceiving or manipulating actual physical objects. One needs a term other than "imagery report" for this process since that term refers to an observable event, and one wants to refer to the unobservable mental process that is the origin of such reports. The basic hypothesis proposed here is that subjects engage in an *imagistic simulation* process wherein a schema assimilates the image of a particular system and produces expectations about its behavior in a subsequent image. I take the co-occurrence of a dynamic imagery report and a prediction (as described in the previous section) as providing some evidence that an imagistic simulation is occurring.

Figure 9.4 gives an overview of this process. Here it is assumed that the physical intuition about how an object behaves is an expectation embodied in a permanent and somewhat general schema. In the case of S2 imagining twisting a rod, the imagistic simulation is the process of applying a schema capable of controlling real actions for the twisting of objects. The schema is applied to a particular image of a one-foot–long bar of metal. This initial static image may have been generated in a previous process in period 1 in Figure 9.4. In period 2, the schema assimilates the image, "runs through an action on it," and generates an expectation about its behavior. (In actuality the subject presumably goes through two simulations with a short and a long rod here, after which he is able to compare them.) In Figure 9.4 the terms "schema," "image," and "simulation" describe hypothesized cognitive structures or processes, whereas "depictive hand motions," "imagery reports," "stated predictions," and "intuition reports" are terms for observable behavior patterns. Time moves from left to right in the figure.

It is assumed that all of the cognitive processes shown in Figure 9.4 can be nonverbal in character. Since the subject is asked to think aloud as much as possible however, there must also be an auxiliary description process that enables the subject to describe his thinking as or after it occurs. This process is not shown explicitly in the diagram.[2]

---

[2] Figure 9.4 shows a process for the case where the knowledge stored in the schema is nonverbal. In cases where explicit verbal rules are already stored with the schema, imagery may not be necessary.

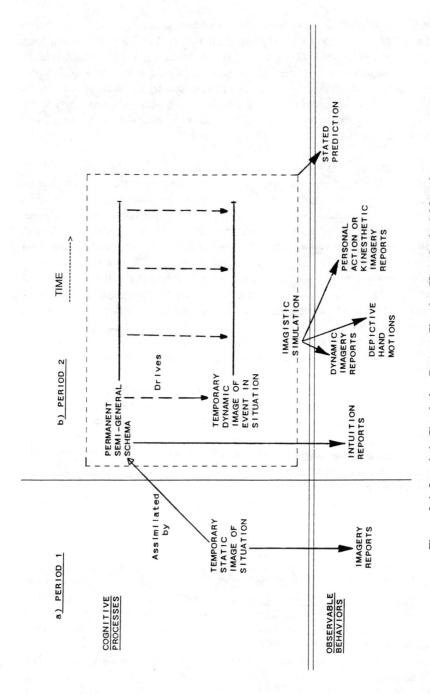

Figure 9.4. Imagistic Simulation Process Showing Hypothesized Mental
Processes Producing Observable Behaviors

The *best* evidence supporting the hypothesis that an imagistic simulation has taken place would be the co-occurrence of all the observable behaviors shown below the horizontal line in Figure 9.4. However, such evidence is very likely to be incomplete in any one episode. It would seem improbable for subjects to be so obliging as to actually verbalize all of these indicators spontaneously. Nevertheless a number of such cases were observed, such as the previously cited passage from S2, lines 137–141. More often though, without any retrospective probing by the interviewer, one might expect only an imagery report with a prediction, and most often, simply the prediction.

S5's "paint dots on the spring" protocol. In the following example the subject appears to make repeated attempts to carry out an imagistic simulation before finally becoming satisfied. He has already concluded that the wider spring will stretch more, based primarily on a bending rod analogy very similar to S3's discussed earlier. The interviewer then poses a second part of the question that challenges this model of the spring, namely: "Measurements are taken on a small segments of the spring and it is found that the primary deformation in the segment is a twisting or torsion effect around the axis of wire B. How can stretching a spring twist the wire without bending it much at all?" (A thought experiment not performed by any of the subjects, but which may help the reader envision twisting in the spring wire, is to imagine stretching a circular ribbon cut out of a piece of paper, as shown in Figure 9.5.) In thinking about this question, S5 imagines putting "paint dots" on the spring wire, apparently to help him think about the twisting deformation in the wire. (It was not possible to videotape this interview, therefore there is no data on hand motions.)

022   S5:   . . . suppose I had a big spring and I could make little paint dots on it all along its length, and then I imagine hanging a weight on the spring and saying you know, would I see a torsional displacement of the paint dots. And what would it look like. And I have a hard time imagining that because you know, the torsional displacements that come to mind are very small. So it's not a really gigantic effect. It's hard to imagine—you sense that the twists are going to be such that the outside of the spring moves down.

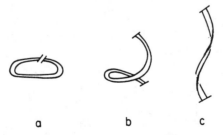

a   b   c

Figure 9.5. Imagery Allowing One to See Twisting in Spring Wire

024 *S5:* (Makes drawing in Figure 9.6a of spring with paint dots on wire) . . . I'm just looking at the very first coil, and if I made a line of little dots down the center of the coil, er, down the outside in the spring in the undeflected position, and then I put a little weight on—there's the dots. And then I have the impression that if I put the weight on, these dots would twist in this direction er, you know

029 *S5:* It looks like it's going to rotate like that. Um, but now when I examine the actual direction closely, I'm not so sure . . . Uhh, I guess . . . it should really go the other way.

031 *S5:* I was looking at this and I was imagining that the thing er, the spring—going down; . . .

031 *S5:* . . . these coils are gonna move down so that would mean that the twist— well, . . . it's opposite to what I had up there.

035 *S5:* (Makes drawing 9.6b.) I guess it's got to be the other way because if I see there that the coils, because their elongating, that means that the coil wants to pull down that way . . .

036 *S5:* So . . . the other parts are going to twist such that . . . little dots on the surface will tend to move up . . .

037 *S5:* (Makes drawing 9.6c)

038 *S5:* . . . The mass is going down and so now—these portions of the spring—— Hmmmm

040 *S5:* . . . I'm just getting a hard time envisioning what's going on 3- dimensional space, and so I'm having a hard time seeing which way this is going to rotate.

041 *S5:* Well I want to imagine that the portion here up to the cross section, I want to say that that's fixed. So I'm pulling down on the weight or the weight's

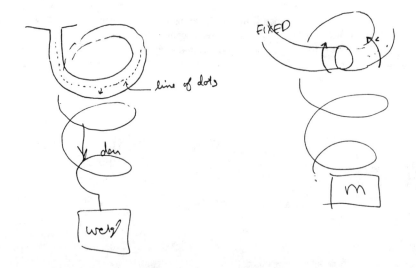

Figure 9.6. S5's Drawings for Spring Problem

pulling itself down, and that's causing these coils to elongate. I'm trying to decide how it's gonna twist this portion of the wire that's coming in here . . .

042 S5:   Suppose we imagine this to be frictionless, then . . . make a nice bearing there . . . if you imagine the extremes, if you pull it up and down, this little line . . . on the outside of the spring you know, would . . . rotate down till it's at the bottom.

044 S5:   In other words, if I had a little frictionless bearing I'm trying to imagine

046 S5:   . . . I guess I'm–I'm quite satisfied with that.

047 S5:   . . . you see that the wire twists in such a way that little portions of the spring move up and over the spring moving towards the center.

Interpretation of S5's protocol. S5 makes a drawing of the spring in line 24. What is the role of a drawing here? Does it replace or support internal imagery? One can argue that it cannot replace the imagery, since he speaks of the imagining movements, and the drawings do not move. Thus the drawings most likely play the role of providing a permanent record of his imagery here, and possibly of helping supporting it. Also, an initial imagery report and prediction occur at the end of line 22 at the beginning of the section just before he makes the first drawing. This makes it reasonable to assume that the drawing reflects static features of the subject's initial image but does not replace it. Taking this view then, there is evidence for dynamic imagery co-occurring with prediction in lines 22, 24, 29, 42 and 44–47, and these processes are probably aided by a perceived drawing.

These interpretations are reinforced by a later, retrospective section where he describes how he was thinking when he determined the direction of twisting. (Retrospective reports should not be given as much weight as concurrent reports, but they are still a relevant source of data to be weighed alongside other data, especially when they occur only a short time later.—

072 1:   . . . Can you describe the kind of thinking you used to actually determine the direction? Were you thinking of an equation or–

073 S5:   Oh, no. This is all er, I think very experimental. What I think I have—this image of this line of paint dots on a spring and you know I'm pulling on the weight. I'm going to pull and release, pull and release and so I'm constantly putting it through its paces. And asking you know, how would I see the dots move if I—put it through its paces. And you know originally I had the direction wrong but then you know now that I've thought about it and . . . done the mental experiment in my mind a lot, I'm more and more convinced that the dots move internally and that there is a twist of that orientation.

Here again we have imagery reports linked to making a prediction, and a clear description of the subject's experience during the simulation process. In addition, there is evidence for the simulation being a process extended over time, for him "asking questions of" the simulation, for the simulation increasing his confidence, and for his substituting a personal action of stretching for the force of the weight. Other statements in S5's protocol that fit the latter interpretation of substituting a personal action include: (35) "the coil wants to pull"; (41) "So I'm pulling down on the weight or the weight's pulling itself down, and that's causing these coils to elongate." Taken together, the observations for this protocol fit almost all of the patterns shown below the horizontal lines in Figure 9.4 and support the hypothesis that the subject is running through imagistic simulations where one or more general schemas operate on the image of a particular system and produce expectations about its behavior in a subsequent dynamic image.

In addition, in speaking about having "a hard time imagining" (line 22) and "having a hard time envisioning what's gong on [in] 3-dimensional space" (line 40), he indicates that the simulation process is not easy here. This implies that it requires mental concentration and effort, and this is also implied by the extended period of several attempts to perform an accurate simulation. The source of trouble here may be the difficulty of applying a schema for twisting to such a strange object, or difficulty in forming and manipulating a detailed spatial representation of a helical spring, or both. The fact that he says "I want to imagine" the situation, the fact that it is difficult for him, and the fact that he makes and extended effort to do it anyway, is evidence that (a) he intends and tries to set up the imagistic simulation as an extended process very different from "remembering a fact" and (b) this process of imagining is important to him as a technique.

S2's Zig zag spring protocol. In another example S2 says (referring to the two-dimensional zig-zag spring analogy in Figure 9.7):

> 23 *S2:*   and when we do [stretch] this, what bends . . . is the bendable bars. . . . and
> that would behave like a spring. I can imagine that it would; I can kines-
> thetically pull on it and it would stretch, and you let it go and it bounces up and
> down (waves hand up and down, palm down, fingers extended). It does all the
> things.

In this example, additional evidence for simulation as a dynamic process occurs when the subject makes depictive hand movements that match the actions he is talking about.

The two main participants in imagistic simulations, a specific image and a more general schema, are discussed in turn in more detail in the next two sections.

Figure 9.7. S2's Zig-Zag Spring

Imagery: Spatial Representations

It is clear that it is not adequate here to claim that subjects simply "look" at a "movie" in their heads and "see" the result. This may describe one's introspective experience, but it is important to attempt to describe the nature of the cognitive processes that give rise to the sense of "seeing" (and "acting in") a "movie." In forming explanations here, based on the work of Shepard (1984), Kosslyn (1980), and others, I will use the idea of a temporary spatial representation (image) capable of representing in at least a skeletal manner (a) shapes of objects, (b) spatial relations among them, and (c) object movements over time. I assume that this spatial representation may use some of the brain's higher level perceptual processing capacity and that various manipulation processes (orienting, transforming and combining images) are available to the subject (Kosslyn, 1980; Shrager, 1989).

The concept of imagery as an internal representation gives one a starting point for understanding imagistic simulations. But it leaves unanswered the questions of how new knowledge can emerge from a new combination of an action and an image in an imagistic simulation. In order to progress further, the concept of physical intuition schemas is developed in the next section.

Physical Intuition Schemas

Argument for the Presence of General Schemas

In this section I give a more detailed argument for the presence of schemas of modest generality as the source of intuitive knowledge used in imagistic simulations. How does S3 know that a short rod will bend less than a long one? How does S2 know that it is more difficult to twist a shorter rod? Where does this knowledge reside? Occasionally a subject may make a prediction based on an episodic memory of a specific concrete experience at a particular time in his past, and this process could also involve dynamic imagery. In most of the cases examined here, however, the subjects make statements of a more general nature that do not refer to a specific episode in the past. I account for this by assuming that the intuitions involved are not based on a specific episodic memory, but exist as a somewhat more general form of knowledge—an expectation for what will happen over a range of circumstances.

To return to S2's intuition about the twisting rod, does this knowledge reside only in the temporary spatial representation (image)? There is reason to assume that it cannot reside solely in the specific temporary image of the situation currently under consideration, since in this case the knowledge is presumably more generally applicable and permanent. Rather, it seems plausible that the temporary image of a particular rod of a certain length acts in conjunction with a permanent schema for twisting objects that can assimilate objects of different sizes and shapes and that embodies the subject's physical intuitions about twisting. In this particular case the twisting schema assimilates (is instantiated by) the image of a rod about one foot long. It is not assumed that the subject has applied the schema to this particular object before; in fact, the image of the object may be a newly constructed one. It is assumed that the schema is general enough and flexible enough to allow its application to a certain range of new objects. This enables one to explain cases such as the application of a bending schema to novel cases like the zig-zag spring.

Intuitions Are Expectation Relations in a Schema

Such a schema is hypothesized to produce the following cognitive effects in the subject. An object or situation that satisfies certain preconditions can be seen as fitting a certain interpretation, and this leads to certain expectations about its behavior, and in some schemas to expectations about the results of an action controlled by the schema. An example of an expectation relation in a schema for twisting objects is the expectation that it takes more effort to twist a shorter object; in a schema for bending objects an example is the expectation that a longer object will bend more under the same force. In other words such schemata embody a structure of relationships between properties of an assimilated object, the expected behavior of the object, and in some cases the expected effects of an action that could be performed on the object by the subject. The model proposed here then is that physical intuitions are embodied in these relationships, and that one experiences a conscious physical intuition when one of these expectation relationships in the schema is an object of conscious attention.

Perceptual Motor Schemas

Presumably imagistic simulations can occur with schemas that are primarily perceptual, as opposed to action oriented, in nature; for example, I can imagine the effects of a glass of water tipping over in a certain way on a certain part of my desk. However, in most of the examples in this chapter the subject refers to a personal action, such as the twisting rod example. Therefore I will frame hypotheses in the discussion that follows in terms of the involvement of a particular type of intuition schema that I will term a "perceptual motor schema." I assume that perceptual motor schemas for twisting and bending objects were built up from the subject's prior experiences in acting on many concrete objects. As shown in Figure 9.8, a perceptual motor schema is hypothesized to contain at least three major subprocesses: a subprocess for assimilating objects in the environment based on preconditions that must be satisfied for the schema to apply; a subprocess for initiating and tuning or adjusting the action so that it is appropriate for this particular object; and a third subprocess embodying the anticipated results of the action—in this case, an image of how far the rod will turn.[3]

Transcript observations were used earlier to suggest four characteristics that a cognitive structure embodying a physical intuition should have: it should be concrete, be self-evaluated, have modest generality, and stand without further explanation or justification. Perceptual motor schemas as previously described would

---

[3] It is not assumed here that the assimilated representation or the anticipation of results are necessarily discrete symbols. Such an anticipation could take the form of a readiness to assimilate certain perceptual events rather than being language-like in character.

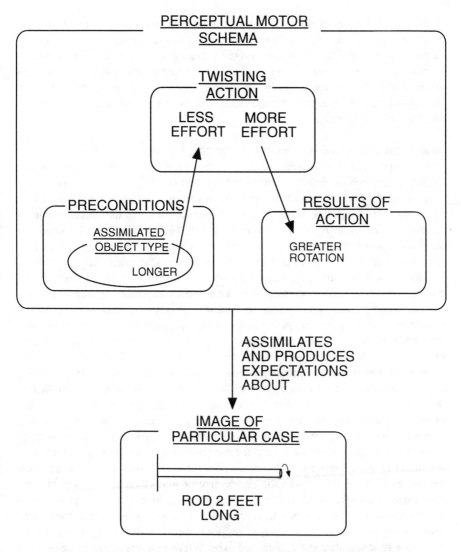

Figure 9.8. Perceptual Motor Schema for Twisting Objects (Shows
expectation relations of a longer object requiring less effort to twist [for
same resulting rotation] and more effort leading to greater rotation [for
the same object length].)

typically posses all of these features, and they are therefore promising candidates
for the cognitive structures embodying these elemental physical intuitions.[4]

---

[4] I make no claims that this initial model of perceptual motor schemes is completely sufficient. Here I
have merely attempted to give a preliminary outline of some of the elements that seem to be needed to
explain data of this kind. This builds on the work of Witz and Easley (Witz, 1975), who used perceptual
motor schemas to explain patterns in the play of young children.

While I have identified schemas with individual intuitions, in more complex cases there may be several intuitions associated with a single schema, each intuition being associated with a different expectation relation in the schema. For the sake of simplicity, in this chapter I sometimes refer to the mental embodiment of a physical intuition as an intuition schema. When more precise language is required, I refer to this knowledge as an intuitive expectation that is one of the relationships in the structure of the schema.[5]

Theoretical and Empirical Support for Perceptual Motor Schemas

Some support for this general perspective can be derived from several sources, including research on motor control and brain theory. Piaget (1976) proposed that very elementary sensorimotor schemas (in his terms, *schemes*) combine to form more complex cognitive structures in the child prior to the development of language. This view is compatible with that of Neisser (1976), who speaks of schemas as accepting information, directing movement, and providing anticipations for what will happen in a situation. He points out that even visual perceptual schemas control actions (e.g., of exploratory eye movements that track objects and seek new information). A schema coordinates processing over time at many levels: sensory, perceptual, cognitive, action, and muscle control. Thus, it is capable of participating in a *continuous proprioceptive interaction with the environment over time* when active. As Neisser (1976) puts it, schemas involve feed forward units and efferents as well as receptors and afferents.

More recent work by authors such as Schmidt (1982) and Arbib (1981) has further developed the concept of schemas or "programs" in motor control theory. Schmidt proposed a theory of motor schemas in his discussions of motor control programs that involve the capability of coordinating parallel overlapping sequences of muscle actions over time. He describes such motor programs as general in the sense that a single program can produce a large variety of responses depending on the values of certain input parameters. He also refers to expectations that anticipate the results of the action. From the perspective of brain theory, Arbib (1981) has emphasized the close coordination of nonverbal perceptual and motor processes as occurring when motor schemas are activated and assembled in a appropriate order before any movement occurs. He also proposes the view that a motor schema can embody a general pattern of actions and expectations with parameters adjusted to a particular situation in the process of tuning.

In addition, physiological research suggests that the motor control system can be involved in imaginal activity, even when no actual movements occur. Jacobson (1930) (one of the inventors of the electromyogram) found that for most subjects, while lying still, instructions to imagine a specific activity such as putting on a coat or pumping a bicycle pump resulted in marked increases in electrical action potentials of muscle groups that would be involved in the activity.

---

[5] As I discuss later, than an intuition is only a part of a schema is also compatible with the idea that an unconscious part of a schema can be made conscious in an imagistic simulation.

Two of the themes I wish to build on then from these researchers are, first, the idea of a dynamic schema as a structure that can coordinate perceptions and motor actions over time in a parallel manner, and second, the idea that even though it is nonverbal and dynamic, such a structure can have at least modest generality and the flexibility to assimilate and act on new cases via adjustment and tuning. The latter flexibility is seen as one of the important mechanisms by which an elemental simulation can produce new knowledge.

Observations from the present transcripts also support the view that perceptual motor schemas are being used that involve action-oriented knowledge. First, there are anthropomorphic action reports where subjects describe projecting a manipulative action of their own into the problem situation. For example, reports such as S2, line 111: "I'm visualizing what will happen when you just take this single coil and pull down on it and it stretches, and it stretches . . ." occur where the subject replaces the weight pulling on the spring with the pulling force of his hand (see also S5, lines 41 and 73, pp. 218–219). This same pattern can also be accompanied by kinesthetic imagery reports. Accompanying depictive hand movements (e.g., Figure 9.3) are a third form of evidence indicating that perceptual motor schemas are involved.

Summary: A Model for Imagistic Simulation

In this view the "running" of certain imagistic simulations involves a permanent physical intuition schema (such as a perceptual motor schema for twisting). The schema assimilates a target object (such as the rod) and drives a temporary sequence of dynamic imagery involving the target object as shown in Figure 9.4. Although the schema does this without actually assimilating a real object, it may produce the associated hand movements. This process involves two major components: a temporary spatial representation that is responsible for the experience of an image of a specific (and perhaps newly constructed) example, and a more general schema that is a permanent resident in memory. Once it has been activated, the schema can generate expectations about the effects of "operating on" the objects in the spatial representation. Thus an imagistic simulation of this kind is not just a "playback" of an image; it is the "playing out" of a general action schema interacting with (adapting to and tuning itself for) a particular imagined example. It involves imagined actions as well as imagined perceptions. Presumably, once the expectations have been generated they can be described verbally via a separate process if sufficient vocabulary is available. Filling in the details of this perspective and rejecting or supporting it with more empirical evidence is an important task for future research.

Perceptual motor schemas may not be the only kind of extant physical intuition, but in the examples discussed here they appear to serve as a simple but important type, involving knowledge of how personal actions affect objects. However, some elemental physical intuitions may derive from schemas that are less action oriented and more perceptually based. This raises the question as to how widely applicable the model developed in this chapter is, and I will offer two comments on this issue.

First, if one assumes that some causal ideas stem from the attribution of personal actions to other objects, elements of the framework presented here may apply more generally to other kinds of causal intuition as well. In this regard I note that even though S2's intuition was about the personal motor action of twisting a rod, he was confident in his assumption that the intuition transfers to instances where another physical object does the twisting instead of his hand.

Second, the main ideas that have been presented may apply to more perceptually based schemas as well. The examples used here suggesting the involvement of more action-oriented schemas do have some advantages for an initial study of physical intuition and simulation. Through the connection to motor control theory, they help make plausible the concept of a schema that is at the same time a nonverbal structure able to drive concrete images of events but also a general structure in its range of application. Also, the presence of action-oriented schemas can be evidenced through the additional observable behaviors of hand motions and reports of imagining personal actions. These observable indicators provide important evidence for the occurrence of a dynamic cognitive process over time in simulations. But although these indicators may make some properties of action-oriented schemas easier to document, I see no obvious reason why the basic elements of the model presented here should not apply to more perceptually based schemas as well.

Implicit Knowledge and Physical Intuitions

This section discusses the following issues. What is the relationship between physical intuition and implicit knowledge? Is an intuition ever implicit in the sense that the subject has not previously been conscious of the intuition? Are intuitions ever implicit in the somewhat weaker sense of being conscious but nonverbal and unarticulated?

The data to be analyzed here suggest that certain intuitions can be implicit in either sense, and that others can be explicit. When an intuitive expectation is conscious during a real or imagined event and is described verbally or mathematically, this is referred to as an explicit intuition. On the other hand, it is plausible that other intuitions embodied in a perceptual motor schema could be implicit in the sense that a parameter could be taken into account in controlling an action without being consciously differentiated perceptually or articulated verbally. For example, subjects may know how to release a sling whirled around their head so that it will hit a target in front of them. But many subjects are quite mistaken about where the release point occurred; as reported in Piaget (1976), release occurs at the side of the subject, since the rock travels in a straight line tangent to the circle after release. I use the term "unconscious knowledge" for this stronger sense of "implicit"—not being consciously aware of certain knowledge. As another example of unconscious knowledge, I am usually not aware of the sequence of action components performed with my tongue and mouth when I am saying the word "with" even though I may be aware that I have said the word.

It may be possible for previously unconscious knowledge to become a conscious intuition. One way this can occur is by watching or attending to what one does more carefully, for example, twirling a long sling at a slow speed and watching where one releases the sling. I will argue that another way this might occur is via an imagistic simulation that would not involve direct observation. For example, I can imagine saying the word "with" without actually saying it, and identify at least two separate component motor movements involved. Here unconscious knowledge is used to produce explicit knowledge.

In this section I examine the possibility that S2's thinking about the twisting rod is a case where the subject's imagistic simulation serves to convert implicit knowledge residing in a physical intuition schema into more explicit knowledge (lines 137–141, p. 214). Here the subject in the end was able to access relevant knowledge of how objects behave when they are twisted. However, this did not appear to be simply a case of immediate recall; rather, he reports making an effort to imagine what would happen as if he were actually performing the actions of twisting. It is as if he wanted to "run through" the experience of twisting the rod in order to "experience" the result.

Mounoud and Bower (1974) describe evidence from arm movements for the implicit, unarticulated anticipatory knowledge in infants 18 months old or less that prepares muscles to exert a larger force in picking up a large object. Presumably such estimates of force level are not encoded as discrete, language-like symbols, but are embedded in control (tuning) processes of a perceptual motor action schema that are parallel and distributed in nature.

Similarly, as S2 reports his expectation about twisting the rod, he may be consciously attending to and articulating it for the first time, even though he may have used the knowledge previously to control actions. This would account for the subject's experience of a hard-to-describe "intuition" or "kinesthetic sense" as the source of knowledge in this case. This account suggests that unconscious, unarticulated knowledge can be experienced, isolated in attention, and subsequently described as the subject simulates an event.

Distinguishing Different Levels of Implicit Knowledge
Rather than a strict dichotomy between implicit and explicit knowledge, it is useful to propose three levels on a dimension running from more implicit to more explicit knowledge, as follows. These levels describe types of knowledge one might use in completing a task or comprehending a scene, for example.

1. *Unconscious Knowledge*: I am unaware of an element of knowledge I use, even as I use it, such as the sequence of individual limb placements during crawling. (I may be aware of a larger unit of knowledge than the knowledge element in question, such as the whole act of crawling and the idea that I am crawling. But this awareness is holistic, and there is not a differentiated awareness of the compo-

nent knowledge elements [limb movement sequences] in question [Piaget, 1976].) Similarly, I am usually not aware of the sequence of actions performed with my tongue and mouth as I say the word "with" even though I may be aware that I have said the word. The knowledge elements are representationally undifferentiated—not separated out from the whole experience.

In particular here I have in mind the perceptual motor knowledge involved in carrying out an action that is performed more or less automatically by subschemas and that is not ordinarily under conscious control. This knowledge comprises the "lower" part of a schema whose other part is in conscious attention. (I am not referring here to other schemas weakly activated at a subliminal level by "horizontal association" to a schema in conscious attention.)

If one takes Neisser's view of a schema as coordinating processing at many levels from sensory up to cognitive and back down to muscle control, one can associate the "upper" or cognitive levels of a schema with more explicit knowledge, and the lower levels with more implicit knowledge. These are represented as being above and below the horizontal lines in Figure 9.9. There an active perceptual motor schema is pictured as a triangle whose upper part embodies only very abbreviated, skeletal, depictive representations of the preconditions and expectations (initial and final states) of an event. The lower part embodies the substructures supporting the extensive distributed and parallel processing in the perceptual and motor systems needed to actually perform the action. When the schema is simply one of a number of schemas being considered in a planning process, only the small upper part of the schema's processing need be in conscious attention for very brief moments. With an intentional effort to focus on a particular feature in an imagistic simulation however, much more of the schema's processing can be brought into conscious attention, revealing knowledge that was previously unconscious.

2. *Conscious but Nonverbal Knowledge*: The entity in question is differentiated from the context (e.g., imagistically), but no verbal or mathematical description in

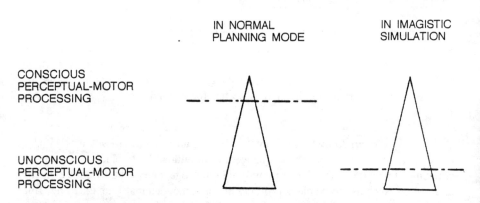

Figure 9.9. Change in Ratio of Conscious to Unconscious Processing During Imagistic Simulation.

terms of discrete symbols has been constructed. For example, a child may be able to watch someone make a sequence of novel arm movements and imitate them afterwards without any need for verbal description. Or I may suddenly notice contrasting types of cloud formations in the sky without describing them verbally. By "differentiated" I mean that the knowledge element is separately represented (e.g., as an image) and recognized as distinct from its context so that it can be attended to and reflected upon.

The example of the tongue and lip movements involved in saying the word "with" is helpful for sorting out several possible sources of confusion. First, I am focusing on the knowledge of an action element, such as the placement of the tongue against the teeth. I claim this is a knowledge element that I have not been conscious of and that has not been verbally described by me. Thus one needs to avoid confusion between the ability to verbally articulate the word "with" (the whole action) with the ability to verbally describe the way the tongue moves (the element of knowledge under consideration). Such confusions are all to easy to make in discussing the topic of implicit knowledge.

Second, with regard to the idea that knowledge is differentiated at level 2, one might object that for someone at level 1 with respect to the movements, these movements are still differentiated, since that person can make the movements precisely and competently. This is a different use of the term "differentiated" however, since to be at level 2 requires a differentiated representation that allows the person to reflect on the movements, not simply to produce an accurate performance of the movements.

Third, even if I am conscious of saying the word "with" *as a whole*, that does not mean I have a conscious representation at level 2 or 3 of the *component movements* involved. Thus it is important to avoid whole–part confusions with respect to the knowledge element one is talking about. In the present approach one first picks either the whole or the part and makes a commitment to the level of knowledge element one is going to describe. That element should then fit into only one level.

3. *Conscious and Verbally Described*: The knowledge element is conscious, differentiated from its context, and verbally or mathematically labeled or described in terms of discrete symbols.

Symbolic descriptions at level 3 can occur at different levels of precision. I may have developed a rough conceptual differentiation and verbal description at level 3 but have not formulated a stable, compact, precise description or proposition amenable to use in deductive inferences. Even though the knowledge has been given an initial description, the description may be unstable in that it is not accessed reliably and accurately. The description may be redundant rather than compact and may be vague or imprecise.

In other cases the knowledge element may become more precise: The knowledge element is fully conscious, stable, and compact; has been precisely described verbally; and involves precisely differentiated components. For some purposes this might be treated as an even higher fourth level of explicitness amenable to use in rigorous problem solving and axiomatic proof.

The terms "implicit" and "explicit" have often been used more simply as a dichotomy that distinguishes level 1 from level 3 only—unconscious from verbally explicable knowledge—ignorning the possibility of conscious but undescribed knowledge at level 2. I will use the term "implicit knowledge" to refer to knowledge of type 1 or type 2 above.[6]

Examples of undescribed knowledge. In relating these concepts to examples, I will describe the role of implicit knowledge not as the only possible way to explain the behavior, but as the hypothesis that appears to be the most plausible. For example, in the twisting rod episode, I have hypothesized that S2 runs through an imagistic simulation in order to (a) activate the knowledge, (b) focus on and differentiate the variables in question, (c) simulate the event and experience an effect, and (d) describe the effect verbally. This is seen as a process for making implicit knowledge more explicit. Evidence that it is at least implicit in the sense of type 2, undescribed knowledge, includes the fact that the subject refers to his "imagining" as the source of his prediction and the co-occurrence of hand motions. These support the interpretation that the source of knowledge here is nonverbal and is described in a subsequent step.

In a second example I refer back to the first transcript segment in this chapter where S2 has an intuition about narrow and wide springs at the very beginning of his solution:

05   *S2:*   I'm going to try to visualize it to imagine what would happen . . . my guess would be . . . a kind of a kinesthetic sense that somehow a bigger spring is looser.

Here again, the subject's effort to attempt a visualization can be explained by the hypothesis that he is accessing implicit knowledge that has not been described before. These two examples appear to discredit several competing hypotheses. In the first part of this quotation, S2 indicates that he anticipates that an extended imagery process (running through a simulation) may be helpful in producing a finding. This argues against the idea that explicit knowledge was retrieved in a direct and ordinary manner—against retrieval of a specific fact. I will elaborate on this argument in the next major section on "Knowledge as Action," where I argue that because of their dynamic character, the imagistic simulations involving physical intuitions discussed in this chapter are more likely to involve an analogue, depictive representation rather than a static, descriptive one. Then in the conclusion I argue that the use of imagistic simulation was an effortful and important process in the thinking of these subjects. These arguments add further support for the hypothe-

---

[6] Karmiloff-Smith (1987) posits an even finer breakdown with a larger number of categories between implicit and explicit knowledge in order to explain data on linguistic development.

sis that some of the knowledge used from these schemas is undescribed—for if it were explicitly described then why go to the trouble to form an image of the situation and run through a simulation of it?

Also, there is no evidence in either example for the competing hypothesis that the situation is a complex construction that would use the simulation as a way to infer the result of coordinating several schema applications in combination. (This might be said of the zig-zag spring case discussed earlier where it is seen as the coordinated action of several bending rods put together.) Here the subject refers to only a single action.

Evidence for unconscious knowledge. For these two examples there is also some weaker evidence that the knowledge used was previously unconscious. The subject in line 05 describes his findings as new information rather than something he has known before but never described. Yet this new information does not appear to come from a chain of inferences. The subject describes it as coming from "visualizing" or "imagining it" and a "kinesthetic sense." Thus a plausible hypothesis here is that the subject is using perceptual motor knowledge that was previously unconscious. This is also true to some extent of the twisting rod episode, where the subject's wording implies that he is realizing for the first time that it will "twist more" rather than remembering it as a familiar image.

Evidence for the use of motoric knowledge in the two examples suggests that the pertinent knowledge resides in a perceptual motor schema. It is reasonable to assume that such schemas can have tuning parameters that are unconscious. This makes plausible the idea that the knowledge needs to be made conscious. As described earlier, evidence for the involvement of motoric knowledge occurs in three forms: references to acting on objects, references to kinesthetic or muscular imagery, and depictive hand motions during thinking. Thus, although the evidence is not conclusive, there is more than one line of support for the hypothesis that unconscious knowledge is being accessed here to form an image that is subsequently "inspected." This hypothesis is not intended to explain all of the transcript examples in this chapter, but the two examples discussed in this section appear to fit this description.[7,8]

---

[7] One may reasonably question whether this "inspection" is conducted by a homunculus containing the "mind's eye" and whether this consequently may be a circular argument that has little explanatory value. To counter this objection we can draw on the view of Shepard (1984) that the "mind's eye" is just the body's extended eye—just the many layers of our single perceptual-cognitive system being driven in a top–down manner rather than a bottom–up manner. Such activiations may not reach down to the retinal level but may still feel somewhat similar to the act of seeing. The number of layers or stages of processing involved during perception is not known, but one might assume for the sake of argument that there were, say, 15 layers in the visual-cognitive system from retina to goal structure. These would include layers that would represent objects and spatial relations between objects in a scene during perception, say in layers six to eight. Then one can hypothesize that the subjective experience of imagery occurs whenever there is significant processing in layers six to eight, in the absence of the real objects. This could happen if they were activated in a top–down manner by higher layers. By extension, kinesthetic imagery would involve top–down activation of intermediate layers in the motor control system, but with suppression of the lowest layers that produce actual movements.

Researchers such as Gelerntner (1959), Larkin and Simon (1987), and Lindsey (1988) have proposed the hypothesis that there is a special mode of nondeductive spatial inferences made possible by diagramatic representations and perhaps by static imagistic representations in general. Such inferences are derived from implicit knowledge of spatial relationships and constraints that become explicit when a static image is "examined" and described. The perspective I am proposing in this section can be viewed as a related idea but in the domain of dynamic actions. That is, there are implicit relationships and constraints that are built into action schemas that can become explicit when the schema is applied to an image of a particular situation with a particular question in mind in an imagistic simulation.

There is also a connection here to the famous example of asking someone how many windows are in his living room (Chase, 1983). One possible interpretation is that for subjects who report imagining being in the room and counting the windows, knowledge that was implicit in their spatial memory of the room becomes explicit in the imaging, focusing, and counting process. Although this is not an example of *physical* intuition, it provides an interesting comparison to the process previously discussed.

Distinguishing "implicit" from "intuitive." The meaning used here for the term "implicit" can be contrasted with a less specific meaning. Some theorists have used the term to mean intuitive knowledge. For example, Westcott (1968) proposed a very broad definition of intuition as "reaching a conclusion on the basis of less explicit information than is ordinarily required to reach that conclusion." Indeed, intuitive knowledge may often begin its developmental course as implicit knowledge.

However, I suggest a narrower use of the term "implicit." That these two concepts can be distinguished can be demonstrated by indicating examples of explicit intuitions. I have a reasonably strong intuition of momentum in the case of large coasting objects such as railroad cars. This knowledge has been made explicit

---

"Inspection" then refers to the act of focusing on a particular feature of the "experience" during the "running" of the schema involving the motor and visual systems. That is, inspection of a new image at level 8 occurs when a second schema at levels 9–12 (such as counting/number) assimilates and interprets the image (such as "windows in my living room") during the time the image is maintained. Thus a certain amount of parallel processing is assumed. This account makes the simplifying assumption that somewhat similar processes account for both imagery and actual perception at each of these levels. There is no infinite regress of homunculi in this view because the buck stops with the schemas interpreting and responding to the image, just as it would stop there during the perception of a real event.

[8] This hypothesis that imagistic simulation can make unconscious knowledge explicit also seems to fit the example of determining movements involved in saying "with." Introspectively, there seem to be separate phases of (a) imaging saying the word and recognizing the separate movements involved and (b) verbally describing each movement. Either actually saying the word "with" or imagining saying it seems to be necessary before description of the movements is possible. Presumably this kind of imagery is the same as that which supports a predictive imagistic simulation. I can predict, for example, that it would be easier to say the word "with" with a peppermint on top of my tongue rather than in front of my tongue.

(differentiated and described) by my training in physics, so that I now have an explicit intuition of momentum that is also supplemented by other representations such as formulas. The final knowledge state in the two cases discussed in this section are additional examples of explicit intuitions. Thus it appears that one can develop explicit and even precisely described physical intuitions. This argues for separating the meanings of "implicit" and "intuitive."[9]

Summary. In summary, the data fit the hypothesis that one can have "experiences" of events over time in a dynamic image (such as twisting an object) without the object being present. In certain cases, one can focus on, identify, and describe "pieces" or elements of the experience in the image that were not previously described, implying that imagistic simulation is a mechanism by which some of the implicit knowledge in physical intuition schemas can be made more explicit. The view that intuitions can take the form of implicit knowledge in a perceptual motor schema helps explain why subjects take them to be "givens" that are not in need of further explanation or justification. They are something the subject just "knows how" to do that requires no justification.

Knowledge as a Flow Over Time

Different Uses of the Term "Simulation"
de Kleer and Brown (1983) have used the terms "simulation" and "envisioning" to describe processes that lead to qualitative predictions about the behavior of a system, usually via chains of causal inferences. A rule of the form "A causes B" or "an increase in A causes an increase (decrease) in B," for example, constitutes an element of knowledge in their approach. These elements are of the same form as many of the intuitive expectations discussed in this chapter (such as the idea that a weight will bend a rod in a certain direction, or that making a rod longer will cause it to turn more under the same twisting effort). de Kleer and Brown focus on how rules for the behavior of a whole system can be derived from a collection of such

---

[9] This differentiation of the terms "implicit" and "intuitive" is also aided by contrasting the intuitive knowledge of the expert with two other major types of knowledge identified by Easley (1978), Clement (1983), and Larkin (1983), namely scientific models and mathematically described principles. They describe at least three types of knowledge representations used in physics: a practical (or naive) representation sufficient for a subject to draw or describe a problem situation in everyday, nonscientific terms (which may draw on intuitions); a scientific (or physical model) representation such as a vector diagram of forces; and mathematical principles such as Newton's laws of motion. Intuitions presumably play a prominent role at least in the first type of representation. For an expert, presumably the physical models and mathematical principles should all be explicit and precise. For a novice, however, they may be imprecise or unstable. The levels of implicit and explicit knowledge given on pp. 227–229 are probably most useful though as a description of different types of intuitive knowledge. Thus, implicit does not mean the same as intuitive in this context. Rather, "degree of implicitness" is a descriptor at a finer level of detail that can be applied to examples of intuitive knowledge; some intuitive knowledge is implicit, while other intuitive knowledge may be explicit.

knowledge elements. A list of these knowledge elements is used to derive new inferences in an information-processing model of causal reasoning.[10] The knowledge elements are treated as passive data structures in the computer model.

.   *Passive strings of symbols.* However, it is rather easy to take the computer metaphor too seriously in such a perspective and to assume that each such knowledge element or expectation in working memory is like a passive string of symbols stored somewhere in the head. While reasoning and learning are thought of as active processes, knowledge is thought of as static and passive "data" elements composed of strings or networks of symbols. Presumably the implicit, underlying metaphor for knowledge in these approaches is the printed word. While it is true that not all features of a model need to be taken as literal candidates for features of the real system to be explained, nevertheless very few authors disavow static symbols as positive and central features of these models. It is still all too easy using their point of view to disregard the possibility of a much richer and more dynamic representation as an alternative basis for knowledge.

Simulation of single actions. de Kleer and Brown speak of "running" a simulation to refer to the process of making *inferences from collections* of causal knowledge elements. However, in this chapter I have used the term to describe a more fundamental process, the process of running through the action and movement involved in a *single* causal knowledge element. (Where one needs separate terms for these two senses one could use "elemental (or knowledge) simulations" and "compound (or reasoning) simulations.") Thus while de Kleer and Brown model reasoning involving many causal knowledge elements as a dynamic process, I wish to go further and also model each knowledge element as a dynamic process. I have already discussed the case of S5 who invests a large amount of time and effort attempting to determine the single causal relationship between stretching and the direction of twisting deformation in the spring wire. This example shows that establishing a single knowledge element of the form "A causes B" can require a substantial effort, and that imagistic simulation can play a major role in such an effort. Observations of this kind have motivated the topic of this chapter—the nature of these single knowledge elements as opposed to rules for combining them.

The Knowledge Experienced in Imagistic Simulations Is Not Static

A more dynamic view of knowledge structures can be derived from evidence that subjects are thinking about *experiencing an event over time* in order to produce a prediction for a single causal relationship. That is, they "run through" the event mentally in real time (or some speeded up or slowed down version of real time). For example, S2 says (referring to the two dimensional zig-zag spring analogy in Figure 9.7):

---

[10] Brown and his colleagues have recently made an attempt to go beyond this view themselves by introducing ideas from Vygotskian linguistics and anthropology (Brown, Collins, & Duguid, 1988).

23   S2:   And when we do this what bends . . . is the bendable bars . . . and that would behave like a spring. I can imagine that it would; I can kinesthetically pull on it and it would stretch, and you let it go and it bounces up and down (waves hand up and down, palm down, fingers extended). It does all the things.

In cases like these the subject

1.   makes an imagery report
2.   makes a prediction
3.   indicates the use of an extended-in-time process either verbally or via hand motions.

S2's imagistic simulation of the twisting rod (see Figure 9.3) also has these features. The subjects' reports of experiencing the effects of actions occurring over time provide a real motive for using the term "simulation." They suggest that the subjects are somehow mentally simulating some aspects of the rich flow of perceptions and/or motor actions over time that would exist if they were actually viewing and/or causing such events. This is a different meaning than a symbol manipulation procedure that steps its way through a series of inference rules operating on a set of wordlike tokens, where the inference that "a longer rod twists more" could be seen as the result of a single discrete step not extending continuously over time.

Further examples of dynamic simulation were provided by S5 in lines 22 to 73 on pages 217–219. Statements such as line 73 indicate that he experiences key elements of knowledge as events over time in dynamic imagery which lead to an expectation.

Summary. These findings relate to the common focus on abstract principles in expert knowledge discussed in the introduction. The examples presented provide evidence that expert thinking can be concrete rather than abstract. In addition, it seems unwise to take it as a given that causal knowledge elements in working memory are simply static language-like symbols. It appears that alternative hypotheses should include the possibility that part of one's knowledge in working memory is based in a dynamic flow of imagined perceptions and/or actions.[11] This would mean that the intuitive knowledge developed in an imagistic simulation does not just consist of an end state of static tokens, but is a process or activity that takes time to experience and to have significance (in the colloquial sense, to be meaningful) for the subject.[12]

---

[11] This interpretation is also compatible with the classic observation of Shepard and Cooper (1982) that subjects take longer to imagine large rotations of a figure than small rotations and with data on "representational momentum" (Freyd & Finke, 1984).

[12] Although the topics are well beyond the scope of this chapter, another strength of the present view is its potential for providing a more adequate view of meaning and consciousness than the view of knowledge as passive data structures. When a perceptual motor schema is activated and interacting with events in the world, this interaction can be seen as a primitive and primary locus of conscious experience and meaning. In this view, a closely related but less direct locus of meaning occurs when the schema is activated and interacting with internal images.

Conclusion: Can Physical Intuitions and Simulations
Play an Important Role in Expert Thought?

It is now possible to summarize the arguments for and against the importance of physical intuition and imagistic simulation in the expert solutions examined here.

Limitations of Physical Intuition and Simulation

The protocols examined indicated that there are limitations to the power of imagistic simulations. First, the subjects' confidence levels in most of the simulations considered here was high, but it was low in others. Second, as with any cognitive process, simulation is vulnerable to error and can at times mislead the subject if used in the absence of checking via alternative approaches. For example, S2's statement in line 26 that the zig-zag spring "would behave like a spring" is correct in terms of macroscopic effects, but not in terms of more detailed effects (there is twisting of the wire in a helical spring, but not in a zig-zag spring). Thus his simulation here failed on its own to reflect an important difference between the situations.

As a second example of limitations, the first simulation identified in S5's transcript produced a predicted direction for twisting in the spring wire, which he rejected later after other simulations. He also complained at the beginning about "having a hard time imagining that." Thus some simulations may be very difficult to carry out.

Indeed, much of the literature on misconceptions in science can be interpreted as documentation of those places where physical intuition leads to conclusions in conflict with currently accepted physical theory. The earlier discussion of the point of release for a sling provides one example. In that case "the way it feels" is not sufficiently imagable or is misleading. Thus physical intuition is by no means infallible. In addition, one would expect simulation processes using intuitions to often be ineffective for determining exact quantitative relationships without the aid of symbolic mathematical tools.

Types of Expertise

Despite these limitations, evidence has been presented that indicates that physical intuition can play a powerful role in expert thought. The remainder of this section summarizes that evidence.

Concrete intuitions versus abstract knowledge. I can now return to the interesting contrast between the focus of experts on concrete intuitions in the current study with the finding of Chi, Feltovich, and Glaser (1981) that experts focus on abstract principles very early on in problem solving. This focus on abstract principles also appears to conflict with retrospective reports of scientists such as the one quoted from Einstein in the introduction.

In the Chi et al. analysis, although experts may use some concrete knowledge to comprehend the surface features of the problem, they quickly make "a brief analysis of the problem statement to categorize the problem . . . into types that are characterized by the major physics principles that will be used in solution" (Chi et al., 1981, p. 150). They describe the role of concrete thought as that of activating and confirming the application of a previously learned, abstracted solution method. The aim of problem solving is described in terms of leaving the concrete stage behind as quickly as possible. Concrete knowledge plays only an initial "start-up" role, at most, in expert thought. In the cases discussed here, however, the role was to reason directly or by analogy from examples for which the subject could generate a clear imagistic simulation. Experts found it desirable to retain concrete cases as anchoring assumptions in their thinking, which added to their satisfaction and understanding of the domain. I expand on this view in the "Evidence for Importance..." section below.

The Chi et al. study cited protocol evidence indicating that an early focus on abstract principles occurred in the solutions they examined, and I am not claiming that their finding is difficult to reproduce. Rather, these contrasting views can be explained in part by assuming that the results are influenced by the particular kind of problems used. Their study used standard elementary textbook problems in contrast to the use of an explanation task for a less familiar situation in the present study. What makes the spring problem in the present study interesting is the fact that, for many experts, the physics principles that apply are not at all easy to determine. Thus in some ways it is more like a real problem on the frontier of science. Thus Chi et al.'s experts may have shown a preponderance of evidence for the use of formal methods because the problems solved were routine problems solvable via well-learned formal procedures.

One might argue that the problem used in the present study is simply too easy; perhaps a simple intuition is all that is needed to quickly solve the problem without more formal methods. But the problem in the present study was in fact considerably harder than those in the Chi et al. study. Many subjects spent longer than 20 minutes working on it and one research physicist spent over 3 hours trying to find an appropriate model for the deformation in the spring wire!

Definitions of expertise. This raises the issue of how to define expertise in science. Studies like the Chi et al. study focus on performance in a domain of problems that have become extremely familiar to the expert, where knowledge approaches the point of routinization. One might use the phrase "domain expertise" for this kind of skill.

On the other hand, many subjects did not have a ready strategy or even set of operators to apply to the problem used in this study. They were all expert problem solvers but not experts in the content area involved—the theory of statics or of springs in particular. Since most subjects began with little knowledge about how springs work, the present study concerns expertise in finding appropriate ways to understand, model, and explain the behavior of an unfamiliar system. The phrase "expertise in scientific modeling" or "generative expertise" (as opposed to "domain expertise") may be apt here. This is presumably the type of thinking Einstein was referring to in his letter to Hadamard. Although physical intuition may be used by experts during routine problem solving, it probably plays a more prominent and visible role in solving unfamiliar problems.

Evidence for Importance of Physical Intuition
and Imagistic Simulation

Sources of evidence that physical intuition and imagistic simulation played an
important role in the solutions can be listed as follows:

1. *Intuitions in simulations played a role in raising confidence.* First, we have
    already seen that subjects can make confident predictions from simulations
    involving physical intuitions, sometimes approaching 100%. Even when this is
    not the case an intuition may improve the subject's confidence by a certain
    amount. This is a valuable contribution since, in any hard problem, the subjects
    are almost never 100% sure of their results.

2. *Subjects value simulations involving intuitions.* Subjects referred to simulations
    involving intuitions as a purposeful part of their solution. For example, S5 says
    "I want to imagine that . . . I'm trying to decide how it's gonna twist . . ."
    (line 41). Here the subject indicates his intention to perform a simulation in
    order to arrive at a conclusion. This argues that the simulation is not simply an
    epiphenomenal side effect of some more formal process, but is rather a useful
    process on its own with a potential payoff that the subject recognizes.

3. *Simulations using intuitions are involved in more than the initial step in
    problem solving.* Two findings from this study argue that this view is too
    limited: (a) physical intuitions in simulations were central to the primary
    method used for solutions here, and (b) they led to an increase in the subject's
    understanding in some cases, not just to the correct answer.

    a. *Physical intuitions were the primary source of knowledge in the solutions.*
        In most of the cases discussed in this chapter, high confidence levels were
        reached *without* the use of formal physics or mathematics. All of these
        subjects indicated that assumptions underpinning their final solution were
        based on physical intuitions.

    b. *Physical intuitions used in simulations led to an increase in understanding.*
        Quotations such as Einstein's cited at the beginning of this chapter lead one
        to suspect that physical intuition can play an important role in a scientist's
        understanding of a physical system, not just a role in generating the answer
        to a particular problem. Specifying a theory of "understanding" and
        detecting changes in it are ambitious tasks beyond the scope of this
        chapter, but here I wish to at least suggest the possibility that physical
        intuition can contribute to an understanding that goes beyond merely
        obtaining a correct prediction. There is an interesting example of S2
        reporting a change in his understanding based in part on his physical
        intuition about twisting long and short horizontal rods. At that point, he
        was considering bending and twisting effects in a model of the spring
        involving square coils. After running through some simulations involving
        the twisting rod, he says:

144 S: And my confidence is now 99% . . . I now feel pretty good about my
          understanding about the way a spring works, although I realize at the same time

> I could be quite wrong. Still, there seems to be something to this torsion business; I feel a lot better about it.
>
> 178 S: Before this torsion insight, my confidence in the answer was 95%, but my confidence in my understanding of the situation was way way down, zero. I felt that I did not really understand what was happening; now my confidence in the answer is near 100% and my confidence is my understanding is like 80%.

Here he separates estimates of confidence in his *answer* from confidence in his *understanding* of the system. His new view of the spring has increased his own perceived level of understanding. This view includes the intuition that longer twisting elements will twist more than shorter ones as an anchoring assumption. Presumably the appeal of such an anchoring intuition is not only that it gives one an answer to the problem, but that it adds satisfaction and conviction to an explanation. Thus in this case one finds that a method used to attain self-evaluated understanding with conviction for such a system is to relate it to a concrete, physical intuition schema. The subject's perceived increase in his own understanding can be explained by the following hypothesis: Many of the desirable properties of his physical intuition knowledge about twisting rods—its dynamic character and imagability or "runability," high certainty, generality, flexibility, and experiential meaningfulness—are inherited by his new square-coil model of the spring. If this view is correct, it means that grounding in physical intuition is an extremely important asset for a scientific model.

In summary, for all of these reasons, it appears that physical intuition and imagistic simulation played an important and sometimes central role in the thinking of these expert subjects.

Effortful simulation argues for knowledge being implicit. Why did subjects bother to run through effortful imagistic simulations? The fact that they did so, and that the knowledge experienced in simulations appears to be analogue and dynamic rather than based in static symbols, supports the hypothesis that in some cases the simulations allowed them to uncover implicit (undescribed or perhaps even unconscious) knowledge. For if it were explicitly described, then why announce the intention to form an image of the situation and make the effort to run through a simulation of it? Why not just report it? Thus the fact that simulations were considered to be effortful is also an argument for the involvement of implicit knowledge.

Summary of an Initial Framework for Modeling Physical Intuition and Imagistic Simulation

One of the goals of this chapter was to construct a plausible initial framework that proposes basic relationships between physical intuitions, perceptual motor schemas, visual imagery, kinesthetic imagery, and simulations. At this point I can attempt to summarize the model that has been developed to account for the elemental simulations documented here. As illustrated in Figure 9.4, the model proposes that a schema and imagery can work together to produce imagistic simulations. Physical intuitions are hypothesized to be individual expectations in the schema.

1. The "running" of an elemental imagistic simulation involves a permanent schema (such as a perceptual motor schema for twisting). When acting on real objects in the world in its normal, nonimaging role, such a schema controls perceptual tracking and/or motor coordination processes over a period of time.
2. As such, at least at the level of organization being discussed, parts of the schema in working memory are analogue and depictive in character, rather than being a propositional and descriptive set of static symbols.
3. The schema can have expectations that "set up" a readiness to perceive certain expected events in a top–down manner.
4. Some of these expectations are implicit (depictive and undescribed or in some cases possibly unconscious).
5. In addition to real situations, the schema can assimilate an image of a situation.
6. It is possible for the expectations to operate in the absence of the real situation and "drive" the temporary dynamic imagery representing an event.
7. The subject can focus on certain new features in the resulting image.
8. The subject can then describe these verbally. In this manner, implicit knowledge in a schema can become explicitly described knowledge.

This separation of a schema activated from permanent memory and an image in temporary memory (generated by a top–down and/or bottom–up process) allows us to separate what is old, familiar, permanent, and more general (the schema) from what can be new, novel, temporary, and more specific (the image of particular objects and movements) in an elemental simulation. (In a more complex simulation several schemas might interact with the same image.)

In this model new knowledge can be learned in a way that does not depend on inferences from chains of wordlike symbols, for example:

1. The subject can apply an existing intuition schema to an image of a new situation, and the schema can assimilate and adjust its expectations about an event via tuning mechanisms. The subject then reports the anticipated result of applying the schema in the new situation.
2. Implicit knowledge in an existing intuition schema can be tapped as previously undescribed expectations in the schema generate images that can be assimilated by other schemas and described, thereby being converted to explicit knowledge. Here it does not matter whether the situation being considered is familiar or new, the point is that the subject can bring a new question to the situation so that an aspect of "running" the schema that has not been described before is attended to and articulated.

Limitations on the generality of the findings. Assuming that the findings in this chapter have some validity, how general are they? The useful generality of findings from a case study is of a different type than that of a statistical study. Case studies are most valuable in underdeveloped areas of science where concepts and models are primitive and the primary need is for the formation of viable hypothesized models that are grounded in (suggested by and constrained by) a body of detailed observations. Rather than extending the results of a narrowly defined experimental setting to a population, the findings are general to the extent that the new empirical and theoretical concepts and models developed can be adapted and applied fruitfully by the reader to other cases involving sometimes rather different settings and samples. Thus their generality derives from giving the reader new conceptual tools to think with in other situations.

My first comment on the generality of these findings is that the models of physical intuition and imagistic simulation developed here were derived from cases of a particular type. The type can be located on a spectrum of uses of imagery in thinking—a spectrum that runs from simple to complex uses: from simple spatial inferences on static images generated from memory, to combinations thereof, to elemental dynamic simulations, to complex simulations of the behavior of a novel system in Gedanken experiments. Again, studies in the past have tended to treat complex simulations as a chain of elemental simulations without modeling the process of an elemental simulation. The present study has concentrated this last goal and is therefore situated midway along this spectrum. Thus the study may help to provide a foundation for understanding mental simulation and the processes underlying Gedanken experiments.

Second, most examples discussed in this chapter were explained in terms of action-oriented perceptual motor schemas. However, it was argued that the basic framework developed for understanding intuitions and imagistic simulations may also be valid for schemas that are less action oriented.

Third, the discussions of implicit knowledge in this chapter were restricted to examples of implicit expectations in perceptual motor schemas. Other types might include implicit knowledge of spatial constraints on the relative position and movement of objects. The degree to which these types of implicit knowledge might be similar or different is an open question for future research. An analysis of how the different roles played by implicit knowledge (and imagery) can be used in combination may help to explain the effectiveness of complex simulations. In fact the most plausible explanation for the zig-zag spring case discussed earlier would seem to require a combination of elemental simulations and spatial inferences from combining the movements in space produced by individual simulations.

In conclusion, this chapter has presented some initial evidence that (a) experts use elemental physical intuitions; (b) intuitions can play an important role in problem solutions; (c) intuitions can play more than simply a "start-up" role in a problem solution—in particular they can play the role of grounding assumptions that underpin explanations constituting the subject's central understanding of a system; (d) their use often involves dynamic imagery in an imagistic simulation, and (e) imagistic simulation can be used to make implicit knowledge more explicit in a physical intuition. In this model new knowledge can be derived from an imagistic simulation that does not depend on inferences from chains of wordlike symbols.

There is evidence that students also use physical intuitions. The literature on misconceptions in science provides many examples, and there is also evidence for useful intuitive preconceptions (Clement, 1979, 1993; Driver, 1973; Clement, Brown, & Zietsman, 1989). Although the separation between experts and naive subjects is large, the fact that experts use physical intuitions makes it less sharp. How subjects select and refine useful physical intuitions and how they coordinate them with other types of knowledge are important topics for further research.[13]

References

Arbib, M. A. (1981). Perceptual structures and distributed motor control. In V. B. Brooks (Ed.), *Handbook of physiology—The nervous system* (pp. 1449–1480). Bethesda, MD: American Physiological Society.

Brown, J. S., Collins, A., & Duguid, P. (1988). Situated cognition and the culture of learning (IRL Report NO. 88-0008, Institute for Research on Learning, Palo Alto, CA). (Shorter version appears in *Educational Researcher, 18*(1), February, 1989)

Chase, W. (1983). Spatial representations of taxi drivers. In D. R. Rogers & J. A. Sloboda (Eds.), *The acquisition of symbolic skills* (pp. 391–411). New York: Plenum Press.

Chi, M., Feltovich, P. J., & Glaser, R. (1981). Categorization and representation of physics problems by experts and novices. *Cognitive Science, 5,* 121–152.

Clement, J. (1979). Mapping a student's causal conceptions from a problem solving protocol. In J. Lochhead & J. Clement (Eds.), *Cognitive process instruction* (pp. 143–146). Philadelphia: Franklin Institute Press.

Clement, J. (1982). Analogical reasoning patterns in expert problem solving. *Proceedings of the Fourth Annual Conference of the Cognitive Science Society* (pp. 79–81). Ann Arbor, MI.

Clement, J. (1986). Methods for evaluating the validity of hypothesized analogies. *Proceedings of the Eighth Annual Conference of the Cognitive Science Society* (pp. 223–234). Hillsdale, NJ: Lawrence Erlbaum Associates, Inc.

Clement, J. (1988a). Observed methods for generating analogies in scientific problem solving. *Cognitive Science, 12,* 563–586.

Clement, J. (1988b). Nonformal reasoning in experts and in science students: The use of analogies, extreme cases, and physical intuition. In J. Voss, D. Perkins, & J. Siegel (Eds.), *Informal reasoning and education* (pp. 345–362). Hillsdale, NJ: Lawrence Erlbaum Associates, Inc.

Clement, J. (1989). Learning via model construction and criticism: Sources of creativity in science. In J. Glover, R. Ronning, & C. Reynolds (Eds.), *Handbook of creativity; Assessment, theory and research* (pp. 341–381). New York: Plenum.

Clement, J. (1993). Using bridging analogies and anchoring intuitions to deal with students' preconceptions in physics. *Journal of Research in Science Teaching, 30*(10), 1241–1257.

Clement, J., Brown, D., & Zietsman, A. (1989). Not all preconceptions are misconceptions: Finding "anchoring conceptions" for grounding instruction on students' intuitions. *International Journal of Science Education, 11,* 554–565.

---

[13] Another issue that is beyond the scope of this chapter is the origin of intuitions. The cases discussed support the idea that some physical intuitions originate in perceptual motor schemes. It is reasonable to assume that most physical intuitions are grounded in personal experience with physical phenomena. Like other knowledge, however, intuitions could be biased during construction by other prior knowledge or rational tendencies that would mean that perception does not play the only role in their construction. Most examples in this chapter were modeled in terms of perceptual motor schemas. But it is not clear that all intuitions, including the notion of symmetry, can be explained in this way. Thus considerable work remains to be done in this area.

de Kleer, J., & Brown, J. S. (1983). Assumptions and ambiguities in mechanistic mental models. In D. Gentner & A. Stevens (Eds.), *Mental models*. Hillsdale, NJ: Lawrence Erlbaum Associates, Inc.

diSessa, A. (1983). Phenomenology and the evolution of intuition. In D. Gentner & A. Stevens (Eds.), *Mental models*. Hillsdale, NJ: Lawrence Erlbaum Associates, Inc.

diSessa, A. (1985). Knowledge in pieces. In G. Forman & P. Pufall (Eds.), *Constructivism in the computer age* (pp. 49–70). Hillsdale, NJ: Lawrence Erlbaum Associates, Inc.

Driver, R. (1973). *The representation of conceptual frameworks in young adolescent science students.* Doctoral dissertation, University of Illinois, Urbana-Champaign, IL.

Easley, J. (1978). Symbol manipulation reexamined. In B. Presseisen, D. Goldstein, & M. Appel (Eds.), *Topics in cognitive development* (Vol. 2, pp. 99–112). New York: Plenum.

Fischbein, E. (1987). The intuitive dimension of mathematical reasoning. In T. Romberg & D. Stewart (Eds.), *The monitoring of school mathematics: Background papers* (Vol. 2.). Wisconsin Center for Education Research, U. of Wisconsin.

Forbus, K. (1984). Qualitative process theory. *Artificial Intelligence, 24,* 85–168.

Freyd, J., & Finke, R. (1984). Representational momentum. *Journal of Experimental Psychology: Learning, Memory, & Cognition, 10,* 126–132.

Gelernter, H. (1963). Realization of a geometry theorem proving machine. In E. Feigenbaum & J. Feldman (Eds.), *Computers and thought* (pp. 134–152). New York: McGraw-Hill.

Gooding, D. (1990). *Experiment and the making of meaning: Human agency in scientific observation and experiment.* Dordrecht: Kluwer.

Hadamard, J. (1945). *The psychology of invention in the mathematical field.* Princeton, NJ: Princeton University Press.

Jacobsen, E. (1930). Electrical measurement of neuromuscular states during mental activities: 11. Imagination and recollection of various muscular acts. *American Journal of Physiology, 94,* 22–34.

Karmiloff-Smith, A. (1987). From meta-processes to conscious access: Evidence from children's meta-linguistic and repair data. *Cognition, 23,* 95–147.

Kosslyn, S. (1980). *Image and mind.* Cambridge, MA: Harvard University Press.

Larkin, J. (1983). The role of problem representation in physics. In D. Gentner & A. Stevens, *Mental models* (pp. 75–98). Hillsdale, NJ: Lawrence Erlbaum Associates, Inc.

Larkin, J., & Simon, H. A. (1987). Why a diagram is (sometimes) worth ten thousand words. *Cognitive Science, 10,* 65–100.

Lindsay, R. K. (1988). Images and reference. *Cognition, 29,* 229–250.

Miller, A. I. (1984). *Imagery in scientific thought: Creating twentieth-century physics.* Boston. Birkhauser.

Mounoud, P., & Bower, T. G. R. (1974). Conservation of weight in infants. *Cognition, 3* (1), 29–40.

Neisser, U. (1976). *Cognition and reality.* San Francisco: W. H. Freeman.

Nersessian, N. J. (1984). *Faraday to Maxwell: Constructing meaning in scientific theories.* Dordrecht: Kluwer.

Nersessian, N. J., & Greeno, J. G. (1990). Multiple abstracted representations in problem solving and discovery in physics. *Twelfth Annual Proceedings of the Cognitive Science Society.* Hillsdale, NJ: Lawrence Erlbaum Associates, Inc.

Piaget, J. (1955). *The child's construction of reality.* London: Routledge & Kegan Paul.

Piaget, J. (1976). *The grasp of consciousness.* Cambridge, MA: Harvard University Press.

Qin, Y., & Simon, H. (1990). Imagery and problem solving. In *Twelfth Annual Proceedings of the Cognitive Science Society* (pp. 646–653). Hillsdale, NJ: Lawrence Erlbaum Associates, Inc.

Schmidt, R. A. (1982). *Motor control and learning.* Champaign, IL: Human Kinetics Publishers.

Schon, D. (1981). *Intuitive thinking? A metaphor underlying some ideas of educational reform.* D.S.R.E. Working paper WP-8, Massachusetts Institute of Technology, Cambridge, MA.

Shepard, R. N. (1984). Ecological constraints on internal representation: Resonant kinematics of perceiving, imagining, thinking and dreaming. *Psychological Review, 91* 417–447.

Shepard, R., & Cooper, L. (1982). *Mental images and their transformations*. Cambridge, MA: MIT Press.

Shrager, J. (1990). Common sense preception and the psychology of theory formation. In J. Shrager & P. Langley (Eds.), *Computational models of scientific discovery and theory formation* (pp. 437–470). San Mateo, CA: Morgan Kaufmann.

Tweney, R. D. (1986). Procedural representation in Michael Faraday's scientific thought. *PSA 1986, 2*.

Westcott, M. R. (1968). *Towards a contemporary psychology of intuition*. New York: Holt, Rinehart and Winston.

Witz, K. (1975). Activity structures in four year olds. In J. Scandura (Ed.), *Research in structural learning* (Vol 2). New York: Gordon and Breach.

10

Philosophical Remarks on Implicit Knowledge and Educational Theory

Jonathan Berg
University of Haifa

I would like to present a philosophical approach to this educational approach to implicit and explicit knowledge, though my remarks might be referred to less pretentiously as some philosophical reactions—or the reactions of some philosopher.

After a few preliminary words on knowledge and belief, I turn to the implicit/ explicit distinction in an effort to see how it might best be construed for the present purposes. On the basis of this I offer a philosophical view—or at least some philosopher's view—of how the notion of implicit knowledge functions in educational theory.

Knowledge and Belief

Since there are so many ways to talk about knowledge and belief—so many different ideas people have in mind when they use those words—I would like to clarify what *I* mean when *I* talk about knowledge and belief. My intention is to describe not merely my own idiolect, but rather a particularly common, natural way of conceiving of knowledge and belief. In fact, I take it to be *the most* common, natural way, both for the person in the street and hence, also for philosophers.

I start from what appear to be "the best examples"—paradigmatic cases—of knowledge and belief. Thus, I take it for granted that I believe that (as I write this) there is a pen in my hand. In fact, I *know* it. And I do not believe that (as I write this) there is an elephant in this room. In fact, I *know* there is not. Furthermore, such assertions about what I know and what I believe are true regardless of the language in which they are asserted; they can be truly asserted in Swedish, for example, despite my total ignorance of the language.

As for beliefs, some are true and some are false. Of course, *I* could not point to any particular belief of *mine* as false; for if I thought it were false, I would not believe it. But we can all easily think of examples of false beliefs held by others, or

I am grateful for the helpful comments of Sid Strauss and other participants in the Sixth Annual Workshop (Implicit and Explicit Knowledge: An Educational Approach) of the Unit of Human Development and Education, Tel Aviv University, October 1988, where an earlier draft of this chapter was read.

even by ourselves at other times, such as my former belief, as a child, that the world is flat.

Belief differs from knowledge in this important respect, since it is impossible to know something that is not true. If someone *knows* that an elephant is standing in front of him, there has to *be* an elephant standing in front of him; if not, then although the individual may *believe* an elephant is there, even with great certainty, he has no such *knowledge,* since there would be no such knowledge to be had.

As trivial as this fundamental point might seem, it is, perhaps consequently, easily overlooked, as when certain misconceptions (false beliefs) that a student shows signs of having are construed as implicit *knowledge.* On the view that I am sketching, such misconceptions might be thought of as implicit beliefs, but they could not be any kind of knowledge, implicit or otherwise, as long as they are indeed misconceptions (hence, false).

Of course, one could always stipulate, just by fiat, nonstandard definitions of belief and knowledge (actually, of the *terms* 'belief,' 'knowledge,' etc.); scientific progress may make this useful, and even necessary. But one must bear in mind the cost. If knowledge can be false, what distinguishes it from belief? The construal of knowledge as possibly false not only deviates profoundly from the standard conception of knowledge, but it also obliterates what would appear to be a useful distinction, between beliefs, in general, and those special beliefs which (among other things) happen to be correct.

Note that requiring knowledge to be true does not carry any heavy metaphysical commitments. In particular it does not commit one to any particular theory of truth, objective or otherwise; truth may be defined in terms of correspondence, coherence, or pragmatic value. All that is needed of truth for the picture I am sketching is that it divide up our beliefs, so that some of them are true and the others are not; what exactly it is that makes the true ones true can be left open. Denying a notion of truth as innocuous as this would surely require considerable argument.

Philosophers traditionally go on to demand more of knowledge than mere true belief, because they want to distinguish between true beliefs one just happens to have (such as a wild guess that turns out to be right), or that one has for the wrong reasons (e.g., "the oracle said so"), from true beliefs for which one has real justification. Now, what counts as "real justification" is a tough philosophical nut, yet to be cracked. And however justification is construed, justified true belief widely seems to fall short of knowledge. But this is not the place for a survey of modern theory of knowledge. (For that see Lehrer, 1974.) The point was to call attention to a commonly recognized difference between knowledge and belief: What is known is therefore true; what is not actually true can at most be believed.

It is for this reason that the present discussion should be carried on in terms of belief, rather than knowledge. For it is belief, rather than knowledge, that is relevant to theories of education. Try as they might to teach only the truth, teachers can be mistaken. But whether what they teach their students is true or false, they go about teaching it in just the same way. Thus, the truth or falsity of what a teacher teaches is in a fundamental way independent of and irrelevant to the educational process. So the subject is really implicit *belief* and educational theory. I shall turn to the latter after an examination of the former.

From Implicit Meaning to Implicit Thought

What is implicit belief? One reason it is hard to say is because the implicit/explicit distinction as it is generally applied is linguistic, rather than epistemological. What, after all, would be a really clear case of such a distinction?

What leaps to mind are cases such as Grice's famous example of conversational implicature, where a letter of reference for a philosophy job candidate reads,

> Mr. X's command of English is excellent, and his attendance at tutorials has been regular. (Grice, 1989, p. 33)

We can easily distinguish here between the laudatory explicit meaning of what was written and the scathing implicit meaning (what is "conversationally implicated").

In addition to conversational implicature, we might take presupposition as illustrating the implicit/explicit distinction. If someone says,

> The waiter pocketed his tip

she may be taken as presupposing, and hence, saying implicitly, that there is in fact a waiter, uniquely specified by the context, that said waiter was given a tip, that he was clothed at the time, and so on.

Indirect speech acts (if indeed there are any) would also be prime candidates for applications of the implicit/explicit distinction. If in asking the question,

> Could you pass the salt?

one thereby requests that the hearer pass the salt, the request may be viewed as implicit, in what explicitly is a question. And in general we may view as implicit any part of the "message" of an utterance (what is conveyed by it) that lies beyond its literal meaning.

How can this distinction between implicit and explicit be extended beyond the narrow realm of linguistic content? We could talk of implicit rules, but if by this we mean un*written* or un*spoken* commands, we remain in the realm of language. The same goes for implicit invitations and other such acts of communication. In logic we speak of implicit premises and implicit conclusions, but here, too, the distinction is applied to linguistic entities, insofar as the inferences or arguments formed by premises and conclusions are viewed as sets of sentences.

In light of all this how can a *belief* be implicit or explicit? If beliefs were something like sentences in the head, then we could think of implicit beliefs as what is implicit in those sentences. The problem with this, of course, is in finding such sentences in the head. Surely nobody buys the most radical form of the brainwriting thesis, according to which our beliefs are *literally* spelled out on brain tissue! So the question is whether there might be some more moderate, plausible version of the brainwriting thesis, on the basis of which implicit belief could be construed as what is implicit in the sentences in one's head.

Could it be that each belief corresponds to a particular cluster of neurons charged in a particular pattern? That beliefs are, indeed, spelled out in the head, but in some kind of neural code? Maybe some neurophysiologists believe this, but clearly it is much more than can reasonably be inferred from the empirical findings to date.

What brain scientists are more likely to hold, if they go for any form of brainwriting at all, would be that beliefs are "written" in the brain the way that what my son had for dinner is "written" on his face, or (better yet) the way genetic endowments (at the highest level of abstraction) are "written" into DNA. That is, maybe there are some regular causal connections between beliefs and complex neural states. (Even this may seem pretty farfetched, but suppose, for the sake of argument, it is not.)

The problem with this, as far as the characterization of implicit belief goes, is that it does not distinguish implicit from explicit, because this way *everything* is implicit. To put the point more generally—as soon as the brainwriting thesis is weakened to the point where the beliefs are not being written down in a language that is enough like natural language to support a distinction between literal and nonliteral content, then the possibility of a belief's being *explicit* is lost! So either the brainwriting thesis is too strong to be plausible, or else it is too weak to yield *e*xplicit belief (qua explicit content of sentences in the head).

Belief Without Awareness

What about distinguishing implicit belief from explicit belief on the basis of awareness? (This is suggested in this volume by Efraim Fischbein [Chap. 4] and John Clement [Chap.9].) One might say that a belief is implicit if the individual who has it is unaware of it, that is, unaware that he has the belief.

But what is it to be unaware of a belief one has? The easy answer to this question is the Freudian line: The beliefs of mine that I am unaware of are my subconscious beliefs. The problem with this is that it does not get us anywhere, in that unless one has already accepted the Freudian story, the resort to the subconscious will not help. That is, explaining implicit belief as subconscious belief merely leads to the reformulation of the question about implicit belief as a question about subconscious belief.

What is it to believe something subconsciously? The difficulty posed by this question should not be underestimated. It appears that one believes something subconsciously if (a) one would deny believing it, yet (b) some of one's actions not otherwise explainable would be easier to explain if one *did* believe it. But at least on the face of it this is very strange, if not absurd. For we generally refrain from ascribing to people beliefs they would explicitly deny having. I am not saying, of course, that there can be no theoretical justification for some useful notion of subconscious belief. But for one thing, such a notion would be fundamentally different from the notion of belief as it is most commonly construed. Moreover, theories relying on such a notion would thereby be committed to the controversial theories (or at least some of them) from which that notion derives whatever theoretical value it might have. The notion of subconscious belief seems problematic enough (and controversial enough) that one would not want to rest one's theories on it, if one did not absolutely have to. (Besides, there seems to be a lot more to the Freudian notion of subconscious belief than just unawareness.)

How else can we have a belief without being aware of it? Another famous name that might come to mind here after Freud's is that of Michael Polyani. But his notion of tacit knowledge is nothing like subconscious belief or belief without awareness. As Polyani explains, "the triad of tacit knowledge consists in subsidiary things (B) bearing on a focus (C) by virtue of an integration performed by a person (A); we may also say that in tacit knowing we attend *from* one or more subsidiaries *to* a focus on which the subsidiaries are brought to bear" (1969, p. 182). Polyani, himself, explicitly warns that "it would be a mistake to identify subsidiary awareness with subconscious or pre-conscious awareness" (p. 194). As opposed to the relatively static implicit/explicit distinction, according to which our beliefs more or less divide into the implicit and the explicit (or the more implicit and the more explicit), Polyani's notion of the subsidiary element of knowledge is dynamic, its extension varying in accordance with an element's role in particular instances of knowing. "It is the *function* of a subsidiary item that counts in classing it as subsidiary" (p. 194), he explains; the same item may function as subsidiary in one instance and as focal in another. Indeed, on Polyani's view there simply is no strictly explicit knowledge (p. 195).

Alternatively, one might try to cash in implicit belief in terms of the implications (i.e., the logical consequences) of our beliefs (cf. Fishbein's discussion of situations in which one is aware of a model one is using but not of all of its implications). The problem with construing implicit belief as that which is merely *implied* by what we believe is that, except for those of us who are logically omniscient, our beliefs are not closed under logical consequence. That is, just because something follows from our beliefs, it does not follow that we believe it; there are surely many logical consequences of our beliefs that we do not believe, not even implicitly. As Gilbert Harman concedes, "One cannot be expected even implicitly to believe a logical consequence of one's beliefs if a complex proof would be needed to see the implication" (1986, p. 14). (If we believed all the logical consequences of our beliefs, we would all be brilliant mathematicians!) So we must distinguish between our beliefs and the implications thereof. For there is no reason to assume that those implications of our beliefs of which we are *not* aware are *beliefs* of ours, altogether.

Nevertheless, one might suppose, as does Harman, that we *do* believe— implicitly—at least *some* of the consequences of our (explicit) beliefs—namely, those consequences that are "easily inferable" (1986, p. 13) from explicit mental representations. The trick here is to explain what it is for a consequence to be "*easily* inferable." Harman's inclination is simply to take some notion of (psychologically) *immediate implication* as fundamental (p. 18). Hartry Field seems to be similarly satisfied with talk of "obvious consequences" (1978, p. 83) of core beliefs. But as William Lycan (1986) has persuasively argued, it is hard to imagine how a line could effectively be drawn between those consequences that are "obvious" or "easily inferable" and those that are not. And so, a satisfactory analysis of implicit belief along such lines does not seem feasible.

Implicit Methods

It may be telling that when Clement (see Chap. 9, this volume) describes the greatest degree of implicitness, he speaks of being unaware of the *knowledge* one is *using*, thus tying implicitness to *action* rather than mere mental states. Given the distinction between knowing *that*—such as knowing that spiders eat flies—and knowing *how*—such as knowing how to drive a car—we can distinguish between cases where we can verbally *express* what we know how to do and cases where we cannot. Then (in keeping with the initial linguistic conception of the implicit/ explicit distinction) we may construe as implicit knowledge the latter—the knowledge how (know-how) that we cannot express. Take the example of crawling—we know how to do it, but we cannot *say* how we do it. Or better yet, take the example of language—we know how to speak grammatically, but explicitly stating that knowledge is notoriously beyond us. (This is not to suggest, of course, that know-how never entails propositional knowledge. Knowing *how* to speak grammatically entails knowing *that* certain sentences are grammatical and *that* certain sentences are not. But such knowledge *that* would be knowledge one could explicitly state; what would be implicit would be only the means by which such determinations are made.)

Appearances notwithstanding, construing "implicit knowledge" this way, as knowing how without being able to say how, does not bring us back to talk about *knowledge*, proper. For know-how is not really a kind of knowledge (in the relevant sense). Rather, it is the possession of an ability, or a method or a way of doing something. There is clearly something decidedly nonepistemic about being able to act in a certain way, as opposed to merely believing something. (I allow myself to ride roughshod here over analyses according to which *all* knowledge consists in nothing other than the possession of various abilities, on the assumption that such analyses do not allow for explicit mental representations in the first place.) On this view, then, implicit knowledge amounts to no more than implicit method, where implicitly having a method is simply having a way of doing something such that one is not sufficiently aware of it to be able to spell it out (to describe it fully in words).

Implicit Knowledge in Educational Theory

What about education? My guess is that in the present discussion of implicit knowledge, from an educational approach (or from educational approaches), what is actually being discussed (as "implicit knowledge") is either implicit methods, in the particular sense previously described, or simply misconceptions, in the sense of false beliefs. (I use the word 'misconception' nonpejoratively, merely to refer to a belief that happens not to be true, no matter how reasonable it may be for a particular individual in particular circumstances to adopt it.)

Consider, first, misconceptions. There are clearly many ways in which misconceptions—false beliefs—can give students trouble, leading them to false conclusions (more misconceptions). So obviously, one of a teacher's aims must be to correct misconceptions (at least some of them). And doing this (in a straightforward way) requires being *aware* of the misconceptions. But what does this mean? What is it to be aware or to be unaware of a certain misconception—a false belief— that one has?

There is an important ambiguity here. On the one hand, being unaware of a certain misconception may consist in being unaware of the belief *altogether*—but, on the other hand, it may consist merely in being unaware of *the falsity of* the belief. Being unaware of a misconception in the latter sense—unaware merely of its falsity—does *not* require anything as dubious as having a belief while being altogether unaware of it. In other words, no notion of implicit knowledge or implicit belief is needed to describe the case where a student suffers from a misconception. Naturally, the *student* would be unaware of the fact that her belief is false—but that does not mean that she has any beliefs (or knowledge) of which she is not aware.

For example, my beginning logic students (among others) are often inclined to commit what is commonly known as the fallacy of affirming the consequent, whereby the converse of a conditional is inferred from the conditional ("If P then Q; therefore, if Q then P"). Their inclination to commit this fallacy may be seen as the result of their having a certain misconception, namely that every conditional is equivalent to its converse. Of course, they might not be prepared to formulate this belief by themselves, but whether they are or not, what counts pedagogically is that they would accept it as true—as something they believe—once it is put to them (the technical terms having been explained). And they, of course, do not recognize it as a *mis*conception; if they *realized* that it is false, they naturally would *not* believe it. *I*, however, *do* recognize it as a misconception; and this is important and useful to me as their teacher, because it allows me to teach them something important, by showing them how this belief of theirs is actually false.

Implicit methods are also pedagogically significant. For a student may acquire, without being aware of it, a way of doing something that does not work so well. (Maybe it used to work well, in some restricted domain of application, but it does not work in some new domain.) This does not necessarily mean that the student suffers from some particular false belief, but just that in certain situations he proceeds in a certain way (a) that he is not fully able to describe and (b) that is not satisfactory for such situations. Since teachers are concerned with imparting not only beliefs but also abilities or skills, it follows that when a student is using an inadequate method—of which he may be entirely unaware—the teacher should want to make him aware of the inadequacy of this method, and hence, must herself become aware of the method the student is using.

An example that comes to mind here is one in problem solving. Here is the problem:

> Two trains set out on the same track at the same time, one from Station A on its way to station B, the other from station B on its way to station A. A fly on the front of the engine of the train from station A also set out at the very same time, flying along the track to the front of the engine of the train from station B, then back to the train from A, then back to the train from B, and so on. If the distance between A and B is 100 miles (by rail), and the trains traveled at the (constant) speed of 50 miles per hour, and the fly flew at the (constant) speed of 100 miles per hour, then how far did the fly manage to fly until being squashed in the head-on collision? (It may be assumed that the fly is one-quarter of an inch long.)

One way to proceed when faced with such a problem may be called the "Method of Sums," by which a measure is calculated as the sum of certain other measures. This method would seem particularly natural for determining the distance of a course that clearly divides into easily distinguishable segments. To proceed this way in solving the problem at hand, one would calculate the distance the fly flew until first meeting the train from B, then the distance it flew until returning to the train from A, and so on (until the distance to fly between the trains did not exceed the length of the fly). Solving this problem by the Method of Sums could clearly involve a lot of messy calculations. Alternatively, one might calculate the total distance the fly flew, not on the basis of the separate distances it flew, but on the basis of the total *time* it flew, easily determined as the time the trains traveled until they crashed.

Now it is easy to see how it would be useful for the teacher to be aware of it when students would unwittingly proceed here by the Method of Sums. But such students need not be described as having any relevant misconceptions (false beliefs). (It might even be wrong to describe them as having the false belief that the way to solve this problem is by the Method of Sums, since they might not know what the Method of Sums is, nor even be able to understand an explanation of it.) But they also need not be described as having any mysteriously implicit knowledge or belief. They could be simply described as doing something in a certain way without being aware of it—as implicitly having a certain method, if you will. But to me this is much less mysterious (and much more intelligible) than talk of "implicit knowledge."

A Disclaimer

This is an essay in conceptual analysis. None of my remarks are intended to have any substantial empirical consequences; to construe them as such would be to misunderstand them. Rather, my aim has been to show how (certain) talk of implicit knowledge might be reformulated in terms that are prima facie less problematic. To this end I have suggested how the role(s) played in (some) educational theory by the concept of implicit knowledge could be played as well by the concepts of misconception (false belief) and of implicit method (a way that one has of doing something but that one cannot fully describe). Theories formulated in terms of the latter are preferable for their being more easily accommodated by the conceptual apparatus we already have.

References

Field, H. (1978). Mental representation. *Erkenntnis, 13*, 9–61.

Grice, H. P. (1989). *Studies in the way of words.* Cambridge: Harvard University Press.

Harman, G. (1986). *Change in view: Principles of reasoning.* Cambridge: Bradford/MIT.

Lehrer, K. (1974). *Knowledge.* Oxford: Oxford University Press.

Lycan, W. G. (1986). Tacit belief. In R. J. Bogdan (Ed.), *Belief: Form, content, and function* (pp. 61–82). Oxford: Clarendon Press.

Polyani, M. (1969). Sense-giving and sense-reading. In M. Polyani (Ed.), *Knowing and being.* London: Routledge & Kegan Paul.

Author Index

A

Acredolo, C., 183, *201*
Adams, N., 68, *82*
Al Fakhri, S., 183, *201*
Allen, T. W., 183, *202*
Arbib, M. A., 224, *243*
Ariel, S., 84, *93*
Arnon, I., 200, *202*
Astington, J. W., 84, 85, 88, 90, 91, 92, *93, 94*

B

Baillargeon, R., 65, *80*
Bairstow, J. P., 183, *201*
Baker, K., 129, *130*
Bamberger, J., 170, *180*
Baron-Cohen, S., 86, *93*
Bartsch, K., 90, *95*
Behr, M. J., 70, *80*, 112, *129*
Bell, A. W., 111, 113, *129*
Bellugi, U., 60, *81*
Benenson, J., 64, *82*
Bergson, H., 108, *109*
Bertenthal, B. I., 183, *201*
Bishop, Y., 188, *201*
Bower, T. G. R., 227, *244*
Bradbury, A., 183, *201*
Brouwer, L. E. J., 152, *167*
Brown, A. L., 56, 71, *80*
Brown, D., 243, *243, 244*
Brown, J. S., 205, 233, 234n, *243, 244*
Bruner, J. S., 83, *93*
Bullock, M., 66, *80*

C

Camp, C., 243, *243*
Campbell, R., 85, 89, *94*

A (right column)

Caramazza, A., 101, *109*
Caramuel, J., 152, *167*
Carey, S., 56, *80*
Carpenter, B., 183, *202*
Carpenter, J. T., 183, *202*
Carpenter, T. P., 70, *80*, 112, *129*
Carraher, D. W., 68, 69, *80*
Carraher, T. N., 68, 69, *80*
Chase, W., 232, *243*
Chi, M., 205, 234, *243*
Clement, C., 23, *52*
Clement, J., 101, *109*, 120, *129*, 182, *202*, 211, 233n, 237, 238, 240, 243, *243, 244*
Cobb, P., 134, 134n, 135, 136, 137, 151, *167*
Cohen, M., 58, 74, 77, *81*
Collins, A., 234n, *243*
Cooper, L., 235n, *244*
Corbitt, M. K., 70, *80*, 112, *129*
Curtis, L. E., 68, *82*

D

DeCorte, E., 113, *130*
de Kleer, J., 16, *52*, 205, 133, *244*
de la Rocha, O., 69, *81*
DeLoache, J., 87, *93*
Deri, M., 77, *80*, 103, *109*, 112, 113, *130*
diSessa, A. A., 2, 2n, 9, 34, 36, 42, 45, *52*, 109, *109*, 206, 211, 212, 238, *244*
Driver, R., 120, *129*, 243, *244*
Duguld, P., 234n, *243*
Duranti, A., 91, *93*

E

Easley, J., 233n, *244*
Eben Shushan, A., 197, *202*
Erickson, G., 101, 102, *109*

Subject Index

A

Arithmetic operations
  addition and subtraction, 68, 153-155
  multiplication and division, 68, 79,
      111-112, 117-118, 120-129
  explicit beliefs about, 117-118
  implicit beliefs about, 117-118,
    123-127
  implicit models of, 111-112
  nonconservation of, 111
  overcoming misconceptions about,
    120-129
  sources of misconceptions about,
    127
Awareness (and consciousness)
  of discrepancies, 121-122, 124-127
  of ideas about written language, 172,
    178-179
  of intuitive models of operations,
    99-109, 120-129
  as a means for distinguishing implicit
    beliefs, 226-233, 248-250
  of mental states, 88
  and nonverbal knowledge, 226,
    228-229
  of plurality, 137
  of preconceptions and misconceptions,
    108-109, 120-125, 178-179,
    251-252
  and symbolization, 83, 92-93
  and unconscious knowledge, 226-228,
    231-233
  of the use of the minimum quantity
    principle, 178-179
  of uncertainties in the results of
    operations, 164
  and verbal descriptions, 229-230

B

Beliefs
  concept of, 90

  explicit, 117-119
  false, 85, 87-90, 245-246, 251
  implicit, 117-118, 123-127, 179,
    246-248
  and knowledge, 245-247
  and symbolization, 86
  true, 245-246

C

Cognition
  factors involved in genesis of, 3-51
    feedback, 4
    principles of invention, 5
    problems, 4
    resources, 5-51
      alpha level, 7-18
      beta level, 7, 10, 18-36
      gamma level, 8, 10, 36-38
      prior, 5-51
  mechanisms of, 1-3, 36-38
  perceptions of, 1-3, 18-20, 27-28, 34,
    46-50
    Hume, 1
    Kant, 18-19, 27, 48
    Newell, 1-2
    Piaget, 2-3, 19-20, 28, 34, 46-50
Cognitive development
  constructivist account of, 61-62
  empiricist account of, 61-62
  rational-constructivist account of, 57
  from sensory to perceptual to abstract,
    62, 79
Constructivism
  and the genesis of cognition, 6
  and the law of frequency, 61
    need for a theory of, 56
    relevant input for learning, 56-57,
      60
      about fractions, 70
      about meaning of verbs, 60-61
      about novel instances in a